Communications in Computer and Information Science 2110

Rationale

The CCIS series is devoted to the publication of proceedings of computer science conferences. Its aim is to efficiently disseminate original research results in informatics in printed and electronic form. While the focus is on publication of peer-reviewed full papers presenting mature work, inclusion of reviewed short papers reporting on work in progress is welcome, too. Besides globally relevant meetings with internationally representative program committees guaranteeing a strict peer-reviewing and paper selection process, conferences run by societies or of high regional or national relevance are also considered for publication.

Topics

The topical scope of CCIS spans the entire spectrum of informatics ranging from foundational topics in the theory of computing to information and communications science and technology and a broad variety of interdisciplinary application fields.

Information for Volume Editors and Authors

Publication in CCIS is free of charge. No royalties are paid, however, we offer registered conference participants temporary free access to the online version of the conference proceedings on SpringerLink (http://link.springer.com) by means of an http referrer from the conference website and/or a number of complimentary printed copies, as specified in the official acceptance email of the event.

CCIS proceedings can be published in time for distribution at conferences or as post-proceedings, and delivered in the form of printed books and/or electronically as USBs and/or e-content licenses for accessing proceedings at SpringerLink. Furthermore, CCIS proceedings are included in the CCIS electronic book series hosted in the SpringerLink digital library at http://link.springer.com/bookseries/7899. Conferences publishing in CCIS are allowed to use Online Conference Service (OCS) for managing the whole proceedings lifecycle (from submission and reviewing to preparing for publication) free of charge.

Publication process

The language of publication is exclusively English. Authors publishing in CCIS have to sign the Springer CCIS copyright transfer form, however, they are free to use their material published in CCIS for substantially changed, more elaborate subsequent publications elsewhere. For the preparation of the camera-ready papers/files, authors have to strictly adhere to the Springer CCIS Authors' Instructions and are strongly encouraged to use the CCIS LaTeX style files or templates.

Abstracting/Indexing

CCIS is abstracted/indexed in DBLP, Google Scholar, EI-Compendex, Mathematical Reviews, SCImago, Scopus. CCIS volumes are also submitted for the inclusion in ISI Proceedings.

How to start

To start the evaluation of your proposal for inclusion in the CCIS series, please send an e-mail to ccis@springer.com.

Ioannis Kostavelis · Dimitrios Folinas ·
Dimitrios Aidonis · Charisios Achillas
Editors

Supply Chains

5th Olympus International Conference, ICSC 2024
Katerini, Greece, May 24–26, 2024
Proceedings, Part I

Springer

Editors
Ioannis Kostavelis
International Hellenic University
Kateríni, Greece

Dimitrios Folinas
International Hellenic University
Kateríni, Greece

Dimitrios Aidonis
International Hellenic University
Kateríni, Greece

Charisios Achillas
International Hellenic University
Kateríni, Greece

ISSN 1865-0929 ISSN 1865-0937 (electronic)
Communications in Computer and Information Science
ISBN 978-3-031-69343-4 ISBN 978-3-031-69344-1 (eBook)
https://doi.org/10.1007/978-3-031-69344-1

This Springer imprint is published by the registered company Springer Nature Switzerland AG
The registered company address is: Gewerbestrasse 11, 6330 Cham, Switzerland

Preface

Undeniably, logistics and supply chain management play a huge role within today's globalized economy, as they support the movement and flow of goods, together with many economic transactions. According to the European Commission, the growing importance of global supply chains has fundamentally changed the way the economy and goods manufacturing are organized. However, the recent Covid-19 pandemic brought to the surface the vulnerability of the modern economy, as the pandemic disrupted many supply chains at its outbreak, and the subsequent economic recovery led to massive further pressure on the global supply system. Indisputably, supply chain resilience may improve through international cooperation, diversification and the accelerated uptake of digital technologies. The primary objective of the 5th Olympus ICSC was to offer an international platform for the presentation and publication of the latest scientific research findings in the field of Supply Chain Management. This conference provided valuable opportunities for delegates to exchange innovative ideas, establish research and business connections, and foster global partnerships for potential collaborations. We sincerely anticipate that this conference will significantly contribute to the advancement of knowledge in relevant scientific and academic domains.

The 5th Olympus ICSC 2024 received 92 submissions, out of which 51 papers were accepted as oral presentations in the main conference track. The conference also hosted three workshops and a poster session. Each paper was reviewed in a double-blind mode by at least two members of the Program Committee and the authors of accepted submissions were asked to submit their final versions taking into consideration the comments and suggestions of the reviewers. The best paper of the conference was selected by the General and Program Chairs, after suggestions from the Program Committee. Accepted papers covered a broad spectrum of issues falling under the wider scope of supply chain management in real-life applications, including among others, digital supply networks, decision making in logistics, humanitarian logistics, city-logistics, standards in supply chain and robotics and automation in logistics. Among them, the three most represented topics were Digital Twins with Simulation, Robotic Applications and IoT Data Processing, proving the dedication of the community to adopting Industry 4.0 technologies in the contemporary supply chain domain.

The framework of the technical program of the 5th Olympus ICSC 2024 was outlined by 3 invited speakers. First, J. Rod Franklin, (Kühne Logistics University) through his speech entitled: "*Resilience in a contemporary context: Geopolitics, state based cyber threats, and an angry mother nature - Oh my!*" provided holistic insights regarding the components that affect contemporary logistics challenges. The second invited speaker, Lazaros Nalpantidis (Technical University of Denmark), with his speech entitled "*Autonomous Robotics in Agriculture: Digitalizing Agricultural Production*" provided a comprehensive description of state-of-the-art technologies in machine learning for robotic applications in real-life agricultural applications. The third invited speaker, Dimitrios Giakoumis (Centre for Research and Technology Hellas) through his speech entitled "*Service robots in logistics; from warehouse through to transport and retail operations automation*" outlined state-of-the-art research findings and applications of robotics towards Warehouse 4.0 transition.

Three workshops were selected and organized in conjunction with the main conference. The "*Workshop on Research findings on procurement management in Greece*" was organized by Dimitrios Folinas, Antonios Mademlis, Aristotelis Mavidis and Efthimios Spiridopoulos. The "*Workshop on City Logistics*" was organized by Charisios Achillas, Dimitrios Tsitsamis, Naoum Tsolakis and Emmanouil Vlachogiannis. The "*Workshop on Challenges and solutions in agrifood supply chain*" was organized by Evangelos Lioutas, Christina Manosi, Christos Mourtziopoulos, Stavros Papadopoulos and Konstantinos Rotsios.

We wish to thank the Department of Supply Chain Management of the International Hellenic Univeristy and, mostly, we feel the need to thank the people who made the 5th Olympus ICSC 2024 happen, our Workshop & Tutorial Chairs Dimitrios Folinas, Charisios Achillas and Evangelos Lioutas, our Publication Chair Ioannis Kostavelis, our Local Chair Dimitrios Triantafullou, the 33 members of our Program Committee, as well as all the authors who submitted their work to the 5th Olympus ICSC 2024.

May 2024

Ioannis Kostavelis
Dimitrios Folinas
Dimitrios Aidonis
Charisios Achillas

Organization

Conference General Chairs

Dimitrios Folinas	International Hellenic University, Greece
Dimitrios Aidonis	International Hellenic University, Greece

Program Committee Chairs

Ioannis Kostavelis	International Hellenic University, Greece
Dimitrios Folinas	International Hellenic University, Greece
Dimitrios Aidonis	International Hellenic University, Greece
Charisios Achillas	International Hellenic University, Greece

Program Co-chairs

J. Rod Franklin	Kühne Logistics University, Germany
Lazaros Nalpantidis	Technical University of Denmark, Denmark
Dimitrios Giakoumis	Centre for Research and Technology Hellas, Greece

Workshop Chairs

Dimitrios Folinas	International Hellenic University, Greece
Charisios Achillas	International Hellenic University, Greece
Evangelos Lioutas	International Hellenic University, Greece

Publicity Chair

Charisios Achillas	International Hellenic University, Greece

Publication Chair

Ioannis Kostavelis	International Hellenic University, Greece

Local Chair

Dimitrios Triantafyllou	International Hellenic University, Greece

Program Committee

Bochtis Dionysis	Center for Research and Technology Hellas, Greece
Desislava Petrova-Antonova	Sofia University, Bulgaria
Diamantis Vasilis	Democritus University of Thrace, Greece
Diego Casado Mansilla	University of Deusto, Spain
Diego López de Ipiña	University of Deusto, Spain
Gasteratos Antonios	Democritus University of Thrace, Greece
Haralambides Hercules	University of Rotterdam, Netherlands
Kateris Dimitris	Center for Research and Technology Hellas, Greece
Kelemis Athanasios	International Hellenic University, Greece
Keramydas Christos	International Hellenic University, Greece
Kladovasilakis Nikolaos	International Hellenic University, Greece
Krinidis Stelios	International Hellenic University, Greece
Lioutas Evangelos	International Hellenic University, Greece
Michailidou Alexandra	Aristotle University of Thessaloniki, Greece
Nalpantidis Lazaros	Technical University of Denmark, Denmark
Naserentin Vasilis	Chalmers University of Technology, Sweden
Nenes George	University of Western Macedonia, Greece
Ntziachristos Leonidas	Aristotle University of Thessaloniki, Greece
Peleka Georgia	Centre for Research and Technology Hellas, Greece
Preslav Dimitrov	South-West University "Neofit Rilski", Bulgaria
Remigio Berruto	University of Torino, Italy
Siozios Konstantinos	Aristotle University of Thessaloniki, Greece
Sofia Panagiotidou	University of Western Macedonia, Greece
Stafyla Amalia	International Hellenic University, Greece
Teneketzis Demosthenis	University of Michigan, USA
Tsarouchas Panagiotis	International Hellenic University, Greece
Tsolakis Naoum	International Hellenic University, Greece

Tsongas Konstantinos	International Hellenic University, Greece
Tzetzis Dimitrios	International Hellenic University, Greece
Vidovic Milorad	University of Belgrade, Serbia
Vlachokostas Christos	Aristotle University of Thessaloniki, Greece
Vlachos Dimitrios	Aristotle University of Thessaloniki, Greece

Contents – Part I

Contents – Part II

Humanitarian Logistics-Tourism and Accessibility

Modern Approaches and Technologies in Agri-food Domain

Supply Chain Embraces Industry 4.0 Technologies

Industry 4.0 Technologies in Distribution Centers: A Survey

Adamos Daios(✉) and Ioannis Kostavelis

Department of Supply Chain Management, International Hellenic University, Kanellopoulou 2, 601 32 Katerini, Greece
adamdaio@ihu.gr

Abstract. Industry 4.0 technologies are gaining traction with every aspect of modern manufacturing and distribution procedures. In the context of supply chain management, where the flow of products and information is of the utmost importance, these technologies play a crucial role in achieving accuracy, speed, and flexibility while being cost effective. A central node of each supply chain is the distribution center. The main functionalities of distribution centers concern receiving, storing, packaging and dispatching goods, while managing all necessary information related to them. The paper at hand provides a short yet representative literature survey for the Industry 4.0 technologies that have been adopted so far in the logistics applications of contemporary distribution centers. The standard processes are outlined and examined in terms of their automation with novel applied or theoretical technological solutions. In addition, the emerging processes of distribution centers are discussed including demand forecasting and automation in last-mile delivery. Discussions and future trends are also presented, and the adoption pace of the new technologies is analyzed.

Keywords: industry 4.0 · distribution center · robotics · IoT · cloud computing · warehouse automation

1 Introduction

The Fourth Industrial Revolution (Industry 4.0) merged virtual and physical worlds by introducing the concept of cyber physical systems. But the growing interest in the term "Industry 4.0" has yet to be fully explored in the Supply Chain sector and more specifically inside distribution centers, on the grounds that these technologies remain costly and challenging for companies [1]. Industry 4.0 technologies are physical and digital based [2]. Physical technologies are additive manufacturing, sensors, robots, and drones, while their digital counterparts are cloud computing, artificial intelligence, blockchain, big data analytics and simulation.

A distribution center is a type of warehouse where the permanent storage of goods is somewhat limited and the focus of this establishment is on constant

I. Kostavelis et al. (Eds.): ICSC 2024, CCIS 2110, pp. 3–11, 2025.
https://doi.org/10.1007/978-3-031-69344-1_1

product movement, along with the information concerning this flow [3]. The main standard processes of a distribution center are receiving and sorting inbound goods, storing for a limited time of such goods, order picking and assembly to fulfill customer needs and shipping such orders to customers. All this product flow is accompanied by information collection and reporting and is managed by a Warehouse Management System (WMS).

The scope of the paper is to present and review all relevant technologies stemming from Industry 4.0 that have been proposed or/and applied in the processes of a distribution center, both standard and emerging ones. Although the papers presented here are addressed to warehouse environments, their applicability to distribution centers, a specific type of warehouse, is also accepted and welcomed since they are a more demanding in terms of technology and communications.

2 Standard Processes of Distribution Centers

2.1 Receiving

The location of moving pallets in distribution centers can be determined by utilizing several sensors onboard the forklift responsible for these tasks [4]. Forklifts are industrial vehicles always present in a warehouse environment and responsible for transporting pallets. Onboard sensors can reconstruct the forklift trajectory and orientation, thus determining the location of the pallet at the time of its unloading. The authors in the discussed work proposed the use of onboard Radio Frequency Identification system at the ultra-high frequency band paired with an inertia measurement unit and an optical flow sensor, which can estimate the forklift pose over time. The system was evaluated in a real warehouse with results that deem it suitable for further deployment.

2.2 Storing

Automated Storage and Retrieval Systems (AS/RS) handle complex combinatorial and sorting tasks. A novel approach to these systems is by employing multiple objective ant colony optimization [5], which is a class of optimization algorithms that are modelled on the actions of an ant colony. This approach is useful in problems that deal with locating better paths through graphs and each solution is optimally updated after each simulation iteration. Results showed that ant colony optimization is a viable candidate for planning automated storage systems.

2.3 Inventory Management

An innovative technique for inventory counting in warehouses with a wide range of general or specialized items was presented in [6]. A worker takes images of the stored items with a smart device and then these images are processed, correlated with the database and finally the items are recognized and counted. The proposed architecture has been designed with the minimum computational cost and least assets approach.

Micro aerial vehicles (MAVs) can be employed for a high-performance autonomous inventory counting inside warehouses with the help of a multi-modal sensor setup (RFID reader, high resolution cameras) [7]. The MAV is localized within the warehouse environment with the help of 3D Lidar. The system was evaluated in various scenarios with high-level inspection missions in a full-automated mode and is suitable for live deployment.

A similar approach that employed Unmanned Aerial Vehicles (UAV) with an added function of information validation was proposed in [8]. The items to be counted are tagged with RFID, while the system uses a blockchain and a distributed ledger to validate all the collected inventory data by UAVs and make them available to external parties. Tests concerning data collection were conducted in real warehouses outperforming traditional manual tasks, and furthermore the proposed blockchain-based architecture was also evaluated in many scenarios.

Automated Guided Vehicles (AGVs) are crucial in inventory management since they are used to automate routine tasks. A dynamic route-planning system based on Artificial Intelligence (Machine Learning using an Artificial Neural Network) is suitable for the implementation of AGVs in warehouses with limited computing resources [9]. The system was tested in Gazebo simulation environment to produce results with testing accuracy up to 98

In cases where AGVs are working collaboratively with humans, the need arises for creating and maintaining a safe environment for both parties [10]. Workers assisted with Augmented Reality (AR) devices can interact with AGVs' planned paths, add virtual objects and walls to their cyber-physical navigation view thus creating areas that are off limits for mobile robots.

2.4 Picking

In picking scenarios where picking tasks and arrival times are not known a priori, an architecture [11] was proposed for multi-agent task allocation and execution. A team of autonomous robots place bids (cost-estimates for completing currently available tasks) in a central auctioning system, which solves a combinatorial problem and assigns these tasks to the agents. The auctioning system runs at a constant rate that allows newly added tasks to be a part of the auctioning. Researchers have evaluated the proposed framework in a lab environment. The authors in [12] introduced a novel autonomous pallet truck equipped with cameras and LiDARS capable of autonomous navigating in warehouse environment, detecting and picking pallets in order to transport them from one location to another.

AR plays a vital role in assisting logistics workers with their picking duties. The implementation of Smart glasses in warehouse management [13], as observed in four companies (DHL, Samsung, Coca-Cola & Intel) that use Vision Picking, increased productivity, performance, safety, speed, accuracy, and reduced errors.

The use of AR in warehouse environments are a novelty that begins to show its potential, although in larger scale companies due to increased deployment costs.

Following the growing employment of AR in the picking process inside distribution centers, gamification elements were used to enhance AR and ultimately increase motivation and job satisfaction [14]. These two integrated modules, an AR picking module and a Gamification module, are connected to an existing WMS. While the AR picking module is responsible for supporting the worker with picking duties, the Gamification module provides a new working experience and keeps track of each worker's progress, reports, and rewards.

2.5 Order Fulfillment

Automated warehouses are fine examples of complex logistics systems, where order-picking and fulfillment are highly-managed operations [15]. A simulation-based Digital Twin can dynamically adjust the parameters under various conditions, providing managers with data-driven decision support. A full-scale discrete event simulation model can serve as an integral part of the Digital Twin, since the model integrates with operational data, monitors the automated warehouse, and provides tested and high-quality solutions to everyday operations. Authors attest that the Digital Twin concept provides invaluable information, based on data analytics, and a decision support tool in such a demanding environment as a distribution center.

An extensive literature review of mixed palletizing methods for smart warehouse environments was conducted by researchers [16]. Proposals from a variety of disciplines (Reinforcement Learning, Quantum Computing, Big Data Analytics, Simulation, Robotics, Augmented Reality) were presented to produce an efficient and effective way to place heterogeneous packages on a pallet. Although the main approach to deal with this long-standing problem was based on exact and heuristic algorithms, industry 4.0 technologies provided a new foundation for exploring innovative solutions. Algorithm-based mixed palletizing methods, such as quantum computing, big data analytics and reinforcement learning are being employed for solving diverse mixed palletizing scenarios. Technology-based methods, such as augmented reality, robotics and simulation are being utilized to apply such solutions, either by humans (AR) or robots (Robotics) and evaluate them with Simulation technology.

2.6 Shipping

A Smart Scheduling model [17] combines first mile and last mile operations of different logistics companies and produces an optimization method that solves real-time scheduling tasks in the interconnected logistics network. The cooperation of the different logistics companies is based on Industry 4.0 solutions including vehicle reidentification, GPS-based methods, and smartphone-based monitoring. The real-time optimization of open tasks assignment to the scheduled routes relies on the gathered information from all agents and is solved with a combined meta-heuristic algorithm (Black Hole Optimization & Big Bang Big Crunch algorithm).

Figure 1 shows the flow of goods inside a distribution center and how Industry 4.0 technologies affect them in every step.

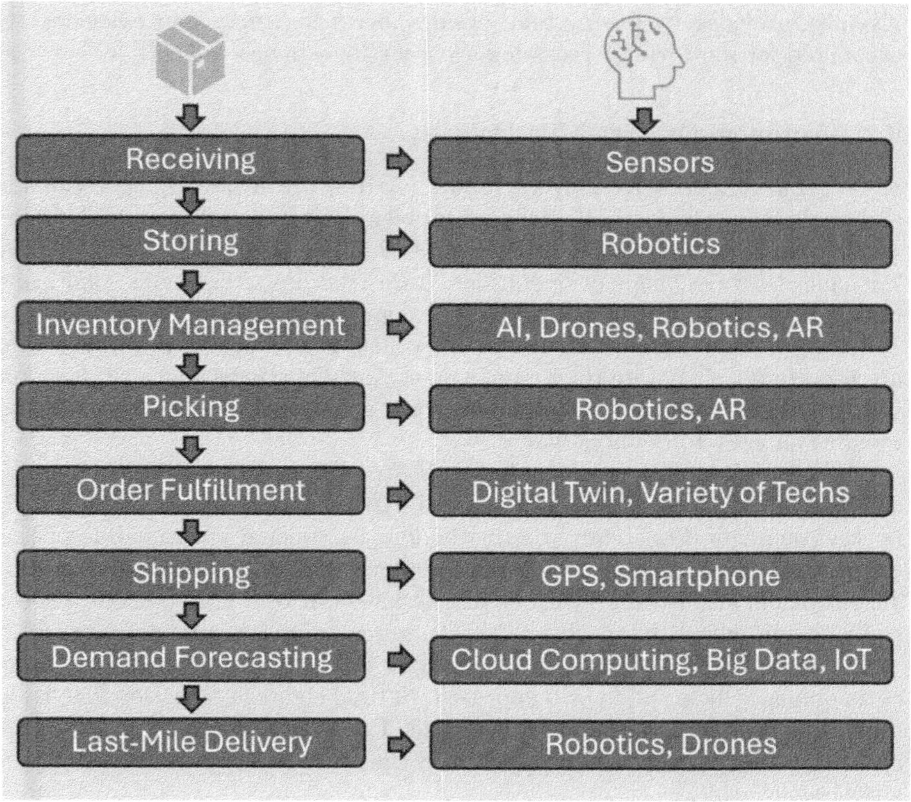

Fig. 1. Flow of goods inside a distribution center and relevant technologies.

3 Emerging Processes of Distribution Centers

3.1 Demand Forecasting

A predictive analysis for customer behavior [18] can be employed for an optimization model that determines the allocation of goods to different distribution centers. This model is based on multiple factors such as travelling time, transportation costs and confidence of the prediction results. Cloud computing facilitates the management of the Big Data that is generated from all available distribution channels, while a genetic algorithm is used to generate an almost optimal solution for anticipatory shipping.

In another case, a system was proposed to use Internet of Things in warehouse management by using Node-RED (open-source programming tool for connecting hardware and software) and MongoDB (tool for storing data) [19]. Every product entering the warehouse is attached to an RFID tag which holds and updates relevant information, such as product name, production date, expiry date, location in warehouse and weight. The huge boost in real-time warehouse visibility provided by this system, besides increasing speed and efficiency, was accounted for improving forecasting accuracy by as much as 56%.

3.2 Autonomous Last-Mile Delivery

Self-driving autonomous delivery robots (ADRs) are a developing technology and could solve the last-mile delivery problem [20] in an effective and efficient way. This review showed that there are four major aspects of using ADRs for last-mile deliveries, namely operations, infrastructure, regulations, and acceptance. ADRs will provide with more secure and faster deliveries, reducing costs and transportation pollution, but to do so major investments in infrastructure are necessary to facilitate their employment. Regulations have not yet been universally created or applied to urban areas and acceptance of ADRs by pedestrian remains an issue to be investigated.

A technical solution was introduced [21] from JD.com (a leading E-commerce company in China) to the autonomous last-mile delivery in complex traffic environments. Concretely, the methodologies used in each module of their autonomous vehicles were presented, together with safety guarantee strategies. The autonomous last-mile delivery vehicle has been tested on realistic yet controlled environment. In another work, the processes of last mile delivery of food were assessed [22] in a simulation scenario for different kind of agents e.g. drone, autonomous vehicle and hybrid approach. In total eighteen scenarios were tested differing in terms of demand and fleet size. The results showed that the hybrid robot-drone delivery system outperformed the other two approaches (drone and autonomous vehicle).

Table 1 gives a summary of Industry 4.0 technologies in distribution centers. For this work we selected only recent representative works related to automation of Supply Chain applications and specifically on the logistics and last mile delivery tasks. It can be conceived that although there is a force towards automating the procedures, the adoption pace is slow and this relies on specific challenges and applications related to the operational environment, the type of goods to be handled, and the regulation limitations.

4 Discussion

This paper has presented a selective literature survey to reveal that there is an increased scientific activity for the transformation of the existing supply chain processes into contemporary smart ecosystems, by exploiting the added value

Table 1. Industry 4.0 technologies in distribution centers.

Reference	Industry 4.0 technology	Applied	Process
Motroni et al. (2021)	Sensors	Yes	Receiving
Brezovnik et al. (2015)	Robotics	No	Storing
Daios et al. (2024)	Artificial Intelligence	No	Inventory Management
Beul et al. (2018)	Drones	Yes	Inventory Management
Fernández et al. (2019)	Drones	Yes	Inventory Management
Nguyen et al. (2020)	Artificial Intelligence	No	Inventory Management
Papcun et al. (2019)	Augmented Reality, Robotics	No	Inventory Management
Dahlquist et al. (2023)	Robotics	No	Picking
Tsiogas et al. (2021)	Robotics	Yes	Picking
Husár et al. (2021)	Augmented Reality	Yes	Picking
Plakas et al. (2020)	Augmented Reality	No	Picking
Ashrafian et al. (2023)	Digital Twin	No	Order Fulfillment
Daios et al. (2024)	Variety of Technologies	Yes & No	Mixed Palletizing
Bányai et al. (2018)	GPS, Smartphone	No	Shipping
Lee (2017)	Cloud Computing, Big Data	No	Demand Forecasting
Hamdy et al. (2022)	Internet of Things	No	Demand Forecasting
Alverhed et al. (2024)	Robotics	No	Last-mile Delivery
Li et al. (2020)	Robotics	Yes	Last-mile Delivery
Samouh et al. (2020)	Robotics, Drones	No	Last-mile Delivery

of Industry 4.0 technologies. This domain is significantly impacting distribution centers, enhancing various processes such as receiving, storing, inventory management, picking, order fulfillment, and shipping. These technologies offer solutions to improve accuracy, speed, flexibility, and cost-effectiveness in supply chain operations.

Digital Twins, Internet of Things, Robotics, Cloud Computing, and Warehouse Automation are identified as key technologies driving advancements in distribution center operations. These technologies enable real-time communication, data-driven decision-making, and optimization ultimately improving overall efficiency and performance. From the literature review it can be concluded that Industry 4.0 technologies have only begun to demonstrate their potential to revolutionize enterprise operations. Despite challenges such as cost and complexity, there is a clear trend towards the adoption of these technologies in distribution centers, indicating a significant potential for transformation in the near future.

Acknowledgement. The paper has been funded under the Horizon Europe project entitled "TOURAL: Multidimensional model of tourism verticals driving the sustainable balanced growth among rural& remote grids and urban clusters of rural regions, fostering macro-regional cooperation" with GA number 101132489

Disclosure of Interests. The authors have no competing interests to declare that are relevant to the content of this article.

References

1. Efthymiou, O.K., Ponis, S.T.: Industry 4.0 technologies and their impact in contemporary logistics: a systematic literature review. Sustainability **13**, 11643 (2021). https://doi.org/10.3390/su132111643
2. Bai, C., Dallasega, P., Orzes, G., Sarkis, J.: Industry 4.0 technologies assessment: a sustainability perspective. Int. J. Prod. Econ. **229**, 107776 (2020). https://doi.org/10.1016/j.ijpe.2020.107776
3. Higginson, J.K., Bookbinder, J.H.: Distribution centres in supply chain operations. In: Langevin, A., Riopel, D. (eds.) Logistics Systems: Design and Optimization, pp. 67–91. Springer, Boston (2005). https://doi.org/10.1007/0-387-24977-X_3/COVER
4. Motroni, A., Buffi, A., Nepa, P.: Forklift tracking: industry 4.0 implementation in large-scale warehouses through UWB sensor fusion. Appl. Sci. **11**, 10607 (2021). https://doi.org/10.3390/app112210607
5. Brezovnik, S., Gotlih, J., Balič, J., Gotlih, K., Brezočnik, M.: Optimization of an automated storage and retrieval systems by swarm intelligence. Procedia Eng. **100**, 1309–1318 (2015). https://doi.org/10.1016/j.proeng.2015.01.498
6. Daios, A., Xanthopoulos, A., Folinas, D., Kostavelis, I.: Towards automating stocktaking in warehouses: challenges, trends, and reliable approaches. Procedia Comput. Sci. **232**, 1437–1445 (2024). https://doi.org/10.1016/j.procs.2024.01.142
7. Beul, M., Droeschel, D., Nieuwenhuisen, M., Quenzel, J., Houben, S., Behnke, S.: Fast autonomous flight in warehouses for inventory applications. IEEE Robot. Autom. Lett. **3**, 3121–3128 (2018). https://doi.org/10.1109/LRA.2018.2849833
8. Fernández-Caramés, T.M., Blanco-Novoa, O., Froiz-Míguez, I., Fraga-Lamas, P.: Towards an autonomous industry 4.0 warehouse: a UAV and blockchain-based system for inventory and traceability applications in big data-driven supply chain management. Sensors **19**, 2394 (2019). https://doi.org/10.3390/s19102394
9. Nguyen Duc, D., Tran Huu, T., Nananukul, N.: A dynamic route-planning system based on industry 4.0 technology. Algorithms **13**, 308 (2020). https://doi.org/10.3390/a13120308
10. Papcun, P., Cabadaj, J., Kajati, E., Romero, D., Landryova, L., Vascak, J., Zolotova, I.: Augmented reality for humans-robots interaction in dynamic slotting "chaotic storage" smart warehouses. IFIP Adv. Inf. Commun. Technol. **566**, 633–641 (2019). https://doi.org/10.1007/978-3-030-30000-5_77/FIGURES/4
11. Dahlquist, N., Lindqvist, B., Saradagi, A., Nikolakopoulos, G.: Reactive multiagent coordination using auction-based task allocation and behavior trees. In: 7th IEEE Conference on Control Technology and Applications (CCTA) (2023)
12. Tsiogas, E., Kleitsiotis, I., Kostavelis, I., Kargakos, A., Giakoumis, D., Bosch-Jorge, M., Ros, R.J., Tarazon, R.L., Likothanassis, S., Tzovaras, D.: Pallet detection and docking strategy for autonomous pallet truck AGV operation. In: IEEE International Conference on Intelligent Robots and Systems, pp. 3444–3451 (2021). https://doi.org/10.1109/IROS51168.2021.9636270
13. Husár, J., Knapčíková, L.: Possibilities of using augmented reality in warehouse management: a study. Acta Logistica **8**, 133–139 (2021). https://doi.org/10.22306/al.v8i2.212
14. Plakas, G., Aretoulaki, E., Ponis, S.T., Agalianos, K., Maroutas, T.N.: A proposed technology solution for enhancing order picking in warehouses and distribution centers based on a gamified augmented reality application. In: Proceedings of the 14 th International Conference on Interfaces and Human Computer Interaction 2020 and

13 th International Conference on Game and Entertainment Technologies 2020, pp. 217–221. IADIS Press (2020). https://doi.org/10.33965/ihci_get2020_202010C030
15. Ashrafian, A., Pedersen, S.: Digital twin for complex logistics systems: the case study of a large-scale automated order picking and fulfillment system. IFAC-Papers OnLine **56**, 11056–11061 (2023). https://doi.org/10.1016/j.ifacol.2023.10.808
16. Daios, A., Kladovasilakis, N., Kostavelis, I.: Mixed palletizing for smart warehouse environments: sustainability review of existing methods. Sustainability **16**, 1278 (2024). https://doi.org/10.3390/su16031278
17. Bányai, T., Illés, B., Bányai, Á.: Smart scheduling: an integrated first mile and last mile supply approach. Complexity **2018**, 1–15 (2018). https://doi.org/10.1155/2018/5180156
18. Lee, C.K.H.: A GA-based optimisation model for big data analytics supporting anticipatory shipping in retail 4.0. Int. J. Prod. Res. **55**, 593–605 (2017). https://doi.org/10.1080/00207543.2016.1221162
19. Hamdy, W., Al-Awamry, A., Mostafa, N.: Warehousing 4.0: a proposed system of using node-red for applying internet of things in warehousing. Sustain. Futures **4**, 100069 (2022). https://doi.org/10.1016/j.sftr.2022.100069
20. Alverhed, E., Hellgren, S., Isaksson, H., Olsson, L., Palmqvist, H., Flodén, J.: Autonomous last-mile delivery robots: a literature review. Eur. Transp. Res. Rev. **16**, 1–13 (2024). https://doi.org/10.1186/S12544-023-00629-7/FIGURES/3
21. Li, B., Liu, S., Tang, J., Gaudiot, J.L., Zhang, L., Kong, Q.: Autonomous last-mile delivery vehicles in complex traffic environments. Computer (Long Beach Calif) **53**, 26–35 (2020). https://doi.org/10.1109/MC.2020.2970924
22. Samouh, F., Gluza, V., Djavadian, S., Meshkani, S., Farooq, B.: Multimodal Autonomous Last-Mile Delivery System Design and Application. In: 2020 IEEE International Smart Cities Conference (ISC2), pp. 1–7. IEEE (2020). https://doi.org/10.1109/ISC251055.2020.9239082

"Charting the Future of Public Procurement: Insights from the First Round of a Delphi Study on Emerging Technologies in the EU Context"

Mavidis Aristotelis(✉) and Folinas Dimitrios

International Hellenic University, Katerini, Greece
armavid@yahoo.g

Abstract. This paper presents the initial findings from the first round of a Delphi study, a method chosen for its proven efficacy in fostering iterative consensus-building among a panel of experts under conditions of anonymity, aimed at developing a technology roadmap for integrating emerging technologies into public procurement in alignment with European Union strategic goals. The study engages a panel of experts to identify and assess the potential impact of cutting-edge technologies in revolutionising procurement processes. The methodology section details the selection of experts and the survey's design, ensuring a comprehensive understanding of the current landscape and future possibilities. The results from this round offer valuable insights into the consensus and diverse opinions on various technologies such as artificial intelligence, Blockchain, and data analytics. These findings highlight the key areas of agreement and debate among experts and shed light on the challenges and opportunities inherent in adopting these technologies within the EU framework. The paper discusses the implications of these results for the subsequent rounds of the Delphi study and outlines preliminary conclusions that begin to shape a strategic technology roadmap. This study is pivotal in guiding policymakers and stakeholders towards effective and innovative procurement strategies, ensuring alignment with the broader objectives of the European Union.

Keywords: Delphi study · Emerging technologies · Public procurement · European Union

1 Introduction

Adopting emerging technologies in public procurement represents a promising avenue to enhance efficiency, transparency, and innovation [1–5]. This paper delves into the role of technologies like Blockchain, AI, and IoT in revolutionising the procurement cycle, assessing their fit, implementation urgency, and potential to meet EU strategic goals [6–11]. Embarking on the initial phase of a Delphi method-based study to construct a technology roadmap for integrating emerging technologies within the European Union's public procurement sector signifies a pivotal step towards realising a strategic and harmonised digital transformation aligned with EU objectives and regulations

I. Kostavelis et al. (Eds.): ICSC 2024, CCIS 2110, pp. 12–38, 2025.
https://doi.org/10.1007/978-3-031-69344-1_2

[12–14]. This approach gathers and refines expert insights on adopting transformative technologies such as Blockchain, AI, and IoT. It ensures a deep understanding of their practical implications, strategic fit, and potential to enhance public procurement transparency, efficiency, and innovation [15]. The significance of this research lies in its methodical consolidation of expert consensus, offering a robust framework for overcoming adoption barriers and aligning technological integration with the overarching goals of EU directives. By preparing the formalisation of a comprehensive technology roadmap, this study guides policy formulation and procurement practices and sets a precedent for future research in public procurement innovation, ensuring the strategic deployment of emerging technologies in a sector critical to the European Union's economic and social fabric. The suitability of emerging technologies varies across the procurement cycle's phases—planning, tendering, contract awarding, and management. AI and data analytics are particularly suitable for the planning phase, enabling predictive analytics for market analysis and needs assessment. Blockchain can ensure integrity and transparency during tendering, while AI streamlines proposal evaluations. IoT technologies enhance contract management and performance monitoring. The urgency of implementation is dictated by the technology's maturity level and the specific challenges it addresses in each phase. Emerging technologies stand to significantly contribute to the EU's objectives of transparency, value for money, and innovation in public procurement. Blockchain technology, by design, enhances transparency and trust in transactions [16–18]. AI and data analytics can optimise procurement processes, ensuring value for money through efficient decision-making. IoT fosters innovation in service delivery and infrastructure management, aligning with EU directives that encourage innovative solutions in public procurement. The deployment of these technologies aligns with several key EU directives aimed at modernising public procurement. These include directives advocating for greater efficiency and transparency (Directive 2014/24/EU), the promotion of electronic procurement (e-procurement), and the encouragement of innovative procurement practices [19]. The paper discusses how these technologies integrate with and support the principles outlined in EU procurement directives. Despite their potential, several barriers hinder the integration of emerging technologies into the public procurement process. These include technical challenges, such as interoperability and scalability issues; legal and regulatory challenges, particularly data privacy and security; and organisational challenges, including resistance to change and skills shortages [20, 21]. The paper analyses these barriers in-depth and suggests potential mitigation strategies. The paper concludes by presenting findings from a survey of experts in the field, aiming to gauge the level of agreement on the use and prioritisation of emerging technologies in public procurement. Initial findings suggest a broad consensus on the importance of AI and Blockchain, though opinions vary regarding implementation timelines and prioritisation of technologies. Emerging technologies offer the transformative potential for the public procurement sector. Their strategic adoption and integration into procurement processes could significantly contribute to the EU's transparency, efficiency, and innovation objectives. However, realising this potential requires addressing existing barriers and fostering consensus among stakeholders on technology prioritisation and implementation strategies. In our paper, we employ the Delphi method, a choice driven by its proven efficacy in fostering iterative consensus-building among a panel of experts under conditions of anonymity [12, 13, 22]. This methodology is particularly pertinent for developing a technology roadmap to navigate the intricate landscape of integrating emerging technologies such as AI, Blockchain, and IoT into the European Union's public procurement processes. The Delphi method's capacity to amalgamate diverse expert opinions into a coherent strategy is invaluable, given the complexities and uncertainties these technologies entail. Moreover, its structured approach ensures that the resulting technology roadmap is not only a reflection of collective expert wisdom but also anticipates future challenges and opportunities. The Delphi method facilitates a strategic, well-informed approach to fostering innovation in public procurement by aligning technological integration with the EU's strategic objectives and regulatory frameworks. This methodology choice underscores our commitment to producing a forward-looking roadmap deeply rooted in expert consensus, ensuring it is a robust guide for policymakers and practitioners navigating the evolving intersection of technology and public procurement within the EU context.

2 Literature Review

Public procurement represents 14% of the EU's Gross Domestic Product (GDP) and catalyses competitiveness and expansion [23]. It has become a more significant policy tool for fostering enhanced market integration following the economic downturn [24]. The pivotal role of public procurement in influencing economies and societies cannot be overstated [25]. Its capacity to promote innovation [26], facilitate sustainable development [5, 27], and drive business activities underscores its significance. Nonetheless, the efficacy of procurement policies hinges on their adept management of innovation [28], market dynamics, and societal objectives. Therefore, meticulous attention to the design of procurement procedures and assessing their results is imperative to optimise advantages while mitigating adverse economic and societal effects. Digitalising public procurement is crucial for promoting sustainable and efficient fiscal resource management, vital for a country's development [29]. Emerging technologies enhance public value in e-government services by promoting anti-corruption, transparency, and access to public information, with technology serving as a crucial mechanism for public value generation [9, 30, 31].

The European Union (EU) employs various robust framework tools and strategies to govern public procurement, ensuring transparency, competition, and value for money. These include the Public Procurement Directives, which establish legal principles and procedures [32]. Innovation Partnerships and Pre-Commercial Procurement (PCP) foster innovation, while Green Public Procurement (GPP) integrates environmental considerations [33]. Strategic procurement aligns purchasing with broader policy objectives, promoting social inclusion [34], SME support [35], and innovation [36, 37].

In the European Union (EU), adopting emerging technologies in public procurement is gaining traction as governments seek to modernise and optimise their procurement processes [30, 38]. These technologies offer various benefits, such as increased efficiency, transparency, and cost-effectiveness. Blockchain technology, for example, is being explored for its potential to enhance the security and integrity of procurement transactions by providing an immutable ledger of records [8, 10, 39, 40]. Artificial intelligence (AI) and machine learning algorithms are being utilised to automate routine tasks, improve decision-making, and identify patterns and trends in procurement data [21, 41, 42].

Moreover, e-procurement systems are becoming increasingly prevalent across EU member states, facilitating electronic communication between buyers and suppliers, streamlining bidding processes, and reducing administrative burdens. Digital marketplaces and platforms are also emerging to connect buyers with a wider pool of suppliers, promoting competition and driving innovation. Additionally, the EU has been proactive in promoting the use of digital tools in public procurement through initiatives such as the European Single Procurement Document (ESPD) and the European Single Procurement Vocabulary (ESPD) [29]. These initiatives aim to standardise procurement procedures and terminology across member states, making it easier for businesses to participate in public procurement processes across borders. Overall, the EU is witnessing a transformation in public procurement practices driven by the adoption of emerging technologies, which are expected to continue shaping the future of procurement in the region [29, 43–45].

Technology Roadmapping is crucial in this transformation path because it is a strategic tool illustrating the linkages between specific technology areas, products, and market dynamics [13, 14]. However, it traditionally falls short in providing in-depth insights into the challenges associated with each technology or research and development benchmark across leading nations. By incorporating the Delphi method with technology Roadmapping, we introduce a layer of rich, varied, and quantitatively detailed insights from Delphi study findings into the Roadmapping process. This integration transforms conventional roadmaps into more comprehensive 'three-dimensional' visualisations. This approach underpins our use of the Delphi method for Technology Roadmapping, as it significantly enriches the roadmap with diverse expert perspectives and detailed data, thereby enhancing the strategic planning and decision-making process for technology implementation in public procurement [13, 14].

3 Methodology

3.1 Scope

The scope includes evaluating emerging technologies for their suitability, urgency, and alignment with EU public procurement objectives and directives and identifying barriers and challenges to their implementation. The culmination of this study is the formulation of a strategic technology roadmap. This roadmap will be substantiated by the consensus derived from expert inputs and meticulously aligned with the EU's strategic objectives and regulatory directives. It is intended to serve as a blueprint for the progressive adoption of emerging technologies in public procurement, guiding stakeholders through the complexities of digital transformation.

3.2 Objectives

This study is conducted to comprehensively understand the integration of emerging technologies within the European Union's public procurement cycle, framework and strategic objectives. Five key objectives drive our research:

Assessment of Technological Suitability and Urgency
We endeavour to accurately identify which emerging technologies are aptly suited for each distinct phase of the public procurement cycle. Concurrently, we seek to determine the immediacy with which these technologies must be implemented, ascertaining their relevance and criticality to public procurement practices' current and future state.

Facilitation of EU Strategic Objectives
The research aims to evaluate the potential contribution of these technologies in fulfilling the strategic objectives set forth by the EU for public procurement. This encompasses analysing how technology can enhance transparency, efficiency, and equitable competition whilst ensuring compliance with legal mandates and promoting sustainability and innovation.

Alignment with EU Directives-Gap Analysis
A focal point of our investigation is to scrutinise how these emerging technologies are congruent with extant EU directives governing public procurement. This involves thoroughly examining the synergies and discrepancies between the innovative technological capabilities and the established regulatory frameworks. Also, we are concentrating on uncovering and addressing critical gaps within the existing EU public procurement framework that can be mitigated or resolved by applying emerging technologies, thereby enhancing procurement processes' efficiency, transparency, and innovation.

Identification of Barriers and Challenges
Recognising that the path to technology adoption is often fraught with obstacles, our study is also geared toward pinpointing the barriers and challenges that impede the assimilation of these technologies into the public procurement process. We seek to unearth both systemic and operational hindrances that must be addressed to facilitate a smooth transition to a technologically advanced procurement system.

These objectives are anticipated to yield a holistic and strategic perspective on incorporating emerging technologies in EU public procurement, setting a precedent for future research and practical applications in the field.

3.3 Research Questions

Through these Research Questions, the research aims to provide a comprehensive understanding of the transformative impact of these technologies on the procurement landscape within the EU context.

Suitability and Implementation Urgency of Emerging Technologies in Public Procurement Phases
RQ1. Which emerging technologies are most suitable for enhancing each phase of the public procurement cycle (planning, tendering, contract awarding, and management)?

RQ2. Given the current challenges and technological readiness within the public procurement sector, what is the urgency of implementing these technologies?

Contribution of Emerging Technologies Towards Achieving EU Strategic Objectives in Public Procurement
RQ3. How do emerging technologies such as Blockchain, Artificial Intelligence (AI), and the Internet of Things (IoT) contribute to achieving the European Union's strategic objectives of transparency, value for money, and innovation within public procurement processes?

Alignment of Emerging Technologies with EU Public Procurement Directives
RQ4. In what ways do emerging technologies align with the principles and requirements outlined in the European Union's public procurement directives?

RQ5. Which gaps in the current EU public procurement policies could be effectively bridged by integrating emerging technologies, and how can these integrations facilitate improvements in the procurement lifecycle?

Barriers and Challenges in Integrating Emerging Technologies into Public Procurement
RQ6. What are the principal barriers and challenges to integrating emerging technologies into public procurement?

3.4 Research Design

The research employed the Delphi method's first round to harness expert consensus on integrating emerging technologies in EU public procurement. This structured approach entailed selecting a diverse expert panel across relevant fields, crafting a comprehensive questionnaire probing the suitability, urgency, and alignment of technologies like AI/ML, Blockchain, and IoT with EU procurement directives, and identifying implementation barriers. Responses underwent meticulous analysis, blending qualitative insights from literature with quantitative consensus measures from experts. The iterative feedback loop facilitated clarification and refinement of expert opinions, aiming to build consensus on pivotal issues. This methodology's rigour and inclusivity underpin the formulation of a strategic technology roadmap, aligning emerging technologies with EU procurement objectives, thereby contributing a structured dialogue to the academic discourse on public procurement modernisation. In constructing our expert panel for this research, we employed rigorous selection criteria, focusing on academic credentials, professional experiences, and relevance to our study's objectives [46]. This multidisciplinary group of 21 experts was curated to encompass a broad spectrum of knowledge areas, including law and economics, data analysis, EU policy, emerging technologies, public administration research, and cybersecurity, among others [47]. Their diverse backgrounds ensured comprehensive coverage of the technological, legal, and policy-oriented aspects of public procurement within the EU context [47]. Selection filters prioritised individuals with demonstrated expertise in integrating technology into procurement processes, active engagement in EU policy-making or analysis, and innovative contributions to public sector digital transformation [48]. This deliberate and strategic expert aggregation facilitated a rich, nuanced exploration of emerging technologies' potential to revolutionise EU public procurement, ensuring the research outcomes were grounded in a wide-ranging, authoritative consensus. Our methodology section presents a structured approach encapsulated in Fig. 1, which outlines our comprehensive research framework. This visual representation illustrates the sequential process from expert selection to the formulation of a technology roadmap, depicting the interconnectivity of each phase and its components.

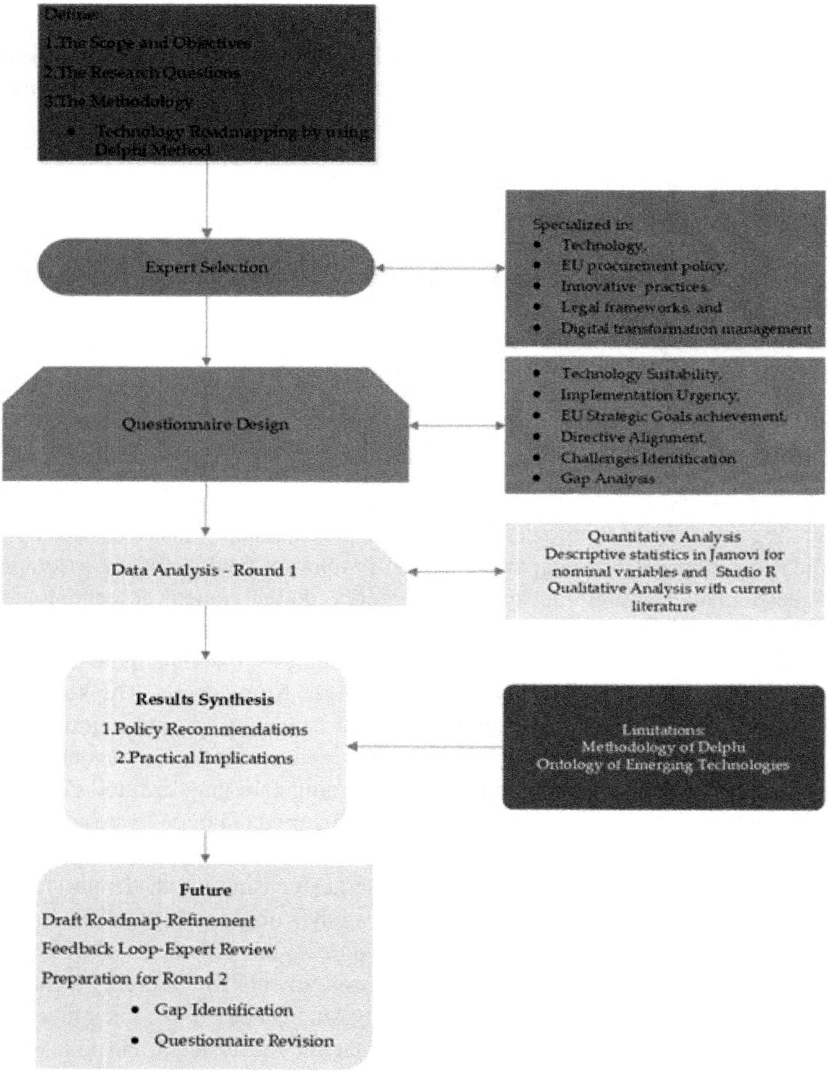

Fig. 1. Research Framework for the Integration of Emerging Technologies in EU Public Procurement

3.5 Data Collection Methods

Our study's data collection method was meticulously designed to capture a wide array of expert insights into integrating emerging technologies in EU public procurement. Utilising Google Forms facilitated an efficient and accessible mechanism for gathering responses, ensuring comprehensive participation from a globally dispersed panel of experts. These individuals were strategically identified through an extensive search on professional platforms like LinkedIn and ResearchGate, as well as through participation in pivotal EU workshops and conferences, notably the Freshminds initiative by the Joint Research Centre and engagements with the European Commission's Directorate General for Digital Services, specifically the Unit B2 on Interoperability and Digital Government. This methodological approach enabled the inclusion of diverse voices, from policymakers and industry practitioners to researchers and technologists, all contributing valuable perspectives on leveraging technology to enhance EU public procurement processes [49, 50]. This rich dataset forms the basis for our analysis, driving the development of a nuanced technology roadmap aligned with the strategic objectives of the European Union [51, 52].

3.6 Analysis Methods

To analyse data collected on integrating emerging technologies in EU public procurement, our study employed a two-tiered approach to ensure both accuracy and depth in our findings. Initially, we utilised Jamovi for descriptive statistics, which provided a foundational understanding of our data's distribution and central tendencies [53]. Jamovi, being user-friendly and open-source, facilitated an initial exploration of the responses, enabling us to visualise patterns, frequencies, and percentages of the various identified gaps, technological suitability, and perceived urgency levels across different procurement phases.

Building upon this preliminary analysis, we refined our data and sought deeper insights using RStudio, specifically targeting consensus rates among experts [54]. RStudio's versatile environment allowed for more complex statistical procedures, enabling us to disaggregate and re-aggregate data based on emerging themes and consensus levels [54, 55]. In Delphi method research for nominal variables, specific consensus measures like the mode for most common responses and percentage agreement among experts are used to gauge consensus. Weighted Kappa statistics can assess agreement levels across rounds [56], focusing on how expert opinions converge or diverge on categorical choices, offering a nuanced view of consensus development and stability over time [57]. Through custom scripts and the application of packages like dplyr and tidyr, we could accurately calculate the percentage of consensus for each identified challenge, barrier, and the alignment of technologies with EU directives [58]. This approach enhanced the reliability of our findings and provided a nuanced understanding of expert opinions on the potential impact of emerging technologies on public procurement.

A consensus threshold of 70% is particularly noted for its use in various studies, and we have also used it in our research when it is applicable [59].

This methodical analysis, leveraging the strengths of both Jamovi and RStudio, underscored the critical gaps and opportunities within the current EU public procurement framework. It paved the way for formulating a strategic technology roadmap grounded in empirical evidence and expert consensus to guide the EU toward a more efficient, transparent, and innovative procurement system.

4 Results Analysis and Discussion

Researching the suitability of emerging technologies in the EU's public procurement framework is essential for creating effective technology roadmaps [12–14].

In addressing the suitability of emerging technologies across different phases of the public procurement cycle, our study solicited insights from a panel of 21 experts through the first round of Delphi method research. The consensus on the application potential of specific technologies—Artificial Intelligence/Machine Learning (AI/ML), Blockchain, Big Data Analytics, Business Intelligence, Robotic Process Automation (RPA), Robots and Drones, and Augmented and Virtual Reality (AR/VR)—within the phases of Preparation and Planning, Tendering, Awarding, Contract Management, and Monitoring and Evaluation [60]. The consensus results are presented in Table 1.

Table 1. Consensus Rates for the Suitability of Emerging Technologies Across Public Procurement Cycle Phases

Phase	Blockchain (%)	AI/ML (%)	Big Data Analytics (%)	Business Intelligence (%)	RPA (%)	Robots and Drones (%)	AR/VR (%)	IoT (%)	3D Printing (%)
Preparation and Planning	60	70	80	79.0	76.6	16.6	23.1	38.10	19.05
Tendering	70	85	75	79.1	70.7	24.9	38.5	14.29	0.00
Awarding	75	90	55	68.6	47.2	8.3	7.7	19.05	4.76
Contract Management	80	70	70	52.7	64.8	33.2	23.1	52.38	14.29
Monitoring and Evaluation	65	60	85	84.4	35.4	74.9	53.9	66.67	9.52

The compiled data presents a nuanced analysis of the suitability of various emerging technologies across the public procurement cycle. Blockchain, AI/ML, and Big Data Analytics emerge as frontrunners, demonstrating high suitability percentages across multiple phases, particularly in Contract Management and Monitoring and Evaluation. This consensus underscores the technologies' potential to significantly enhance transparency, efficiency, and innovation within procurement processes. Conversely, 3D Printing and AR/VR technologies show selective suitability, indicating a more niche application within the procurement cycle. The findings highlight a strategic opportunity for the EU to harness these technologies in alignment with its procurement directives and strategic objectives. The study advocates for a meticulously crafted technology roadmap by addressing identified barriers and leveraging expert consensus, guiding the EU towards a more transparent, efficient, and innovative procurement landscape.

Table A7 in the Appendix below marks those technologies that meet or exceed a 70% consensus threshold for their suitability in each phase of the public procurement cycle The consensus analysis on emerging technologies within the EU public procurement cycle underscores the suitability of Blockchain, AI/ML, and Big Data Analytics, particularly in phases like Awarding and Contract Management. This reflects their potential to enhance transparency, efficiency, and decision-making accuracy. Business Intelligence and Robots and Drones also show targeted applicability, emphasising the importance of data-driven insights and automation in modern procurement practices. However, despite their potential, technologies such as 3D Printing and AR/VR do not meet the consensus threshold, suggesting a need for further exploration of their use cases.

The urgency assessment conducted with 21 experts on implementing emerging technologies in public procurement phases illuminates strategic priorities for modernisation efforts. Urgency is critical in technology roadmap development because it ensures timely adaptation and implementation of innovations, keeping pace with rapidly changing markets and technological advancements [12–14]. The consensus in Table 2 underscores a compelling urgency for integrating Blockchain and Artificial Intelligence/Machine Learning (AI/ML), particularly emphasising their significant impact on the Tendering and Contract Management phases. These findings suggest a keen recognition of Blockchain's potential to enhance transparency and security, while AI/ML is valued for its capacity to optimise decision-making through data analytics and automation. Furthermore, the strong inclination towards Big Data Analytics and Business Intelligence in the Preparation and Planning and Monitoring - Evaluation phases indicate an acknowledgement of their critical role in enhancing data-driven strategies and operational efficiencies. This collective insight from experts prioritises technological adoption in areas most susceptible to immediate improvements and aligns with overarching objectives to advance the efficiency, transparency, and integrity of the EU public procurement framework.

Table 2. Consensus Rates for the Urgency of Emerging Technologies Across Public Procurement Cycle Phases

Phase	Blockchain (%)	AI/ML (%)	Big Data Analytics (%)	Business Intelligence (%)	RPA (%)	Robots and Drones (%)	3D Printing (%)	AR/VR (%)	IoT (%)
Preparation and Planning	42.86	80.95	80.95	66.67	9.52	0.0	0	4.76	23.81
Tendering	66.67	66.67	38.10	19.05	57.14	4.76	4.76	9.52	9.52
Awarding	52.38	57.14	38.10	14.29	9.52	0.0	4.76	0	9.52
Contract Management	61.90	71.43	38.10	28.57	47.62	9.52	0	14.29	61.9
Monitoring and Evaluation	38.10	52.38	76.19	66.67	23.81	14.29	0	4.76	38.1

Table A8 reflects a consensus among experts of over 70% about the urgency of implementing emerging technologies in public procurement in each phase. The urgency of incorporating emerging technologies into the public procurement cycle is a pivotal concern in contemporary governance and administrative practices. Table A8 presents a comprehensive assessment of consensus levels regarding the imperative integration of various emerging technologies across distinct phases of the procurement process. The discernible consensus on the urgency of AI/ML and Big Data Analytics in the preparation and planning phase underscores their recognised significance in informed decision-making and strategic planning. Conversely, the absence of consensus across all technologies during the tendering and awarding phases suggests a less pronounced perceived urgency for technological intervention in these procedural stages. While there's unanimity regarding AI/ML's urgency in contract management and Big Data Analytics in monitoring and evaluation, the disparate consensus levels on other technologies underscore the nuanced considerations influencing their adoption throughout the procurement cycle. This subtle understanding underscores the complexity of technology adoption within public procurement contexts, necessitating a judicious and context-sensitive approach to implementation.

The simultaneous consensus on suitability and urgency in a technology roadmap ensures strategic alignment, efficient resource allocation, and risk mitigation in public procurement. It accelerates impactful technology adoption, prioritising technologies critical for immediate needs while preparing for future challenges and optimising investments for transformative efficiency, transparency, and effectiveness improvements.

In our study, by comparing Tables A7 and A8 we can discuss that across the public procurement cycle, Big Data Analytics consistently emerges as both a suitable and urgent technology in various phases (preparation and planning, monitoring and evaluation), underscoring its pivotal role in transforming public procurement processes. AI/ML is frequently regarded as suitable and considered urgent in the preparation, planning, and contract management phases, suggesting a growing recognition of its potential to drive efficiencies and improve decision-making. Blockchain's suitability in the awarding and contract management phases without corresponding urgency indicates its potential benefits, though not immediately critical for implementation. The results suggest a nuanced view among experts on prioritising and integrating these technologies, with a clear emphasis on the transformative potential of Big Data Analytics across the procurement cycle.

Table 3 presents the consensus rates for how each technology can help achieve EU objectives. Each row represents a different EU objective, and each column represents a technology, with the consensus rate (%) indicating the level of agreement among experts on that technology's contribution to achieving the objective.

Focused analysis reveals significant insights in evaluating the technological impacts on European Union (EU) objectives where consensus surpasses the 70% threshold. Blockchain technology's unparalleled strength in "Improving Transparency and Accountability" is unanimously recognised, with a 100% consensus rate, underscoring its potential to foster a new era of trust and transparency in digital transactions. Similarly, AI/ML technologies command a noteworthy consensus in "Ensuring Value for Money" and "Fostering Innovation", each with an 80.95% agreement among experts. This mirrors the broad acknowledgement of AI/ML's transformative capabilities in optimising resources and spearheading innovative solutions across sectors.

Table 3. Consensus Rates (%) of Technologies' Contributions Towards Achieving EU Objectives

EU Objective[a]	Blockchain (%)	AI/ML (%)	Big Data Analytics (%)	Business Intelligence (%)	RPA (%)	Robots and Drones (%)	3D Printing (%)	AR/VR (%)	IoT (%)
Improve Transparency-Accountability	100.00	38.10	52.4	95.2	33.33	4.76	-	-	38.10
Ensure Contract Compliance	80.95	42.86	52.4	76.2	38.10	14.29	-	14.29	57.14
Legal Compliance	80.95	52.38	28.6	76.2	42.86	-	-	4.76	9.52
Ensure Fair Competition	57.14	23.81	47.6	57.1	9.52	4.76	-	19.05	4.76
Ensure Value for Money	42.86	80.95	66.7	38.1	28.57	4.76	19	9.52	23.81
Sustainability-Cycle Economy	42.86	23.81	33.3	42.9	9.52	28.57	57	-	38.10
Foster Innovation	33.33	80.95	52.4	28.6	19.05	14.29	43	42.86	19.05
Social Responsibility	33.33	33.33	38.1	28.6	9.52	14.29	24	9.52	19.05
Increase Efficiency	38.10	76.19	76.2	38.1	80.95	42.86	24	19.05	42.86
Improve Supplier Performance	19.05	76.19	47.6	28.6	4.76	23.81	29	19.05	38.10

[a]Please note, the table uses "-" for objectives not explicitly mentioned for a technology, indicating no data was provided for that particular objective and technology combination. This comprehensive overview allows for a direct comparison of the perceived effectiveness of various technologies in addressing EU objectives.

Business Intelligence (BI) notably excels in Improving Transparency and Accountability, achieving a 95.2% consensus. This high rate of agreement highlights BI's critical role in extracting actionable insights from data, thus enhancing decision-making processes and ensuring accountability. Robotic Process Automation (RPA) is identified as a leading force in Increasing Efficiency, with an 80.95% consensus, reflecting its efficiency in automating routine tasks, optimising operational processes and reducing manual errors. The comprehensive analysis of consensus rates across emerging technologies about EU strategic objectives in public procurement delineates a clear categorisation of technologies with high and moderate impacts. At the forefront, Blockchain, AI/ML, and Business Intelligence (BI) are identified as high-impact technologies, each uniquely contributing towards the modernisation and efficiency of public procurement processes. With its unparalleled ability to foster transparency and accountability through secure and immutable records, Blockchain is unanimously recognised for its profound impact. Blockchain is pivotal for enhancing trust in public transactions and instrumental in ensuring contract and legal compliance, addressing two critical facets of public procurement. AI/ML technologies emerge as crucial drivers for providing value for money and fostering innovation, receiving substantial consensus above 80%. By harnessing the power of data analytics and machine learning, AI/ML can optimise procurement strategies, predict market trends, and introduce innovative solutions, significantly contributing to cost efficiency and the advancement of procurement practices [61]. Business Intelligence, with a notable 95.2% consensus in improving transparency and accountability, underscores the technology's effectiveness in providing deep insights into procurement operations. BI tools enable stakeholders to make informed decisions, ensuring that procurement activities align with strategic objectives and comply with regulatory standards.

In the moderate impact category, RPA and IoT demonstrate their utility in enhancing efficiency and ensuring contract compliance. RPA's automation capabilities streamline administrative tasks, reducing errors and operational costs [62]. IoT's real-time monitoring and data collection capabilities offer valuable insights into the procurement lifecycle, ensuring adherence to contract terms and conditions [10, 63].

These categorisations prompt a strategic dialogue on adopting and integrating these technologies into EU procurement policies. While high-impact technologies offer transformative potential, moderate-impact technologies play essential roles in complementing and enhancing the procurement ecosystem.

Table 4 summarises how well each of the emerging technologies aligns with existing EU directives on public procurement based on the frequencies and percentages provided:

Table 4. Alignment of Emerging Technologies with Existing EU Directives on Public Procurement: A Comparative Overview

Technology	Strongly Align (%)	Moderately Align (%)	Weakly Align (%)	Do Not Align (%)	Unsure (%)
Blockchain	71.4	28.6	-	-	-
AI and Machine Learning	45.0	40.0	10.0	5.0	-
Internet of Things (IoT)	30.0	55.0	5.0	-	10.0
Augmented/Virtual Reality	9.5	47.6	33.3	4.8	4.8
Big Data Analytics	71.4	28.6	-	-	-
Robotic Process Automation	38.1	57.1	-	-	4.8
3D Printing	-	38.1	28.6	-	33.3
Business Intelligence	57.1	33.3	4.8	-	4.8
Robots and Drones	-	47.6	19.0	-	33.3

The results indicating the alignment of emerging technologies with existing EU directives on public procurement can be interpreted through the lens of specific EU directives, such as Directive 2014/24/EU[1] on public procurement and Directive 2014/25/EU on procurement by entities operating in the water, energy, transport, and postal services sectors. These directives aim to increase the efficiency of public spending, ensure greater transparency, and promote innovation and sustainability in procurement processes. Blockchain[2] and Big Data Analytics[3] show high rates of strong alignment (71.4%), suggesting that these technologies are perceived as highly compatible with EU directives' goals of transparency and efficient data management. With its immutable ledger, Blockchain enhances the traceability and integrity of procurement records, directly supporting transparency and anti-corruption measures emphasised in EU directives. Similarly, Big Data Analytics can significantly contribute to strategic decision-making and market analysis, aligning with the directives' push for more data-driven and efficient procurement processes [45, 64, 65]. AI, and Machine Learning[4]and Business Intelligence[5], which also shows a strong alignment, can be interpreted as valuable tools for facilitating directive-driven objectives such as innovation and the tailored assessment of bids based on criteria beyond cost, including quality, environmental benefits, and lifecycle costs. Their ability to process large datasets and provide actionable insights can help procurement entities make more informed decisions, a key aspect of the modernisation efforts encouraged by the directives. Robotic Process Automation (RPA)[6] and IoT, which have a considerable alignment, could be seen as technologies supporting operational efficiencies and real-time monitoring capabilities. RPA can automate routine tasks, reducing manual errors and improving process efficiency. IoT's role in real-time tracking aligns with the directive's emphasis on contract performance and effective contract management. Augmented/Virtual Reality (AR/VR) and 3D Printing present mixed results in alignment, indicating areas where the current directives may not fully capture these technologies' potential benefits. AR/VR's applications in training and simulation for procurement professionals and 3D Printing's implications for sustainability and innovation might require more explicit acknowledgement and guidance within the EU procurement framework. Robots and Drones showing moderate to low alignment and higher levels of uncertainty suggest a need for clearer guidance or amendments in

[1] Directive 2014/24/EU outlines the need for digitization and online management tools essential for ensuring competition and transparency in public procurement, setting substantial conditions for legal activities in electronic form at a European level [20].

[2] The European Interoperability Framework and the EU Strategy for Blockchain promote seamless operation and innovation in blockchain technology.

[3] European Strategy for Data and the Digital Europe Programme, are aligned with big data analytics.

[4] The AI Act and the Digital Europe Programme are EU initiatives specifically designed to align with and foster the development and application of AI and Machine Learning technologies.

[5] The Digital Single Market Strategy and European Strategy for Data support business intelligence by enabling big data use for innovation and better decision-making across sectors.

[6] The Digital Europe Programme and the Single Digital Gateway Regulation support the integration of Robotic Process Automation (RPA) by promoting digital transformation and automation across EU sectors.

directives to address these technologies' roles in procurement, particularly regarding operational deployment and ethical considerations.

The consensus percentages for perceived gaps in current EU public procurement policies regarding the integration of emerging technologies are presented in the table below:

Table 5. Consensus on Perceived Gaps Hindering the Integration of Emerging Technologies in EU Public Procurement

Gap	Count	Consensus %
Technological (Lack of Standardisation, Limited Technical Expertise…)	21	100.00%
Regulatory (Unclear Guidelines…)	13	61.90%
Strategic Gaps (Lack of Long-term Vision, Inadequate Stakeholder Involvement…)	11	52.38%
Organisational (Resistance to Change, Skill Gap, Misalignment with Objectives…)	9	42.86%
Financial (Budget Constraints…)	5	23.81%
Ethical and Social Considerations	1	4.76%

Table 5 clearly illustrates that Technological gaps are unanimously identified as the most critical barrier, with 100% consensus. This underscores a universal recognition of the need to standardise and enhance technical expertise in the field. Regulatory issues and Strategic Gaps also emerge as significant concerns, indicating a need for clearer policy guidelines and more inclusive, forward-thinking strategic planning. The technology's interaction with EU laws, particularly the General Data Protection Regulation, is a topic of ongoing analysis, highlighting how legal frameworks must adapt to maximise the benefits of Blockchain in public procurement [18]. The search for an AI regulatory model in the EU is based on principles that aim to balance democratic values with the need for a clear framework, diverging from more abstentionist or overly regulatory models seen in other regions. With the advent of the EU AI Act, rules are being set out for AI-driven products and services, emphasising data protection under the General Data Protection Regulation (GDPR). The interactions between the AI Act/AI systems and GDPR present challenges, highlighting the need for an evolving regulatory framework [66]. An ongoing effort is to harmonise AI usage within public procurement across member states, ensuring best practices and compliance with EU directives. Organisational challenges highlight internal barriers to change [20], while Financial constraints reflect resource-related hurdles. Ethical and Social considerations, however less cited, remain an important area for attention. Addressing these gaps is essential for successfully integrating emerging technologies in EU public procurement, fostering innovation, efficiency, and transparency.

In our discussion on the integration challenges of emerging technologies in public procurement, the consensus results, as outlined in the accompanying table, provide a compelling narrative on the breadth and depth of barriers encountered. This quantitative analysis unequivocally highlights regulatory constraints as the most significant hurdle, with a unanimous 100% of respondents identifying compliance issues as a major impediment to technology adoption. This consensus underscores the pressing need for regulatory frameworks to evolve with technological advancements, ensuring that legal guidelines are clear and conducive to innovation. Data privacy and security concerns, cited by 90.48% of stakeholders, emerge as another critical area, reflecting the high stakes involved in managing sensitive procurement data. The overwhelming agreement on this point emphasises the need for stringent data protection measures and underscores the urgency of aligning emerging technologies with data privacy regulations such as the GDPR [18].

Furthermore, the table reveals that organisational barriers, including resistance to change and skill gaps, are acknowledged by 76.19% of respondents. This significant consensus points to the internal challenges within procurement entities, highlighting the need for cultural shifts and targeted training programs to facilitate the adoption of new technologies. Financial barriers and technical limitations, identified by over half of the respondents, further complicate the adoption landscape, indicating concerns over cost-effectiveness and the practicality of integrating new systems. The consensus on vendor lock-in and interoperability issues, noted by nearly half of the stakeholders, amplifies the call for strategic measures to ensure flexibility and open standards in technology deployment.

This detailed consensus, derived from Table 6, illustrates the complex challenges hindering the effective implementation of emerging technologies in public procurement. It underscores the imperative for a holistic and strategic approach that addresses these multifaceted barriers, paving the way for leveraging technology to achieve the EU's objectives of enhancing efficiency, transparency, and innovation in procurement processes.

Table 6. Consensus Percentages on Challenges to Emerging Technology Integration in EU Public Procurement

#	Challenge	Count	Consensus of Experts %
1	**Regulatory Constraints (e.g., Compliance Issues)**	21	**100.00%**
2	**Data Privacy and Security Concerns**	19	**90.48%**
3	**Organisational Barriers (Change Resistance, Skill Gap, etc.)**	16	**76.19%**
4	Financial Barriers (High Initial Costs, Uncertain ROI, etc.)	11	52.38%
5	Technical Limitations (Interoperability, Complexity, etc.)	10	47.62%

(continued)

Table 6. (*continued*)

#	Challenge	Count	Consensus of Experts %
6	Vendor Lock-in (Dependency on Single Vendor…)	10	47.62%
7	Interoperability Issues	8	38.10%
8	Ethical and Social Considerations	7	33.33%
9	Cultural and Organisational Resistance	7	33.33%
10	Lack of Clear Strategy and Leadership	7	33.33%
11	Complex Integration Processes	4	19.05%
12	Scaling Challenges	4	19.05%
13	Evolving Technological Landscape	3	14.29%
14	Cost and Budget Constraints	1	4.76%
15	Capacity Building and Skill Development	1	4.76%

5 Recommendations and Implications

5.1 Policy Recommendations

In light of the empirical data presented in Table 1, which delineates the consensus rates for the suitability of various emerging technologies across public procurement cycle phases, this paper posits a series of policy recommendations.

The data reveals a progressive increase in the suitability of Blockchain from 60% in the Preparation and Planning phase to 80% in Contract Management, indicating its vital role in enhancing transparency and security as procurement advances. Consequently, policies should be crafted to encourage the strategic deployment of Blockchain where its impact is most pronounced. Similarly, AI/ML's peak suitability of 90% during the Awarding phase underscores the necessity for policies promoting AI/ML integration for advanced decision-making support during this critical phase. With Big Data Analytics and Business Intelligence showing high suitability, especially in the Monitoring and Evaluation phase (85% and 84.4%, respectively), there is a clear directive for policies facilitating the widespread integration of data analytics tools. Such policies would ensure that data-driven insights continuously inform procurement processes, enhancing efficiency and strategic decision-making.

Considering the insights gained from the discerned consensus rates showcasing the pivotal role of Blockchain, AI/ML, Business Intelligence (BI), and Robotic Process Automation (RPA) in enhancing EU public procurement objectives, this paper recommends a targeted policy framework to harness these technologies effectively. Recognising Blockchain's unparalleled contribution to transparency and accountability, policies should foster its integration by establishing secure, transparent transaction protocols. Concurrently, AI/ML's profound impact on fostering innovation and ensuring value for money necessitates the development of ethical guidelines and support for AI-driven solutions in procurement processes. The significant role of BI in decision-making underscores the need for policies promoting data literacy and the adoption of analytics tools. Lastly, RPA's efficiency in process automation calls for investment in digital infrastructure to facilitate widespread implementation. These policy recommendations collectively aim to optimise emerging technologies' transformative potential, ensuring they contribute substantively towards achieving strategic, efficient, and innovative procurement practices within the EU framework.

For enhanced efficiency, transparency, and innovation, EU policymakers should proactively revise public procurement directives to better integrate and leverage emerging technologies, particularly Blockchain, AI/ML, and IoT. Establishing comprehensive guidelines for the ethical use and deployment of AR/VR and 3D Printing within procurement practices is crucial. Furthermore, encouraging cross-sectoral collaborations can facilitate the seamless integration of these technologies, driving the modernisation of public procurement processes in alignment with evolving EU objectives and standards.

Policy recommendations must prioritise the harmonisation of regulatory frameworks with the pace of technological innovation, ensuring legal clarity and compliance facilitation. Strengthening data privacy and security protocols is critical to safeguard sensitive procurement information [17]. Additionally, policies should support organisational change, addressing resistance and skill gaps through comprehensive training programs. Financial and technical barriers require strategies for cost management and system interoperability, alongside measures to prevent vendor lock-in, promoting a competitive and flexible technological ecosystem in public procurement.

5.2 Implications for Practice

The varying rates of suitability and urgency across technologies and procurement phases suggest a strategic layering of technological integration, where the focus shifts from planning and market analysis (AI/ML and Big Data Analytics) towards ensuring transaction integrity (Blockchain) and operational efficiency (RPA, IoT) as the procurement process progresses. This underscores the importance of adopting a phase-specific approach to technology implementation, leveraging each technology's strengths to address each procurement phase's unique challenges and objectives. Practically, this means that procurement professionals must be agile, adopting a multi-technology strategy that aligns with each phase's specific needs and challenges to enhance the procurement process's overall efficacy and integrity. Procurement entities must tailor their technology strategies to leverage the strengths of specific technologies at different stages of the procurement cycle, such as utilising RPA for efficient documentation processing in the early phases and capitalising on IoT for effective contract management and monitoring.

The empirical consensus on the transformative role of Blockchain, AI/ML, Business Intelligence (BI), and Robotic Process Automation (RPA) in advancing EU strategic objectives in public procurement provides profound implications for practice. Blockchain's unanimous endorsement for enhancing transparency mandates its prioritisation for secure, immutable transaction records, reinforcing trust in public transactions [16]. On the other hand, AI/ML emerges as a powerhouse for ensuring value for money and driving innovation, with an 80.95% consensus rate signalling its pivotal role in predictive analytics, market analysis, and automated decision-making processes. This indicates a pressing need for procurement systems to embrace AI-driven solutions that optimise costs and introduce dynamic, innovative procurement strategies. Similarly, the significant role of BI in enhancing decision-making capabilities, with a high consensus rate, highlights the importance of a data-driven approach in procurement. Investing in analytics tools and training for procurement professionals can transform procurement data into actionable insights, leading to strategic, informed decisions that align with EU procurement objectives. Lastly, RPA's endorsement for its efficiency in automating routine tasks underlines the necessity of adopting automation technologies to streamline operations, reduce errors, and free up resources for strategic procurement activities.

Furthermore, the critical role of technologies like AI/ML and Big Data Analytics in procurement highlights the urgent need for investment in digital infrastructure and training. Procurement professionals require ongoing education to navigate these technologies effectively, ensuring they can leverage data analytics for insights and AI for enhanced decision-making capabilities. The study's results indicate that public procurement practitioners should prioritise integrating technologies like Blockchain and Big Data Analytics, which align strongly with EU directives. Additionally, there's a clear call for regulatory evolution to accommodate emerging technologies such as AR/VR, ensuring the procurement framework remains adaptive and inclusive of technological advancements.

In practice, the consensus on challenges necessitates procurement entities to navigate regulatory landscapes, proactively ensuring alignment with technological innovations. Emphasising data security and privacy becomes paramount, alongside cultivating an organisational culture receptive to change and technological adoption. Addressing financial and technical barriers involves strategic investments in cost-effective solutions and interoperable systems. Practitioners must also mitigate vendor lock-in risks by diversifying technology sources, ensuring flexibility and sustainability in procurement practices, and enhancing public procurement processes' efficiency, transparency, and innovation.

5.3 Future Research Directions

Future research should delve into the longitudinal impact of emerging technologies on public procurement outcomes, assessing their long-term efficiency, transparency, and innovation enhancements. Comparative studies across EU member states can provide insights into varying adoption rates and success factors, offering a blueprint for optimised implementation strategies. Additionally, exploring the intersection of technology adoption with sustainable and socially responsible procurement practices can broaden the understanding of achieving broader EU policy goals. The role of emerging technologies in mitigating procurement fraud and enhancing cybersecurity warrants focused investigation, given the increasing digitalisation of procurement processes. Lastly, examining the effects of technological integration on supplier diversity and SME participation in public procurement can contribute to more inclusive and equitable procurement ecosystems. This study's reliance on expert consensus may introduce subjectivity, potentially overlooking broader stakeholder perspectives. The rapid pace of technological evolution also challenges the timeliness and relevance of findings. Future research should incorporate various stakeholder views and continuously update to reflect the latest technological advancements and regulatory changes.

The next step of our research will be the second Delphi round, which aims to refine a technology roadmap for integrating emerging technologies in EU public procurement [13]. This phase will prioritise technologies, assess their impacts, and outline implementation strategies, considering regulatory, infrastructural, and skill-related factors. It seeks expert consensus on key milestones and challenges, guiding policymakers and stakeholders through a phased adoption approach. This roadmap will align technology integration with EU objectives, enhancing procurement efficiency, transparency, and innovation while addressing potential barriers to successful implementation.

6 Conclusion

6.1 Summary of Key Findings

The comprehensive analysis of the suitability and urgency of emerging technologies across the public procurement cycle phases offers pivotal insights for integrating innovative solutions within the EU's strategic procurement framework. This study reveals that the strategic deployment of technologies like AI/ML, Blockchain, Big Data Analytics, and IoT, tailored to specific phases of the procurement process, is crucial for enhancing transparency, efficiency, and innovation.

In the Preparation and Planning phase, the emphasis on AI/ML and Big Data Analytics underscores the importance of leveraging predictive analytics and market intelligence early on to inform strategic decision-making. As the process advances to the Tendering and Awarding phases, the increased suitability and urgency of Blockchain highlight its critical role in ensuring transaction integrity and fostering trust through transparent and secure processes [16]. During Contract Management, the convergence of Blockchain and IoT's high suitability and urgency marks a shift towards ensuring robust contract execution and compliance, facilitated by real-time tracking and performance monitoring capabilities. In the Monitoring and Evaluation phase, the pronounced focus on Big Data Analytics and BI and IoT's applicability underscores the need for technologies that offer deep analytical insights into procurement outcomes, driving continuous improvement and strategic alignment with EU procurement objectives. This analysis concludes that a dynamic, phase-adjusted approach to technology integration is paramount. Tailoring technology adoption to address each procurement phase's unique requirements and challenges ensures the realisation of strategic objectives. Furthermore, this phased approach highlights the necessity for ongoing investment in digital infrastructure, skills development, and policy frameworks that accommodate and foster the adoption of these emerging technologies. The key finding from merging suitability and urgency data reveals Big Data Analytics as the sole technology identified as both suitable and urgent for the Preparation and Planning, and Monitoring and Evaluation phases, emphasising its critical role in enhancing public procurement processes.

The study also reveals that Blockchain and Big Data Analytics align highly with EU procurement directives, enhancing transparency and data-driven decision-making. AI/ML and Business Intelligence also align strongly, promoting innovation and informed evaluations. However, AR/VR, 3D Printing, and Robots and Drones indicate a need for updated regulatory guidance to exploit their potential in public procurement fully, emphasising the necessity for legislative adaptation to technological advances.

Expert consensus about challenges and barriers underscores the necessity for evolving EU procurement directives to align with rapid technological advancements. Key challenges identified include regulatory constraints, data privacy concerns, and organisational barriers, emphasising the need for strategic policy reforms. Experts advocate for robust data security protocols, cultural adaptation towards technology, and workforce upskilling. Addressing financial and technical hurdles, alongside mitigating vendor lock-in, is crucial. This collective insight calls for a multidisciplinary approach to seamlessly integrate emerging technologies, enhancing public procurement processes' transparency, efficiency, and innovation.

Expert consensus underscores the necessity for evolving EU procurement directives to align with rapid technological advancements. Key challenges identified include regulatory constraints, data privacy concerns, and organisational barriers, emphasising the need for strategic policy reforms. Experts advocate for robust data security protocols, cultural adaptation towards technology, and workforce upskilling. Addressing financial and technical hurdles, alongside mitigating vendor lock-in, is crucial. This collective insight calls for a multidisciplinary approach to seamlessly integrate emerging technologies, enhancing public procurement processes' transparency, efficiency, and innovation.

6.2 Contribution to Knowledge

This study significantly contributes to the knowledge base by elucidating the nuanced roles of emerging technologies across different phases of the EU public procurement cycle. Mapping the suitability and urgency of technologies like AI/ML, Blockchain, and IoT provides a strategic framework for integrating digital innovations in procurement processes. This research offers a novel, phase-specific approach to technology adoption, underpinning the importance of tailoring technological solutions to enhance procurement efficiency, transparency, and innovation, thereby aligning with EU strategic objectives.

By mapping the contours of technology suitability and urgency across the procurement cycle, this paper contributes to formulating a nuanced roadmap for digital transformation in EU public procurement. Such a roadmap will align with the EU's overarching goals and set a benchmark for leveraging technology to achieve a transparent, efficient, and innovative procurement ecosystem.

This research also enhances knowledge of the alignment of emerging technologies with EU procurement directives, revealing varying degrees of compatibility. It highlights Blockchain and Big Data Analytics' strong alignment, identifies gaps in current directives for technologies like AR/VR, and underscores the necessity for legislative updates to leverage technological advancements in public procurement fully.

This study also enriches understanding by illuminating the consensus among experts on the challenges of integrating emerging technologies in EU public procurement. It highlights the critical need for regulatory adaptation, emphasises data security, and identifies organisational readiness as pivotal. The findings contribute to shaping strategic policy and practice reforms, advancing the discourse on technological transformation within public procurement frameworks.

6.3 Limitations and Mitigation

While providing valuable insights into the integration of emerging technologies in EU public procurement, this study has certain limitations that necessitate consideration. First, the reliance on expert consensus through the Delphi method, while robust, may introduce subjectivity, reflecting the perspectives and experiences of the selected panel. Subjectivity can potentially skew the understanding of technology suitability and urgency. Future research should diversify the panel of experts to mitigate this limitation, including a broader range of stakeholders from various EU member states and sectors. Additionally, complementing the Delphi method with quantitative data analysis could offer a more objective assessment of the impacts of technology adoption. Second, the dynamic nature of technology evolution means that the findings may quickly become outdated. The rapid pace at which new and existing technologies evolve could alter their suitability and urgency in the procurement process [60]. Ongoing research and periodic reassessment of the technology landscape are essential to maintain the relevance of the findings. Incorporating adaptive frameworks that can evolve with technological advancements will ensure that policy recommendations and strategic implementations remain effective over time. Lastly, the study's focus on EU strategic objectives and public procurement may limit its applicability in different geopolitical contexts or private sector procurement practices. Expanding future research to include comparative analyses between public and private sector procurement and different international procurement frameworks could enhance the generalizability of the findings. Future research would provide a more comprehensive understanding of how emerging technologies can be effectively integrated across various procurement ecosystems. Methodological limitations derive from the Delphi method, employed to gauge expert consensus on the integration of emerging technologies in EU public procurement, which encounters inherent limitations, notably the potential for subjectivity and bias. The method's reliance on expert opinions may reflect a narrow perspective if the panel lacks diversity across sectors and geographies [12, 13, 22, 46, 48, 50, 57, 59].

Additionally, the rapid evolution of technology challenges the Delphi method's iterative process, as findings might quickly become outdated, limiting their applicability. Moreover, the consensus-driven nature may inadvertently prioritise prevailing views over innovative insights. Addressing these limitations necessitates strategically selecting a diverse expert panel and integrating quantitative data to complement and validate the qualitative findings, ensuring a more comprehensive and future-proof analysis. To mitigate the limitations of the Delphi method in assessing emerging technologies in public procurement, strategies include diversifying the expert panel for broader perspectives, integrating quantitative data for objective validation, conducting iterative rounds for updated insights, and fostering open dialogue among experts. These steps ensure a comprehensive, bias-minimised, and dynamic consensus-building process.

Appendix

Table A7. "Consensus on the Suitability of Emerging Technologies Across Public Procurement Cycle Phases: A Checkmark ('✔') Indicates a Consensus Above the 70% Threshold, While a Cross ('✘') Denotes Suitability Below the Threshold."

Phase	Blockchain	AI/ML	Big Data Analytics	Business Intelligence	RPA	Robots and Drones	AR/VR	IoT	3D Printing
Preparation and planning	x	x	✔	✔	✔	x	x	x	x
Tendering	x	✔	✔	✔	✔	x	x	x	x
Awarding	✔	✔	x	x	x	x	x	x	x
Contract Management	✔	x	x	x	x	x	x	x	x
Monitoring and Evaluation	x	x	✔	✔	✘	✔	x	x	x

Table A8. "Consensus on the Urgency of Emerging Technologies Across Public Procurement Cycle Phases: A Checkmark ('✔') Indicates a Consensus Above the 70% Threshold, While a Cross ('✘') Denotes Urgency Below the Threshold."

Phase	Blockchain	AI/ML	Big Data Analytics	Business Intelligence	RPA	Robots and Drones	3D Printing	AR/VR	IoT
Preparation and Planning	x	✔	✔	x	x	x	x	x	x
Tendering	x	x	x	x	x	x	x	x	x
Awarding	x	x	x	x	x	x	x	x	x
Contract Management	x	✔	x	x	x	x	x	x	x
Monitoring and Evaluation	x	x	✔	x	x	x	x	x	x

References

1. Wu, C.: Disruptive Technologies in Public Procurement, Washington, D.C. (2021)
2. Uyarra, E., Zabala-Iturriagagoitia, J.M., Flanagan, K., Magro, E.: Public procurement, innovation and industrial policy: rationales, roles Capabilities and Implementation. Res. Policy **49**, 103844 (2020). https://doi.org/10.1016/J.RESPOL.2019.103844
3. Hickok, M.: Public procurement of artificial intelligence systems: new risks and future proofing. AI Soc. (2022). https://doi.org/10.1007/s00146-022-01572-2

4. Rabuzin, K., Modrušan, N.: Prediction of public procurement corruption indices using machine learning methods. In: Proceedings of the Proceedings of the 11th International Joint Conference on Knowledge Discovery, Knowledge Engineering and Knowledge Management, pp. 333–340. SCITEPRESS - Science and Technology Publications (2019)
5. Hochstetter, J., Vásquez, F., Diéguez, M., Bustamante, A., Arango-López, J.: Transparency and e-government in electronic public procurement as sustainable development. Sustainability **15**, 4672 (2023). https://doi.org/10.3390/su15054672
6. Ubaldi, B., et al.: State of the Art in the Use of Emerging Technologies in the Public Sector, Paris (2019)
7. Mavidis, A., Folinas, D.: Industry 4.0 and E-Public Procurement: A Profitable Coexistence, May 2022
8. Rodríguez Bolívar, M.P., Prados Prados, M.: Open technologies for public tendering. blockchain technology impact on transparency and efficiency of public procurement processes. In: Janssen, M., et al. (ed.) EGOV 2022. LNCS, vol. 13391, pp. 196–211. Springer, Cham (2022). https://doi.org/10.1007/978-3-031-15086-9_13
9. Modrušan, N., Rabuzin, K., Mršić, L.: Review of public procurement fraud detection techniques powered by emerging technologies. Int. J. Adv. Comput. Sci. Appl. **12**, 575–583 (2021). https://doi.org/10.14569/IJACSA.2021.0120272
10. Mircea, M., Stoica, M., Ghilic-Micu, B.: Analysis of the Impact of Blockchain and Internet of Things (BIoT) on public procurement. IEEE Access **10**, 63353–63374 (2022). https://doi.org/10.1109/ACCESS.2022.3182656
11. European Union Emerging Technologies in Public Procurement: Study Results | ISA^2. https://ec.europa.eu/isa2/news/emerging-technologies-public-procurement-study-results_en/. Accessed 18 May 2023
12. Antonio, L., Junior, L., Vasconcellos, E., Luís, F., Guedes, L., Vasconcellos, L.: Using Delphi as a Basis to Design a Technology Roadmap (2016)
13. Kanama, D.: Development of technology foresight: integration of technology roadmapping and the delphi method. In: Moehrle, M., Isenmann, R., Phaal, R. (eds.) Technology Roadmapping for Strategy and Innovation, pp. 151–171. Springer, Heidelberg (2013). https://doi.org/10.1007/978-3-642-33923-3_10
14. de Alcantara, D.P., Martens, M.L.: Technology Roadmapping (TRM): a systematic review of the literature focusing on models. Technol. Forecast. Soc. Change **138**, 127–138 (2019). https://doi.org/10.1016/j.techfore.2018.08.014
15. Rejeb, A., Rejeb, K., Appolloni, A., Kayikci, Y., Iranmanesh, M.: The landscape of public procurement research: a bibliometric analysis and topic modelling based on Scopus. J. Public Procure. (2023). https://doi.org/10.1108/JOPP-06-2022-0031
16. Chen, P.: The Relationship between Blockchain and government regulation and governance—the distinctions between different countries. Appl. Comput. Eng. **5**, 731–735 (2023). https://doi.org/10.54254/2755-2721/5/20230685
17. Carvalho, R.: Blockchain and public procurement. Eur. J. Comp. Law Gov. **6**, 187–225 (2019). https://doi.org/10.1163/22134514-00602002
18. Finck, M.: Blockchain Regulation and Governance in Europe. Cambridge University Press (2018). ISBN 9781108609708
19. European Parliament and the Commission. Directive 2014/24/EU of the European Parliament and of the Council of 26 February 2014 on Public Procurement and Repealing Directive 2004/18/EC Text with EEA Relevance 2014, OJ L (2014)
20. Garcia, M.J.G.: Digitalization in public sector procurement and consequences from an organizational point of view in the EU, pp. 74–90 (2022)
21. Tangi, L., van Noordt, C., Rodriguez Müller, A.P.: The challenges of AI implementation in the public sector: an in-depth case studies analysis. In: Proceedings of the 24th Annual

International Conference on Digital Government Research, pp. 414–422. ACM, New York, USA (2023)
22. Linstone, H.A., Turoff, M. (eds.): The Delphi Method: Techniques and Applications–1975 (2008)
23. Bovis, C.: The priorities of EU public procurement regulation. ERA Forum **21**, 283–297 (2020). https://doi.org/10.1007/s12027-020-00608-8
24. Pircher, B.: EU public procurement policy: the economic crisis as trigger for enhanced harmonisation. J. Eur. Integr. **42**, 509–525 (2020). https://doi.org/10.1080/07036337.2019.1666114
25. Grandia, J., Meehan, J.: Public procurement as a policy tool: using procurement to reach desired outcomes in society. Int. J. Public Sect. Manag. **30**, 302–309 (2017). https://doi.org/10.1108/IJPSM-03-2017-0066
26. Lenderink, B., Halman, J.I.M., Voordijk, H.: Innovation and public procurement: from fragmentation to synthesis on concepts, rationales and approaches. Innov.: Eur. J. Soc. Sci. Res. **35**, 650–674 (2022). https://doi.org/10.1080/13511610.2019.1700101
27. Miranzo Díaz, J.: Hacia Una Administración Pública Sostenible: Novedades En La Legislación Europea de Contratación Pública. Actualidad Jurídica Ambiental 1–40 (2017). https://doi.org/10.56398/ajacieda.00093
28. Kijek, A.: The effect of public procurement and its spillovers on innovativeness of enterprises in European countries. Eur. Res. Stud. J. **XXII**, 103–111 (2019). https://doi.org/10.35808/ersj/1410
29. Bertocchi, E., et al.: Accelerating transparency and efficiency in the public procurement sector for a smarter society: enotification and ESPD integration for developing e-procurement. In: Uskov, V.L., Howlett, R.J., Jain, L.C. (eds.) SEEL 2022. Smart Innovation, Systems and Technologies, vol. 305, pp. 269–287. Springer, Singapore (2022). https://doi.org/10.1007/978-981-19-3112-3_25
30. Deloitte. European Commission Study on Up-Take of Emerging Technologies in Public Procurement (2020)
31. Valle-Cruz, D.: Public value of e-government services through emerging technologies. Int. J. Public Sect. Manag. **32**, 530–545 (2019). https://doi.org/10.1108/IJPSM-03-2018-0072
32. Janssen, W.A.: Public procurement law in the European union. In: Grandia, J., Volker, L. (eds.) Public Procurement, pp. 39–56. Palgrave Macmillan, Cham (2023). https://doi.org/10.1007/978-3-031-18490-1_3
33. European Commission. Directorate General for the Environment. ICLEI – Local Governments for Sustainability. Buying Green!: A Handbook on Green Public Procurement, 3rd edn. Publications Office: LU (2016)
34. Kokocińska, K.: The importance of public procurement for the strategic objectives of national socio-economic development. Ruch Prawniczy, Ekonomiczny i Socjologiczny **85**, 15–25 (2023). https://doi.org/10.14746/rpeis.2023.85.1.03
35. Ferreira, A.C., Silva, Â.: Supplier selection and procurement in SMEs: insights from the literature on key criteria and purchasing strategies. Eng. Manag. Prod. Serv. **14**, 47–60 (2022). https://doi.org/10.2478/emj-2022-0030
36. Obwegeser, N., Müller, S.D.: Innovation and public procurement: terminology, concepts, and applications. Technovation **74–75**, 1–17 (2018). https://doi.org/10.1016/j.technovation.2018.02.015
37. Haim Faridian, P.: Innovation in public management: is public e-procurement a wave of the future? a theoretical and exploratory analysis. Int. J. Public Adm. **38**, 654–662 (2015). https://doi.org/10.1080/01900692.2014.953175
38. Milenković, M., Rašić, M., Jovančević, R.: Public Procurement of Innovative and Technological Solutions in the EU. In: Proceedings of the 2022 45th Jubilee International Convention on Information, Communication and Electronic Technology (MIPRO), pp. 1258–1263 (2022)

39. Triana Casallas, J.A., Cueva-Lovelle, J.M., Rodríguez Molano, J.I.: Smart contracts with blockchain in the public sector. IJIMAI **6**, 63 (2020). https://doi.org/10.9781/ijimai.2020.07.005
40. European Commission. Joint Research Centre. Blockchain for Digital Government: An Assessment of Pioneering Implementations in Public Services. Publications Office: LU (2019)
41. CAHAI. Artificial Intelligence in Public Sector (2021)
42. Nai, R., Sulis, E., Meo, R.: Public procurement fraud detection and artificial intelligence techniques: a literature review. In: Proceedings of the CEUR Workshop Proceedings, vol. 3256 (2022)
43. European Commission The European Commission's Priorities. European Commission - European Commission (2019)
44. Smuha, N.A., et al.: How the EU can achieve legally trustworthy AI: a response to the European commission's proposal for an artificial intelligence act, Rochester, NY (2021)
45. Adam, I., Fazekas, M.: Big data analytics as a tool for auditors to identify and prevent fraud and corruption in public procurement. ECA J. **2**, 172–179 (2019). https://www.govtransparency.eu/wp-content/uploads/2019/05/ECA-JOURNAL19_02.pdf
46. Avella, J.R.: Delphi panels: research design, procedures, advantages, and challenges. Int. J. Dr. Stud. **11**, 305–321 (2016). https://doi.org/10.28945/3561
47. Devaney, L., Henchion, M.: Who is a Delphi 'expert'? reflections on a bioeconomy expert selection procedure from Ireland. Futures **99**, 45–55 (2018). https://doi.org/10.1016/j.futures.2018.03.017
48. Skinner, R., Nelson, R.R., Chin, W.W., Land, L.: The Delphi method research strategy in studies of information systems. Commun. Assoc. Inf. Syst. **37** (2015). https://doi.org/10.17705/1CAIS.03702
49. Okoli, C., Pawlowski, S.D.: The Delphi method as a research tool: an example, design considerations and applications. Inf. Manag. **42**, 15–29 (2004). https://doi.org/10.1016/j.im.2003.11.002
50. Rowe, G., Wright, G.: The Delphi technique as a forecasting tool: issues and analysis. Int. J. Forecast. **15**, 353–375 (1999). https://doi.org/10.1016/S0169-2070(99)00018-7
51. Bovis, C.: Public Procurement in the European Union. Palgrave Macmillan, London (2005). https://doi.org/10.1057/9780230501447_1. ISBN 978-1-349-51836-4
52. Bobowski, S., Gola, J.: E-Procurement in the European Union (2017)
53. jamovi (Version 2.5) The Jamovi Project (2024)
54. R Core Team R: A Language and Environment for Statistical Computing (2021)
55. Holey, E.A., Feeley, J.L., Dixon, J., Whittaker, V.J.: An exploration of the use of simple statistics to measure consensus and stability in Delphi studies. BMC Med. Res. Methodol. **7**, 52 (2007). https://doi.org/10.1186/1471-2288-7-52
56. Cohen, J.: Weighted kappa: nominal scale agreement provision for scaled disagreement or partial credit. Psychol. Bull. **70**, 213–220 (1968). https://doi.org/10.1037/h0026256
57. McMillan, S.S., King, M., Tully, M.P.: How to use the nominal group and Delphi techniques. Int. J. Clin. Pharm. (2016).https://doi.org/10.1007/s11096-016-0257-x
58. Dayal, V.: RStudio and R. In: Dayal, V. (ed.) Quantitative Economics with R, pp. 9–27 Springer, Singapore (2020). https://doi.org/10.1007/978-981-15-2035-8_2
59. Diamond, I.R., et al.: Defining consensus: a systematic review recommends methodologic criteria for reporting of Delphi studies. J. Clin. Epidemiol. **67**, 401–409 (2014). https://doi.org/10.1016/j.jclinepi.2013.12.002
60. Uyarra, E., Kundu, O.: Public procurement. In: Elgar Encyclopedia of Public Management, pp. 288–291. Edward Elgar Publishing Limited (2022)
61. Tiwari, M.K., Kumar, M.R., Rofin, T.M., Mitra, R.(eds.): Applications of Emerging Technologies and AI/ML Algorithms. Springer Nature Singapore, Singapore (2023). https://doi.org/10.1007/978-981-99-1019-9. ISBN 978-981-99-1018-2

62. Uskenbayeva, R., Kalpeyeva, Z., Satybaldiyeva, R., Moldagulova, A., Kassymova, A.: Applying of RPA in administrative processes of public administration. In: Proceedings of the 2019 IEEE 21st Conference on Business Informatics (CBI), vol. 02, pp. 9–12 (2019)
63. van der Wees, A., Breeuwsma, J., van Sleen, A.: IoT societal impact – legal considerations and perspectives. In: Digitising the Industry Internet of Things Connecting the Physical, Digital and VirtualWorlds, pp. 215–235. River Publishers, New York (2022)
64. Sosa, D., Paciello, J.: Data lake: a case of study of a big data analytics architecture for public procurements. In: Proceedings of the 2021 Eighth International Conference on eDemocracy eGovernment (ICEDEG), pp. 194–198 (2021)
65. Uddin Murad, M.A., Cetindamar, D., Chakraborty, S.: Public Procurement, Big Data Analytics Capabilities, and Healthcare Supply Chain Sustainability (2021)
66. Artzt, M., Dung, T.V.: Artificial intelligence and data protection: how to reconcile both areas from the European law perspective. Vietnam. J. Legal Sci. **7**, 39–58 (2022). https://doi.org/10.2478/vjls-2022-0007

Modeling and Optimization of Processes in a Mixed-Use Harbor

Asimina Dimara[1,2(✉)], Alexios Papaioannou[1], Stelios Krinidis[1,3], and Christos-Nikolaos Anagnostopoulos[2]

[1] Management Science and Technology Department, Democritus University of Thrace (D.U.Th.), Kavala, Greece

[2] Intelligent Systems Lab, Department of Cultural Technology and Communication, University of the Aegean (UAEGEAN), Mytilene, Greece

minadimara@gmail.com

[3] Management Science and Technology Department, International Hellenic University (IHU), Kavala, Greece

Abstract. The present research addresses the complicated challenges of modelling and enhancing processes in mixed-use harbors, focusing on Volos, where the convergence of many activities necessitates customized solutions for effective administration. This research initiates a case-specific investigation in response to the changing marine industry landscape, which is represented by the integration of shipping, recreation, and tourism inside the harbor of Volos. Real-world data from the Volos harbor was gathered using a hybrid methodology that blends mathematical modeling and simulation methodologies to inform the dynamic models. Volos is a microcosm that captures the challenges in establishing a balance between tourist, , commercial ships, and recreational boating. The modeling strategy provides a comprehensive representation of processes by taking interactions and possible conflicts into consideration. It is based on well-established harbor models that have been modified for mixed-use areas. In addition, cutting-edge optimization methods were used, considering environmental impact, traffic control, and resource use. Findings, which were obtained in the particular setting of the Volos harbor, show significant gains in resource allocation and operational efficiency, offering important new information for harbor management.

Keywords: Mixed-use Harbor Optimization · Harbor Process Enhancement · Modeling and Simulation · Traffic Control Strategies

1 Introduction

Harbours are considered as one the main transport hubs where commercial activities take place while enhancing the economic development of nearby areas. The ports play an important role in developing their host cities, influencing their economic, social and environmental dynamics. Since ancient times, cities with

I. Kostavelis et al. (Eds.): ICSC 2024, CCIS 2110, pp. 39–53, 2025.
https://doi.org/10.1007/978-3-031-69344-1_3

natural harbours have enjoyed greater economic and commercial growth. Specifically, the success of coastal cities in attracting investments, trade, and population growth has been mainly determined through the optimal location of ports, emphasizing the importance of maritime facilities urban design and financial planning [1]. Nowadays, ports have developed into complex technological hubs, where the careful management of many different and heterogeneous factors such as the movement of ships, containers and travellers, energy management, environmental sustainability, security and others are required. These challenges call for the integration of advanced technologies such as information management systems, and artificial intelligence for predictive maintenance and optimisation of operations, as well as technologies to reduce the environmental footprint, such as the implementation of clean energy solutions and waste management [2].

There are different types of ports, divided mainly by the purpose they serve such as freight and/or passenger transport needs [3]. Container ports are specialised in the handling of containers. Bulk Ports focus mainly on the handling of bulk cargo, such as coal, grain and other unpackaged materials (bulk). General cargo ports handle a variety of cargo, including bulk cargo, heavy equipment and sometimes containers. Ro-Ro ports mainly have vehicles moving in and out of the ships. These ports often serve both commercial vessels and passenger ships. Moreover, Cruise Ports focuses mainly on passenger services. Ferry ports serve passenger and vehicle transport over shorter distances. Finally, ports that serve mixed purposes, handle freight and passenger transport and have complex facilities. These facilities are designed to serve the various transport needs. In the context of mixed-use ports, these facilities serve the loading and unloading of cargo and the embarkation and disembarkation of passengers [4]. This multi-functionality requires careful planning and design to ensure efficient operations and safety for all users.

The management of mixed-use ports, which should be able to serve both freight and passenger transport, involves managing and dealing with several complex and often interrelated situations [5]. In particular, these ports must be able to balance the needs of the various stakeholders while ensuring efficient, safe and sustainable operations. The complexity of these ports underlines the need for complex management, from technological innovations and risk assessments to operational strategies and environmental considerations. Meeting all these challenges requires a holistic approach that can take into account all port activities and the economic, environmental and social impacts of these port activities [6]. One of the key challenges of managing a mixed-use port is the digitalization and modelling of port processes and services. This modelling should optimise services while reducing environmental impacts and waiting times for cargo and passengers. In such a complex process large investments are required and results are likely to be uncertain, as collaboration between many parties is required [7].

Within this context, this paper presents an in-depth analysis and discussion of the issues associated with operating mixed-use ports. The research topic addresses the specific challenges that arise when a port must satisfy a wide range of demands, including transportation for passengers, commercial ships, and leisure activities. Through the use of a hybrid methodology that blends simulation and computational modelling, this study aims to develop dynamic models. Through the use of this approach, port operations can potentially be optimized while mitigating their negative impact on the environment and improving efficiency and safety. It additionally provides an increased awareness of the relationships and potential conflicts between various port activities. Specifically, the study provides insight into the way advanced technological approaches, like real-time data analytics, AI-driven predictive maintenance, and green energy initiatives, could potentially be incorporated into the port's operations to meet the various challenges it meets.

The remainder of the paper is structured as follows: Sect. 2 analyzes the main processes and entities of a mixed-use harbour. Section 3 presents the specific details needed to model a mixed-Use harbour while describing the main events and port operations for such a port. Moreover, it summarizes the methodology needed to optimize port operations. Section 4 presents details for the Port of Volos while addressing the simulation results for the suggested method. Finally, the Conclusions are summarized in the last section.

2 Main Processes of a Mixed-Use Harbor

To analyze, estimate, and improve the efficiency, safety, and satisfaction of users of port operations, it is necessary to simulate and model the main processes at a port that controls both cargo and passenger operations. This is done by establishing models that represent the various systems and flows. Several significant procedures need to be modelled:

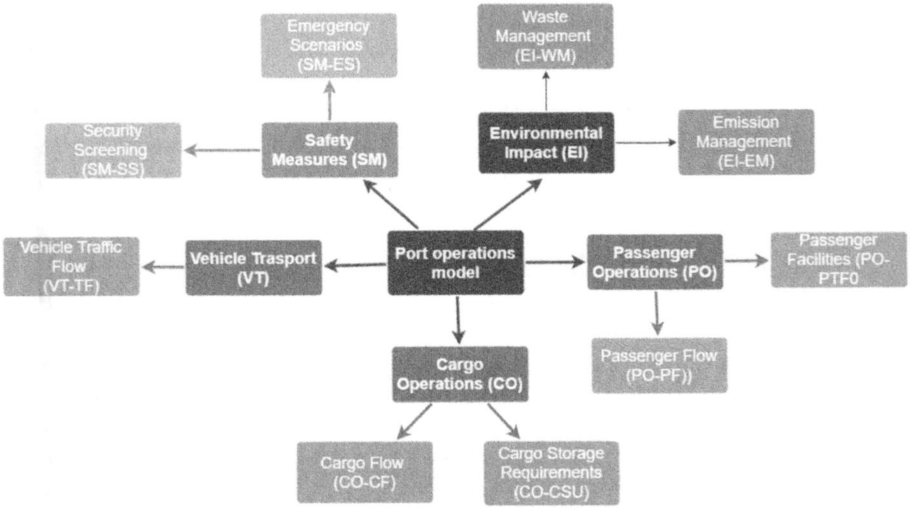

Fig. 1. Main processes for the port operational model

I Cargo Operations (CO). The primary objective of CO is to control the handling and transport of various kinds of cargo, CO include the loading, unloading, storage, and transportation of goods and products inside a port. To model those operations the main processes include:
   - Cargo Flow (CO-CF). It involves the simulation of the flow of goods and products through the port, beginning with their entry by sea and finishing with their unloading, storing, and ultimately terrestrial shipment, or the reverse.
   - Cargo Storage Requirements and Utilization (CO-CSU). It involves the modelling of all types of storage facilities such as open storage areas, and/or warehouse capacity. This process will model the total amount of space needed for different cargo kinds, such as dangerous, bulk, and containerized items.

II Passenger Operations (PO). The primary objective of POs is to facilitate passengers to board or get off ships while providing facilities and services in terminals. To model those operations the main processes include:
   - Passenger Flow (PO-PF). It involves monitoring and predicting passenger flow throughout the port, including arrival, check-in, security check, boarding, and the reverse procedure for passenger disembarkation.
   - Passenger Terminal Facilities (PO-PF). It involves monitoring and predicting the capacity and layout of passenger terminals to efficiently accommodate passengers, including waiting areas, ticket counters, customs and immigration facilities.

III Vehicle Transport (VT). The primary objective of VT is to improve the efficiency and relationship of the logistics chain, VT operations manage the transport and transfer of products and passengers between various modes of transportation, such as from ship to rail or road. To model those operations the main processes include:
   - Vehicle Traffic Flow (VT-TF). it involves monitoring and predicting the circulation of various types of vehicles within the port, such as internal transport vehicles, buses, trucks, and passenger automobiles.

IV Safety Measures (SM). The primary objective of SM is to ensure the implementation of specific regulations and procedures to prevent accidents and ensure the safety of both employees and passengers. To model those operations the main processes include:
   - Security Screening (SM-SS). It involves monitoring and modelling the transit of people and goods through security checkpoints.
   - Emergency Scenarios (SM-ES). It involves the design and modelling of enhanced emergency response protocols and evacuation processes, and simulations of potential emergency events (fires, spills, medical issues).

V Environmental Impact (EI). The primary objective of EI is to monitor how the decisions and processes impact the environment. This includes changes to ecosystems, preservation of biodiversity and changes to the quality of the air, water, and soil. To model those operations the main processes include
   - Emission Management (EI-EM). It involves monitoring and predicting the environmental impact of port operations, including emissions from ships, vehicles, and infrastructures.

- Wast Management (EI-WM). It involves monitoring and predicting waste generation, to identify potential mitigation strategies and sustainability practices.

While the aforementioned processes are fundamental, there are additional considerations such as stakeholder engagement, employee management, and various management strategies unique to each port. It's important to recognize that all these processes are interconnected or affect each other. For example, efficient cargo flow directly impacts vehicle traffic flow by influencing the number of trucks needed for cargo transport, which in turn affects emission management through the emissions generated by these vehicles mainly during idling. This interconnection underlines the complexity of port operations and the need for comprehensive modelling to enhance port efficiency, safety, and environmental sustainability. The main processes needed for the port operational model are presented in Fig. 1.

3 Methodology

3.1 Modeling Details: Entities and Relationships

The main key entities involved in the port operation model are ships, cargo, vehicles, passengers, and all the infrastructure components (e.g., docks, storage facilities, passenger terminals) [8]. Furthermore, each of those entities includes further attributes to describe them. The attributes for each entities are:

- Ships: Ships are characterized by their type (e.g., cargo ships, passenger liners, recreational boats), and their entities include attributes like size, capacity, and type of cargo and/or number of passengers.
- Cargo: Cargo is characterized by type (e.g., container, bulk goods, liquid cargo) and their entities include attributes like volume, weight, and handling requirements.
- Vehicles: Vehicles are characterized by type (e.g., trucks for cargo, trucks for transport, buses, cars) and their entities include attributes like capacity and type.
- Passengers: Passenger entities include attributes like destination, ticket type, and special needs (e.g., accessibility requirements).
- Infrastructure: Infrastructure includes als the port's infrastructure like Docks (e.g.,cargo docks, passenger terminals), storage facilities (e.g., warehouses, open storage areas), and equipment (e.g., cranes, forklifts, tugs).

Furthermore, there are certain relationships among the entities. The main relationships for the port operational model are:

- Ship relationships:
  - Uses Docks
  - Loads/Unloads Cargo (if cargo ship)
  - Carries Passengers (if passenger liner)

- Cargo relationships:
  - Transported by Ships
  - Stored in Storage Facilities
- Vehicles relationships:
  - Transports Cargo (if truck)
  - Transports Passengers (if bus or car)
  - Accesses Infrastructure (Docks, Storage Facilities)
- Passengers relationships:
  - Travel on Ships
  - Use Vehicles (Buses, Cars)
  - Access Infrastructure (Passenger Terminals)
- Infrastructure relationships:
  - Docks serve Ships
  - Storage Facilities store Cargo
  - Equipment is used for handling Cargo at Docks and/or in Storage Facilities

The above description of the entities and their relationship describes the primary elements of the port operations model ans is depicted in Fig. 2.

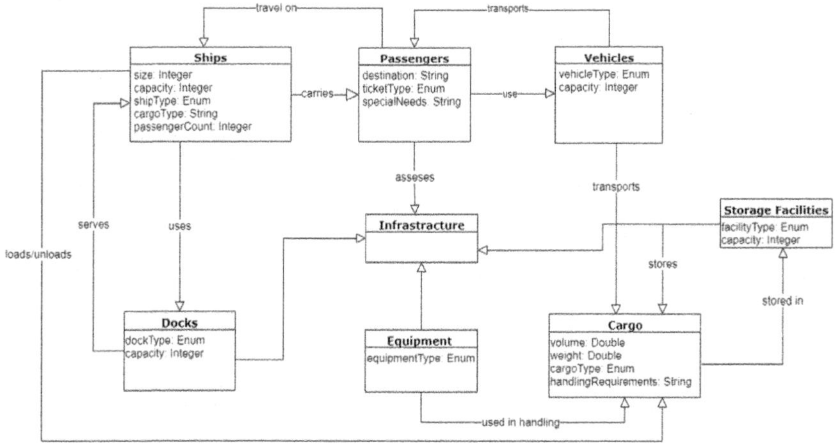

Fig. 2. Class diagram for modelling the port operational processes

3.2 Common Events in Port Operations

Common events in port operations include various processes like ship arrival and departure, loading and unloading of cargo, passenger boarding and disembarking, and vehicle arrivals and departures. Each event has associated parameters (e.g., time of occurrence, location, involved entities) and required resources and changes the state of the entities. The events and their parameters that change the entities are:

- Ship Arrival. The main parameters are time of occurrence, location, ship, and required resources(List of Infrastructure or Equipment).
- Ship Departure. The main parameters are time of occurrence, location, and ship.
- Loading Cargo and Unloading Cargo. The main parameters are time of occurrence, location, cargo, ship, and required resources.
- Passenger Boarding and Passenger Disembarking. The main parameters are time of occurrence, location, passengers, and ship.
- Vehicle Arrival and Vehicle Departure. e main parameters are time of occurrence, location, vehicle.

The operations within the port and the above events are depicted in Fig. 3.

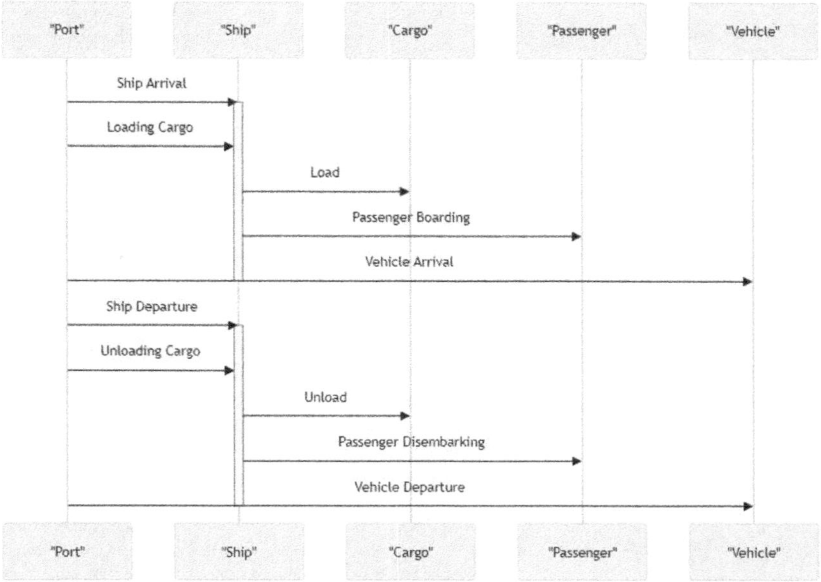

Fig. 3. Sequence Diagram of Common events in port operations

3.3 Port Operation Modelling the Main Process Flow and Constraints

To map the process flow for each of the above entities type through the port comprises a sequence of events from arrival to departure, the decisions made at each juncture, and the resources required. Moreover, certain limitations and regulations impact port operations. As a result, the constraints must be integrated into the modelling to reflects real-world operational limits. The processed along with the constraints are presented to Tables 1, 2, 3 and 4.

Table 1. Ship Process Flow

Process Step	Event	Decision	Resources	Constraints
Arrival	Ship Arrival	Assignment to a dock-based on ship type, size, and availability	Tugboats for maneuvering, dock space	Limited dock availability based on ship size and type Restrictions on simultaneous docking of large vessels due to space or safety regulations
Loading/Unloading Operations	Loading Cargo/ Unloading Cargo	Allocation of cranes and labor based on cargo type and priority	Cranes, forklifts, labor	Equipment availability, Labor shifts and working hours affecting the timing and speed of loading /unloading
Passenger Boarding/ Disembarking	Passenger Boarding/ Passenger Disembarking	Assignment of terminal gates and timing to avoid congestion	Customs agents, terminal facilities, security personnel	Terminal capacity limits to avoid overcrowding Security and customs processing times, which can delay operations
Departure	Ship Departure	Clearance based on completed operations and harbor traffic	Tugboats for maneuvering, harbor traffic management	Harbor traffic control measures, dictating departure windows to prevent congestion Weather conditions impacting the feasibility of departures

Table 2. Cargo Process Flow

Process Step	Event	Decision	Resources	Constraints
Arrival with Ship	Ship Arrival	Unloading sequence based on cargo priority and destination		
Storage		Allocation to storage area based on cargo type (e.g., hazardous materials)	Storage facilities, security monitoring	Limited storage space, requiring efficient allocation and turnover. Special requirements for hazardous or temperature-sensitive goods, limiting storage options
Transportation Out	Vehicle Arrival (for external transport)	Scheduling of trucks or rail for outbound transportation	Loading equipment, logistics scheduling systems	Availability of external transport (trucks, rail) aligned with cargo readiness. Scheduling constraints based on external logistics networks

Table 3. Passenger Process Flow

Process Step	Event	Decision	Resources	Constraints
Arrival at Terminal	Passenger Arrival	Processing sequence	Terminal facilities, staff for check-in and baggage	Limited check-in counters and staff, leading to potential delays during peak times. Restricted terminal access during high-security alerts or events
Boarding	Linked to Passenger Boarding Event	Gate assignment and boarding sequence	Security screening, boarding passes processing	Fixed boarding times and sequences to ensure timely departures. Gate capacity limits, affecting boarding efficiency
Disembarking and Departure	Linked to Passenger Disembarking Event	Customs and immigration processing based on origin/destination	Customs agents, baggage claim facilities, transport options from terminal	Immigration and customs processing capacity, potentially creating bottlenecks

Table 4. Vehicles Process Flow

Process Step	Event	Decision	Resources	Constraints
Arrival	Vehicle Arrival	Direction to parking or loading area based on vehicle type	Parking spaces, loading docks	Limited parking and loading dock space, especially during peak operations. Specific entry protocols for heavy vehicles
Loading/ Unloading	Linked to Loading Cargo/Unloading Cargo Events	Timing and location for loading/unloading operations	Loading equipment, dock space	Coordination with cargo operations to ensure vehicle loading/unloading aligns with ship schedules Physical space constraints in loading areas, limiting the number of vehicles
Departure	Vehicle Departure	Exit scheduling to manage traffic flow	Traffic management systems	Traffic management systems dictating exit times to avoid congestion within the port area. Security checks

3.4 Optimizing Port Operations

For each of the main entities, a framework must be designed to enhance the operations while considering any constraints. Specifically, ship operations, include dock allocation, scheduling, tugboat efficiency, ship arrival coordination, and speed optimization while defining objective functions and constraints to model these processes.

$$F_{ship} = w_1 \cdot (T_{wait}) + w_2 \cdot (T_{tug}) + w_3 \cdot (E_{total}), \tag{1}$$

where T_{wait}, T_{tug}, and E_{total} represent the actual total waiting time for ships, total tugboat operation time, and total emissions, respectively. The w_1, w_2, and w_3 are the weights assigned to each objective, indicating their relative importance in the optimization process. And:

$$T_{\text{wait}} = \min \sum_{i=1}^{N} (t_{\text{dockAssigned},i} - t_{\text{arrival},i}) \tag{2}$$

$$T_{\text{tug}} = \min \sum_{j=1}^{M} t_{\text{operation},j} \tag{3}$$

$$E_{\text{total}} = \min \left(\sum_{i=1}^{N} e_{\text{idle},i} + \sum_{k=1}^{K} e_{\text{travel},k} \right) \tag{4}$$

The constraints to be followed are:

- Dock Allocation Constraints:

$$\forall i \in \text{Ships}, \exists!\ d \in \text{Docks} : \text{size}(i) \leq \text{capacity}(d)$$

- Tugboat Availability:

$$\forall j \in \text{Tugboats}, t_{\text{start},j} \leq t_{\text{operation},j} \leq t_{\text{end},j}$$

- Ship Arrival Coordination:

$$t_{\text{arrival},i} + \Delta t_{\text{speedOptimization},i} \approx t_{\text{dockAvailable},i}$$

- Speed Optimization Constraints

$$v_{\text{min}} \leq v_i \leq v_{\text{max}}$$

A genetic algorithm [9] is exploited to optimize the ship operations based on the objective function and constraints for these operations as described in Algorithm 1.

Algorithm 1. Genetic Algorithm for Optimizing Ship Operations

1: **Initialization:** Generate an initial population of solutions encoding dock allocations, tugboat schedules, and ship speeds.
2: **Evaluation:** Compute the fitness of each solution using the objective function F_{ship}, taking into account the operational constraints.
3: **Selection:** Select individuals for reproduction based on their fitness scores, preferring solutions that minimize the objective function.
4: **Crossover:** Create offspring by combining aspects of the parent solutions, ensuring that constraints are not violated.
5: **Mutation:** Introduce random changes to offspring solutions to explore new parts of the solution space, maintaining compliance with constraints.
6: **Replacement:** Update the population with the new generation of solutions, potentially retaining some of the best solutions from the current generation.
7: **Termination:** Repeat the process until a satisfactory fitness level is achieved.

Likewise, for the rest of the port operations, cargo handling, passenger management, and vehicle management the specific optimization functions aimed at improving operational efficiency, and the constraints that bound these operations are adressed in Table 5.

4 Simulation Results for Port Operations

4.1 Port of Volos

The port of Volos is the main gateway connecting mainland Greece with the Sporades islands. In the port there are 3 piers, 2 of which cover commercial activities and are located on the western side. Passenger ships depart from the main pier [10]. Situated at the entrance of the Pagasitikos Gulf, the Port of Volos is the third largest port in Greece. The Port of Volos is run and managed by Volos Port Authority SA (Fig. 4). A breakwater that guards the port keeps ships safe and provides cover for the harbour. The distance between the port entrance and its anchorage area is approximately 2 nautical miles [12].

The major facilities that are available in the Port of Volos are presented in Table 6 [12].

Table 5. Objective functions and constraints for passenger, vehicle, and cargo optimization

Area	Optimization Function	Constraints
Cargo Handling	Minimize total loading/unloading time: $T_{\text{load/unload}} = \sum(t_{\text{end}} - t_{\text{start}})$	Cargo volume vs. capacity: $V_{\text{capacity}} \geq V_{\text{cargo}}$
	Maximize storage efficiency: $S_{\text{efficiency}} = \frac{V_{\text{utilized}}}{V_{\text{total}}}$	Storage time vs. requirements: $T_{\text{storage}} \geq T_{\text{required}}$
Passenger Management	Minimize queue time: $T_{\text{queue}} = \sum(t_{\text{service}} - t_{\text{arrival}})$	Counter availability: $N_{\text{counters}} \geq N_{\text{required}}$
	Maximize passenger throughput: $P_{\text{throughput}} = \frac{N_{\text{processed}}}{T_{\text{total}}}$	Terminal capacity: $C_{\text{capacity}} \geq N_{\text{passengers}}$
Vehicle Logistics	Minimize idle time: $T_{\text{idle}} = \sum t_{\text{idle}}$	Parking/loading slots: $L_{\text{slots}} \geq N_{\text{vehicles}}$
	Minimize emissions: $E_{\text{emissions}} = \sum e_{\text{idle}}$	Optimal traffic flow: $T_{\text{traffic flow}} \leq T_{\text{optimal}}$

Fig. 4. Port of Voles

Table 6. Facilities of the Port of Volos

Ro-Ro Berths	Available
Cranes	Nine(9) Shore Cranes of 8–30 ton capacity Various private crane companies with greater capability operate in Volos greater area
Forklifts	Available/Six (6) 2, 5 ton , two (2) 4 ton , one (1) straddle carrier of 40 ton Also available from private companies
Tugs	Available
Mooring Boats	Available
Cargo Boats	Available
Water Burges	Available
Fresh Water/Shore	Available
Surveyors	Available
Transport (Air)	Athens International Airport 240 km/Thessaloniki 330 km
(Rail)	Available Locally
(Private)	Bus Station , Mini Buses , Tax
Garbage/Sludge	Disposal Available - Compulsory

4.2 Real Time Data

The numerical data analysis displayed in Fig. 5 presents a summary of the port operations in Volos for the period of 2000-2023, over two decades. The table is notable for reflecting several indicators that fluctuate, with noticeable peaks occurring in 2001 and 2011, indicating more activity. On the other hand, an important decrease was observed in 2020, which may be related to global occurrences that have an impact on trade and shipping. The port has generally been rising until 2020 when it noticed a time of recovery. This information indicates the scale of the port's operations.

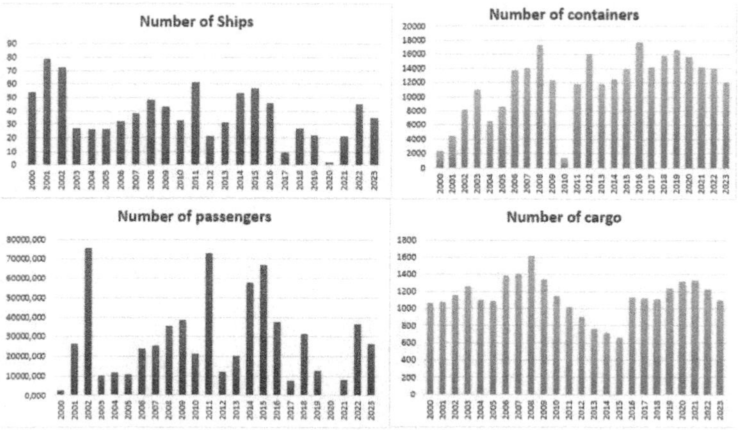

Fig. 5. Statistics of the port of Volo

Moreover, a provider of maritime data analysis, Marine Traffic which provides users the ability to view real-time data on ship movements and whereabouts in harbours and ports may be exploited (Fig. 6). A database including specifics about the vessels, such as the place of construction, size, gross tonnage, and International Maritime Organization (IMO) number, is accessible.

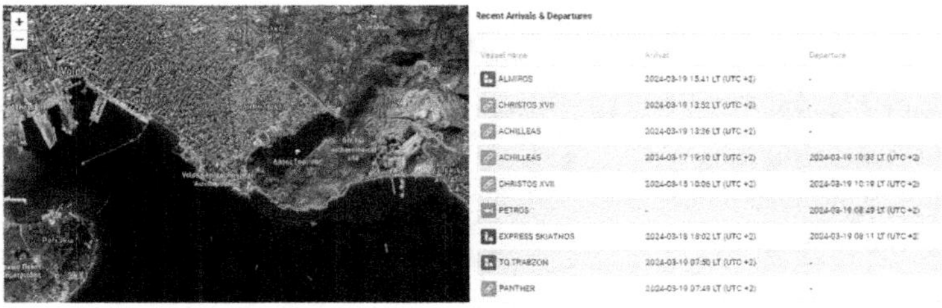

Fig. 6. Volos real-time data: Marine traffic

4.3 Simulation Scenario: Peak Season Operation at the Port of Volos

The simulated scenario focuses on the busiest month of the Port of Volos when tourists travelling the Sporades Islands contribute to increased passenger and ship flow. The simulation will evaluate the port's ability to handle increasing dock, tugboat, and resource demands while preserving operational safety and environmental sustainability. The details of the scenario are presented in the Table 7.

Table 7. Simulation scenario for the Port of Volos during peak activity

Aspect	Detail	Ideated Numbers/Conditions
Initial Conditions	Start Date	August 1st
	Baseline Ship Arrivals	20 ships per day
	Baseline Passenger Arrivals	5,000 passengers per day
	Available Docks	5 docks for passenger ships
	Tugboat Availability	3 tugboats
Resource Constraints	Dock Utilization	95% capacity
	Tugboat Utilization	90% capacity
	Waiting Time Threshold	2 h maximum for docking
Traffic Flow	Peak Hour Ship Arrivals	5 ships during peak hours (10 am–2 pm)
	Peak Hour Passenger Arrivals	1,500 passengers during peak hours
	Average Docking Time	1 h per ship
	Average Turnaround Time	4 h per ship

4.4 Simulation Scenario Results

Based on the aforementioned simulation scenario for the Port of Volos during peak activity in August, Table 8 illustrates the optimization results. These results demonstrate the improvements and efficiencies gained through the implementation of the optimization algorithms and other measures.

Table 8. Simulation Scenario results

Optimization Metric	Before Optimization	After Optimization	Improvement
Dock Utilization Efficiency	85%	95%	10%
Average Docking Wait Time	120 min	60 min	−50%
Tugboat Turnaround Efficiency	75%	90%	20%
Passenger Processing Time	90 min	45 min	−50%
Emission Levels During Peak Hours	100 units	80 units	−20%

5 Conclusions

in this research paper, a comprehensive analysis into optimization of operations in the mixed-use Port of Volos is provided. A particular emphasis is given on handling the difficulties during the peak travel season. The simulation results demonstrate significant gains, including a 10% increase in port utilization efficiency and a 50% reduction in average docking wait times and passenger processing times. A 20% increase in tugboat efficiency allowed for more seamless operations. The assessment also indicates a noteworthy 20% mitigation in emissions during peak hours, demonstrating a strong dedication to environmental sustainability. These results imply that the use of genetic algorithms can significantly improve port operations, increasing productivity and lowering environmental impact while also improving harbour management techniques. The findings should be tested with real-time data.

Acknowledgement. This work is partially supported by the TOURAL project funded by the EU H2020 under Grant Agreement No. 101132489.

References

1. Xiao, G., et al.: Evaluation of ship pollutant emissions in the ports of Los Angeles and Long Beach. J. Mar. Sci. Eng. **10**(9), 1206 (2022)
2. Dimara, A., et al.: A low-cost business-oriented seaport energy effective management platform. Int. J. Appl. **11**(1), 62–90 (2022)
3. Tijan, E., et al.: The role of port authority in port governance and port community system implementation. Sustainability **13**(5), 2795 (2021)

4. Mahmud, K.K., Chowdhury, M.M.H., Shaheen, M.M.A.: Green port management practices for sustainable port operations: a multi method study of Asian ports. Maritime Policy Manag. **50**, 1–36 (2023)
5. Chen, K., et al.: Port sustainability through integration: a port capacity and profit-sharing joint optimization approach. Ocean Coast. Manag. **245**, 106867 (2023)
6. Kuakoski, H.S., et al.: Marketing, entrepreneurship, and innovation in port management: trends, barriers, and research agenda. Maritime Policy Manag. 1–18 (2023)
7. Almeida, F.: Challenges in the digital transformation of ports. Businesses **3**(4), 548–568 (2023)
8. Singh, A.: Port development: history, present and future challenges. In: Infrastructure Planning and Management in India: Opportunities and Challenges, pp. 25–34. Springer Nature Singapore, Singapore (2022)
9. Dimara, A., et al.: Personalized thermal comfort modeling through genetic algorithm. In: Energy Sources, Part A: Recovery, Utilization, and Environmental Effects, pp. 1–22 (2021)
10. Port of Volos. https://www.port-volos.gr/cgi-bin/pages/index.pl?arlang=English&type=index. Accessed 02 Feb 2024
11. MarineTraffic. https://www.marinetraffic.com/en/ais/details/ports/591?name=VOLOS&country=Greece. Accessed 04 Feb 2024
12. Port of Volos details. https://www.tsansizis.gr/ports/volos-port

BladeWorks: A Novel Manufacturing-as-a-Service Platform for the Development of Customized Knives

Nikolaos Kladovasilakis[1](✉), Paschalis Charalampous[1], Athanasios Panagiotis Pelekoudas[1], Ioannis Kostavelis[2], Dimosthenis Ioannidis[1], and Dimitrios Tzovaras[1]

[1] Centre for Research and Technology Hellas, Information Technologies Institute, 6th km Charilaou-Thermi Road, 57001 Thessaloniki, Greece
nikoklad@iti.gr

[2] Department of Supply Chain Management, School of Economics and Business Administration, International Hellenic University, 60100 Katerini, Greece

Abstract. In recent years, the business model of Manufacturing-as-a-Service (MaaS) has gained increased interest in Industry 4.0 activities paving the way for Industry 5.0. MaaS emphasizes on-demand and scalable manufacturing services allowing common people to have access to the development and fabrication processes of their products. More specifically, MaaS enables industries to have access to several manufacturing procedures without the need for extensive inhouse production facilities. In this context, the BladeWorks platform aims to offer a groundbreaking approach to MaaS in the knife-manufacturing industry. BladeWorks is a web-based tool, where the users can produce the desired blade design employing Artificial Intelligence (AI) and numerical methodologies. In the first approach, a novel AI-retrieval module was developed, where the input of the software is a simple blade picture, and BladeWorks proposes a design that best fits the query image. In the second tool, the desired design is generated in real-time considering the actual geometrical characteristics of the input picture. Then, the users can validate the produced design via an online finite element analyses (FEA) tool and modify it based on the simulated results. Finally, the user can choose the manufacturing process considering a list of available fabrication methods derived from the platform's connectivity with workshops and receive an instant cost estimation along with an estimated time of arrival for their product. In the future, this platform could expand to numerous other applications, such as mechanical component crafting, minimizing the intermediary steps and revolutionizing the current manufacturing and supply chain processes.

Keywords: Manufacturing-as-a-Service · Customized Blades · Machine learning · Finite Element Analysis

I. Kostavelis et al. (Eds.): ICSC 2024, CCIS 2110, pp. 54–65, 2025.
https://doi.org/10.1007/978-3-031-69344-1_4

1 Introduction

The European directions of Industry 5.0 aim to infusion into the production and manufacturing systems the elements of human-centricity, sustainability and resilience [1]. Towards this direction, Manufacturing-as-a-Service (MaaS) has emerged as an on-demand, agile and scalable manufacturing business model addressing the main elements of Industry 5.0 [2]. Nowadays, more and more companies and organizations in numerous industries, such as clothing, automotive, etc., employ the MaaS model to offer customized solutions to their clients and increase the client's involvement in the production of their items [3]. More specifically, MaaS models consist of a cloud-based platform where the potential customer can use a wide range of smart and interactive tools to design and develop their products according to their needs and schedule their production. These smart tools are usually artificial intelligence algorithms that allow the design and analysis of the desired product without having any prior experience.

In this context, one of the most crucial design tools for the MaaS platform is the retrieval of design from the design library or even from a single picture of a product. The integration of AI into the processes of 2D retrieval and contour extraction signifies a substantial advancement in manufacturing, especially within the Manufacturing-as-a-Service (MaaS) framework. Leveraging AI, these operations attain unprecedented accuracy and efficiency, facilitating the seamless conversion of user inputs into custom-designed products. AI's adeptness at parsing and interpreting complex visual data is revolutionizing the way designs are conceptualized, retrieved, and refined in the manufacturing domain. In the realm of 2D retrieval, AI algorithms—utilizing a combination of advanced image processing techniques and Principal Component Analysis (PCA) for feature extraction—excel at navigating through vast design databases to pinpoint matches closely resembling user-submitted images [4–6]. This capability not only streamlines the design selection process but also ensures that the final products are profoundly personalized. Similarly, in contour extraction, AI-driven processes, specifically with Convolutional Neural Networks (CNNs) and the Mask R-CNN architecture, meticulously analyze product images to extract precise geometric details, enabling the creation of accurate and customized product outlines with minimal manual oversight. These advancements highlight AI's transformative role in advanced design and manufacturing, enhancing both product quality and customization.

Moreover, MaaS models often integrate analytical tools in order to numerically test and evaluate the produced designs. These tools provide vital information about the design correctness to the customers enabling the proper assessment and evaluation of the customized design without the need for engineering experience. The most common of these tools is the FEA, which assesses the developed design under realistic operation conditions in a short time and with high accuracy. FEAs can highlight the weak region of the product that should be redesigned, i.e. the regions with high stress concentration, and extract the overall mechanical performance of the developed product, such as maximum strength and deformation. Based on these results, a design optimization process can occur to produce more functional and mechanically superior object.

In this context, the current study aims to develop a holistic cloud-based platform to be integrated into the MaaS model for knife manufacturing. The novelty of this paper is focused on the employment and integration of image process and pattern recognition tools in the design platform in order to produce the desired knife design with minimal user intervention. Therefore, the users are able to create/design the desired knife geometry without having any design knowledge or experience in a short time period. Furthermore, in the developed platform, a FEA-based module was developed and integrated in order to provide the rapid testing, evaluation and optimization of the designed knife. It is worth mentioning that the FEA module is embedded in the platform and its usage is focused on specific cutting scenarios and pre-selected construction material models. In this way, the user intervention in FEA remains minimal widening its utilization for all types of users (experts, intermediate, amateurs). Figure 1 graphical summarize in a flowchart of the architecture of the proposed MaaS platform. The forthcoming sections explore the aforementioned tools and methodologies deployed in the BladeWorks platform, illustrating how AI technologies are pivotal in refining and augmenting the platform's knife design and production capabilities.

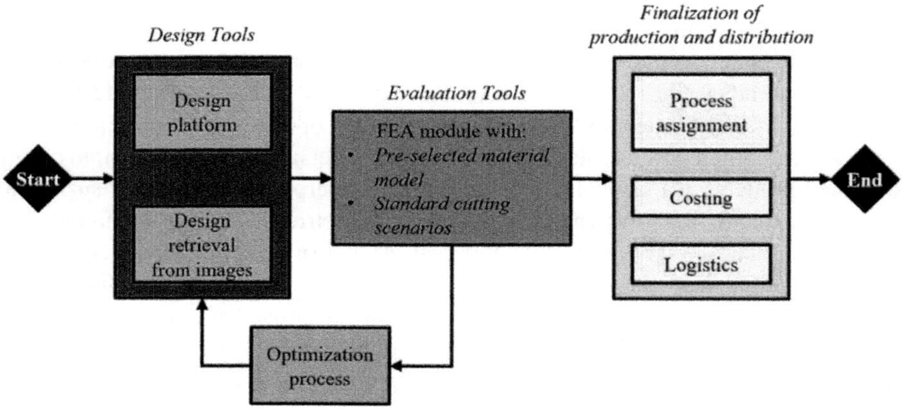

Fig. 1. Flowchart of the architecture of the BladeWorks MaaS platform.

2 Methodologies

2.1 Design Tool Using 2D Retrieval

To actualize the first tool of the BladeWorks platform, a novel approach was adopted, leveraging a 2D blade retrieval model, which takes as input a knife outline image (query image), searches through a database of different knife designs and produces as output the most similar knife design image to the input, accompanied by its corresponding design.

The most common architectures that could accomplish this task consist of databases that host both images and semantic descriptions. Furthermore, a model is required for the input image encoding that will project an image from the field of pixels into a new vector space, making that way the comparison between images easier. The resulting representation then is compared with the representations stored in the database. The database consists of two components: the vector representations of the images and the available images themselves. The database entry that has the closest distance measure to the query image is also the one that will be returned as output. The 2D blade retrieval model utilizes a method that eschews traditional CNN architectures in favor of a different approach that integrates image processing techniques with PCA for feature extraction and dimensionality reduction [7]. Instead of relying on pre-trained neural networks, this model utilizes computer vision algorithms to pre-process the images from a pre-existing knife template dataset, extracting significant contours and augmenting that dataset by generating mirrored and rotated versions of each image, significantly enhancing the robustness and variability of the dataset. This pre-processing phase ensures that each knife image is standardized in size and orientation, facilitating consistent feature extraction across the dataset. The custom knife dataset plays an integral role in our methodology, serving as the foundation for both the PCA-based feature extraction and the subsequent image retrieval mechanism. Initially, the images are meticulously processed to highlight their most defining characteristics, such as precise shape outlines and prominent edge contours, thus preparing them for detailed analysis Subsequently, PCA is employed to transform these detailed images into a condensed vector space, resulting in the creation of "eigenknives" [8]—a set of principal components that capture the fundamental attributes of the dataset. Figure 2 portrays a schematic representation of workflow for knife/retrieval and matching system.

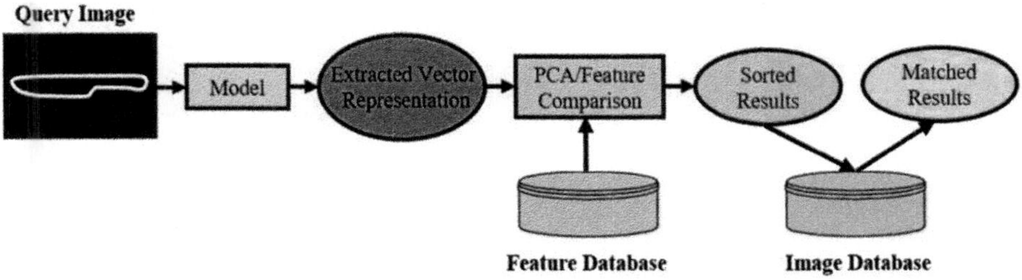

Fig. 2. Schematic representation of the process flow of the 2D knife/retrieval and matching system.

2.2 Design Tool Using Contour Extraction

In order to implement the second tool of the BladeWorks platform, another innovative approach was followed using a contour extraction model, which accepts as input a knife image, and initially detects the knife object on the image and then extracts the contour outline of the knife by applying a series of computer vision processes to ensure the accuracy of the contour. Briefly, this tool effectively converts an input knife image into a detailed contour outline of the detected knife.

The contour extraction model within the BladeWorks platform strategically opts for Convolutional Neural Networks (CNNs) due to their unparalleled efficiency in analyzing visual imagery. Specifically, the model employs the Mask R-CNN architecture [9], which is pre-trained on the comprehensive COCO dataset [5]. This dataset is a large-scale and richly annotated collection of images that encompass a wide variety of everyday objects, enabling the CNN to effectively learn features ranging from simple edges to complex shapes, crucial for accurate visual recognition. The pre-training on the COCO dataset equips Mask R-CNN with a rich knowledge base of object characteristics, allowing it to adeptly detect objects within new images by comparing learned features. This prior knowledge is crucial, as it significantly enhances the model's ability to discern and extract the contours of knives from images, leveraging learned patterns to identify similar objects efficiently. The Mask R-CNN framework operates in two stages. In the first stage, the model scans the input image with a backbone architecture to generate a feature map. This stage, often referred to as the Region Proposal Network (RPN), identifies potential object candidates or Regions of Interest (RoIs) [10]. In the context of the contour extraction model, when a knife image is inputted, the model leverages this back-bone architecture to discern textural, colour, and shape features relevant to knives. The RPN then proposes candidate bounding boxes that likely contain a knife based on these features. The second stage of Mask R-CNN is where the model precisely delineates the knife from the background. This stage refines the bounding boxes proposed by the RPN and simultaneously predicts the object class and generates a high-resolution mask for each instance. For knife detection, this means the model not only localizes the knife within the image but also generates a pixel-wise mask delineating the exact shape of the knife [11]. This process is driven by a combination of convolutional neural network layers and a fully connected network, ensuring precise boundary detection and shape prediction. Figure 3 shows the Mask R-CNN architecture for knife detection.

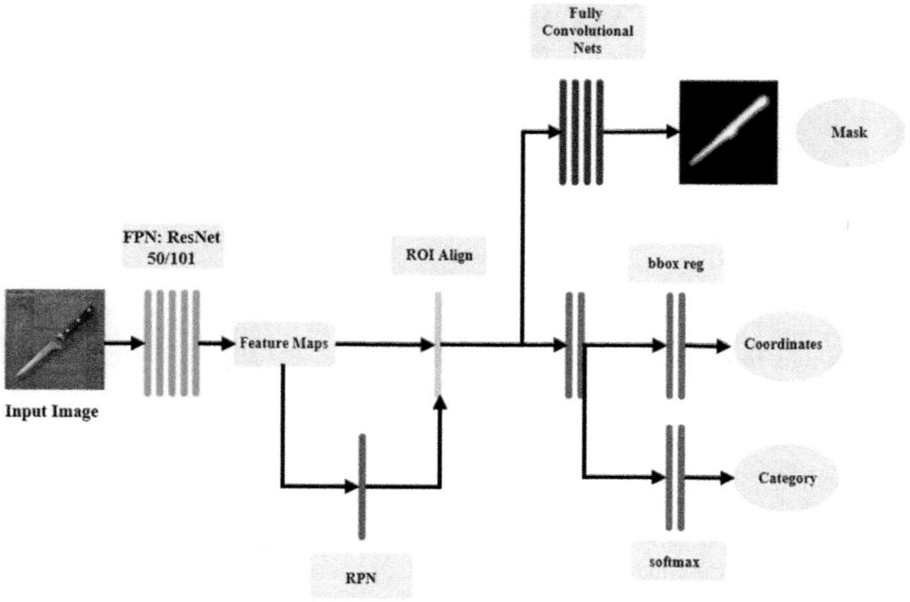

Fig. 3. The Mask R-CNN architecture for the knife detection from an input image.

Following the Mask R-CNN's identification and segmentation of knives in images, the next critical phase is the post-processing of the prediction masks. Initially, masks predicted as knives are filtered and isolated. If multiple knife instances are detected in an image, their masks are aggregated into a single combined mask. This combined mask is then subjected to a clipping process to maintain binary values within [0, 1]. Following this, a thresholding step is applied where pixel values below a certain threshold are set to 0 (absence of a knife), and those equal to or above are set to 1 (presence of a knife), thereby sharpening the mask's accuracy. This process results in a clear, binary mask that precisely delineates the shape and presence of knives in the image.

In the BladeWorks platform, the integration of Mask R-CNN and advanced computer vision techniques for contour extraction of detected knives represents a significant stride in image processing and analysis. After the Mask R-CNN model successfully detects and segments a knife within an image, delineating its mask, the next vital step is the extraction and refinement of the knife's contour. The process begins with the application of the Sobel operator, a discrete differentiation operator that computes an approximation of the gradient of the image intensity function. By employing separate convolutions in both the x and y directions, the Sobel operator highlights regions of high spatial frequency, which correspond to edges. The resultant edges are then combined using the Euclidean norm, creating a comprehensive edge map. This edge map is then refined through binary thresholding and morphological closing. The morphological closing is particularly crucial as it helps in closing small gaps in the detected edges, thus ensuring a more continuous contour. After these steps, the edge map is masked with the knife mask to isolate the knife edges. Subsequently, the largest contour, representing the knife's outline, is extracted. To smooth this raw contour and reduce irregularities, a Gaussian filter is applied. This low-pass filter diminishes high-frequency components by convolving the contour with a Gaussian kernel, where the value of the sigma parameter dictates the smoothing level. The resultant smoothed contour is then subjected to additional image processing techniques like morphological gradients and thinning to produce a clear, one-pixel-thick outline of the knife. This final contour represents a precise and visually refined depiction of the knife's edge, which is a critical output of the contour extraction model's analysis pipeline.

2.3 Numerical Simulation Environment

In the present study, a numerical simulation module was established, where the main objective is to incorporate a feature where the user will be able to examine the functionality of the proposed knife design via an automated approach. Through this simulation, the efficiency of the cutting process in relation to the geometry of the knife and the workpiece material can be investigated. The simulation scenarios will examine the operation of the knife at critical wear points and the final output of the module shall compose the evaluation of the examined knife's mechanical behavior. With the aid of FEA, discrete simulation scenarios will be applied to estimate critical points of the knife design aiming to identify potential weaknesses of the blade itself during the cutting procedure. Considering the development of the simulation environment, the open-source software FreeFEM++ was utilized [12]. This software is based on the C++ programming language, enabling the programming and automation of the simulation process for the mechanical behavior of the blade. FreeFEM++ is open-source software used for numerical solutions of differential equations, where it provides a programming and problem-solving environment for nonlinear mechanics, acoustics, fluid dynamics, and more. Regarding the automatic simulation using the FreeFEM++ library, the following aspects must be considered: a) the geometrical characteristics of the blade, b) the material of the blade, c) the workpiece material, and d) the cutting trajectory.

Geometrical characteristics are essential for the development of an accurate Finite Element Model (FEM) model regarding the precise geometric models that are necessary to represent the system under study. Hereupon, the geometry of the involved components plays a crucial role in a successful FE simulation, as it impacts the accuracy, reliability, and performance of the model [13]. It must be noted that in the examined case, the selected knife will act as the input to the simulation environment. In addition, the utilization of precise and reliable material data is necessary to ensure that simulations faithfully reflect the behavior of the examined case, hence a library of materials was created for the blade and the workpiece material. Moreover, the boundary conditions on a FEA model determine how the system interacts with its environment. If not defined correctly, the simulation may produce inadequate or ineffective results. Within the developed simulation module, the regions of the boundary conditions, both for external loads and for constraints, will be provided by the end-user. Finally, it should be emphasized that creating a suitable mesh is necessary for the application of simulation methods, so in the present study, the discretization and the solving will be accomplished with the aid of the library provided by FreeFEM++. All of the above-mentioned are illustrated in Fig. 4, where the geometry of an investigated knife is imported and automatically meshed using the appropriate tools and functions provided by the FreeFEM++ library. In particular, an example of a blade is exhibited, on which external loads (red arrows) and constraints (purple triangles) were applied taking into account inputs from the user regarding these regions. Moreover, the discretization was accomplished using the function provided by FreeFEM++, where it should be noted that a fairly uniform mesh was created. Finally, the user selects the materials of the blade itself and the workpiece that lead to different magnitudes on the external loads and mechanical behavior of the system.

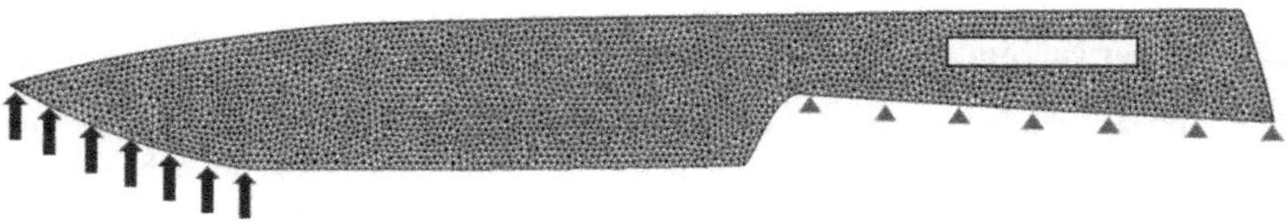

Fig. 4. Geometrical characteristics of the investigated meshed knife model and the corresponding boundary conditions.

3 Results and Discussion

After the presentation of the developed tools for design extraction and numerical analysis, the next step is the demonstration of the results of these through the BladeWorks platform. First of all, the main web-based design platform is illustrated in the indicative image of Fig. 5. In this platform, the aforementioned tools were integrated in order to extract the desired knife geometry and tested in a fast, accurate and reliable manner.

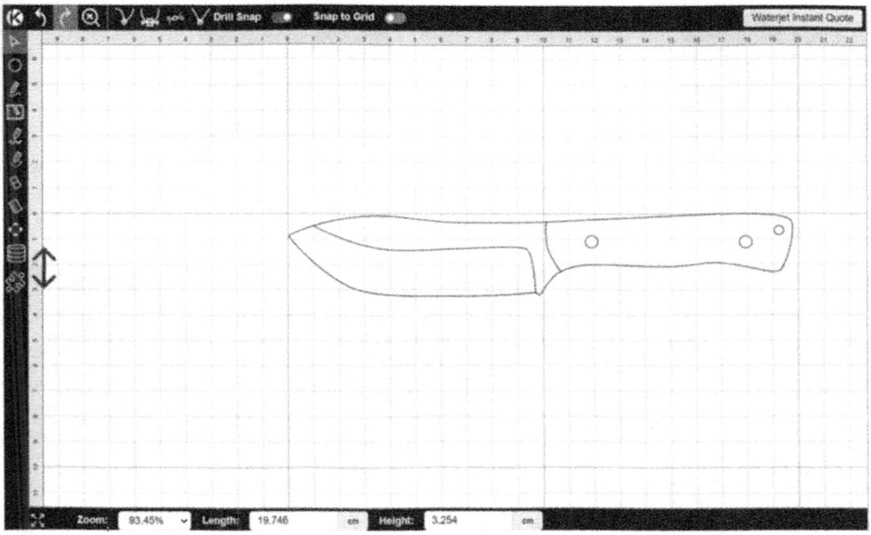

Fig. 5. Indicative image of the design environment for the customized knives along with all the designed tools.

3.1 Design Extraction

During the retrieval phase, a query image is subjected to an identical preprocessing and feature extraction pipeline. Its resultant PCA-derived feature vector is then systematically compared against those of the images within the dataset using Euclidean distance as a metric to measure similarity. This comparison method effectively quantifies the visual and structural resemblance between the query image and each dataset image, determining the "closeness" based on the computed distances. The system adeptly ranks the images based on their similarity scores, thereby ensuring that the image with the closest match, which exhibits the highest visual and structural congruence to the query image, is accurately identified and returned as the outcome of the retrieval process. Figure 6 presents indicative results of the 2D image retrieval model for different types of knives.

Following the knife object detection and its segmentation by Mask R-CNN, the subsequent contour extraction and refinement are vividly demonstrated. The completed process is illustrated in Fig. 7 through a sequence of detailed images, showcasing the main stages of the user-submitted image for a kitchen knife in the BladeWorks platform.

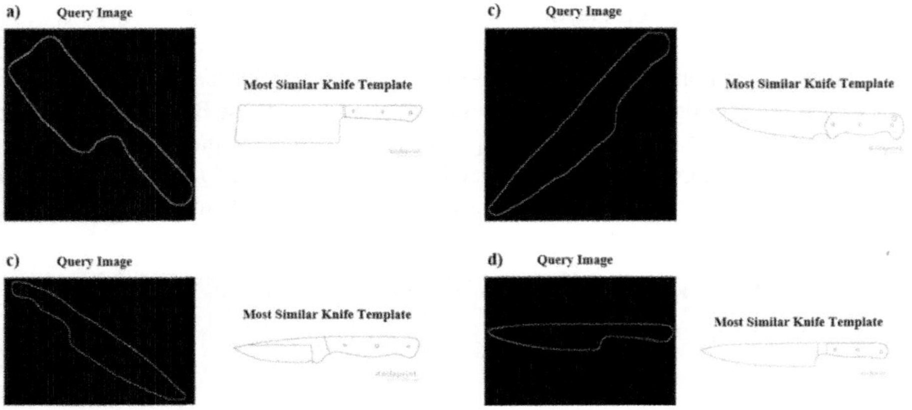

Fig. 6. Indicative results of the 2D image retrieval model for four different types of knives: a) cleaver, b) hunting, c) skinner and d) kitchen knife.

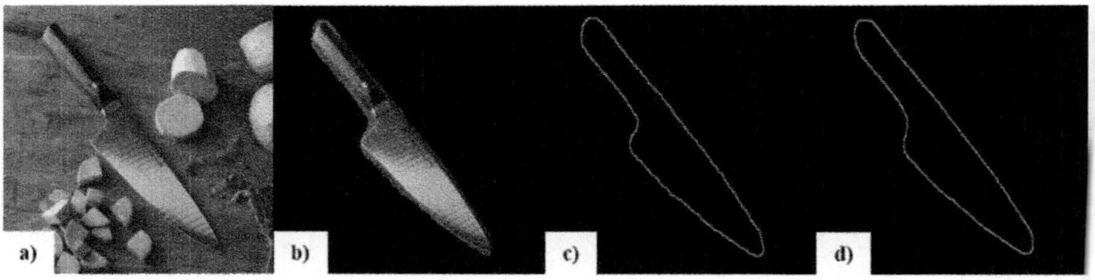

Fig. 7. Indicative results of the contour extraction model: (a) Input Image, (b) Knife Mask Prediction, (c) Contour Extraction based on Sobel Operator and (d) Refined Contour Outline/Output Image

3.2 Finite Element Analysis Results

Results of the developed simulation tool are displayed in Fig. 8, where the left part depicts the 3D model of the blade before the application of the external load and the right part after the execution of the numerical simulation. As expected, the tip of the blade shifted parallel to the direction of the external load. It should be noted that a scaling factor has been applied to the displacements to facilitate the presentation of the simulation results.

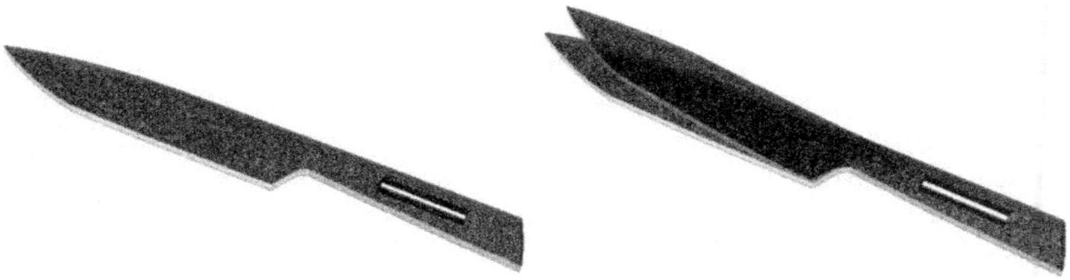

Fig. 8. 3D Geometry (left) and the developed displacements (right) in the simulation environment.

In addition, the results from the simulation were stored in Visualization Toolkit format (.vtk) in order to be visualized using the ParaView software [14]. The corresponding results are depicted in Fig. 9, where the developed Von Mises stresses are presented in the upper part of the figure and the displacements on the bottom part. It must be emphasized that the outcomes using the developed simulation module are consistent with the theoretical one [15]. Specifically, the highest values on the displacement are located at the tip of the blade where the loads are applied, and the maximum equivalent stress occurs at the bending point right after the handle of the knife. Taking into account the results from the numerical simulation, a safety factor can also be measured to ensure the reliability and safety of the designed knife under various loading conditions. The safety factor is typically defined as the ratio of the maximum load that a structure can withstand to the maximum load it is expected to experience during normal operation. This ratio provides a margin of safety, ensuring that the designed blade will not fail even under unexpected or extreme conditions. Hereupon, various cutting scenarios as well as several geometries for the designed knives could be investigated utilizing the developed simulation module without the need for time-consuming and costly experimental procedures.

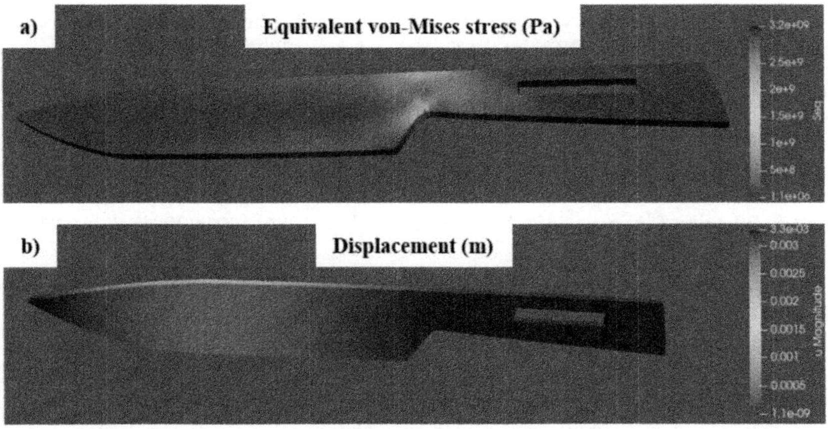

Fig. 9. Developed a) von Misses stresses [Pa] and b) Displacements [m] on the examined scenario.

4 Conclusions

In the context of this paper, a series of advanced design and numerical tools were developed and integrated into a web-based design platform in order to employ the MaaS business model in the knife design and development industry. In detail, through the design tools, the user can easily and accurately extract the desired design from a single picture with a noisy background or choose the most "matching" for the existing knife library. Then, the user can modify and customize the obtained design in order to properly fit specific needs and specifications. Moreover, the users can test the mechanical performance of their designs through the developed FEA tool in a user-friendly, rapid and reliable manner. This testing could assist in the further design optimization of the produced knives leading to higher quality products. Finally, the developed tools of design extraction and FEA can be easily employed with small modifications in the MaaS framework for other industries, such as the sheet metal industry, highlighting the high impact of the current work.

Acknowledgments. This research was supported by the project "BladeWorks" (Project code: KMP6-0082416) under the framework of the Action "Investment Plans of Innovation" of the Operational Program "Central Macedonia 2014–2020", that is co-funded by the European Regional Development Fund (ERDF) of the European Union and Greece.

Disclosure of Interests. The authors have no competing interests to declare that are relevant to the content of this article.

References

1. Breque, M., De Nul, L., Petridis, A.: Industry 5.0 – Towards a sustainable, human-centric and resilient European industry. European Commission, Directorate-General for Research and Innovation, Publications Office of the European Union (2021). https://data.europa.eu/doi/10.2777/308407
2. Rauschecker, U., Meier, M., Muckenhirn, R., Yip, A.L.K., Jagadeesan, A.P., Corney, J.: Cloud-based manufacturing-as-a-service environment for customized products. In: Cunningham, P., Cunningham, M. (eds.) eChallenges e-2011 Conference Proceedings (2011)
3. Bulut, S., Wende, M., Wagner, C., Anderl, R.: Impact of manufacturing-as-a-service: business model adaption for enterprises. Procedia CIRP **104**, 1286–1291 (2021). https://doi.org/10.1016/j.procir.2021.11.216
4. He, K., Zhang, X., Ren, S., Sun, J.: Deep residual learning for image recognition. In: Computer Vision and Pattern Recognition, pp. 770–778 (2015)
5. Lin, T.Y., et al.: Microsoft COCO: common objects in context. In: Fleet, D., Pajdla, T., Schiele, B., Tuytelaars, T. (eds.) ECCV 2014. LNCS, vol. 8693, pp. 740–755. Springer, Cham (2014). https://doi.org/10.1007/978-3-319-10602-1_48
6. Szegedy, C., et al.: Going deeper with convolutions. In: Computer Vision and Pattern Recognition, pp. 1–9 (2015)
7. Sirovich, L., Kirby, M.: Low-dimensional procedure for the characterization of human faces. J. Opt. Soc. Am. A **4**(3), 519–524 (1987)
8. Turk, M., Pentland, A.: Eigenfaces for recognition. J. Cogn. Neurosci. **3**(1), 71–86 (1991)
9. He, K., Gkioxari, G., Dollár, P., Girshick, R. Mask R-CNN. In: 2017 IEEE International Conference on Computer Vision (ICCV), pp. 2980–2988 (2017)
10. Lin, T.Y., Dollár, P., Girshick, R., He, K., Hariharan, B., Belongie, S.: Feature pyramid networks for object detection. In: Proceedings of the IEEE Conference on Computer Vision and Pattern Recognition, pp. 2117–2125 (2017)
11. Dai, J., Li, Y., He, K., Sun, J.: R-FCN: object detection via region-based fully convolutional networks. In: Advances in Neural Information Processing Systems, pp. 379–387 (2016)
12. Hecht, F.: New development in FreeFem++. J. Numer. Math. **20**(3–4), 251–266 (2012)
13. Yakupov, S.N., Kiyamov, H.G., Yakupov, N.M., Mukhamedova, I.Z.: A new variant of the fem for evaluation the strength of structures of complex geometry with heterogeneous material structure. Case Stud. Constr. Mater. **19**, e02360 (2023). https://doi.org/10.1016/j.cscm.2023.e02360

14. Ahrens, J., Geveci, B., Law, C.: ParaView: An End-User Tool for Large Data Visualization, Visualization Handbook. Elsevier, Amsterdam (2005)
15. Alok, G., Singh, S.K., Gobinath, R., Saivratha, T., Sushmitha, A., Reddy, V.S.: Finite element analysis of polycarbonate knife cum peeler. Mater. Today: Proc. **39**(1), 250–257 (2021). https://doi.org/10.1016/j.matpr.2020.07.039

Text Mining in Supply Chain Risk Management: A Bibliometric Analysis

Georgios Gelastopoulos(✉), Christos Keramydas, and Naoum Tsolakis

Department of Supply Chain Management, School of Economics and Business Administration, International Hellenic University, 570 01 Thermi, Greece
gelageo@ihu.gr

Abstract. In Supply Chain Risk Management (SCRM), the use of text mining is gaining increasing attention as the application of modern algorithms enable rapid, real-time interpretation of huge volume of unstructured data. Online data has the potential to provide critical insights for proactive risk identification and mitigation in the complex and interconnected global supply chain networks, especially in periods of man-made disasters or crises such as the Ukrainian-Russian conflict. This paper delivers an overview of how text mining of online data is being used in SCRM. More specifically, by using bibliometric methodologies, this study identifies primary areas of focus and collaborative networks in SCRM's research field. The most common analysis methods such as citation analysis, co-authorship patterns, keyword co-occurrence, and publication trends take place as a comprehensive corpus of peer-reviewed articles from Scopus database is collected and analyzed. By employing bibliometric tools and network analysis measures the study explores how the use of text mining techniques is evolving for the past ten years, and where it is heading. This is achieved by visualizing the networks with suitable programmes, by using indices like the modularity index and with cluster analysis which are applied to the networks created from the bibliographic data. This study aims to uncover trends, disciplines, and how individual studies are related to one another. The results suggest thematic clusters, influential studies and authors, and research methods that are significant to the field and they map trends and future directions, providing valuable insights for both academic researchers and industry practitioners.

Keywords: Bibliometric Analysis · Supply Chain Risk Management · Text Mining · Online Data

1 Introduction

The effects of supply chains changing from simple to complex global networks are significant in terms of the disruptions they can experience, as highlighted by the COVID-19 pandemic. This health crisis has uncovered crucial weak points in the management of supply chain (SCM) systems. The challenges caused by the pandemic made companies to quickly change their methods by using various suppliers, raising inventory levels and accepting new technologies to enhance resilience in supply chains (Li and Zobel 2020; Trkman and McCormack 2009).

I. Kostavelis et al. (Eds.): ICSC 2024, CCIS 2110, pp. 66–75, 2025.
https://doi.org/10.1007/978-3-031-69344-1_5

In today's intricate and globally-connected business environment, managing supply chain risks (SCRM) has turned into a critical element for companies. SCRM concentrates on recognizing, evaluating and reducing dangers in the operations of supply chains. This process involves multiple stages such as identifying risk, evaluating it, implementing a management strategy to deal with the risks identified and then monitoring them over time (Manuj and Mentzer 2008).

The digitalization of SCM, especially with advanced algorithms and real data analysis can be a very promising direction to enhance resilience against global uncertainties, such as political unrest and economic challenges (Livelli 2024). Text mining, which is a method to extract useful information from unstructured text data, can offer insights based on data and news, and can be a strong asset for a company to mitigate risks (Howells 2020).

Text mining has been acknowledged for its value in different academic areas. However, there still exists a significant underutilization of this potential within SCM (Toorajipour et al. 2021; Ghadge et al. 2012). The broad utilization of text mining in different fields of study has shown its efficiency in managing and analyzing textual data. However, the complete potential of text mining for processing huge amounts of textual information like technical papers, news articles and online content is not yet tapped into significantly in the field of SCM.

The purpose of this study is to shed light on how text mining can improve SCRM. This review, which performs a bibliometric analysis of research papers that use text mining on online data for Supply Chain Management, shows where these works are published, from which countries they come more often and with keyword analysis - it points out what areas have received most attention and are deserving further investigation. The analysis provides groundwork for closing down the divide between potential in text mining and its real-world application; this is an important step towards fortifying supply chain defenses against future, unexpected threats.

2 Article Selection

This study uses a systematic literature review process to investigate the literature in text mining of online data in Supply Chain Risk Management. The main stages are three: planning the review, conducting the review and reporting the review (Tranfield et al. 2003).

The Scopus database was used to search for journal articles, using the keywords ("supply chain" OR "global supplier") AND ("text mining" OR "text analytics") as the search terms. The review was limited to the past ten years, and it included papers written only in English language. After examining the resulted papers, only the ones that utilize text mining techniques on online data for supply chain management were selected, resulted in 53 papers.

3 Bibliometric Analysis

3.1 Publications Per year

In Fig. 1, it can be seen that in 2014 there were no papers published, but in 2015, a single influential paper named "Insights from hashtag #supplychain and Twitter analytics: Considering Twitter and Twitter data for supply chain practice and research" was published and it was cited 367 times, hinting this paper was a key contribution to the field. In 2016 as well as in 2019 were not published any new papers, and in 2017 and 2018, only a few papers came out each year.

Starting in 2020, five papers were published, which is not a very big number, however these five papers are highly cited indicating the recognition and influence they have. In 2021 it is noticed an increase, where 15 documents were published. This may be stemmed from improved text mining algorithms and the profound impact of the COVID-19 pandemic, which may have spurred more studies. The year 2023 stands out with the most papers published—17 in total. Even though the data for 2024 has just started, there is already one paper published.

Regarding the number of citations, it is noticed that the single paper in 2015 by Chae (Chae 2015)was highly cited, while the papers in 2017 and 2018 were not at the same level. However, the papers published in 2020 and 2021 although they are considered recent papers are very highly cited. In 2022 and 2023 it is noticed a decline in citations number but this is justified over the fact that papers need some time to be read and then cited in subsequent work and it is anticipated that the citation frequency will grow as the field continues to advance.

Over the ten years, research activity visibly escalated at the last four years, which are the years that the Covid-19 pandemic hit. Alongside with the technological advancements in text mining and Artificial Intelligence techniques, this indicates that text mining is an emerging field for SCRM with an expanding significance and it has the potential to be a cornerstone technique for the SCRM (Fig. 2).

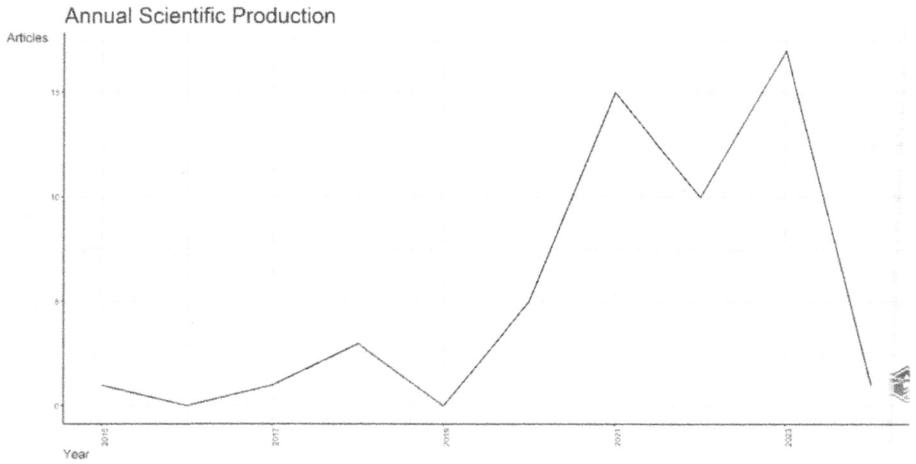

Fig. 1. Number of Publications from 2014 to 2024 plotted along with total citations.

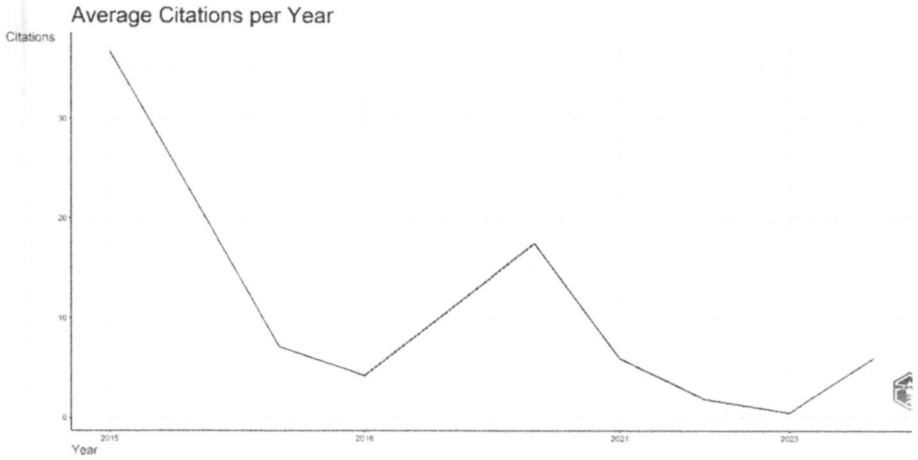

Fig. 2. Average Citations per Year.

3.2 Authors and Co-citation Analysis of Authors

In this section, we identify the most prolific authors. The analysis showed that the 53 papers were published by 170 authors. In order to identify the most important authors an analysis using VOSviewer was performed. A co-authorship network with authors as unit of analysis was created and the minimum number of documents of an author was set to 1. The most cited author is Bongsug Chae with 368 citations, followed by Anirban Adhikary, and Sourav Bikash Borah and Amalesh Sharma with 297 each. Lin Wang, Binrong Wu and Yu-Rong Zeng have 78 citations and Sirui Wang, Chih-Yuan Chu and Gül E. Kremer have 74, 72 and 72 citations respectively (Fig. 3).

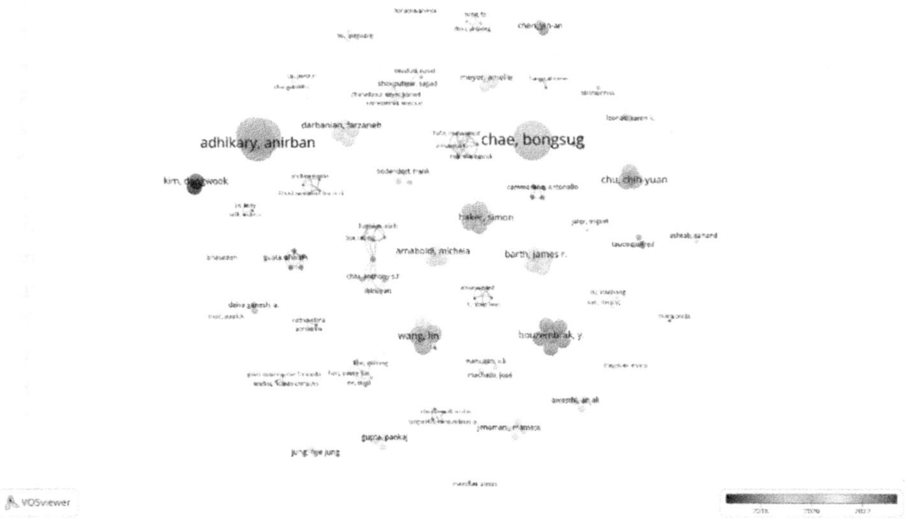

Fig. 3. Network of authors. The citations were used as weight for the node size.

The co-citation analysis of authors reveals the pivotal place of specific authors, how they are cited and how they are connected to each other. The clusters identified by VOSViewer, as it can be seen in Fig. 4, are five main clusters and a sixth smaller cluster (purple color). Based on the structure of the network, it can be deduced that although we have diverse themes, these are highly connected to each other. This suggests that while researchers are working on specialized areas with different objectives, their work is not isolated. The methods they use connect to each other and findings on one field can influence the research on a different one.

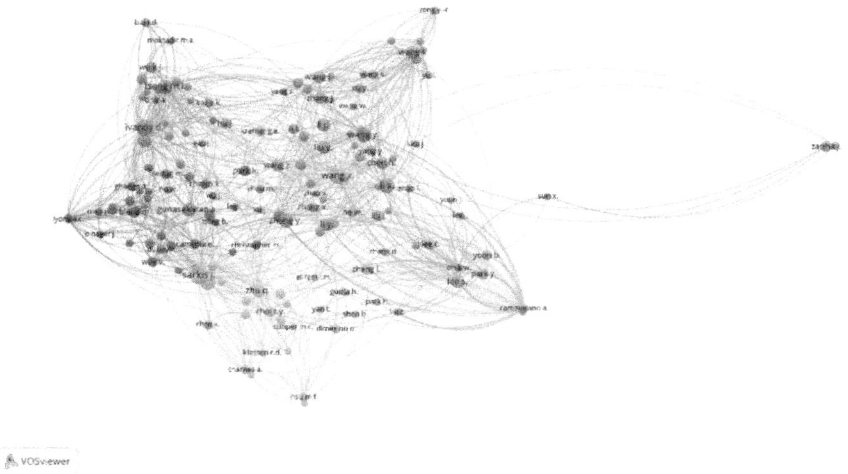

Fig. 4. Co-citation network with authors as unit of analysis. (Color figure online)

In total there are 7548 authors at the references of the papers, of which 160 meet the threshold of having at least 5 number of citations. We can identify influential authors in each cluster. In cluster with color blue, we can identify Tseng M. L. (19 citations), Ivanov D. (23 citations), and Dolgui A. (16 citations), who are strongly connected to the rest of the network. Sarkis J, is the most influential author in the yellow cluster and in the whole network with 30 citations and a total link strength of 1092. According to the papers that authors in the yellow cluster publish, the yellow cluster can be characterized as green supply chain management or environmental supply chain management. In the yellow cluster Seuring S. is also a top author having 22 citations and 667 total link strength. Li X. is the top author in green cluster having 20 citations. The green cluster can be characterized as a cluster that contains computational and data analytics papers. Wang X. has 21 citations in the turquoise cluster. Park K. is the most influential author in red cluster with 11 citations and 319 total link strength. Lastly, Li J. is the most influential author in the purple cluster with 15 citations (Table 1).

Table 1. Top 5 most cited authors from the references of documents.

N.	Author	Cluster	Links	Total link strength	Citations
1	Sarkis J.	4	131	1092	30
2	Ivanov D.	3	113	810	23
3	Seuring S.	4	119	667	22
4	Wang L.	2	90	664	16
5	Tseng M. L.	3	107	660	19

3.3 Contribution of Countries

Regarding the contribution of countries to the topic, the most productive country is the United States with 11 papers published highlighting the influence this country has in the field. China and United Kingdom have 8 publication each, followed by India and with 7 publications (Table 2).

Table 2. Top Countries contributing during 2014–2024.

Country	TP	TC
United States	11	814
China	8	98
United Kingdom	8	185
India	7	355

Notes: TP = Total Publications; TC = Total Citations.

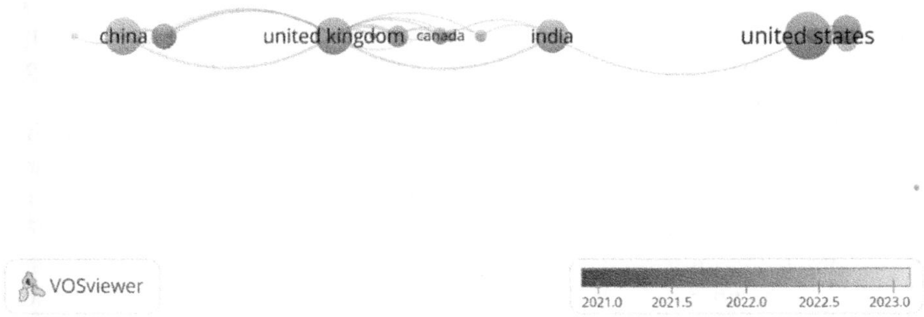

Fig. 5. Co-authorship network diagram of countries.

In Fig. 5 the network of co-authorship countries is visualized. The bigger nodes are the ones with the most publications, that is United States, United Kingdom, India and China. Greece, Germany, Columbia and Australia do not share publications with other countries; hence they are missing from the network (Fig. 5). In total there are 29 countries of which 20 are connected with 39 edges. Five groups are evident and the interaction between the groups can easily be observed from the network. The proximity among clusters and countries, represents the collaboration between them. The width of the edges represents the volume of collaboration. The largest cluster consists of 8 countries: Canada, Finland, France, India, Italy, Netherlands and Portugal. In this group it is noticed that United Kingdom collaborates more with Netherlands and India, and also with China which belongs to another group consisting of Hong Kong, Pakistan and Philippines. USA collaborates more with Austria, Iran and Switzerland. The fourth cluster consists of Korea which collaborates with USA and Indonesia. The fifth more isolated cluster that doesn't connect to the rest of the network consists of two countries: Japan and Bangladesh.

3.4 Keyword Analysis

A total of 200 keywords were identified. The keyword *text mining* is the most prevalent, appearing in 21% of the papers. It is followed by *covid-19* which appears in 9% of the documents. *Social media* and *supply chain* follow appearing in 7% of the documents.

The keyword network was also exported in GML format and analyzed in the open-source software Gephi (Bastian et al. 2009), in order to use the community detection algorithms, and more specifically the modularity index (Blondel et al. 2008). Usually, a modularity value above 0.3 suggests that the network does indeed have a significant community structure. The modularity index was found equal to 0.54. This suggests a strong structure of communities within the network: certain keywords tend to group together much more frequently than would be expected in a random network, indicating that there are distinct themes or topics studied in the literature. The algorithm grouped the 200 keywords in 19 communities that represent a different topic. This can be interpreted as that the research landscape is diverse and specialized. The size distribution in Fig. 6, shows that most communities are small in size, with only a few larger ones. This suggests a few dominant research areas and several more focused on specialized topics.

Figure 7 shows the co-occurrence network visualized in VOSviewer, in which the color of the nodes indicates the year the papers were published and the size of the nodes indicates the number of occurrences of the keyword. The hub node of the network is the keyword *text mining* with 28 occurrences connecting to other nodes with 111 links. It is connected to other central nodes that appear in the literature frequently such as *covid-19* (13 occurrences), *supply chain* (9 occurrences), *social media* (9 occurrences), *sustainability* (7 occurrences), and *sentiment analysis* (7 occurrences). From this, it can be deduced that the impact of covid-19 in supply chains is a topic that researchers approached with text mining techniques. Another topic that draws major attention is sustainability. Lastly, the size of *social media* keyword indicates that social media is a big source of data that researchers analyzed. From the network, some of the most mentioned text mining techniques and algorithms become evident, such as *topic modelling*, *sentiment analysis* and *natural language processing*. The yellow cluster, contains

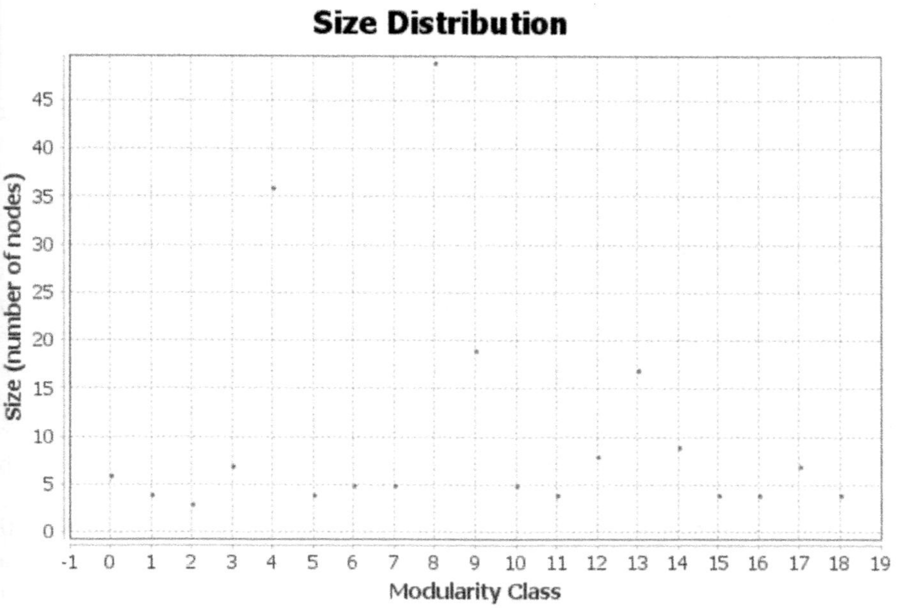

Fig. 6. Size distribution of communities in the keyword network.

the most recent keywords suggesting that *smartphone*, *supplier selection* and *artificial intelligence* are among the most recent topics, reflecting the direction of the research. The fact that 174 keywords out of 200 appear only once suggests the multidisciplinary nature of the research, where they apply various techniques to solve different problems.

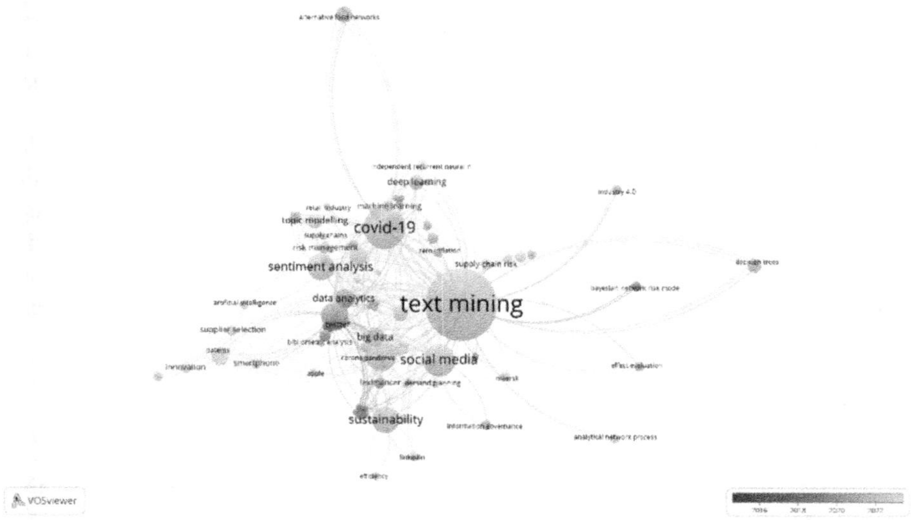

Fig. 7. The keyword network visualization. (Color figure online)

4 Discussion

The aim of this study was to quantify the research on text mining on online data for SCRM by conducting a bibliometric analysis. The results indicate that application of text mining techniques on online data for Supply Chain Risk Management has been very recently adopted by researchers – the last three years have been the most productive on the topic – and it is a very promising path that can been utilized in numerous ways and for very diverse objectives.

The most cited author is Bongsug Chae with 368 citations, making his paper *Insights from hashtag #supplychain and Twitter Analytics: Considering Twitter and Twitter data for supply chain practice and research* (Chae 2015) one of the most influential in the field. This paper discusses how Twitter is a significant platform for supply chain professionals and organizations to share information, discuss a wide range of topics, and gauge public sentiment towards supply chain management practices. Chae is followed by Anirban Adhikary, Sourav Bikash Borah and Amalesh Sharma (Sharma et al. 2020), whose paper *Covid-19's impact on supply chain decisions:*

Strategic insights from NASDAQ 100 firms using Twitter data received 297 citations so far. This study concluded in four major themes that Twitter data revealed. Demand-Supply Challenges: Some sectors experiencing a decline in demand (e.g., automobiles, crude oil, transportation), while others saw spikes (e.g., technology firms). Technological Challenges. Building a Resilient Supply Chain. Sustainable Supply Chain Challenges. These studies collectively highlight a growing recognition of the value of social media analytics as a critical tool for real-time monitoring, risk assessment, and strategic planning within supply chain management.

Based upon the findings, several promising areas emerge for future research in the application of text mining within Supply Chain Risk Management. As a critical area stands out the utilization of different and advanced techniques such as deep learning and machine learning which can provide better insights. Given the emphasis observed in the current literature, another focus area for future research is sustainability within supply chains. Researchers can explore more ways to improve sustainable practices like sustainable sourcing, and reduce environmental impact, helping in climate change challenges.

Considering the size of the research conducted on Covid-19's impact on supply chain, future studies could include various types of disruptions, such as geopolitical tensions, natural disasters, or financial crises. Utilizing text mining to forecast risk for supply chains could be very beneficial for a more robust ecosystem. The analysis suggested that social media is a significant source of data. Using diverse data sources, such as weather conditions or satellite images, and combining them, could offer a more comprehensive approach in mitigating risks.

References

Bastian, M., Heymann, S., Jacomy, M.: Gephi: an open source software for exploring and manipulating networks. Proc. Int. AAAI Conf. Web Soc. Media **3**(1), 361–362 (2009). https://doi.org/10.1609/icwsm.v3i1.13937

Blondel, V.D., Guillaume, J.-L., Lambiotte, R., Lefebvre, E.: Fast unfolding of communities in large networks. J. Stat. Mech: Theory Exp. **2008**(10), P10008 (2008). https://doi.org/10.1088/1742-5468/2008/10/P10008

Chae, B.K.: Insights from hashtag #supplychain and Twitter analytics: considering twitter and twitter data for supply chain practice and research. Int. J. Prod. Econ. **165**(July), 247–259 (2015). https://doi.org/10.1016/j.ijpe.2014.12.037

Ghadge, A., Dani, S., Kalawsky, R.: Supply chain risk management: present and future scope. Int. J. Logist. Manag. **23**(3), 313–339 (2012). https://doi.org/10.1108/09574091211289200

Howells, R.: The Importance of Real-Time Data in Times of Supply Chain Disruption (2020). https://www.forbes.com/sites/sap/2020/04/28/the-importance-of-real-time-data-in-times-of-supply-chain-disruption/?sh=3f42bc035563

Li, Y., Zobel, C.W.: Exploring supply chain network resilience in the presence of the ripple effect. Int. J. Prod. Econ. **228**(October), 107693 (2020). https://doi.org/10.1016/j.ijpe.2020.107693

Livelli, F.: What Does Supply Chain Resilience Mean in 2024? (2024). https://www.thebci.org/news/what-does-supply-chain-resilience-mean-in-2024.html

Manuj, I., Mentzer, J.T.: Global supply chain risk management strategies. Int. J. Phys. Distrib. Logist. Manag. **38**(3), 192–223 (2008). https://doi.org/10.1108/09600030810866986

Sharma, A., Adhikary, A., Borah, S.B.: Covid-19's impact on supply chain decisions: strategic insights from NASDAQ 100 firms using Twitter data. J. Bus. Res. **117**(September), 443–449 (2020). https://doi.org/10.1016/j.jbusres.2020.05.035

Toorajipour, R., Sohrabpour, V., Nazarpour, A., Oghazi, P., Fischl, M.: Artificial intelligence in supply chain management: a systematic literature review. J. Bus. Res. **122**(January), 502–517 (2021). https://doi.org/10.1016/j.jbusres.2020.09.009

Tranfield, D., Denyer, D., Smart, P.: Towards a methodology for developing evidence-informed management knowledge by means of systematic review. Br. J. Manag. **14**(3), 207–222 (2003). https://doi.org/10.1111/1467-8551.00375

Trkman, P., McCormack, K.: Supply chain risk in turbulent environments—a conceptual model for managing supply chain network risk. Int. J. Prod. Econ. **119**(2), 247–258 (2009). https://doi.org/10.1016/j.ijpe.2009.03.002

Blockchain-Enabled Green Supply Chain Management: Innovating Agricultural Plastic Waste Recovery and Reverse Logistics

Dimitra Tzanetou, Stavros T. Ponis(✉), George Plakas, and Theodoros Nikolaos Maroutas

School of Mechanical Engineering, National Technical University Athens, Heroon Polytechniou 9, 15780 Athens, Greece
staponis@central.ntua.gr

Abstract. In the scientific field of green supply chain management and reverse logistics, addressing the escalating issue of plastic pollution stands as a critical challenge, particularly within the agricultural sector. The integration of sustainable practices and innovative technologies in managing agricultural plastic waste is paramount to advancing environmental stewardship and operational efficiency. In that direction, the research presented in this paper delves into the development of a novel approach that harmonizes with the principles of reverse logistics and green supply chain management, aiming to mitigate the environmental footprint of agricultural plastics. Central to this study is the exploration of an advanced system for the management of agriplastic waste, leveraging Blockchain technology to foster a transparent, efficient, and sustainable supply chain. This system proposes a decentralized platform that enables seamless interaction between stakeholders, including farmers and waste collectors, facilitating the effective tracking, collection, and recycling or energy recovery of agricultural plastics. By establishing a reliable network for the detailed reporting of agriplastic usage and disposal, the research underscores the potential of digital ledger technologies to enhance traceability and accountability in waste management processes. Furthermore, this research emphasizes the importance of reverse logistics in the lifecycle management of agricultural plastics, from their initial deployment to their final disposal or repurposing. Through the creation of a mobile application and the formulation of a comprehensive business model, the study aims to facilitate the recovery and recycling of materials and thus, to contribute to the reduction of environmental pollution, the promotion of sustainable agricultural practice and the broader objectives of environmental conservation and sustainability.

Keywords: Green Supply Chain Management · Blockchain · Agricultural plastic waste · Reverse Logistics · Circular Economy · Waste-to-energy

1 Introduction

Plastic pollution is a critical global issue, exacerbating environmental, economic, health, and aesthetic challenges with each passing day (Soares et al. 2021). The surge in plastic usage across various agricultural operations over recent decades has notably contributed

I. Kostavelis et al. (Eds.): ICSC 2024, CCIS 2110, pp. 76–80, 2025.
https://doi.org/10.1007/978-3-031-69344-1_6

to this dilemma. Although the agricultural sector is not the primary culprit, its substantial utilization of plastics in numerous applications adds significant strain (Batista et al. 2022). This issue is particularly pronounced in countries like Greece, where the absence of effective agri-plastic waste management systems results in a substantial portion of waste being improperly discarded on land, in the sea, or being illegally burned, thereby inflicting a broad spectrum of environmental damages (Andrea et al. 2020). Adding to the complexity, research indicates that the improper disposal of agricultural plastics can lead to soil degradation, water contamination, and a reduction in biodiversity, highlighting an urgent need for sustainable waste management practices (Hajam et al. 2023). Furthermore, studies emphasize the potential of recycled agricultural plastics in creating economic opportunities through the production of value-added products, thus underscoring the economic as well as environmental benefits of recycling (Hoffman et al. 2023). The environmental impact of plastic waste in oceans has also been well-documented, with agricultural plastics contributing to the vast expanses of marine litter that harm marine life and ecosystems (Thushari and Senevirathna 2020). Moreover, the health implications for humans through the bioaccumulation of toxic substances from plastics in the food chain have been a growing concern among scientists (Smith et al. 2018).

Given these multifaceted impacts, there is a critical need to design, develop, and implement comprehensive systems for the detection, tracking, recovery, and, where feasible, the energy utilization or safe disposal of agri-plastics. Such systems would not only aim to mitigate agri-plastic waste pollution but also promote the agricultural sector's alignment with sustainability and circular economy principles. By embracing innovative solutions and fostering international collaboration, it is possible to address the pressing challenges posed by agricultural plastic pollution, thereby ensuring a more sustainable future for global agriculture and the environment at large. BLOCK AGROWASTE attempts to accommodate this need by developing a state-of-the-art, environmentally friendly and economically viable innovative agri-plastic waste management system. The project will focus on the development of a decentralized platform based on Blockchain technology, providing continuous communication between contract farmers and collectors of agri-plastic waste. In particular, the objective of the proposed project is to create a highly reliable information network for all stakeholders, through which, farmers will be able to inform the collectors about the type, quantity, date of placement and geographical location of agri-plastics in their greenhouses, using an online distributed ledger. At a later stage and after the end of the useful/ functional service life of the agri-plastics, the registered quantity will be able to be declared available for recycling, while the collectors will be notified accordingly through a specially designed mobile application. The latter will collect the waste and transport it to suitable units for further processing, recycling and energy utilization, thus successfully completing its management cycle.

The successful implementation of the proposed project will lead to the development of an effective agri-plastic waste management system, capable of enhancing the traceability of agri-plastics at the end of their useful life and their final use as waste, i.e. their separation by type and gathering by farmers, their collection by non-hazardous waste collection companies, and finally, their utilization by waste-to-energy companies. The ultimate goal of BLOCK AGROWASTE is to formulate a detailed business plan for the sustainable and commercially successful introduction of a complete solution, exploitable in both domestic and international markets, by issuing thorough technical instructions to potentially participating companies, regarding the creation of cooperative relations aimed at the collection, transport, management and utilization of agri-plastic waste.

2 Methodology of the Proposed Project

In order to fulfill the objectives outlined for the BLOCK AGROWASTE initiative, the research methodology adheres to a structured framework comprising four sequential phases: **(a)** an investigative study into the prevailing circumstances within the agri-plastic waste management domain alongside technological exploration for the development of the information system; **(b)** the construction of the project's technological infrastructures; **(c)** rigorous evaluation and testing to ensure functionality and system interoperability; and **(d)** pilot implementation followed by a comprehensive analysis of the project outcomes. Delving further into the methodological steps, the approach is delineated into five key points crucial for the project's success:

- The comprehensive documentation of the current state of agri-plastic waste management, including all types of plastic waste distinguished by their chemical properties (e.g., PE films, HDPE, etc.), utilization, disposal timelines, and requirements for pre-recovery treatment processes.
- The smart design of an innovative agri-plastic management system designed for optimal accumulation and transportation to suitable facilities for subsequent recycling and processing. This system bifurcates into two technological pillars: a subsystem dedicated to the collection and analysis of big data, which will collect real-time data for visualization purposes, and an application subsystem, which will be utilized as the project's backbone, to deliver services of high importance to both farmers and agri-plastic waste collectors.
- The successful integration of technology to ensure the operational efficiency of the system and the seamless progression of agricultural activities through the adoption of a Blockchain platform. This enables farmers to join a networked ecosystem, facilitating the dissemination of agri-plastic waste data as streaming inputs to a cloud computing setup for further analysis. Conversely, collectors of agri-plastic waste are apprised of plastic quantities through an easy-to-use Web UI/UX accessible via their mobile devices.
- The seamless development of the Blockchain platform's data collection and analytic subsystem, alongside the effective data processing and visualization, plays a critical role in reinforcing the successful execution of the agri-plastics management framework.
- The emphasis on the mobile application's user-friendly design is anticipated to augment its acceptability among end-users, namely, the farmers and agri-plastic waste collectors. The application interface is designed to be intuitive, directing farmers in the disposal of agri-plastic waste and assisting collectors in the acquisition and subsequent transport for recycling, processing, and energy recovery.

These methodological facets collectively constitute the foundation upon which the BLOCK AGROWASTE project aspires to revolutionize agri-plastic waste management, leveraging state-of-the-art technologies to address environmental challenges, thus steering the agricultural sector towards sustainability and circular economy paradigms.

3 Conclusions

In summary, the BLOCK AGROWASTE project adopts a holistic approach, initiating with an evaluation of existing waste management methods and the creation of a sophisticated information system. It proposes a dual-component system that integrates extensive data gathering and analysis with a user-friendly mobile app. This initiative aims to enhance the efficiency of collecting, transporting, and recycling agricultural plastics by employing blockchain technology for the instant sharing and processing of data. The approach emphasizes the integration of technology, ease of use, and the project's pilot testing to verify its effectiveness and potential for expansion. Furthermore, the project is a deliberate effort to reduce the environmental footprint of agricultural plastic waste. Through the application of advanced technology and a systematic strategy, it seeks to provide a sustainable solution that not only tackles the current challenges of waste management in the agricultural sector but also supports wider objectives of sustainability and the circular economy. This effort is expected to significantly better the handling of agricultural plastics, diminish pollution, and promote a more sustainable agricultural sector.

Acknowledgments. This research has been co-financed by the European Regional Development Fund of the European Union and Greek national funds through the Operational Program Attica 2014–2020, for the Action Entitled "Research synergies and Innovation in the Region of Attica" (project code: ATTP4-0325411).

Disclosure of Interests. The authors have no competing interests to declare that are relevant to the content of this article.

References

1. Andrea, V., Mpeza, P., Barelos, D., Stylios, C.: Unraveling the role of plastic waste pollution in the Amvrakikos wetlands national park, Greece: the stakeholders' views. J. Mar. Sci. Eng. **8**(8), 549 (2020)
2. Batista, T., et al.: Dealing with plastic waste from agriculture activity. Agronomy **12**(1), 134 (2022)
3. Hajam, Y.A., Kumar, R., Kumar, A.: Environmental waste management strategies and vermi transformation for sustainable development. Environ. Chall. **13**, 100747 (2023)
4. Hofmann, T., et al.: Plastics can be used more sustainably in agriculture. Commun. Earth Environ. **4**(1), 332 (2023)
5. Smith, M., Love, D.C., Rochman, C.M., Neff, R.A.: Microplastics in seafood and the implications for human health. Curr. Environ. Health Rep. **5**, 375–386 (2018)

6. Soares, J., Miguel, I., Venâncio, C., Lopes, I., Oliveira, M.: Public views on plastic pollution: knowledge, perceived impacts, and pro-environmental behaviours. J. Hazard. Mater. **412**, 125227 (2021)
7. Thushari, G.G.N., Senevirathna, J.D.M.: Plastic pollution in the marine environment. Heliyon **6**(8), e04709 (2020)

Evaluating Trends and Identifying Research Gaps: A Thematic and Evolutionary Bibliometric Analysis of Deposit Refund Systems (1938–2024)

Konstantinos Rotsios[1,2], Aristotelis Mavidis[3], Dimitris Folinas[3](✉), and Thomas Fotiadis[2]

[1] Department of International Business, Perrotis College, American Farm School, 551 02 Thessaloniki, Greece
krotsi@afs.edu.gr

[2] Department of Production Engineering and Management, Democritus University of Thrace, 671 00 Xanthi, Greece

[3] Department of Supply Chain Management, International Hellenic University, 601 00 Katerini, Greece
armavid@yahoo.gr, folinasd@ihu.gr

Abstract. This study presents a novel bibliometric analysis of Deposit Refund Systems (DRS) from 1938 to 2024, aiming to describe the thematic evolution and identify key research trends within the field. By utilizing data extracted from Scopus and applying a refined search strategy encompassing terms such as "deposit refund system," "reverse vending machine," and "container deposit legislation", among others, we gather relevant publications for analysis.

The study employs a series of bibliometric tools, including co-word analysis, thematic maps, trend topic analysis, and Treemaps, to dissect the complex landscape of DRS research. Through these methodologies, the research elucidates how dominant themes have shifted over the decades, highlights the emergence of new research areas, and underscores technology integration in DRS practices.

Key findings reveal a significant focus on 'recycling' and 'waste management' as central themes, with emerging interests in 'plastic waste' and 'technological advancements'. The analysis also identifies gaps in current research, particularly in the socio-economic impacts of DRS and its effectiveness across different geopolitical contexts.

This paper significantly contributes to understanding DRS dynamics, offering valuable insights for policymakers, practitioners, and researchers. It suggests areas for future research and underscores the need for a multidisciplinary approach to enhance DRS's effectiveness in promoting sustainable waste management practices globally, thereby providing practical guidance for implementing and improving DRS systems.

Keywords: Deposit Refund Systems · Bibliometric Analysis · Recycling Trends · Waste Management · Thematic Evolution

I. Kostavelis et al. (Eds.): ICSC 2024, CCIS 2110, pp. 81–101, 2025.
https://doi.org/10.1007/978-3-031-69344-1_7

1 Introduction

Deposit Refund Systems (DRS) have emerged as a critical solution to tackle the challenges associated with waste management and recycling [1–3]. However, it is not just about the system; it is about the consumers[4]. Initially developed to encourage the return and recycling of beverage containers, DRS has expanded its scope to include a wide range of recyclable materials such as plastics, glass, electronics, and more [1, 2, 5–7]. This system plays a pivotal role in promoting sustainable consumption and disposal practices by implementing a financial incentive mechanism: consumers pay a small deposit at the time of purchase, which is refunded upon the return of the empty container [1, 7, 8].

The significance of DRS extends beyond simple waste reduction; it also contributes to significant decreases in litter, increases in recycling rates, and reductions in landfill use [8, 9]. These systems ensure that returned materials are clean and sorted, significantly enhancing the efficiency of the recycling process. As a result, DRS has been instrumental in diverting waste from landfills and improving the quality of recycled materials, which is essential for the sustainability of recycling industries [3, 10].

DRS are not just a local solution but a global one. Their adaptation varies worldwide, reflecting diverse environmental priorities, economic conditions, and consumer behavior [4]. In regions where DRS is established, there is tangible evidence of improved recycling rates and increased public participation in waste management practices. For instance, countries like Germany [11], Sweden [12], and Finland [10] have set a high standard with their DRS, achieving remarkable container recovery rates and inspiring other nations to follow suit. The systematic review by Guang-wei Zhou et al. (2020) comprehensively analyses the operating modes, key parameters, and development trends of beverage packaging DRS across 40 countries. This review underscores the effectiveness of DRS in transferring waste streams to reuse or recycling but also highlights the need for integration with intelligent collection, ecological design, and a diversified profit model for optimal development [7].

The evolving complexity of waste, particularly with the surge in single-use plastics and electronic waste, poses new challenges and opportunities for DRS. Modern DRS must adapt to handle diverse waste streams effectively and incorporate advanced technologies such as digital deposit tracking, automated sorting, and data analytics to enhance operational efficiency [2, 3, 7, 12–15]. The rise of data analytics and more sophisticated methodological approaches has enabled deeper insights into the operational aspects of DRS and its broader implications. Enhanced capabilities include modelling and simulation of different scenarios, impact assessments, and leveraging big data for tracking and optimising DRS performance [16].

DRS is a key component of broader environmental strategies promoting a circular economy. This involves expanding the materials in these systems and integrating them with other sustainable practices and technologies. As environmental pressures increase, the flexibility and effectiveness of DRS will be crucial in shaping future waste management and recycling efforts globally, making it a significant area for continued research and policy innovation [2, 3, 8, 10, 11, 17]. Zhou et al.'s research calls for the increased application of Internet communication technology and the Internet of Things to make the DRS process more controllable and verifiable [7].

The significance of this study lies in its thorough exploration of Deposit Refund Systems (DRS), which are pivotal for advancing global recycling rates and effective waste management. Through detailed bibliometric analysis, the study uncovers the evolution, prevailing themes, and emergent trends within DRS research, offering crucial insights and identifying gaps in the literature. This foundational knowledge equips policymakers, practitioners, and researchers with a deeper understanding of DRS efficiencies and challenges, guiding future strategies and innovations. Consequently, the findings contribute substantially to pursuing sustainable waste practices and the broader environmental goal of transitioning towards a circular economy.

2 Literature Review

2.1 Current State of DRS

The current state of Deposit Refund Systems (DRS) reflects a sophisticated integration of environmental strategy, technological innovation, and regulatory frameworks tailored to enhance recycling efficiency and waste management. Globally, DRS has proven effective in encouraging recycling behaviours through financial incentives for returning containers and other recyclable materials [2]. Technologically, systems are increasingly adopting automation and real-time data analytics to improve collection rates and processing efficiency [18]. Regulatory approaches vary significantly across jurisdictions but aim to support waste reduction goals while adapting to local economic and environmental contexts [19]. However, challenges remain in achieving uniform participation and in handling complex waste streams like plastics and electronics, pressing the need for ongoing innovation and adaptation in DRS practices.

2.2 Historical Evolution and Future Trends

The historical evolution of Deposit Refund Systems (DRS) research highlights a trajectory from foundational studies focused on basic recycling processes to sophisticated analyses involving policy impacts and technological innovations. Initially centered on the environmental benefits of recycling, the scope has expanded to include economic analyses, technology integration, and socio-political factors [1]. Mrozek (2000) especially highlights the theoretical underpinnings and practical implications of DRS, emphasising their role in environmental regulation where direct emissions monitoring is challenging. His study is particularly insightful in dissecting the economic mechanics behind DRS, illustrating how these systems, traditionally aimed at improving recycling rates, have also been configured to achieve revenue neutrality—where no net revenues accrue to the government, thereby altering the dynamics of incentive structures [20].

Future trends will likely emphasise the integration of digital technologies like A.I. and IoT to optimise DRS operations, address the increasing complexity of waste materials, and enhance global sustainability efforts [7]. Research is expected to increasingly focus on these areas to drive effective and scalable DRS solutions.

2.3 Find and Fill Gaps in Current Research

The bibliometric analysis identified several gaps in current Deposit Refund Systems (DRS) research. Firstly, there is limited exploration of the socio-economic impacts of DRS on diverse demographic groups, which could provide deeper insights into adoption barriers and incentives. Additionally, research on the effectiveness of DRS in non-traditional settings like developing countries remains sparse. There is also a need for comparative studies that evaluate different DRS models across various regulatory environments to ascertain best practices and tailor strategies to specific regional contexts.

3 Methodology

3.1 Scope and Relevance of the Study

This study comprehensively explores the Deposit Refund Systems (DRS), utilising bibliometric analyses to map the evolving research landscape from 1938 to 2024. It identifies core themes, emerging trends, and technological integrations within DRS. It highlights its relevance to enhancing recycling rates and informing policy decisions to bolster global environmental sustainability and waste management practices.

3.2 Objectives and Research Questions

The objectives and relevant research question for this study are clearly articulated as follows:

1. To conduct a bibliometric analysis that maps the evolution of research within the Deposit Refund System (DRS) from 1938 to 2024, identifying core themes, their development, and interconnections.
2. To evaluate how technological advancements have been integrated into DRS research and practices over the studied period.
3. To assess the impact of identified research themes on the formulation and evolution of DRS-related environmental policies.

Research Question:

How have the dominant and emerging themes within DRS research influenced policy decisions, and how have technological advancements impacted the effectiveness of DRS practices over time?

These objectives aim to deepen understanding of the DRS field, revealing how research trends align with or influence policy development and technological integration.

3.3 Data Collection Strategy

For this study, data was meticulously collected from Scopus [21–23], one of the leading scientific databases known for its comprehensive coverage of peer-reviewed literature. The data collection was strategically designed to encompass many publications about Deposit Refund Systems (DRS). The search was structured using the following query:

ALL ("deposit refund system" OR "reverse vending machine" OR "container deposit legislation" OR "bottle deposit" OR "deposit return scheme" OR "beverage container recycling"). This query was crafted to include a broad spectrum of terms relevant to DRS, ensuring the inclusion of diverse research focusing on various aspects of the system—from legislative approaches and specific technologies like reverse vending machines to broader recycling schemes. The choice of keywords aimed to capture all pertinent studies, thus enabling a comprehensive analysis of the thematic evolution, technological impacts, and policy influences within the DRS research landscape. This strategy ensured that the data collected was relevant and representative of the field, providing a robust foundation for the subsequent bibliometric analysis.

3.4 Bibliometric Analysis Using Biblioshiny

The bibliometric analysis conducted using Biblioshiny provided an in-depth exploration of the academic landscape surrounding Deposit Refund Systems (DRS). This tool, which is an extension of the R package 'bibliometrix', facilitates a comprehensive review of scholarly publications, allowing researchers to uncover patterns, trends, and networks within extensive datasets [24].

The thematic map parameters were set to analyse the top 250 documents with a minimum occurrence of 4 for each term. Single-word n-grams were included, without stemming, reflecting exact term usage. For clarity, node size was scaled down to 0.3, and only three labels per community were displayed. Synonym consolidation was applied to vending and plastic recycling terms, while the 'article' term was excluded. The Walk trap algorithm guided the cluster analysis. The thematic evolution parameters indicate a focus on documents from 2019, analysing the top 250 most relevant ones. A minimum frequency of 5 was required to include terms, with single-word n-grams considered. The visualisation scaled nodes to 30% of their standard size, highlighted the top three labels per cluster, and applied the Walktrap method for clustering without repelling overlaps or stemming modifications [25].

3.5 Data Interpretation Strategy

The data interpretation strategy for this study involved a systematic approach to analyse the bibliometric data collected from Scopus. Initially, the data was categorised based on thematic relevance using keyword frequency and clustering techniques. Subsequently, co-word analysis identified interrelationships between themes, while thematic maps and trend analyses illuminated the evolution and prominence of topics over time. Statistical tools were employed to assess the impact and centrality of themes [24]. This multifaceted approach ensured a comprehensive understanding of the Deposit Refund System (DRS) research landscape.

4 Results and Discussion

4.1 Preliminary Analysis of Publications

This bibliometric analysis of Deposit Refund Systems (DRS) in Table 1 spans an extensive period from 1938 to 2024, encompassing 910 documents across 545 sources, illustrating a rich, interdisciplinary field with an annual growth rate of 4.53%. The foundational and recent research averages 9.03 years in age per document, indicating a balanced academic interest over time. Each document garners an average of 25.42 citations, highlighting the significant impact and relevance of DRS studies within the scholarly community. Notably, the corpus contains 4,242 'Keywords Plus' and 2,245 author-generated keywords, reflecting the diverse and evolving nature of DRS research. This study also uncovers robust collaboration dynamics, with an average of 3.02 co-authors per document and 18.35% international co-authorships, emphasising the global and cooperative effort in advancing DRS discourse.

Additionally, the data reveals a variety of document types, with articles (592) leading, followed by conference papers (123), book chapters (75), and reviews (75). This diversity underscores the broad academic and practical engagement with DRS topics. Moreover, 2,302 authors, including 165 solo authors, showcase a vibrant and collaborative research community dedicated to exploring and expanding the DRS field.

Table 1. Main information of DRS Bibliometric Research

Description	Results
MAIN INFORMATION ABOUT DATA	
Timespan	1938:2024
Sources (Journals, Books, etc.)	545
Documents	910
Annual Growth Rate %	4.53
Document Average Age	9.03
Average citations per doc	25.42
References	52964
DOCUMENT CONTENTS	
Keywords Plus (ID)	4242
Author's Keywords (DE)	2245
AUTHORS	
Authors	2302
Authors of single-authored docs	165

(continued)

Table 1. (*continued*)

Description	Results
AUTHORS COLLABORATION	
Single-authored docs	200
Co-Authors per Doc	3.02
International co-authorships %	18.35
DOCUMENT TYPES	
article	592
book	45
book chapter	75
conference paper	123
review	75

4.2 Co-occurrence Analysis Results

The network data in Table A1 and Fig. 1 highlights "recycling" and "waste management" as central nodes, indicating their pivotal role in DRS discourse. High betweenness centrality for these terms suggests they function as gateways, connecting diverse research themes within the network, which is supported by their high PageRank values, indicating influential concepts. Clusters within the network show the thematic groupings of DRS research. The first cluster, dominated by terms like "environmental impact," "sustainable development," and "circular economy," suggests a strong emphasis on sustainability and environmental considerations in DRS studies. The presence of "China" and "economic" terms within the same cluster reflects an integration of geographic-specific economic analyses with environmental concerns. The second cluster, with "human," "environmental policy," and "public policy," indicates a focus on the human dimensions of DRS, policy-making, and its implications for society. This cluster's prominence signals an interdisciplinary approach to DRS research, intersecting social sciences with environmental studies. The third cluster, including "plastic recycling," "bottles," and "reverse vending machines," points to specific technologies and processes in DRS. This cluster's existence underlines the importance of operational aspects of DRS and their evolution over time. This co-word network [26, 27] underscores the complexity of DRS research and its dynamic nature, which is reflective of evolving societal, environmental, and technological contexts. The co-word analysis sheds light on the interconnectivity of key DRS concepts, revealing how central ideas like 'recycling' and 'waste management' are to the field's knowledge structure. It showcases the interdisciplinary nature and evolving priorities within DRS research.

Fig. 1. Co word network

4.3 Thematic Mapping and Thematic Evolution Findings

4.3.1 Thematic Map

In the evolving landscape of Deposit Refund Systems (DRS) research, our bibliometric thematic map in Fig. 2 provides an incisive visualisation of the field's structure and priorities. Anchored by foundational themes of 'recycling', 'sustainable development', and 'deposits', the map underscores their critical role as the backbone of DRS discourse, reflecting robust academic engagement and established knowledge bases. Their findings align with the central themes identified in our thematic map analysis [28, 29], which underscores 'recycling' and 'sustainable development' as pivotal research areas.

Adjacent to these are the 'Motor Themes'—'waste management', 'waste disposal', and 'human factors', which serve as the current drivers of the field's evolution. These pivotal themes indicate an active area where policy meets practice and scholarly efforts could have profound real-world implications. In the ongoing discourse regarding waste management strategies, Doe et al. (2024) emphasise the role of innovative recycling technologies in enhancing material recovery [6].

At the periphery lie 'Niche Themes' such as 'computer vision', revealing a sophisticated, although less central, fusion of DRS with emerging technologies. While currently peripheral, these specialised areas may hold the key to innovative approaches in DRS research. The 'Emerging or Declining Themes' quadrant showcases areas like 'reverse vending machines' and 'Internet of Things', signifying emerging trends or areas that may be phasing out of focus. Their potential for growth or decline offers strategic insight for future research trajectories. Together, these insights from the thematic map not only narrate the current state of DRS research but also offer a strategic foresight into its potential directions, underscoring the importance of adaptability and forward-thinking in environmental management research.

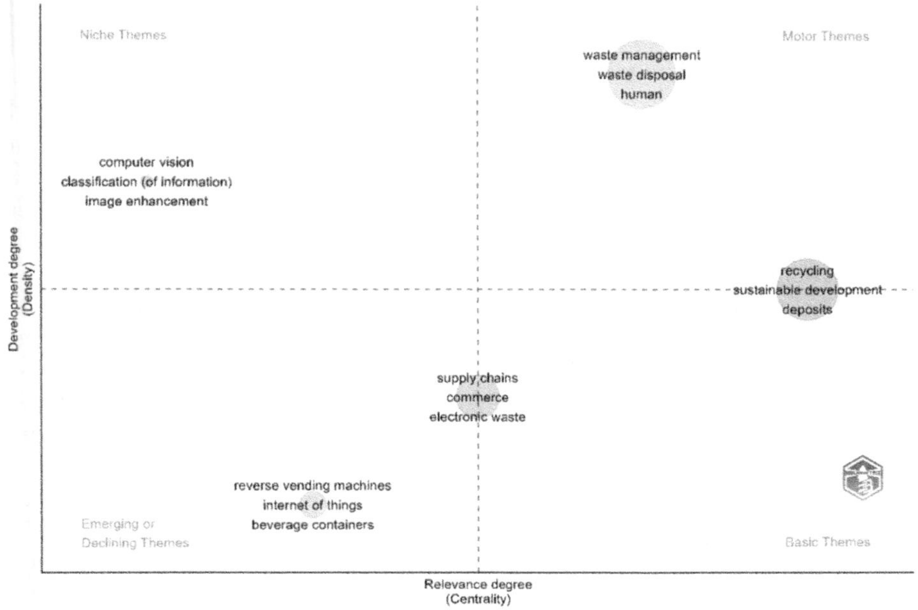

Fig. 2. Thematic Map Depicting the Landscape of Deposit Refund System Research: Core, Niche, Motor, and Emerging Themes

4.3.2 Thematic Evolution

The thematic evolution between 1938–2019 and 2020–2024 illustrates a pivotal shift in Deposit Refund System (DRS) research, mirroring broader environmental and technological trends. Initially, the research was captured by overarching themes like 'climate change' and 'environmental management', highlighting a period where DRS was primarily contextualised within global and ecological narratives.

Entering the 2020–2024 timeline, there is a pronounced transition towards 'plastic recycling' and 'electronic waste', marking a response to urgent environmental concerns over plastic pollution and the management of technological refuse [30–32]. The thematic revolution of 2020–2024 mirrors a global push towards more sustainable materials management and the circular economy [10, 15, 17, 33].

Significantly, the persistence of 'recycling' across both eras underscores its fundamental role within DRS studies. However, its evolution reflects a refined focus that now includes the intricacies of 'human' interaction and 'deposits' systems. The latter suggests increased attention to the economic mechanisms of DRS, such as incentivisation [34, 35] and financial frameworks for waste management [30, 36].

This visualisation captures the chronological progression of themes within DRS scholarship, from broad environmental concerns to targeted strategies addressing specific waste streams. It integrates socio-economic dimensions, revealing the adaptability and depth of DRS research in addressing the multifaceted challenges of waste management in modern societies.

4.4 Trend Topic Analysis and TreeMap

4.4.1 Trend Topic Analysis

The trend topics graphic in Fig. 3 reveals a chronological narrative of research within the Deposit Refund System (DRS) field, highlighting how the academic focus has shifted and expanded in response to global developments. From 1988 to the early 2000s, terms like 'recycling', 'solid waste', and 'environmental impact' were consistently present, signalling the foundational concerns related to waste management and its environmental repercussions in DRS research.

As the timeline progresses towards the 2010s, topics are subtly diversified. Terms like 'economic instruments' and 'cost-benefit analysis' surface more frequently, suggesting a paradigm shift. In this era, the efficiency of recycling processes and the economics of sustainability are examined through a more rigorous, analytical lens, often intersecting with policy development, underscored by the increasing prominence of 'environmental policy' as a key term.

The late 2010s and early 2020s demonstrate an intensified focus on specific waste materials, with 'plastic waste' and 'electronic waste' standing out [12, 30–32, 37, 38]. This era points towards a response to the plastic pollution crisis and the growing concern over the disposal of electronic goods, both of which present significant environmental challenges.

Interestingly, the term 'human' has gained prominence in recent years, suggesting a research pivot towards the human element in DRS—from consumer behaviour to public engagement—emphasising the role of societal attitudes and behaviours in successful DRS implementation [4]. An understanding emerged that the success of any DRS heavily relies on human behaviour. Research thus shifted towards studying how consumer behaviour affects recycling rates and how people respond to various incentives and policy measures.

Overall, the trend topics illuminate a route from broad environmental themes towards a multifaceted approach that links the practicalities of waste management with economic considerations, policy implications, and the crucial role of human factors.

Furthermore, The 'Trend Topics' figure showcases the DRS research expansion reflecting EPR principles with a growing emphasis on 'take-back mandates' and 'deposit-refund', indicating a shift towards integrating environmental considerations within producer responsibilities and consumer recycling practices, as discussed by Tsai, Wu, & Hwang (2013) [39].

Initially, the research predominantly centered around the environmental impacts of waste management—specifically recycling, reducing landfill usage, and managing solid waste. Over time, the focus expanded to include economic aspects such as the cost-effectiveness of DRS policies, the economic incentives for consumers and businesses to participate in recycling programs, and the financial impacts of implementing such systems. This evolution echoes the global discourse on sustainability as the DRS research community seeks comprehensive solutions to the complex challenge of resource recovery and waste reduction. As the field matured, the importance of policy-making in shaping effective waste management systems became obvious. Studies likely began comparing the efficacy of various policy models from different countries or regions, examining how local contexts influence the success of DRS initiatives.

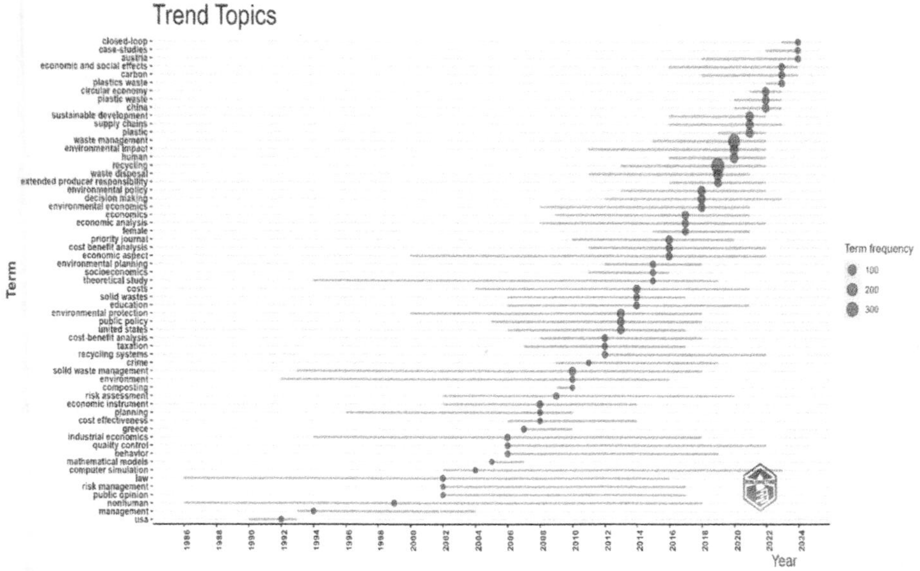

Fig. 3. Chronological Frequency of Key Terms in Deposit Refund System Research (1938–2024): A Trend Topic Analysis

4.4.2 Treemap

The Treemap provides in Fig. 4 a compelling visual breakdown of research focus areas within the Deposit Refund System (DRS) landscape, represented by the frequency and proportion of associated research topics. Dominating the Treemap is 'recycling', encompassing 15% of the research, underscoring its central role in DRS studies. Subsequently, 'waste management' comprises 10% of the research, underscoring the significance of effective management practices in the recycling ecosystem. Smaller yet notable segments such as [40–42], 'sustainable development' [9, 17], and 'environmental impact' reflect the multidimensional nature of DRS research, integrating sustainability and environmental stewardship concerns. The presence of 'human', 'public policy', and 'economic instruments' reveals an acknowledgement of DRS's socio-economic drivers and policy implications. The inclusion of 'plastic waste' [43, 44], 'electronic waste' [30–32], and '[33, 45, 46]' points towards a targeted approach to specific waste streams. At the same time, mentioning geographic regions like 'China', 'European Union', and 'United States' indicates a global research effort with localised studies.

Emerging concepts such as 'game theory' and 'supply chains' suggest an analytical and systemic approach to optimising DRS. Xin Li et al. (2020) demonstrate how 'game theory' can optimise DRS policy, increasing E.V. battery recycling rates, but suggest further subsidy adjustments for greater impact [47]. Meanwhile, 'circular economy' and 'sustainability' reflect the field's alignment with broader global goals for sustainable development. This Treemap depicts the multifaceted and evolving research areas within Deposit Refund Systems (DRS), highlighting how classical themes integrate cutting-edge technologies, evolving policy structures, and objectives for sustainable development.

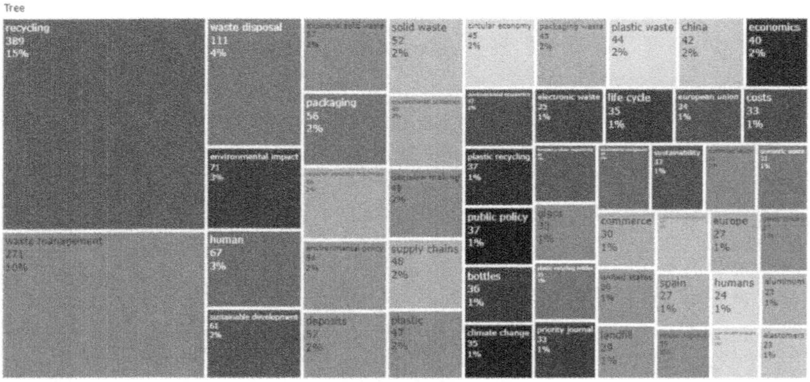

Fig. 4. Treemap Visualization of Dominant Research Themes in Deposit Refund System Studies (1938–2024)

4.5 Discussion on Key Findings

The co-word network exposed the interconnection of core DRS themes, with 'recycling' and 'waste management' emerging as central hubs, indicating their critical roles in shaping the DRS discourse. The interlinkage between 'environmental impact', 'sustainable development', and 'policy-making' highlighted an interdisciplinary approach, connecting ecological concerns with governance and policy implications.

Thematic maps further nuanced this understanding by identifying 'recycling', 'sustainable development', and 'deposits' as foundational research pillars while positioning 'waste management' as a motor theme, signifying its pivotal influence on the field's direction. Emerging themes like 'reverse vending machines' suggested new areas of technological innovation. In contrast, niche themes such as 'computer vision' indicated a specialised but significant corner of DRS research focusing on technology's role in recycling processes.

Trend topic analysis revealed shifts over time, with early research concentrated on broad environmental issues and later transitioning towards specific challenges like 'plastic waste' and 'electronic waste', signalling a response to pressing environmental concerns and reflecting an adaptive research community. The thematic evolution depicted a chronological narrative of the research field, with traditional themes evolving to encompass new technologies, policy frameworks, and sustainability goals. From general environmental concerns, the focus has narrowed to material-specific challenges and socio-economic considerations, echoing the necessity for sustainable development.

Our analysis aligns with recent models developed by Gong et al. (2021), who explored the impact of DRS in an electronic closed-loop supply chain [8]. Their study quantifies how DRS can influence key supply chain decisions, such as recovery rates, remanufacturing costs, and market demand. The research by Gong et al. demonstrates that introducing a DRS can optimise the closed-loop supply chain's performance by balancing economic incentives with environmental outcomes [48]. Their findings corroborate our bibliometric insights, suggesting an increasing scholarly focus on integrating economic instruments into sustainability practices [9, 17, 49, 50].

Treemaps provided a visual quantification of research emphasis [51], underscoring 'recycling' and 'waste management' as the most prolific areas of inquiry [4, 9, 51]. Smaller segments pointed to an increasing diversification of topics, including economic and social dimensions, thus indicating a holistic approach to DRS research. As evidenced in the Treemap Figure ... the predominance of 'recycling' in DRS research reflects environmental commitment and economic prudence, supporting Atstāja et al. (2019), who find DRS to reach financial payback within a decade [52].

4.6 Implications for Policy and Practice

The insights from bibliometric analyses, encompassing co-word networks, thematic maps, trend topics, Treemap, and thematic evolution, hold several implications for policy and practice in Deposit Refund Systems (DRS). The policy implications are various. First, the analysis suggests a need for robust infrastructure investment to support comprehensive recycling systems. This goes beyond household collection [53] to include processing facilities capable of handling diverse materials, reflecting the centrality of 'recycling' within DRS research. Second, the recurrent theme of 'economic instruments' implies that policies should leverage financial mechanisms to incentivise producers and consumers. For instance, deposit schemes might be modernised to increase appeal and efficacy, while producer responsibility programs could encourage manufacturers to produce more recyclable and less environmentally impactful products. The research emphasises specific streams like 'plastic waste' and 'electronic waste' points for targeted policies that address the challenges associated with these materials, including product design, collection, and processing.

The emergence of the human dimension in DRS studies also translates into a policy requirement for community engagement and educational initiatives promoting sustainable behaviours and practices. It is about understanding consumer behaviour and creating a participatory culture in recycling efforts [4].

Practically, the findings suggest that waste management strategies should be increasingly data-driven and technologically advanced, incorporating smart systems for resource management and recycling processes. Potential enhancements could involve using A.I. to sort recyclables or employing blockchain to improve transparency in the supply chain.

Lastly, the thematic evolution underlines the field's shift toward integrating sustainability within all production, consumption, and waste management levels. For practitioners, this means adopting holistic, circular approaches that look beyond waste disposal to material recovery and reintegration into the production cycle.

The bibliometric analysis directs policy and practice toward a harmonised, technology-informed approach that matches environmental goals with economic viability and social acceptance. This approach is crucial in ensuring that DRS initiatives are theoretically sound, practically successful, and sustainable in the long term.

5 Conclusions

5.1 Summary of Key Findings

The bibliometric analysis of Deposit Refund Systems (DRS) research offers key insights: 'Recycling' remains the key player, with growing nuances around 'plastic' and 'electronic waste', reflecting environmental and technological challenges. Economic factors like 'cost-benefit analysis' have risen, emphasising the need for financially viable sustainability practices. 'Human' elements indicate a shift towards understanding consumer behaviour and societal impacts on recycling efficacy. 'Supply chains' and 'closed-loop systems' suggest a trend towards integrating recycling within broader economic processes. Technological advances, inferred from terms like 'computer vision', suggest an increasing role for automation and smart systems in optimising DRS processes. The thematic evolution displays a research shift from broad environmental topics to specific, actionable aspects within DRS. These findings highlight an interdisciplinary approach to DRS, integrating environmental sustainability with economic and technological considerations against social dynamics shaping policy and practice in waste management.

5.2 Limitations of the Study

This study's limitations, particularly in its use of thematic maps, thematic evolution, co-word networks, Treemaps, and topic trend analysis, stem primarily from intrinsic constraints associated with bibliometric methods [26, 27, 51, 54, 55]. These limitations include dependency on the availability and accuracy of keywords in the published literature, which can impact the detection and interpretation of research trends and thematic relationships.

Thematic Maps and Thematic Evolution analyses may not fully capture shifts in research focus due to changes in terminology over time or across different research communities [28, 29, 56, 57]. The reliance on keyword frequency might overlook nuanced or emerging topics that are pivotal but not yet prevalent in the literature.

Co-word Network analysis is limited by its dependence on the consistency and accuracy of keyword usage. Variations and synonyms are not automatically consolidated, which can lead to fragmented thematic representations or exaggerated importance of less central themes. Co-word analysis might distort thematic structures by indexing synonyms or related terms differently, fragmenting themes [58].

While Treemap effectively visualises data proportionality [51], they are contingent on the comprehensive indexing of articles and do not reflect the qualitative impact or the interdisciplinary breadth of the research topics depicted [51]. In Topic Trend Analysis, emerging trends may be underrepresented due to the lag in accumulating substantial research outputs, whereas established topics might appear overly dominant due to their extensive historical literature [24].

These limitations underscore the need for careful interpretation of bibliometric analyses. They highlight the importance of supplementing these findings with additional qualitative assessments and continuous updates to accurately capture the field's evolving dynamics.

5.3 Recommendations for Future Research

To strengthen the scope and impact of future research on Deposit Refund Systems (DRS), a strategic approach should be adopted based on insights gleaned from this study's findings and inherent limitations. The following comprehensive set of recommendations is essential to address these.

Future studies should incorporate qualitative research methods to capture the complex and nuanced aspects of DRS that bibliometric analyses may overlook. Techniques such as in-depth interviews, focus groups, and case studies can provide richer, contextual insights into DRS implementations' practical challenges and successes [59–61].

Moreover, to mitigate potential biases stemming from the predominance of English-language and limited database sources, future research should include a wider array of international databases and consider studies published in multiple languages. This broader approach will enhance the global comprehensiveness of the research, reflecting a more diverse range of experiences and practices. To keep pace with the evolving field, researchers should continuously update the keywords and search terms used in their bibliometric analyses. Keyword updating involves adapting to new terminology and developing a set of related terms that reflect the interdisciplinary nature of DRS research. With the rise of themes like technological innovation in DRS and sustainability impacts, future studies should focus on these areas. Research could explore the integration of advanced technologies in DRS processes and assess the long-term sustainability outcomes of these systems. There is a need for longitudinal research that tracks the effectiveness and adaptability of DRS policies over time. Such studies would provide valuable insights into the dynamic interactions between policy implementations, technological advancements, and environmental impacts [62, 63]. By embracing these recommendations, future research can significantly enhance our understanding of DRS, contributing to more effective and sustainable waste management practices globally.

Disclosure of Interests. The authors have no competing interests to declare that are relevant to the content of this article.

Appendices

Table A1. Key Thematic Nodes and Metrics in Deposit Refund System (DRS) Research: A Bibliometric Network Analysis (1938–2024)

Node	Cluster	Betweenness	Closeness	PageRank
recycling	1	124,300339	0,02040816	0,08468155
waste management	1	59,4498039	0,02040816	0,06687697
article	1	40,0448645	0,02040816	0,05826678
environmental impact	1	8,75467792	0,01960784	0,02629009
sustainable development	1	4,3019145	0,01818182	0,01885383
municipal solid waste	1	6,00196069	0,01886792	0,02396425
packaging	1	7,45842293	0,01818182	0,02694923
deposits	1	8,93673489	0,01923077	0,02355397
supply chains	1	1,77678538	0,01449275	0,01412949
plastic	1	3,06909451	0,01639344	0,01966709
circular economy	1	2,63714488	0,01639344	0,01821692
packaging waste	1	1,86896295	0,01694915	0,01761366
plastic waste	1	3,82424956	0,01724138	0,02084595
China	1	0,93248163	0,01449275	0,01222478
economics	1	3,37376144	0,01818182	0,0197284
environmental economics	1	1,28964212	0,01587302	0,01363098
climate change	1	0,47361572	0,01388889	0,00839687
electronic waste	1	0,66989322	0,01282051	0,01144658
life cycle	1	2,07935696	0,01515152	0,01730523
costs	1	1,45395052	0,01515152	0,01467392
extended producer responsibility	1	1,24440043	0,01538462	0,01474237
glass	1	1,26983593	0,015625	0,01383208
environmental management	1	1,28512666	0,015625	0,0144358
controlled study	1	4,31202613	0,01851852	0,02197523
commerce	1	1,00696454	0,01449275	0,01116827
solid waste management	1	1,46832557	0,015625	0,01663124
game theory	1	0,11724084	0,01204819	0,00709171
aluminium	1	0,27505322	0,01369863	0,00911526

(continued)

Table A1. (*continued*)

Node	Cluster	Betweenness	Closeness	PageRank
waste disposal	2	23,2648903	0,02040816	0,04400445
human	2	16,8145817	0,02	0,03955614
environmental policy	2	4,03533354	0,01785714	0,02082755
solid waste	2	2,96010766	0,01754386	0,02221149
environmental protection	2	2,27118587	0,01612903	0,01711839
decision making	2	1,79232923	0,01538462	0,01539093
public policy	2	0,28049443	0,01369863	0,01182152
European union	2	0,39400632	0,01388889	0,0101946
priority journal	2	3,74004168	0,01754386	0,02288885
sustainability	2	0,45108886	0,01408451	0,0120496
domestic waste	2	1,11989815	0,01587302	0,01556019
united states	2	0,33000139	0,01428571	0,01223759
landfill	2	0,95064343	0,01612903	0,01488362
Europe	2	0,09481346	0,01333333	0,0098413
Spain	2	0,09852056	0,01265823	0,00941385
refuse disposal	2	2,20297162	0,01612903	0,01957726
humans	2	0,36459234	0,01408451	0,01420459
cost-benefit analysis	2	0,35821656	0,01470588	0,01030661
plastic recycling	3	1,68333527	0,01470588	0,01509488
bottles	3	1,22607466	0,01428571	0,01302761
reverse vending machines	3	0,46640611	0,01315789	0,00931828
plastic bottles	3	1,42383638	0,01470588	0,01416222

References

1. Kulshreshtha, P., Sarangi, S.: "No return, no refund": an analysis of deposit-refund systems. J. Econ. Behav. Organ. **46**, 379–394 (2001). https://doi.org/10.1016/S0167-2681(01)00161-5
2. Walls, M.: Deposit-refund systems in practice and theory. SSRN Electron. J. (2011). https://doi.org/10.2139/ssrn.1980142
3. Berck, P., Sears, M., Taylor, R.L.C., Trachtman, C., Villas-Boas, S.B.: Reduce, reuse, redeem: deposit-refund recycling programs in the presence of alternatives. Ecol. Econ. **217**, 108080 (2024). https://doi.org/10.1016/j.ecolecon.2023.108080
4. Konstantoglou, A., Fotiadis, T., Folinas, D., Falaras, A., Rotsios, K.: Accessing consumer perceptions of the effectiveness of the deposit refund system. Sustainability **15**, 9429 (2023). https://doi.org/10.3390/su15129429
5. Kursah, M.B., Baabereyir, A.: Willingness to pay for sachet water plastic waste management through deposit-refund system. Int. J. Environ. Waste Manag. **23**, 141–155 (2019). https://doi.org/10.1504/IJEWM.2019.097612

6. Georgakellos, D.A.: The use of the deposit-refund framework in port reception facilities charging systems. Mar. Pollut. Bull. **54**, 508–520 (2007). https://doi.org/10.1016/j.marpolbul.2007.02.005
7. Zhou, G., et al.: A systematic review of the deposit-refund system for beverage packaging: operating mode, key parameter and development trend. J. Clean. Prod. **251**, 119660 (2020). https://doi.org/10.1016/j.jclepro.2019.119660
8. Gong, Y., Chen, M., Wang, Z., Zhan, J.: With or without deposit-refund system for a network platform-led electronic closed-loop supply chain. J. Clean. Prod. **281**, 125356 (2021). https://doi.org/10.1016/j.jclepro.2020.125356
9. Schneider, D.R., Tomić, T., Raal, R.: Economic viability of the deposit refund system for beverage packaging waste – identification of economic drivers and system modelling. J. Sustain. Dev. Energy Water Environ. Syst. **9**, 1–33 (2021). https://doi.org/10.13044/j.sdewes.d9.0386
10. Mayanti, B., Helo, P.: Circular economy through waste reverse logistics under extended producer responsibility in Finland. Waste Manag. Res.: J. Sustain. Circ. Econ. **42**, 59–73 (2024). https://doi.org/10.1177/0734242X231168801
11. Schmidt, S., Laner, D.: The environmental performance of plastic packaging waste management in germany: current and future key factors. J. Ind. Ecol. **27**, 1447–1460 (2023). https://doi.org/10.1111/jiec.13411
12. Lu, Z., Hasselström, L., Finnveden, G., Johansson, N.: Cost-benefit analysis of two possible deposit-refund systems for reuse and recycling of plastic packaging in Sweden. Clean. Waste Syst. **3**, 100048 (2022). https://doi.org/10.1016/j.clwas.2022.100048
13. Hao, H., Xu, W., Wei, F., Wu, C., Xu, Z.: Reward–penalty vs. deposit–refund: government incentive mechanisms for E.V. battery recycling. Energies (Basel) **15** (2022). https://doi.org/10.3390/en15196885
14. Du Rietz, S.: Making up circular consumers: young adults' personal accounting and counter earmarking within a circular deposit-refund scheme. Account. Forum **47**, 525–552 (2022). https://doi.org/10.1080/01559982.2022.2149045
15. Sakji, I., Ndhaief, N., Rezg, N.: From linear to circular economy: the potential of glass deposits in smart city supply chains. In: Proceedings of the ICNSC 2023 - 20th IEEE International Conference on Networking, Sensing and Control (2023)
16. Kokoulin, A.N., Kokoulin, R.A.: The development of a system for objects recognition in reverse vending machine using machine learning technologies. In: Proceedings of the 2021 International Conference on Data Analytics for Business and Industry, ICDABI 2021, pp. 578–582 (2021)
17. Maguire, S., Robson, I.: Sustainable Development Through Global Circular Economy Practices (2023). ISBN 9781837535903
18. Görgün, E., et al.: Deposit refund system for beverage containers as a best practice example for recycling maximization. Environ. Res. Technol. **4**, 199–205 (2021). https://doi.org/10.35208/ert.862611
19. Özdemir-Akyildirim, Ö.: Deposit-refund system vs. compliance scheme membership: how to comply with producer responsibility regulations? Int. J. Prod. Econ. **162**, 25–44 (2015). https://doi.org/10.1016/j.ijpe.2014.12.027
20. Mrozek, J.R.: Revenue neutral deposit/refund systems. Environ. Resour. Econ. (Dordr.) **17**, 183–193 (2000). https://doi.org/10.1023/A:1008338622801
21. Gray, A.: LibGuides: Scopus: Techniques for Searching
22. Liu, W.: Accuracy of funding information in scopus: a comparative case study. Scientometrics **124**, 803–811 (2020). https://doi.org/10.1007/s11192-020-03458-w
23. Scopus Support Center How Can I Best Use the Advanced Search? - Scopus: Access and Use Support Center. https://service.elsevier.com/app/answers/detail/a_id/11365/supporthub/scopus/~/how-can-i-best-use-the-advanced-search%3F/. Accessed 10 May 2023

24. Aria, M., Cuccurullo, C.: Bibliometrix: an R-tool for comprehensive science mapping analysis. J. Informetr. **11**, 959–975 (2017). https://doi.org/10.1016/j.joi.2017.08.007
25. Hieu, D.D., Ha Duong, P.T.: Detecting communities in large networks using the extended Walktrap algorithm. In: Proceedings of the 2022 RIVF International Conference on Computing and Communication Technologies (RIVF). IEEE, pp. 100–105 (2022)
26. Ding, Y., Chowdhury, G.G., Foo, S.: Bibliometric cartography of information retrieval research by using co-word analysis. Inf. Process. Manag. **37**, 817–842 (2001). https://doi.org/10.1016/S0306-4573(00)00051-0
27. Callon, M., Courtial, J.P., Laville, F.: Co-word analysis as a tool for describing the network of interactions between basic and technological research: the case of polymer chemistry. Scientometrics **22**, 155–205 (1991).https://doi.org/10.1007/BF02019280
28. Clarke, V., Braun, V.: Thematic Analysis. J. Posit. Psychol. **12**, 297–298 (2017). https://doi.org/10.1080/17439760.2016.1262613
29. Tennekes, M.: Thematic maps in R. J. Stat. Softw. **84** (2018). https://doi.org/10.18637/jss.v084.i06
30. Kaur, H., Lin, J.: Economic Instruments for Electronic Waste Management in India (2023). ISBN 9781000873115
31. Ma, H., Wang, X., Chang, P., Jiang, L.: Establishing the recycled supply chain network of waste electrical and electronic equipment. In Proceedings of the Proceedings - International Conference on Management and Service Science, MASS 2009 (2009)
32. Botelho, A., Ferreira Dias, M., Ferreira, C., Pinto, L.M.C.: The market of electrical and electronic equipment waste in Portugal: analysis of take-back consumers' decisions. Waste Manag. Res. **34**, 1074–1080 (2016). https://doi.org/10.1177/0734242X16658546
33. Niero, M., Hauschild, M.Z.: Closing the loop for packaging: finding a framework to operationalize circular economy strategies. Proc. Procedia CIRP **61**, 685–690 (2017)
34. Blose, J.E., Mack, R.W., Pitts, R.E., Xie, H.Y.: Exploring young U.S. and chinese consumers' motivations to recycle. J. Int. Consum. Mark. **32**, 33–46 (2020). https://doi.org/10.1080/08961530.2019.1618776
35. Moqbel, S., El-tah, Z., Haddad, A.: Anti-littering in developing countries: motivating the people of Jordan. Waste Manag. Res. **38**, 726–733 (2020). https://doi.org/10.1177/0734242X19900654
36. Ma, J., Hipel, K.W.: Exploring social dimensions of municipal solid waste management around the globe – a systematic literature review. Waste Manag. **56**, 3–12 (2016). https://doi.org/10.1016/j.wasman.2016.06.041
37. Sterner, T., Coria, J.: Policy Instruments for Environmental and Natural Resource Management, 2nd edn. (2013). ISBN 9781315780894
38. Orset, C., Barret, N., Lemaire, A.: How consumers of plastic water bottles are responding to environmental policies? Waste Manag. **61**, 13–27 (2017). https://doi.org/10.1016/j.wasman.2016.12.034
39. Tsai, T.-H., WU, S.-J., Hwang, H.: Waste recycling policies under extended producer responsibility: take-back mandate versus deposit-refund. Glob. J. Econ. **02**, 1350005 (2013). https://doi.org/10.1142/S2251361213500055
40. Zhang, S., Gao, J., Wang, H.: Research on the recycling and disposal of Chinese pesticide packaging waste based on evolutionary game theory. J. Environ. Sci. Health B. **58**, 565–576 (2023). https://doi.org/10.1080/03601234.2023.2241318
41. Hamilton, S.F., Sproul, T.W., Sunding, D., Zilberman, D.: Environmental policy with collective waste disposal. J. Environ. Econ. Manag. **66**, 337–346 (2013). https://doi.org/10.1016/j.jeem.2013.04.003
42. Ino, H.: Optimal environmental policy for waste disposal and recycling when firms are not compliant. J. Environ. Econ. Manag. **62**, 290–308 (2011). https://doi.org/10.1016/j.jeem.2011.03.007

43. Van Zeben, J., Ross, V.: Plastics: From Resources to Waste and Back Again (2022). ISBN 9781000515145
44. Blasenbauer, D., Lipp, A.-M., Fellner, J., Tischberger-Aldrian, A., Stipanović, H., Lederer, J.: Recovery of plastic packaging from mixed municipal solid waste. a case study from Austria. Waste Manag. 180, 9–22 (2024). https://doi.org/10.1016/j.wasman.2024.02.040
45. Barber, N.: "Green" wine packaging: targeting environmental consumers. Int. J. Wine Bus. Res. **22**, 423–444 (2010). https://doi.org/10.1108/17511061011092447
46. Agnusdei, G.P., Gnoni, M.G., Sgarbossa, F.: Are deposit-refund systems effective in managing glass packaging? state of the art and future directions in Europe. Sci. Total Environ. **851** (2022). https://doi.org/10.1016/j.scitotenv.2022.158256
47. Li, X., Mu, D., Du, J., Cao, J., Zhao, F.: Game-based system dynamics simulation of deposit-refund scheme for electric vehicle battery recycling in China. Resour. Conserv. Recycl. **157**, 104788 (2020). https://doi.org/10.1016/j.resconrec.2020.104788
48. Wang, J., Li, W., Nozomu, M., Adachi, T.: Closed-loop supply chain under different channel leaderships: considering different deposit-refund systems practically applied in China. J. Mater. Cycles Waste Manag. **23**, 1765–1776 (2021). https://doi.org/10.1007/s10163-021-01234-3
49. Sin, L.T., Tueen, B.S.: Plastics and Sustainability: Practical Approaches (2022). ISBN 9780128244890
50. Oldenziel, R., Trischler, H.: Cycling and Recycling: Histories of Sustainable Practices (2015). ISBN 9781782389712
51. Limberger, D., Scheibel, W., van Dieken, J., Döllner, J.: Procedural texture patterns for encoding changes in color in 2.5D treemap visualizations. J. Vis. (Tokyo), **26**, 317–333 (2023). https://doi.org/10.1007/s12650-022-00874-3
52. Atstāja, D., Lukševica, L., Cudečka-Puriņa, N., Vesere, R., Susniene, R.: Analysis and economic evaluation of deposit refund system. Soc. Integr. Educ. Proc. Int. Sci. Conf. 6, 17 (2019). https://doi.org/10.17770/sie2019vol6.3823
53. Thalía, O.B., Gustavo, G.: A perspective of household waste collection methods. In: Iglesias, A., Shin, J., Patel, B., Joshi, A. (eds.) ISBM 2023. LNNS, vol. 834, pp. 425–433. Springer, Singapore (2024). https://doi.org/10.1007/978-981-99-8349-0_33
54. Griffiths, T.L., Steyvers, M.: Finding scientific topics. Proc. Natl. Acad. Sci. **101**, 5228–5235 (2004). https://doi.org/10.1073/pnas.0307752101
55. Blechschmidt, J.: Trend study: in-depth analysis of a trend. In: Blechschmidt, J. (ed.) Trend Management. Business Guides on the Go, pp. 75–84. Springer, Heidelberg (2022). https://doi.org/10.1007/978-3-662-64703-5_7
56. Gentilli, J.: The use of thematic maps to aid research. Cartography **26**, 41–56 (1997). https://doi.org/10.1080/00690805.1997.9714045
57. Squires, V.: Thematic analysis. In: Okoko, J.M., Tunison, S., Walker, K.D. (eds.) Varieties of Qualitative Research Methods. Springer Texts in Education, pp. 463–468. Springer, Cham (2023). https://doi.org/10.1007/978-3-031-04394-9_72
58. Kumar, V., Srivastava, A.: Mapping the evolution of research themes in business ethics: a co-word network analysis. VINE J. Inf. Knowl. Manag. Syst. **53**, 491–522 (2023). https://doi.org/10.1108/VJIKMS-10-2020-0199
59. Thelwall, M., Nevill, T.: Is research with qualitative data more prevalent and impactful now? Interviews, case studies, focus groups and ethnographies. SSRN Electron. J. (2021).https://doi.org/10.2139/ssrn.3833403
60. Case study approach to conducting and designing qualitative investigation for business researchers. Am. J. Arts Educ. Adm. Res. **1** (2022). https://doi.org/10.58314/097878
61. Golam Azam, M.: In-depth case interview. In: Islam, M.R., Khan, N.A., Baikady, R. (eds.) Principles of Social Research Methodology. Springer, Singapore (2022). https://doi.org/10.1007/978-981-19-5441-2_24

62. Ruspini, E.: Longitudinal research: a world to explore. In: The Cambridge Handbook of Research Methods and Statistics for the Social and Behavioral Sciences, pp. 357–377. Cambridge University Press (2023)
63. Keeves, J.P.: Longitudinal research methods. In: Economics of Education, pp. 369–382. Elsevier (1987)

AI, Robotics and Simulation Approaches in Supply Chain

Robotic Depalletizing via Reinforcement Learning of a Pushing Policy

Argyris Dimou[1,2(✉)], Marios Kiatos[3], and Sotiris Malassiotis[1]

[1] Information Technologies Institute (ITI) Center of Research and Technology Hellas (CERTH), 57001 Thessaloniki, Greece
{ardimou,malasiot}@iti.gr
[2] Department of Physics, University of Thessaloniki, 54124 Thessaloniki, Greece
[3] Progressive Robotics, 54645 Thessaloniki, Greece
mk@progressiverobotics.ai

Abstract. Depalletizing, the process of unloading objects from pallets, is a critical task in warehouse automation. Robotic systems face challenges due to the diverse shapes and sizes of objects, often leading to failed grasps in cluttered environments. Pushing actions offer a promising solution to facilitate object singulation. In this work, we employ reinforcement learning (RL) for obtaining optimal pushing policies in depalletizing. We formulate the singulation task as goal reaching, where the target object is moved towards a goal area free from obstacles. Our approach, Goal-FCN (Goal-Driven Fully Convolutional Network), combines feature extraction with a fully convolutional neural network to predict effective pushing actions based on RGB-D images and scene segmentation. Experiments demonstrate the efficacy of our RL-based approach in achieving high success rates in challenging depalletization scenarios.

Keywords: Robotics · Machine learning · Reinforcement learning

1 Introduction

In recent years, depalletizing has emerged as a critical challenge in robotic manipulation, spanning multiple research domains. Past research endeavors have primarily focused on detecting objects within the scene, segmenting them [9], and identifying and planning the most efficient actions to aid in the unloading process [11]. Suction grasping is a widely method used by various robotic systems that enhance speed and accuracy of the process. Researchers have introduced innovative depalletizing solutions, including compact robots by Nakamoto et al. [16] leveraging camera and depth images for speed, and Tanaka et al.'s [22] suction-type end effector for simultaneous extraction and improved load resistance. Krug et al. [14] proposed a novel grasp representation scheme, while Fontanelli et al. [7] utilized a flexible gripper for versatile handling of varied box shapes.

While suction grasping is a common approach in controlled settings, it is often unsuitable for depalletizing tasks in cluttered scenarios. Suction grasping

I. Kostavelis et al. (Eds.): ICSC 2024, CCIS 2110, pp. 105–117, 2025.
https://doi.org/10.1007/978-3-031-69344-1_8

relies on creating a vacuum seal between the gripper and the object's surface, which works well for flat and smooth objects. However, in cluttered environments such as supermarket pallets, objects vary greatly in shape, size, and surface texture, making it difficult for suction-based systems to reliably grasp them. Additionally, suction grippers struggle with porous or irregular surfaces, common characteristics of many items found in depalletizing tasks. Consequently, suction grasping is not a viable option for these scenarios, further emphasizing the need for alternative manipulation strategies. To overcome these difficulties we utilize prehensile grasping. However, in order to be efficient, empty space is needed. To create space, we employ non-prehensile actions [21] like pushing. These actions, offer avenues for creating essential empty spaces and repositioning objects without directly grasping them. By incorporating non-prehensile actions alongside prehensile ones [4,5,13], robotic systems can adeptly negotiate cluttered scenarios, thereby enhancing their overall manipulative capabilitie. A body of research emerged for total or partial singulation of objects using pushing actions, in order to create space around the target object required by the robotic fingers for grasping it. Total singulation [19] refers to the creation of free space around the object, while partial singulation refers to the creation of free space along some object sides.

In this paper, we propose a reinforcement learning approach to tackle the difficulties in depalletizing a pallet including diverse objects. In summary, we:

- We employ a non-prehensile approach to enhance the efficiency of depalletizing, generating space within cluttered environments, similar to a mixed supermarket's pallet.
- Propose a reinforcement learning (RL) framework, specifically the Goal-FCN (Goal-Driven Fully Convolutional Network), for selecting optimal pushing actions.
- Showcase the model's adaptability and generalization capabilities through successful evaluations in two distinct cluttered environments, demonstrating high success rates.

2 Related Work

Recently, a lot of researchers employed learning algorithms for object manipulation. Boularias *et al.* [2] explored the use of reinforcement learning to obtain policies, choosing among grasp and push primitives. They learnt to singulate two specific objects given a depth image of the scene but the agent required retraining for a new set of objects. Zeng *et al.* [25] used Q-learning to train end-to-end two fully convolutional networks in order to learn synergies between pushing and grasping, leading to higher grasp success rates. Yang *et al.* [23] adapted [25] to grasp a target object from clutter by partially singulating it via pushing actions. Kurenkov *et al.* [15] and Novkovic *et al.* [17] used deep reinforcement learning to learn push actions in order to unveil a fully occluded target object. In contrast to singulation, achieving full visibility of the target does not always create free space between the target and surrounding obstacles, which is necessary for prehensile grasping. On the contrary to model-free reinforcement learning approaches, Huang *et al.* [10] proposed a model-based solution for target object retrieval. Specifically, they employed visual foresight trees to intelligently rearrange the surrounding clutter by pushing actions so that the target object can be grasped easily. All the above approaches focus on the partial singulation of objects in order to grasp them.

On the other hand, many works develop methods that totally singulate the objects. Eitel *et al.* [6] trained a convolutional neural network on segmented images in order to singulate every object in the scene. However, they evaluated a large number of potential pushes to find the optimal action. Kiatos *et al.* [12] trained a deep Q-network to select push actions in order to singulate a target object from its surrounding clutter with the minimum number of pushes, using depth features to approximate the topography of the scene. Sarantopoulos and Kiatos [18] extended the work of [12] by modelling the Q-function with two different networks, one for each primitive action, leading to higher success rates and faster network convergence. Finally, Sarantopoulos *et al.* [19] proposed a modular reinforcement learning approach which uses continuous actions to totally singulate the target object. They used a high level policy, which selects between different pushing primitives that are learnt separately. Although, their experiments demonstrated increased success rates over previous works, they considered scenes with low clutter and thus this approach is only beneficial in scenes with enough free space. Our work extends the existing literature by addressing the task of singulating all objects within a pallet, sequentially. While previous methodologies have primarily concentrated on isolating specific objects from cluttered scenes, our approach encompasses the singulation of multiple objects, increasing the level of difficulty.

3 Problem Formulation

The objective is for an agent to perform the optimal pushing actions to effectively singulate all the objects of a pallet of diverse objects, making them available for easy grasps, simplifying the depalletizing process. Given an RGB-D image, the segmentation of the scene and the goal region where the pallet objects should be driven, the agent selects the pushing action that maximizes the probability of singulating the target object.

3.1 Environment

The environment consists of a robotic finger, rigid objects in clutter resting on a rectangular workspace with predefined dimensions $s \times s$ and a single overhead RGB-D camera. The scene comprises a variety of objects such as boxes, cylinders, and bottles, each characterized by dimensions randomly sampled from a predefined range. This diversity contributes to the complexity of the environment, presenting a challenging depalletizing task. Additionally, the pose, geometry, and quantity of obstacles are randomized, further enhancing the variability

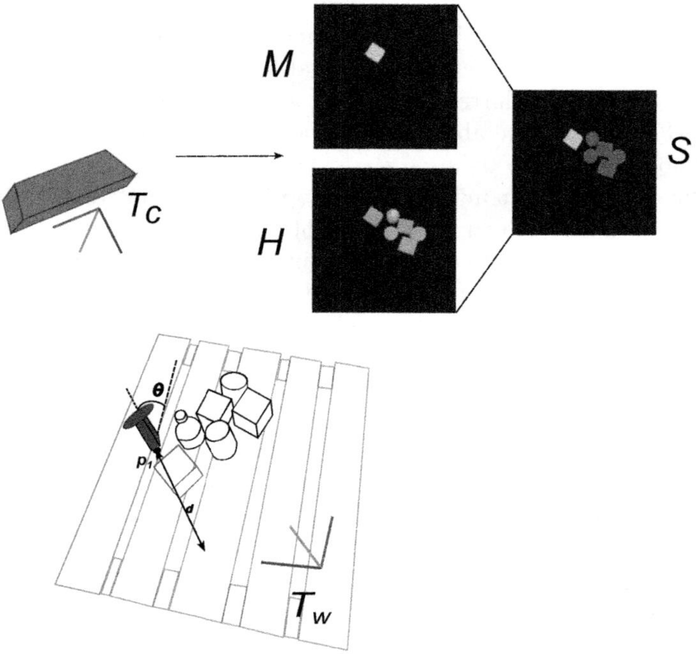

Fig. 1. Illustration of the environment including the support surface, the objects, the robotic finger and the camera. The inertia frame T_w is placed on the center of the table. The visual input $I = \{H, M, S\}$ is a tuple of maps representing orthographic top-down views based on the camera pose T_c. A push action is defined by the initial position $\boldsymbol{p}_1$ that the push starts, the direction angle θ and the pushing distance d. The goal is to singulate the target object (red contour) from the surrounding obstacles. (Color figure online)

and realism of the scenario. The world frame T_w is placed to the center of the workspace with its z-axis being opposite to the gravity direction. An overview of the environment is shown in Fig. 1, where the target object is highlighted in red, and the rest of the objects in black. Note that we choose as initial target the object with the smallest distance from the center of the workspace. Everytime an object is unloaded, we choose as target the object which is closer to the goal region, the same way as a person would operate.

3.2 Visual Representations

We represent the visual input I as a tuple of 2D map images $I = \{M, H, S\}$. To compute these maps, we capture an RGB-D image from a camera as shown in Fig. 1. Given the RGB image, we generate the mask of the target object using a color detector or an advanced object detector. Note that we assume that the target is at least partially visible and can be visually distinguished from the

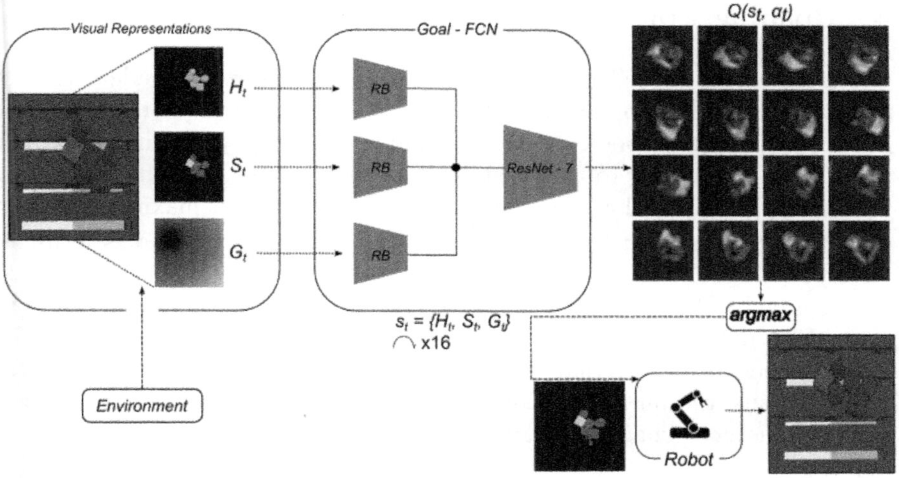

Fig. 2. The heightmap H_t, the segmentation of the scene S_t and the goal G_t are the input of our model Goal-FCN. Initially, we extract features for each image through a residual block RB(c). Then the output features are concatenated and fed to a seven-layer fully convolutional residual network, ResNet-7. The outputs are pixel-wise Q maps with the same size and resolution, which represent the future expected rewards. Robot chooses the pixel with the highest Q-value as the optimal push

obstacles. The mask and depth images are orthographically projected in the gravity direction using known extrinsic and intrinsic parameters of the camera to construct a mask map M and a depth heightmap H respectively. Finally, the heightmap S is an image generated by the fusion of H and M that provides a segmentation of the scene between the target, the obstacles and the support surface. The pixels that belong to the target have the value 0.5, those belonging to an obstacle the value 1 and the rest of them belonging to the support surface the value 0. The edges of the maps are defined with respect to the workspace limits. In our experiments, this area covers 0.5×0.5 m surface. The maps have image resolution 100×100 and thus each pixel $i \in I$ represents a 5×5 mm vertical column of 3-D space in the robot's workspace.

3.3 Actions

The robot executes push actions by moving the robot finger along a line segment $[\boldsymbol{p}_1, \boldsymbol{p}_2] \in \mathbb{R}^2$ parallel to the support surface. The final point is determined by the angle θ with respect to x axis and the pushing distance d, i.e. $\boldsymbol{p}_2 = \boldsymbol{p}_1 + [d\cos(\theta), d\sin(\theta)]^T$. Notice that the height h from the table remains the same during the action execution.

4 Pushing Policy

Our policy is optimized using deep Q-learning. Thus, we formulate the total singulation as a Markov Decision Process (MDP) with time horizon T: at any given state s_t the robot executes a pushing action a_t according to a policy $\pi(s_t)$, then transitions to a new state s_{t+1} and receives an immediate reward $r(s_t, a_t, s_{t+1})$. The goal is to find an optimal policy π^* that maximizes the total expected reward, given by $r_t = \sum_{i=t}^{T} \gamma^{i-t} r(s_i, a_i, s_{i+1})$, where γ is a discount factor.

Inspired by [25], we model the Q-function as a fully-convolutional neural network (FCN). A goal observation G is used as input to the FCN (Goal-FCN), which defines the regions that the target and the obstacles should be depalletized (Fig. 2). Thus, the pushing actions move either the obstacles or the target. To generate the goal image $G \in \mathbb{R}^{H \times W}$, we utilize the empty space around the objects. To simulate a variety of depalletizing scenarios, including both challenging and simpler contexts, we opt for a randomized selection process to determine the center $\boldsymbol{p}^*$ of the goal region within the initial empty space map. This approach introduces variability, allowing for scenarios where the goal area may be either more or less accessible for the entire pallet, mirroring real-world conditions. Taking into account that the segmentation of the scene, which is used to calculate the mask of the target M, could be slightly inaccurate especially in a cluttered scene, we create a goal region slightly larger than the target. Then, we assign the value 0 to the pixels inside a circle with radius $0.65 \times r$ and center $\boldsymbol{p}^*$. This circle is defined in a way that entirely encloses the target's bounding box, i.e. the radius r is computed as slightly larger than the half length of the diagonal that belongs to the target's bounding box. This 0-pixel region defines the goal area that the target should be moved. To the rest of the pixels $g_i \in G$, we assign the value that corresponds to the distance between the position of the pixel i and the circle defined by the goal area. Essentially, we provide to the network the position of each pixel with respect to the area that the target should be moved, which may allow the network to make decisions based on the objects location. Note that the pixels $g_i \in G$ whose distance from the circle is smaller than d_{sing}, compose the singulation area i.e. the area that should be freed from obstacles. To this end, we represent each state $s_t = (H_t, S_t, G_t)$.

4.1 Goal-FCN

The Goal-FCN takes as input the heightmap H_t, the segmentation of the scene S_t and the goal G_t and outputs pixel-wise Q maps with the same size and resolution as the inputs as shown in Fig. 2. Each image is fed to a 2-layer residual block [8] for feature extraction and subsequently the output features are concatenated and fed to a seven-layer fully convolutional residual network similar to the one of [24]. Note that, the ResNet-7 has the following layers: C(3,64)-MP-RB(128)-MP-RB(256)-RB(512)-RB(256)-RB(128)-UP-RB(64)-UP-C(1,1), where C(k, c) is a convolutional layer with $k \times k$ filters and c channels, RB(c) is a residual block with two convolutional layers using 3×3 filters and c channels, MP is a 3×3 max pooling layer with stride = 2, and UP is a bilinear 2× upsampling layer. Each value of pixel $q_i \in Q$ represents the future expected reward of executing a pushing action that starts from a position defined by the pixel i. To simplify learning the angle θ, we account for different pushing directions by rotating the input images into $k = 16$ discrete orientations (different multiplies of 22.5°) and then consider only horizontal pushes to the right. Rotations are done with nearest-neighbor sampling to avoid blurring artifacts, as well as 0-padding to maintain fixed image sizes. Thus, during training each image is rotated according to the angle θ before feeding to the Goal-FCN. On the contrary, during inference we rotate each image $k = 16$ times before feeding to the network. The pixel with the highest Q value across all 16 output maps determines the optimal pushing action. Note that the pushing distance is not a learnable parameter and is kept fixed to 0.1 m. Our pixel-wise parameterization of both state and action spaces enables the use of FCNs as Q-function approximators and provides sample efficiency, since each pixel-wise predictions shares convolutional features for all pushing locations and orientations (i.e. translation and rotation equivariance).

4.2 Rewards

We define a sparse reward scheme. If the agent reduces the target's distance from the optimal pixel $\boldsymbol{p}^*$ or pushes an obstacle out of the singulation area, we assign the value 0.5. If the push results to goal reaching i.e. the target is moved to goal area and there is no obstacle in the singulation area, we assign the value 1. Otherwise, we assign to each push the value 0. To check if the target has reached the goal area, we compute the intersection-over-union (IoU) between the target mask and the 0-pixel area in image G. In this particular problem, we consider more important to demonstrate the ability of the model to singulate all the objects of the pallet in the goal region, rather than the precision of the singulation of each object. Thus, we set the value of the IoU threshold to consider the object singulated, equal to 0.5.

4.3 Terminal States

The episode is terminated when all the target objects reach the goal area, if any object of the scene has fallen out of the support surface, or the predefined maximum number of timesteps T_{max} has been reached. The episode is considered successful only on the first case of goal reaching. In any other case the episode is considered as failed.

4.4 Training

Our Goal-FCN is trained to minimize the temporal difference error δ_t of $Q(s_t, a_t)$ to a fixed target value y_t:

$$\delta_t = |Q(s_t, a_t|\theta_t) - y_t| \tag{1}$$

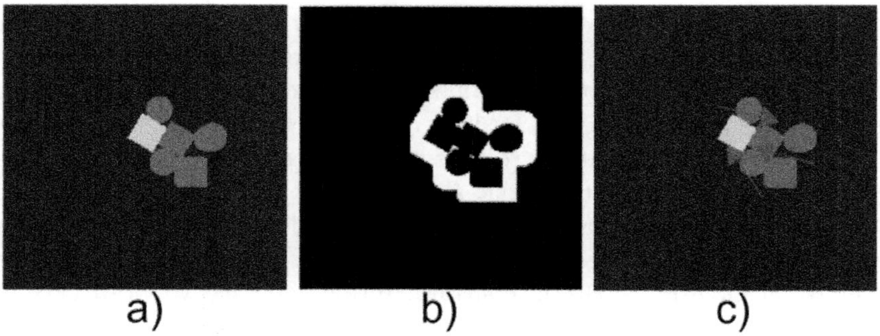

Fig. 3. Illustration of the guided exploration. (a) The state representation S. (b) The set of table pixels around the target from which $\boldsymbol{p}_1$ are sampled. (c) Examples of pushes around the target, with the initial pushing position $\boldsymbol{p}_1$ and the final pushing position $\boldsymbol{p}_2$ depicted by the start and the end of the arrows

$$y_t = r(s_t, a_t, s_{t+1}) + \gamma \max_{a'} Q(s_{t+1}, a'|\theta_t^-)) \tag{2}$$

via Huber loss:

$$L = \begin{cases} \frac{1}{2}\delta_t, \text{if } |\delta_t| \leq 0.1 \\ |\delta_t| - \frac{1}{2}, \text{otherwise} \end{cases} \tag{3}$$

where θ_t, θ_t^- are the parameters of the Goal-FCN and the corresponding target network at time t respectively. The target network is updated with a polyak averaging of 0.999. Similar to [25], we pass gradients only through a single pixel i and thus all other pixels backpropagate zero loss. We train the Goal-FCN using the Adam optimizer with learning rate 10^{-4} and with a discount factor of $\gamma = 0.5$. The model is trained in PyTorch with an Nvidia GeForce RTX 3060. Furthermore, we use prioritized experience replay [20] to balance the data that update the network.

Our exploration strategy is ϵ-greedy with the ϵ initialized at 0.9 then annealed to 0.05. To make the exploration more efficient, we devise prior constraints to reduce the complexity of the action space by performing random exploration and guided exploration with equal probability. During the guided exploration we aim at sample actions that either move the target object or the obstacles from the singulation area. We enforce the initial position $\boldsymbol{p}_1$ to be around the objects of the scene. Specifically, we randomly sample this position as pixels that are around either the target or the obstacles of the scene as shown in Fig. 3. The angle θ is computed by the line that starts from $\boldsymbol{p}_1$ and ends at $\boldsymbol{p}_2$.

During training we generate random goals in order to learn a general goal-reaching policy. This allows to perform data augmentation inspired by hindsight experience replay [1] and thus make the learning more efficient and overcome the difficulties with the sparse rewards. In particular, after experiencing the episode $s_0, s_1, \ldots, s_T$ we store to the replay buffer the non-empty transitions i.e. the transitions that led to a change in the scene, not only with the original goal but also with a goal generated by the position of the target object in state s_T if the target is singulated. Since the goal being pursued does not influence the environment dynamics, we can replay each trajectory using arbitrary goals, assuming we use an off-policy RL algorithm.

5 Results

The objective of the experiments is to evaluate the performance of the policy in the depalletizing task, i.e. the success rate and the mean number of actions before singulating all the objects.

5.1 Evaluation Metrics

To evaluate the policies we run N episodes. An episode is considered successful if the all the objects of the workspace are totally singulated within T_{max} timesteps. In any other case (end of maximum timesteps or fall out of the surface) the episode is considered as failed. For Env-1, $T_{max} = 30$, while $T_{max} = 35$ for Env-2, due to its increased difficulty. We evaluate the performance with 2 metrics 1) the average success rate % over N episodes, which measures the ability of the policy to complete the task, i.e. to singulate all the objects and 2) the average mean number of actions over N episodes, until the task completion (Fig. 4).

5.2 Simulation Experiments

We use the Bullet physics engine [3] to advance simulation. The simulation environment consists of a UR5 robot arm with a rectangular robotic finger, a 0.5×0.5 workspace and a simulated 640×480 RGB-D camera in a top view. The objects used in these simulations include 3 different object types, boxes, bottles, cylinders the shapes and dimensions of which are randomly chosen during experiments. We use $d_{sing} = 3$ cm and keep all the dynamic parameters of the simulation fixed.

Environments. We extensively test the performance of the above policy in two environments. Both environments depict a grid like, initially cluttered scene, where the geometry of the objects is randomly created. The first environment (Env-1) is a 2×2 grid. To test the robustness of the policy in a more cluttered environment, we increase the number of obstacles to 6, a 2×3 grid (Env-2). While we train the policy in Env-1 we evaluate it in both the environments to test its generalization ability.

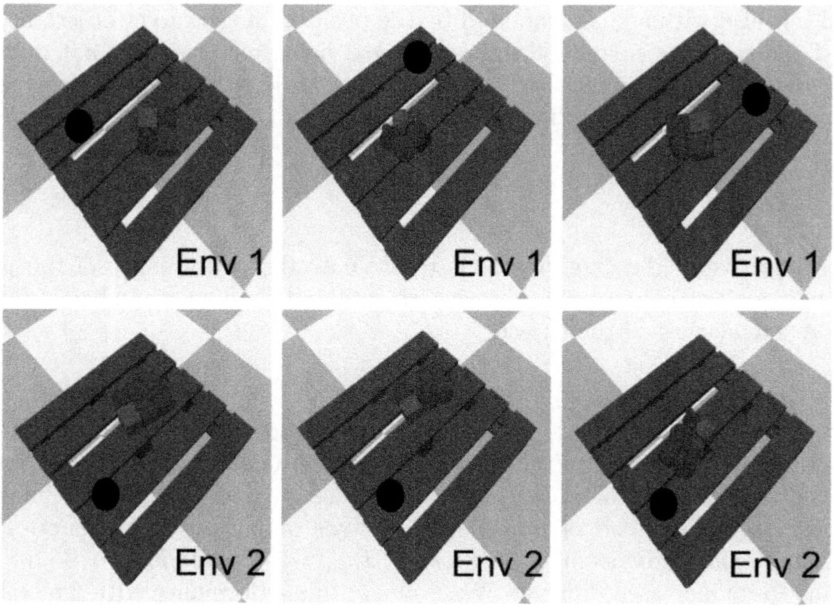

Fig. 4. Samples of scenes from the two different environments, Env 1 and Env 2 that the policies were evaluated. The target object is highlighted in red, the rest of the objects are depicted in blue, while the black areas are the goal regions of the scenes. (Color figure online)

Table 1. Performance evaluation on different environments (Success rate %/Mean actions)

Environment	success rate	mean actions
Env-1	93.6	14.5
Env-2	83.3	22.9

Performance Evaluation. After training the model for 10000 episodes in environment 1, the policy is evaluated for 1000 episodes with different scenes in both environments. Table 1 shows qualitative results for each environment. As we see the results show the efficacy of our RL, Goal driven approach, achieving high success rates in Env-1, without a significant drop of success rate in Env-2. Thus, our model has the ability to generalize in a more challenging environment. Figure 5 shows the relationship between the number of actions and the succcess rate for each environment. The trends of both curves align, indicating a similar progression. However, it's notable that the success rate in the more challenging Env-2 demonstrates a slower increase, requiring a larger number of steps to achieve comparable results.

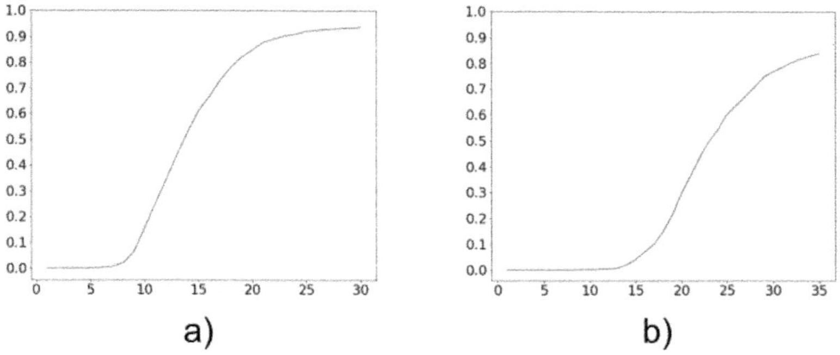

Fig. 5. Number of actions before singulation in the two different environments: (a) Env-1 (b) Env-2.

6 Conclusions

In conclusion, our proposed methodology, based on RL through the Goal-FCN network, offers a solution to the problem of depalletization. By performing non-prehensile pushing actions and incorporating goal regions, our approach demonstrates precision in handling diverse 3D objects within cluttered environments. In our next steps we aim to develop a policy which identifies the optimal goal region, resulting to a more effective unloading process.

Acknowledgments. This work was supported by the European Commission's Horizon Europe Program through the SESTOSENSO project (http://sestosenso.eu/, HORIZON-CL4-DigitalEmerging Grant 101070310).

Disclosure of Interests. The authors have no competing interests to declare that are relevant to the content of this article.

References

1. Andrychowicz, M., et al.: Hindsight experience replay. Adv. Neural Inf. Process. Syst. **30** (2017)
2. Boularias, A., Bagnell, J.A., Stentz, A.: Learning to manipulate unknown objects in clutter by reinforcement. In: Twenty-Ninth AAAI Conference on Artificial Intelligence (2015)
3. Coumans, E., Bai, Y.: Pybullet, a python module for physics simulation for games, robotics and machine learning (2016)
4. Dogar, M., Srinivasa, S.: A framework for push-grasping in clutter. In: Robotics: Science and Systems VII, vol. 1 (2011)
5. Dogar, M.R., Srinivasa, S.S.: A planning framework for non-prehensile manipulation under clutter and uncertainty. Auton. Robot. **33**(3), 217–236 (2012)
6. Eitel, A., Hauff, N., Burgard, W.: Learning to singulate objects using a push proposal network. In: Amato, N.M., Hager, G., Thomas, S., Torres-Torriti, M. (eds.) Robotics Research. SPAR, vol. 10, pp. 405–419. Springer, Cham (2020). https://doi.org/10.1007/978-3-030-28619-4_32

7. Fontanelli, G.A., et al.: A reconfigurable gripper for robotic autonomous depalletizing in supermarket logistics. IEEE Rob. Autom. Lett. **5**(3), 4612–4617 (2020). https://doi.org/10.1109/LRA.2020.3003283
8. He, K., Zhang, X., Ren, S., Sun, J.: Deep residual learning for image recognition. In: Proceedings of the IEEE Conference on Computer Vision and Pattern Recognition, pp. 770–778 (2016)
9. Holz, D., Topalidou-Kyniazopoulou, A., Stückler, J., Behnke, S.: Real-time object detection, localization and verification for fast robotic depalletizing. In: 2015 IEEE/RSJ International Conference on Intelligent Robots and Systems (IROS), pp. 1459–1466 (2015). https://doi.org/10.1109/IROS.2015.7353560
10. Huang, B., Han, S.D., Yu, J., Boularias, A.: Visual foresight tree for object retrieval from clutter with nonprehensile rearrangement. IEEE Rob. Autom. Lett. **7**, 231–238 (2021). https://doi.org/10.1109/LRA.2021.3123373
11. Khairuddin, U., Razi, N.A.Z.M., Abidin, M.S.Z., Yusof, R.: Smart packing simulator for 3d packing problem using genetic algorithm. In: Journal of Physics: Conference Series, vol. 1447, no. 1, p. 012041 (2020). https://doi.org/10.1088/1742-6596/1447/1/012041
12. Kiatos, M., Malassiotis, S.: Robust object grasping in clutter via singulation. In: 2019 International Conference on Robotics and Automation (ICRA), pp. 1596–1600. IEEE (2019). https://doi.org/10.1109/ICRA.2019.8793972
13. Kiatos, M., Sarantopoulos, I., Koutras, L., Malassiotis, S., Doulgeri, Z.: Learning push-grasping in dense clutter. IEEE Rob. Autom. Lett. **7**(4), 8783–8790 (2022). https://doi.org/10.1109/LRA.2022.3188437
14. Krug, R., et al.: The next step in robot commissioning: autonomous picking and palletizing. IEEE Rob. Autom. Lett. **1**(1), 546–553 (2016). https://doi.org/10.1109/LRA.2016.2519944
15. Kurenkov, A., et al.: Visuomotor mechanical search: learning to retrieve target objects in clutter. In: 2020 IEEE International Conference on Intelligent Robots and Systems (IROS) (2020)
16. Nakamoto, H., Eto, H., Sonoura, T., Tanaka, J., Ogawa, A.: High-speed and compact depalletizing robot capable of handling packages stacked complicatedly. In: 2016 IEEE/RSJ International Conference on Intelligent Robots and Systems (IROS), pp. 344–349. IEEE (2016)
17. Novkovic, T., Pautrat, R., Furrer, F., Breyer, M., Siegwart, R., Nieto, J.: Object finding in cluttered scenes using interactive perception. In: 2020 IEEE International Conference on Robotics and Automation (ICRA), pp. 8338–8344. IEEE (2020)
18. Sarantopoulos, I., Kiatos, M., Doulgeri, Z., Malassiotis, S.: Split deep q-learning for robust object singulation. In: 2020 IEEE International Conference on Robotics and Automation (ICRA), pp. 6225–6231 (2020)
19. Sarantopoulos, I., Kiatos, M., Doulgeri, Z., Malassiotis, S.: Total singulation with modular reinforcement learning. IEEE Rob. Autom. Lett. **6**(2), 4117–4124 (2021)
20. Schaul, T., Quan, J., Antonoglou, I., Silver, D.: Prioritized experience replay. arXiv preprint arXiv:1511.05952 (2015)
21. Stüber, J., Zito, C., Stolkin, R.: Let's push things forward: a survey on robot pushing. Front. Rob. AI **7**, 8 (2020). https://doi.org/10.3389/frobt.2020.00008
22. Tanaka, J., Ogawa, A., Nakamoto, H., Sonoura, T., Eto, H.: Suction pad unit using a bellows pneumatic actuator as a support mechanism for an end effector of depalletizing robots. ROBOMECH J. **7**(1), 1–30 (2020)
23. Yang, Y., Liang, H., Choi, C.: A deep learning approach to grasping the invisible. IEEE Rob. Autom. Lett. **5**(2), 2232–2239 (2020). https://doi.org/10.1109/LRA.2020.2970622

24. Zeng, A., Song, S., Lee, J., Rodriguez, A., Funkhouser, T.: Tossingbot: learning to throw arbitrary objects with residual physics. IEEE Trans. Rob. **36**(4), 1307–1319 (2020)
25. Zeng, A., et al: Robotic pick-and-place of novel objects in clutter with multi-affordance grasping and cross-domain image matching. In: IEEE International Conference on Robotics and Automation (ICRA), pp. 1–8. IEEE (2018)

A Simulation Study of Warehouse Loading and Unloading Systems Using Arena

Vasileios Pappas, Nikoleta Xafi, George Tzimas, and Dimitris Folinas(✉)

Department of Supply Chain Management, International Hellenic University, 601 00 Katerini, Greece
{tzimgeo,folinasd}@ihu.gr

Abstract. Warehouse is an important distribution centre. Receiving and delivering are the interface of a warehouse for incoming and outgoing material flow. In this work, the processes in the loading (delivering) and unloading systems (receiving) are carried out simultaneously daily at the warehouse. The processes in the unloading system are the arrival of supplier's lorry, checking, unloading, packing, sealing and storage. On the other hand, arrival of a customer's lorry, processing the delivery order, order picking, sealing, loading and checking are the processes undertaken in the loading system. In this paper, a simulation study was conducted in order to overcome some of the problems at a warehouse in a factory, especially the waiting times at the various processes. These long waiting and total times mean the drivers will lose the opportunity to serve any other distributor and workers at the warehouse have to work overtime. The management realised that the problem is due to lack of facilities and workers. The facilities at the warehouse include forklift, sealing machine, dock, pallet and computer. Therefore, a simulation study was proposed to model the loading and unloading systems in order to find a strategy that will optimise the residence time of any lorry in the warehouse and overcome the overtime problem. In ARENA, a simulation model can be built by putting together predefined modules, which represents processes or logic. Connector lines are used to connect modules and designate the flow of entities. Statistical data, such as cycle time and waiting time are recorded and displayed automatically as reports by ARENA.

Keywords: Simulation · Warehouse · Loading · Unloading · ARENA

1 Introduction

1.1 Inventory Operations

The importance of inventory as a part of supply chains comes from the fact that they constitute a large segment of economic activities. To improve their activities, to gain competitive advantage companies are interested in effective and efficient inventory operations that meet customer expectations. Therefore, the supply chain management (SCM) or logistics tasks to produce and distribute products in the right quantities to the right locations at the right time, while keeping costs down and customer service levels up. In

I. Kostavelis et al. (Eds.): ICSC 2024, CCIS 2110, pp. 118–135, 2025.
https://doi.org/10.1007/978-3-031-69344-1_9

essence, SCM aims to solve these tasks by searching for good trade-offs between system costs and customer satisfaction. Inventory management has been one of the critical factors in many retail sectors for the past few years (Zhang, 2020). Ensuring both product variety and optimal inventory level is always regarded as an operational challenge for retail outlets (Ton, 2010). Quite often, a firm's ability to deliver a differentiated strategy is inexplicably linked with its supply chain and inventory management capabilities (Kartal, 2016). Market demand/supplies are dynamic depending upon various factors like seasons, festivals, and past sales data assist companies to anticipate a massive surge of demand in the market well in advance. However, if the firm does not have proper inventory control measures, it will result in a lost case scenario. Furthermore, with frequent lost sales, the retail shop may lose even regular customers. Consequently, effective inventory management policies should be implemented to improve the inventory performance of the firm. From a customer's point of view, it provides better customer services through fast delivery and low shipping charges, hence meeting their expectations.

The main objectives of inventory management include:

1. Ensure a continuous supply of materials, spares and finished goods such that production is not disrupted and the customer's demand is met in a timely manner.
2. Maintain investment in inventories at the optimum level as required by the operational and sales activities.
3. To avoid both overstocking and under-stocking of inventory.
4. To optimize various costs associated with inventories like purchase cost, carrying a cost, storage cost, etc.

Literature review suggests that simulation models are the most appropriate methodology to analyse different inventory management policies Jackson (2020). Simulation models enable the investigator to analyse various inventory policies, possible results and their implications Bonilla-Enriquez (2020). In studying such issues, modelers typically focus on the following key performance metrics, which eventually can be translated to monetary measures: (1) customer service levels (the rate of totally satisfied customer demands), (2) average inventory levels and backorder levels, (3) rate and quantity of lost sales, (4) inventory cost.

Typically, when an order is performed by a producer or retailer, there is a lag in time (called lead time) after which the order is received. The lead-time demand is the magnitude of demand that arises during lead time and is typically random and therefore can result in stockouts. Consequently, to decrease the uncertainty in lead-time demand, companies constitute safety stock, which is extra inventory stocked to maintain good customer service levels. Companies may also use to place new orders before previous ones are received. Therefore, ordering decisions are typically made based on inventory positions rather than inventory levels, where The Companies to get feasible inventory management use scientific inventory policies which based on mathematical models. These models describe the behaviour of the inventory system.

Inventory models are classified according to whether the demand is known (deterministic) or whether it is random variable having a known probability distribution (stochastic). In the last case the chance of the exact solution is very limited therefore we use simulation.

In this paper, the focus is on simulating a company active in the warehousing and logistics sector, «PRATTEIN S.A.» based in the region of West Attica, using ARENA simulation software.

1.2 Business Process Management Modeling

To make any impact on a business process, it is fundamental to capture and characterize it in some way. A clear description of a business process may serve as a starting point for the design of an IT system, to set up performance measurement, to enact a process by a BPMS, to conduct a simulation study, etc. This wide variety of purposes motivate how process modeling has emerged as a strong tradition within research on BPM. Process modeling is an important and ongoing theme behind the BPM papers in Computers in Industry as well.

One of the earliest papers in Computers in Industry on process modeling is by Ortiz (1999), which introduces a new toolset as follows:

> "FirstSTEP is a comprehensive business process management tool giving business people the power to design, document, analyze, refine, incrementally improve and make a clear business case for process change."

While the work is similar to that of Van der Aalst (2004) in the sense that it assumes a BPMS to exist in the context of the studied problem at hand, it does something extra: It positions the process model as being of direct benefit to managers when they aim for improving business processes. While I already mentioned how one stream in BPM research focuses on the potential of technology, this point makes it clear that another stream positions the process model itself as a means to put BPM into practice.

Work on process modeling has developed along different dimensions over the years, which can be seen in the publications in Computers in Industry. Early papers focus on the use of process models in the context of process improvement projects, e.g. see the work by Krömker (1996) and Kalpic (2002). The main purpose of these papers is to emphasize the importance of the process modeling act itself. The models that are created in the documented projects are presented as assets in and by themselves, which may also serve as reference models in similar contexts.

Soon after the first publications on process modeling, work appeared that moved the focus from the process models itself towards the techniques and tools that can be used for process modeling, e.g. (Mallidi, 1999). This line continues to the present day, as exemplified by a recent paper that provides a building-block approach for manufacturing processes in the form of BPMN models (Erasmus, 2020).

Work on process modeling can be seen to grow in sophistication over the years. For example, Van Nuffel (2012) present a multi-layer, multi-view processes modeling method that aims to support business professionals in their day-to-day decision making. This approach goes well beyond the typical elements captured in a process model; it also goes beyond the typical applications of process models. In a similar vein, the recognition that processes are modeled on different levels of abstraction is what inspired the work by Polancic (2020). The paper proposes a modeling technique for so-called process landscapes. Such models represent organizational processes on a very high level of abstraction, comparable to the concept of value chains. This type of work may well open an entirely new angle for process modeling research.

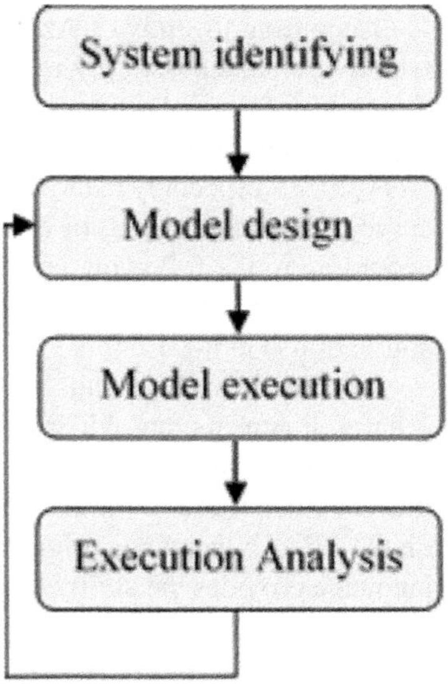

Fig. 1. Simulation Methodology.

Another, very recent example that illustrates the development of research on process modeling is the work by Lamine (2020), which ties BPM to the field of risk management. The work also shows how process modeling can be extended with elements that allow for the management of the entire risk life cycle within an organization. Additionally, it has become clear that for different purposes of process model usage context is an important concept (da Cunha Mattos, 2014). All these advances point at the vitality of process modeling as a research topic within the BPM discipline (Fig. 1).

1.3 Simulation Methodology

Simulation is a process with three mains iterative and interrelated components (see Fig. 3):

- System identifying: In this first step, the system is defined and the necessary data, of the system to simulate, are collected.
- Model design: It is about proposing the tools and structure of models using in the system to simulate.
- Model execution: In this step, the evolution of the conceived model is identified.
- Execution Analysis: Tests are done, on the model data, using specific analyzes. The most basic analysis would simply be to look at the data and derive conclusions from it.

Define the literature on supply chains modelling is mostly extensive, there are several tools and methods to approach simulation (Lee, 2004) according to the case study, using:

- Specialized software: ARENA®, SIMIO®, WINISK®, EXTENDSIM®, Witness®.
- Simulation languages: SIMULA, SIMAN, GPSS, QNAP2.
- Libraries for simulation: JAVASIM, C++ SIM
- General programming languages: C, JAVA, DELPHI

According to study of Azougahg Yassine (2019), a specialized software is chosen, which offers the possibility to describe the models graphically, as a result avoid writing thousands of lines of programming code. For this purpose, the choice of simulation tool, depends on its characteristics beside the other simulation tools, discussed in the study of Dias (2011), especially in the work of Tewoldeberhan (2002) whose reports a benchmark survey of simulation tools by evaluating, a package of discrete event simulation software, according to the following criteria: vendors, model development, input modes, testing and efficiency, execution, animation, output, user, experimental design and coupling simulation-optimization.

According to the results of the benchmark study in agreement with the selection criteria, it appears that ARENA® Rockwell Software is the most powerful tool in this study, which justifies its use in many simulation studies. For these reasons, ARENA® is the tools to model and simulate the case study. ARENA® is a simulation software based on the SIMAN language originating from two words "SIMulation and ANalysis". This language provides the ability to graphically describe the model using d a scheme, which allows avoiding writing programming thousands of lines of code.

1.4 Arena

The user guide of Arena describes it as follows:

«Arena software enables you to bring the power of modeling and simulation to your business. It is designed for analyzing the impact of changes involving significant and complex redesigns associated with supply chain, manufacturing, processes, logistics, distribution and warehousing, and service systems. Arena software provides the maximum flexibility and breadth of application coverage to model any desired level of detail and complexity.

Typical scenarios include:

- Detailed analysis of any type of manufacturing system, including material-handling components
- Analysis of complex customer service and customer management systems
- Analysis of global supply chains that include warehousing, transportation, and logistics systems
- Predicting system performance based on key metrics such as costs, throughput, cycle times, and utilizations
- Identifying process bottlenecks such as queue build ups and over-utilization of resources
- Planning staff, equipment, or material requirements.

Rockwell Software offers a full suite of products to provide enterprise-wide simulation, templates for various vertical markets, and an optimization template.

Arena software is designed for manufacturing or business process consultants and analysts and industrial or systems engineers. It is typically deployed as an enterprise business analysis and productivity tool.

We assume that you are familiar with the basic concepts and terms used in these types of systems. You are interested in improving business or manufacturing productivity and are responsible for evaluating and predicting the impact of proposed strategic and tactical changes to help improve performance.

ARENA is a computer simulation tool with a graphical user interface. Users can model complex systems using the available modules, blocks and elements available in the ARENA templates using simple click-and-drop operations into the model window. Examples of systems that can be modelled are:

- manufacturing plants with people, machines and transport devices,
- bank teller windows, ATMs, and deposit boxes, and
- a computer network with servers, clients and networking capabilities.

ARENA uses SIMAN as the underlying simulation language. So, every time the user places a module in the model window and Alls in the required Aelds, ARENA actually writes its own SIMAN code in the background. The user can view the SIMAN code optionally in a separate window. Each ARENA model and template also has a corresponding Microsoft Visual Basic for Applications (VBA) project. The VBA code is saved in the ARENA Ale with *the.doe* extension, every time the ARENA project is saved. A VBA project consists of a collection of modules. These are classified by their type and are grouped in the VBA project window. The types of modules in the ARENA VBA project are:

1. ARENA objects: Each model has one ARENA object named *ThisDocument*. It is an object reference to the model itself. This is not changeable by the user, but can be extended by adding properties and methods, which can be referenced by code associated with other modules.
2. Code modules: These are user-defined functions, subroutines and variables that can be inserted into a project and referenced from other VBA modules.
3. Class modules: These are similar to code modules, except they can be thought of as objects, rather than simply a collection of functions and properties.
4. Forms: These are user-defined dialogs with controls. They are used to display information or query the user for input (Fig. 2).

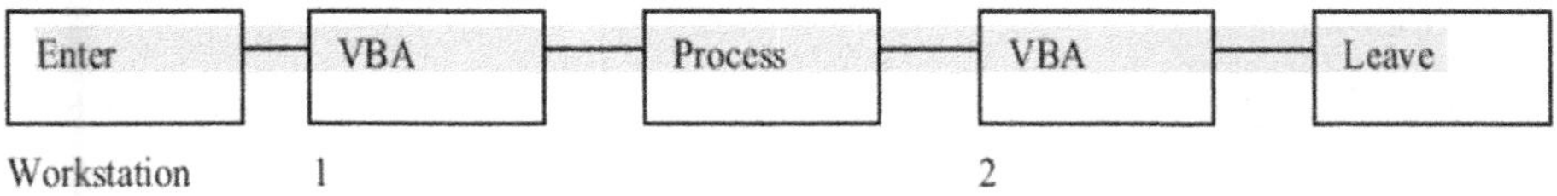

Fig. 2. ARENA model blocks.

2 Problem Statement

The application of the simulation will be presented with a very simple system: storage-picking-distribution, consisting of a 3PL warehousing unit that supplies retailers with products. The product warehouse supplies the retailers and the finished product units are distributed to the market.

We chose a company whose 10% of its turnover comes from the trading of consumer goods (food, carbonated beverages, etc.) and 90% from the provision of logistics services.

The marketing is aimed at small food retailers throughout the prefecture of Attica, catering and distribution outlets. Merchandise is distributed through salesmen, who visit the points of sale daily and record shortages, taking the order form with the customer's approval. It is worth noting that the goods distributed by the company, after being received in its warehouses, are sorted, packed according to the customer's order and distributed directly with the company's own trucks and refrigerators.

Logistic (supply chain) services are provided to large chains of food stores (supermarkets) in the Attica prefecture and involve the receipt, storage, packaging, sorting and distribution of food and carbonated beverages in accordance with the production companies' orders (via salesmen).

The following software is currently installed and operated, either by the company itself or by suppliers:

- Softone: used for invoicing to customers.
- Entersoft: the CRM and ERP modules are used between the vendors and the company.
- SAP: warehouse module connected to Nikas company.
- Aberon: used as warehouse management software WMS.
- Custom (self-produced) software for management and tracking of 24-h orders.

The following technologies and devices are used to operate and support the above:

- Pick by light
- Pick by voice
- Barcode reading and printing devices
- Reading and reading and scanning devices (e.g., barcode readers and readers)
- Portable order picking devices
- Modern local area network

ORDERING, PURCHASING, DISTRIBUTION AND RETURNS PROCEDURES ORDERS

The process concerns orders placed by salespersons. The main actions carried out are as follows:

- The sellers give the orders through the wireless mobile devices connected to the corporate information systems (order proposal).
- The accounting department proceeds to check the accuracy of the order
- The accounting department proceeds to check the available stocks.
- The accounting department proceeds to approve the order with any changes to either the items or quantities.
- The order is printed out in the warehouse, which is received by the warehouse manager.
- Within 10 min the order is prepared in the warehouse. 'All orders are ready by the end of the shift.
- If during the preparation of the order it is found that there is no stock available, the part of this order is entered electronically and at the end of the day a total backorder is created, which is sent to the purchasing and procurement department in order to give the corresponding order orders to the suppliers.

- Orders are loaded onto the trucks in the afternoon.
- Orders are delivered the following morning on the basis of predefined routes.

PURCHASES - SUPPLIES

The responsibility of each department of the Purchasing Department (currently there are four departments) is to forecast purchases and supplies of products based on one of the following conditions:

- fast moving.
- 20-day purchases (usually those not classified as fast moving).
- (mainly due to extraordinary and unforeseen events).
- discount policies for the benefit of the company.
- the method of payment to the supplier (wholesale relationship)

In summary, the main characteristics of the distribution network are as follows:

- 5200 m^2 covered warehouses, built to European Union standards, meeting all safety and hygiene standards for food storage.
- 1400 m^3 cold storage and freezing chambers, with electronic monitoring system for temperature fluctuation, meeting the most modern safety standards.
- 3000 m^2 product handling and parking areas.
- 28 privately owned, well-equipped trucks for transporting refrigerated and dry cargo on a daily basis with a specific prescribed route (one driver per distribution route).
- 70 staff employed, fully trained and 60 salesmen (employees and associates) to take orders on a daily basis.
- 65 suppliers, of which 40 have automatic product identification technology when entering the warehouse.
- Manages a total of 5,500 unique product codes.
- Distributes 800 orders per day (in one shift of operation) or 32 orders per truck

The following assumptions are made:

There is always a sufficient quantity of product in the warehouse, so the process never starves. The product is collected in a pick by light system and the final boxes of products are loaded onto the vehicle. The packaging time follows normal distribution and the truck loading time follows a triangular distribution between 2 (min) and 5 (max) minutes and an average of 3 min.

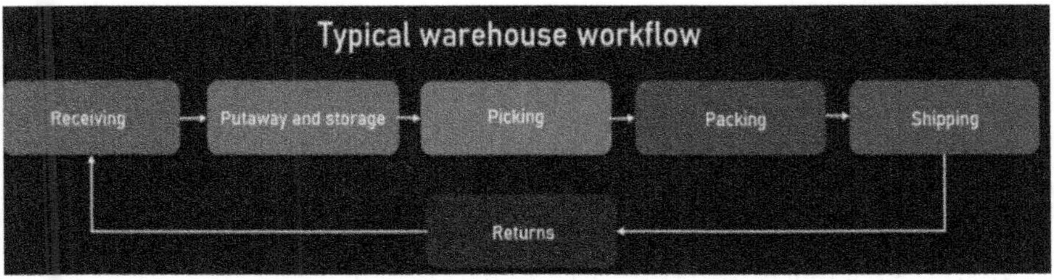

Fig. 3. A generic inventory-distribution system

We are interested in determining the following performance parameters:

- Product picking time
- Total service time per order
- Total distribution time per load

The warehouse-distribution problem described previously, although quite elaborated, is still a simplification of real supply chain systems; however, the applied method can be extended to more realistic problems, including multiple storage stages, distribution arrangements, and so on.

3 Arena Model Construction

For the design and implementation of the simulation model in the ARENA software (version 15), data were taken from orders (49,507 records) as they were prepared and delivered in December 2023, as for the Attica market it is considered a peak season due to the Christmas holiday and the increased demand for codes related to the festive period. During this period of 25 working days, 4,556 orders were prepared and delivered or an average of 182 orders per day. Each order contained, on average, 11 products from a product group of 843 unique codes handled during the period out of a total of 5,500 unique codes handled and distributed by the business on a year basis.

From the set of available data received from the company, 12 high-demand product codes, belonging to 4 product categories, were selected for the simulation model to represent a subset of the processes in place. In particular, the following product codes were selected:

Soft drinks category:

- PEPSI MAX SLEEK 330 CC 4*6PACK
- PEPSI MAX SLEEK 330 CC 4X6PACK
- PEPSI TWIST SLEEK 330 CC 4*6PACK

Coffee category:

- BRAVO CLASSIC 193G 60T/KIB
- BRAVO CLASSIC 95GR 120T/KIB
- STARBUCKS DISC.CAPUCCINO 220 ml 10T

Beer category:

- FIX 500 ML BOX 6
- HENNINGER 500 ML BOX 6
- KAISER 500 ML BOX 6

Biscuits category:

- SOFTKINGS COOKIE DARK CHOCO 10T*160GR
- SOFTKINGS COOKIE TRIPLE CHOCO 10Tx160GR MOB
- SOFTKINGS COOKIE CHOCOLATE 10Tx160GR

From the discussion we had with middle and junior managers in order to understand and record the processes involved in receiving, storing, packaging, sorting and distribution, the corresponding times were obtained. For example, the warehouse department involved in preparing orders using pick by light, which has been the focus of this study, averages 45 orders per hour or 360 orders per hour in the operating shift. Similarly, the average times of loading orders on the trucks were given based on company calculations.

In packaging, we assume that 10 workers and in truck loading are 10 workers available in an eight hour shift.

The Arena environment provides the user the ability to create models using different modules. In order to show the wide applicability when designing the simulation model, three were created, but we will present the results of the last one:

- The first and the second model makes use of the modules of the "Basic Process" panel

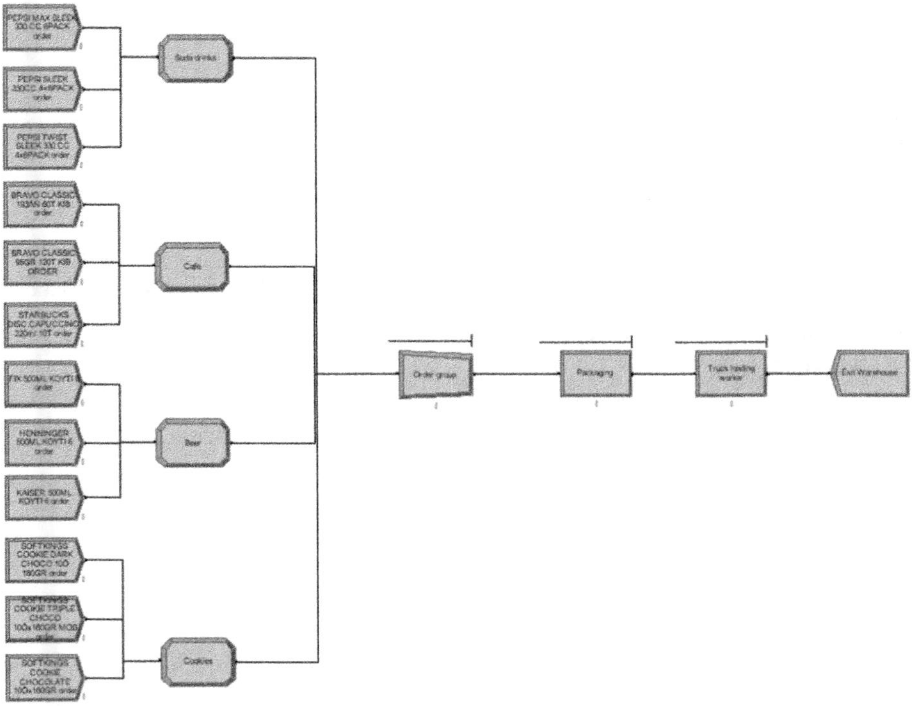

Figure: modules of the first model in the "Flowchart View" area.

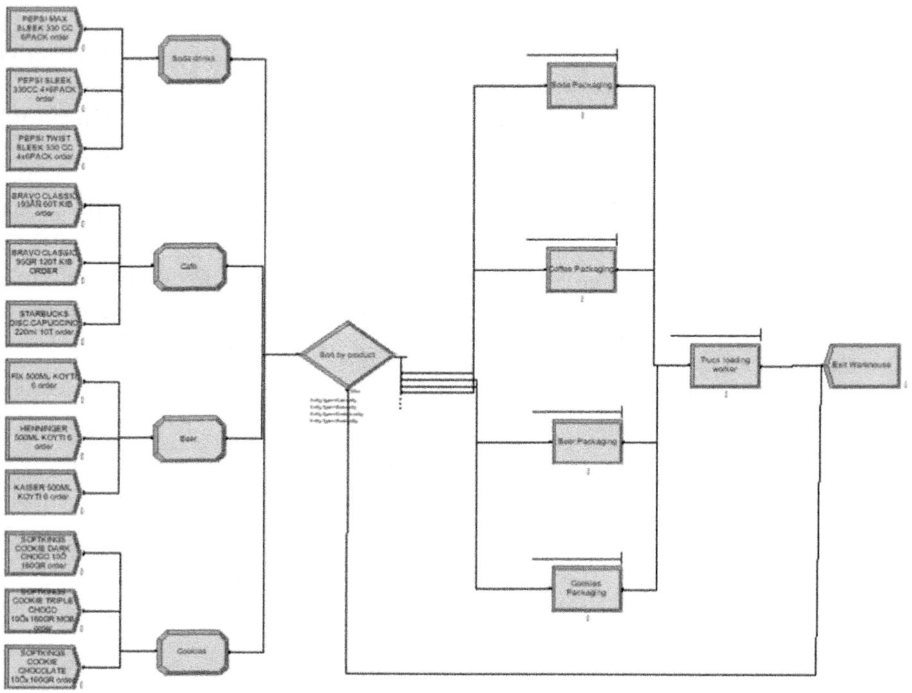

Figure: functional modules of the second model in the "Flowchart View" space

- The third model makes use of the modules of the "Basic Process" and "Advanced Transfer" panel

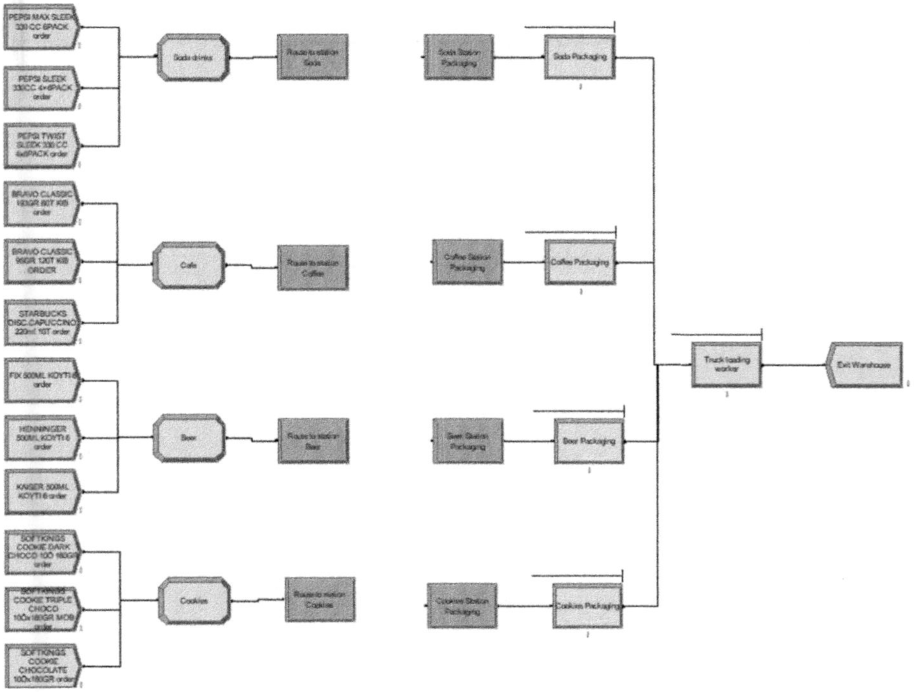

Figure: modules of the third model in the "Flowchart View" area

The simulation period of each Arena model was set to a period of 25 days.

The following steps were applied for each simulation model:

- from the available data, we assumed and estimated the statistical distribution of products and processes in packaging and truck loading.
- for each product, we defined and set the label of the category it belongs, so that it is possible to monitor it from start to finish.
- for each product and process we recorded the most important variables, such as quantitative entity data (inbound, outbound, WIP), resource utilization (jobs, staff availability, staff employment), analysis of waiting queues.

4 Result, Discussion

The result of the simulation produced the following tables:

5tt Olympus ICSC IHU model

Replications: 1 Time Units: Hours

Key Performance Indicators

System	Average
Number Out	1,398

During the simulation period of 25 days, 1.398 products were monitored and recorded.

5tt Olympus ICSC IHU model

Replications: 1 Time Units: Hours

Entity

Time

VA Time	Average	Half Width	Minimum Value	Maximum Value
Beer entity	0.2616	(Insufficient)	0.2153	0.3123
Cafe entity	0.2215	(Insufficient)	0.1852	0.2641
Cookies entity	0.2215	0.001580609	0.1802	0.2699
Soda entity	0.2436	0.002183638	0.2024	0.3070

NVA Time	Average	Half Width	Minimum Value	Maximum Value
Beer entity	0.00	(Insufficient)	0.00	0.00
Cafe entity	0.00	(Insufficient)	0.00	0.00
Cookies entity	0.00	0.000000000	0.00	0.00
Soda entity	0.00	0.000000000	0.00	0.00

Wait Time	Average	Half Width	Minimum Value	Maximum Value
Beer entity	0.00343142	(Insufficient)	0.00	0.1847
Cafe entity	0.00008163	(Insufficient)	0.00	0.02105936
Cookies entity	0.00003282	(Correlated)	0.00	0.01936496
Soda entity	0.00220004	(Correlated)	0.00	0.2115

Transfer Time	Average	Half Width	Minimum Value	Maximum Value
Beer entity	0.03333333	(Insufficient)	0.03333333	0.03333333
Cafe entity	0.03333333	(Insufficient)	0.03333333	0.03333333
Cookies entity	0.03333333	(Correlated)	0.03333333	0.03333333
Soda entity	0.03333333	(Correlated)	0.03333333	0.03333333

Other Time	Average	Half Width	Minimum Value	Maximum Value
Beer entity	0.00	(Insufficient)	0.00	0.00
Cafe entity	0.00	(Insufficient)	0.00	0.00
Cookies entity	0.00	0.000000000	0.00	0.00
Soda entity	0.00	0.000000000	0.00	0.00

Total Time	Average	Half Width	Minimum Value	Maximum Value
Beer entity	0.2984	(Insufficient)	0.2487	0.5171
Cafe entity	0.2549	(Insufficient)	0.2186	0.2974
Cookies entity	0.2548	0.001586521	0.2135	0.3066
Soda entity	0.2792	(Correlated)	0.2358	0.4786

Other

5tt Olympus ICSC IHU model

Replications: 1 Time Units: Hours

Entity

Other

Number In

	Value
Beer entity	204.00
Cafe entity	258.00
Cookies entity	590.00
Soda entity	346.00

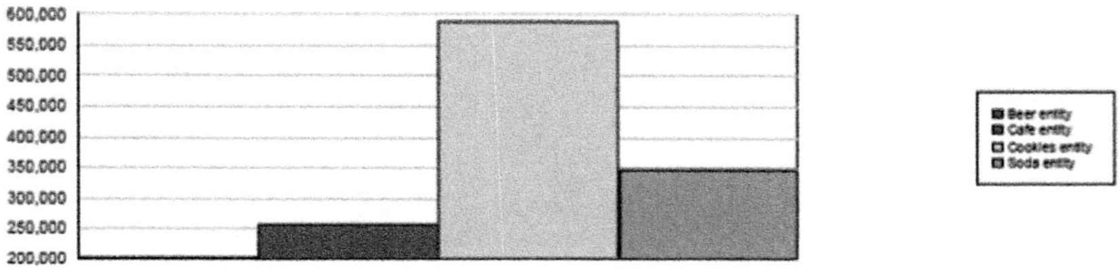

Number Out

	Value
Beer entity	204.00
Cafe entity	258.00
Cookies entity	590.00
Soda entity	346.00

WIP

	Average	Half Width	Minimum Value	Maximum Value
Beer entity	0.1014	0,015391929	0.00	7.0000
Cafe entity	0.1096	0,014814128	0.00	5.0000
Cookies entity	0.2506	0,014117867	0.00	3.0000
Soda entity	0.1610	0,023615197	0.00	9.0000

5tt Olympus ICSC IHU model

Replications: 1 Time Units: Hours

Queue

Time

Waiting Time	Average	Half Width	Minimum Value	Maximum Value
Beer Packaging.Queue	0.00028294	(Insufficient)	0.00	0.03344722
Coffee Packaging.Queue	0.00008163	(Insufficient)	0.00	0.02105936
Cookies Packaging.Queue	0.00003282	(Correlated)	0.00	0.01936496
Soda Packaging.Queue	0.00036381	(Correlated)	0.00	0.03916974
Truck loading worker.Queue	0.00091389	(Correlated)	0.00	0.1724

Other

Number Waiting	Average	Half Width	Minimum Value	Maximum Value
Beer Packaging.Queue	0.00009620	(Insufficient)	0.00	2.0000
Coffee Packaging.Queue	0.00003510	(Insufficient)	0.00	1.0000
Cookies Packaging.Queue	0.00003227	(Insufficient)	0.00	1.0000
Soda Packaging.Queue	0.00020980	(Insufficient)	0.00	4.0000
Truck loading worker.Queue	0.00212937	(Insufficient)	0.00	8.0000

5tt Olympus ICSC IHU model

Replications: 1 Time Units: Hours

Resource

Usage

Instantaneous Utilization	Average	Half Width	Minimum Value	Maximum Value
Packaging worker	0.00627499	0.000483528	0.00	1.0000
Truck load worker	0.04797239	0.002887057	0.00	1.0000

Number Busy	Average	Half Width	Minimum Value	Maximum Value
Packaging worker	0.06274988	0.004835277	0.00	10.0000
Truck load worker	0.4797	0.028870586	0.00	10.0000

Number Scheduled	Average	Half Width	Minimum Value	Maximum Value
Packaging worker	10.0000	(Insufficient)	10.0000	10.0000
Truck load worker	10.0000	(Insufficient)	10.0000	10.0000

Scheduled Utilization	Value
Packaging worker	0.00627499
Truck load worker	0.04797239

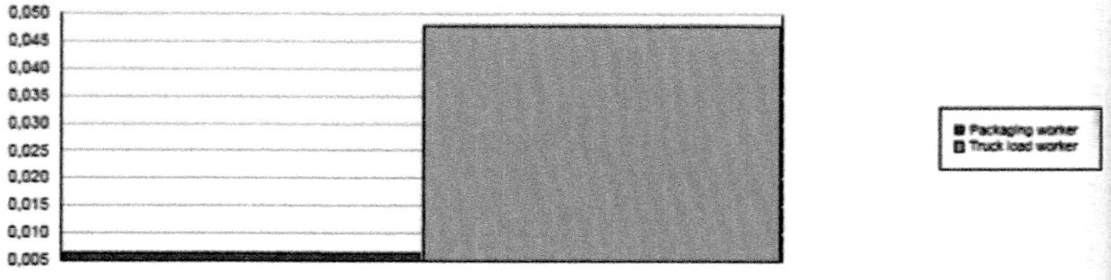

5tt Olympus ICSC IHU model

Replications: 1 Time Units: Hours

Resource

Usage

Total Number Seized

	Value
Packaging worker	1398.00
Truck load worker	1398.00

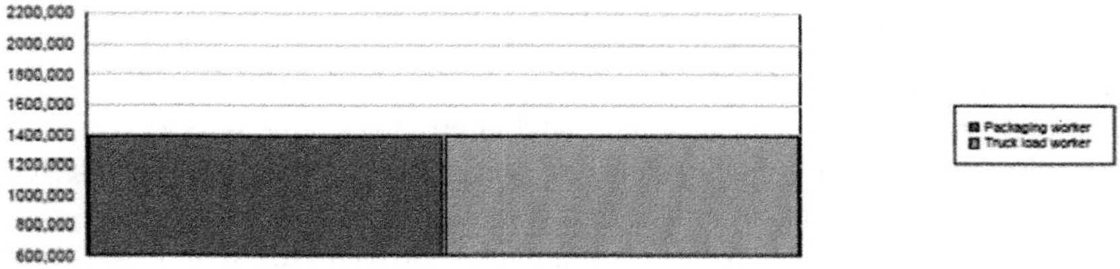

5tt Olympus ICSC IHU model

Replications: 1 Time Units: Hours

Resource

Usage

Total Number Seized

	Value
Packaging worker	1398.00
Truck load worker	1398.00

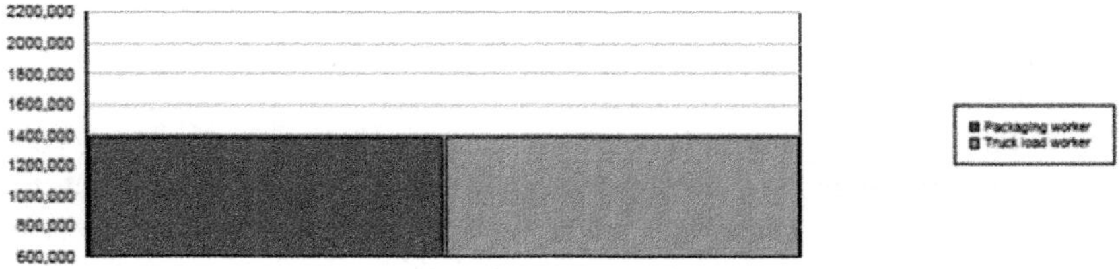

In order to create to evaluate the results in more visual prospect, we created two plots of the usage of workers in packaging and truck loading, during the 25-day period or 600 min.

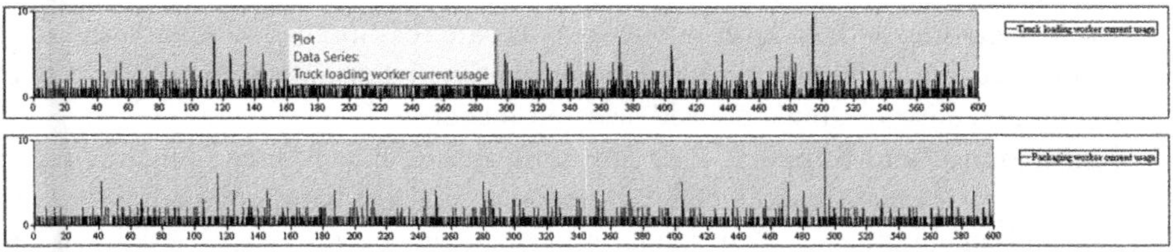

Figure: utilization of workers (packaging, truck loading) during the simulation period

In conclusion, Rockwell Arena simulation software offers several advantages and disadvantages in designing, analyzing, and implementing a 3PL (Third-Party Logistics) warehouse model:

Advantages:

1. **Visualization**: Arena provides a visual representation of the warehouse operations, allowing stakeholders to understand complex processes more easily. This visual aid can enhance communication and decision-making.
2. **Flexibility**: Users can model various scenarios and parameters within the software, enabling them to test different layouts, staffing levels, and operational strategies without incurring real-world costs or risks.
3. **Optimization**: Arena includes optimization features that can help identify bottlenecks, optimize resource allocation, and improve overall efficiency within the warehouse. By fine-tuning parameters, users can strive for the most cost-effective and productive operations.
4. **Risk Reduction**: Using Arena for simulation allows for the identification of potential issues and risks before implementing changes in the real-world environment. This can prevent costly mistakes and disruptions to operations.
5. **Training and Education**: Arena can be used as a training tool for warehouse staff, allowing them to familiarize themselves with new processes and procedures in a virtual environment before implementation.

Disadvantages:

1. **Learning Curve**: Arena simulation software can have a steep learning curve, particularly for users who are not familiar with simulation modeling concepts or the software interface. Training and expertise may be required to effectively utilize all features.
2. **Complexity**: Modeling a 3PL warehouse in Arena requires a deep understanding of the warehouse's operations, processes, and constraints. Creating an accurate model may be time-consuming and complex, especially for large and intricate facilities.
3. **Data Requirements**: Arena simulations rely heavily on accurate input data to produce meaningful results. Gathering, inputting, and validating data can be challenging, particularly if the data is incomplete or unreliable.
4. **Cost**: The initial cost of purchasing Arena software licenses and the resources required to develop and maintain simulation models can be significant. For smaller businesses or projects with limited budgets, this cost may outweigh the benefits.
5. **Validation and Verification**: Ensuring that the simulation accurately reflects real-world operations and produces reliable results requires thorough validation and verification processes. Without proper validation, the simulation outputs may not accurately represent reality, leading to flawed decision-making.
6. **Maintenance and Support**: Like any software, Rockwell Arena requires regular updates, maintenance, and technical support to address bugs, compatibility issues, and evolving user needs. Dependence on vendor support may entail additional costs and potential disruptions in workflow.

In summary, while Rockwell Arena simulation software offers powerful capabilities for designing, analyzing, and implementing 3PL warehouse models, it also presents challenges related to complexity, learning curve, data requirements, cost, and validation. Careful consideration of these factors is essential when deciding whether to utilize Arena for warehouse optimization.

References

Azougahg Yassine, B.K.: Supply chain modeling and simulation using SIMAN ARENA a case study. In: Laboratoire Process, Signaux, Systemes Industriels et Informatique (LAPSSII) (2019)

da Cunha Mattos, T.S.: A formal representation for context-aware business processes. Comput. Ind. **65**, 1193–1212 (2014)

Dias, L.P.: Discrete simulation tools ranking- a commercial software packages comparison based on popularity. In: Proceedings of the Industrial Simulation Conference. Venice (2011)

Erasmus, J.V.: Using business process models for the specification of manufacturing operations. Comput. Ind. **123**, 103297 (2020)

Bonilla-Enriquez, G., Caballero-Morales, S.-O.: Simulation model for assessment of non deterministic inventory control techniques. Asian J. Res. Comput. Sci. **5**, 63–70 (2020)

Kartal, H., Oztekin, A.: An integrated decision analytic framework of machine learning with multi-criteria decision making for multiattribute inventory classification. Comput. Ind. Eng. **101**, 599–613 (2016)

Jackson, I., Tolujevs, J.: Review of inventory control models: a classification based on methods of obtaining optimal control parameters. Trans. Telecom. **21**, 191–202 (2020)

Kalpic, B.B.: Business process modelling in industry – the powerful tool in enterprise management. Comput. Ind. **47**, 299–318 (2002)

Krömker, M.T.-D.: Re-engineering the ship pre-design process. Comput. Ind. **31**, 143–153 (1996)

Lamine, E.T.: BPRIM: an integrated framework for business process management and risk management. Comput. Ind. **117**, 103199 (2020)

Lee, S.U.: Design specifications of a generic supply chain simulator. In: Proceedings of the 2004 Winter Simulation Conference (2004)

Mallidi, K.P.: Process modelling in smallmedium enterprise networks. Comput. Ind. **38**, 149–158 (1999)

Ortiz, A.L.: Building a production planning process with an approach based on CIMOSA and workflow management systems. Comput. Ind. **40**, 207–219 (1999)

Polancic, G.: BPMN-L: a BPMN extension for modeling of process landscapes. Comput. Ind. **121**, 103276 (2020)

Tewoldeberhan, T.W., Verbraeck, A.: An evaluation and selection methodology for discrete-event simulation software. In: Proceedings of the Winter Simulation Conference. San Diego, Calif (2002)

Van der Aalst, W.W.: Process mining: a research agenda. Comput. Ind. **53**, 231–244 (2004)

Van Nuffel, D.D.: Multi-abstraction layered business process modeling. Comput. Ind.. Ind. **63**, 131–147 (2012)

Zhang, Y., Lu, H.: Analysis and optimisation of perishable inventory with stocks-sensitive stochastic demand and two-stage pricing: a discrete event simulation study. J. Simul. **15**, 326 (2020)

Ton, Z., Raman, A.: The effect of product variety and inventory levels on retail store sales: a longitudinal study. Prod. Oper. Manag. **19**, 546–550 (2010)

Simulation Modelling of Dynamic Production Scheduling on Parallel Machines with Sequence-Independent Setups

Anastasia Karamanli[1(✉)], Alexandros Xanthopoulos[1], Ioannis Kansizoglou[1], Antonios Gasteratos[1], and Dimitrios Koulouriotis[2]

[1] Department of Production and Management Engineering, School of Engineering, Democritus University of Thrace, V. Sofias 12, 67100 Xanthi, Greece
{ankarama,axanthop,ikansizo,agaster}@pme.duth.gr
[2] School of Mechanical Engineering, National Technical University of Athens, Heroon Polytechniou 9, 15772 Athens, Greece
jimk@pme.duth.gr

Abstract. More and more emphasis is allocated to production job scheduling by the modern organizations in order to preserve their performance indicators stable. This research addresses the dynamic scheduling of jobs in a production system with a single input queue and parallel machines. The processing times and the times between job arrivals are assumed probabilistic. Jobs belong to different classes and a due date is assigned to each job at the time of its arrival. A machine needs to be setup every time it switches production from some job class to another. In this article, is considered a set of alternative priority rules for dynamic job scheduling using discrete-event simulation. The priority heuristics are compared in respect to several performance metrics in a series of simulation experiments. The behaviour of the scheduling heuristics is assessed under the influence of various parameters. Moreover, are offered managerial insights for scheduling decisions in industry based on the numerical results.

Keywords: Dynamic Scheduling · Stochastic System · Parallel Machines · Sequence-Independent Setups · Discrete-Event Simulation · Priority Rules

1 Introduction

In this article we study a stochastic scheduling problem with parallel machines, dynamic arrivals of jobs and setups. Our motivation for this research originates from the fact that it is substantially relevant to real life applications as elaborated in the following.

The scientific literature often contains static and deterministic scheduling problems. Nonetheless, in real life scheduling applications there are typically dynamic job arrivals and the interarrival times are governed by uncertainty. As Chen et al. [18] claim, a job-shop scheduling problem helps industries achieve improved productivity and equipment utilization. However, production operations frequently deviate from plan because of random factors that cannot be controlled by the scheduler. Dynamic events, such as

I. Kostavelis et al. (Eds.): ICSC 2024, CCIS 2110, pp. 136–147, 2025.
https://doi.org/10.1007/978-3-031-69344-1_10

acceptance or rejection of orders, machines breakdowns or random processing times, could lead to unexpected conditions of the production and as a result to deviation from the schedule, as it is declared in the paper of Wang et al. [19]. Xiong et al. [21] further mentions that the deviation from the production schedule may be caused by urgent orders or jobs, which require reprocessing or reassembling.

There are many real-life occurrences of the production system configuration with parallel machines. For example, an automated assembly line might perform some complex, multi-stage manufacturing process. The bottleneck of the line determines the system throughput as a whole. As a consequence, the manufacturing process in its entirety could be functionally aggregated in a single stage and considered to be a single machine from a production scheduling standpoint. We also encounter often in real world applications the parallel machine setting, because this is a standard approach for production capacity expansion.

In numerous practical situations there are setups of considerable length and/or cost when switching between job families and this is a hard "constraint" imposed by the production technology used which cannot be relaxed. Indicatively, we find such examples in textile manufacturing when switching production from some colour to another, or in plastics fabrication when exchanging molds in injection machines etc.

This paper examines, and tries to offer managerial insights, for research questions such as:

- How do changes in, e.g. job arrival rate and setup times, affect the system's performance?
- Which is the best job priority rule for a given production system and performance metric?
- In what situations does effective production scheduling yields the most substantial benefits?
- Why does some priority heuristic outperform another for certain production environments and criteria?

1.1 Analysis of Related Publications

This article broadly belongs to the research field of priority rules for dynamic scheduling problems with setups. Influential contributions in this field include the survey of scheduling problems with setups of Haned et al. [16], the dynamic scheduling review of Gebreyesus et al. [17], while the influences of production scheduling on Industry 4.0 are discussed in the recent literature review of Zhang et al. [12].

In this paper, we use discrete-event simulation to experiment with the underlying dynamic scheduling condition. Discrete-event simulation is a standard modelling approach for dynamic manufacturing settings, and it is utilized, indicatively, in the papers of Cervenanska et al. [1], Fan et al. [4], Katsios et al. [15] and Palombarini et al. [20].

In this article we examine a scheduling problem with parallel machines and performance metrics related to job completion time; indicative related works is the paper of Haned et al. [16]. Priority rules are established solution approaches to dynamic scheduling problems primarily due to their flexibility and implementation ease. Comparative evaluations of job priority rules are offered, indicatively, in Cervenanska et al. [1], Engenhausen and Lodding [3] and Xanthopoulos and Koulouriotis [9].

A contemporary avenue of research is the application of intelligent solution methods for dynamic scheduling problems including reinforcement learning (Chien and Lan [2], Li et al. [5], Liu et al. [6] and Paraschos et al. [13]), genetic algorithms (Fan et al.[4], Sadeghi et al. [7] and Shady et al. [8]), tabu search (Xie et al. [11]), smart workshop (Zhang et al. [22]) and neural networks (Xanthopoulos and Koulouriotis [9]). More specifically, a reinforcement learning model implemented in a production system could learn the best practices for each state, in order to achieve economic benefits, as Xanthopoulos et al. suggest [14].

1.2 Comparisons with the State of the Art

This article primarily extends the research of Xanthopoulos and Koulouriotis [10]. More precisely, we consider alternative job arrival and processing schemes in addition to due date and setup time mechanisms. Moreover, this research focuses on different job priority heuristics as well as objective functions.

The contribution of this article can be outlined in the following points:

- A novel decision aid model for dynamic production scheduling in parallel machines with setups is introduced,
- Three objective functions are formulated, and their properties are investigated numerically,
- A production system with a job queue of a certain capacity as well as with machines of varying processing speeds is considered,
- Alternative priority heuristics are compared under the influence of job arrival rates, due date allowances and setup factors,
- Based on the simulation experiments, managerial insights for decision makers in industry are offered.

The remainder of this article is structured as follows. Section 2 describes the system, the job scheduling heuristics and the objective functions. Section 3 discusses the simulation methods, the experimental setup and the numerical results. The conclusions of this research and some possibilities for future research are presented in Sect. 4.

2 Materials and Methods

A production system, which is comprised, of an input queue and n parallel machines is studied in this research. We assume that the queue has a certain capacity f, and when is full, new jobs are declined. If there are available jobs positions in the input queue, jobs enter the queue and remain there until they are assigned to some machine for processing. A job cannot be processed simultaneously by more than one machines. No machine is allowed to idle if the input queue of pending jobs is not empty.

We assume parallel machines with different processing speeds and 100% availability, i.e. no machine failure, maintenance etc. is modelled. A machine processes incoming jobs one-by-one. The no-preemption and no-blocking assumption is also made; the processing of some job is completed in a single run and, at that time, the respective machine is made idle instantaneously.

We consider a setting where jobs are categorized to m job families, or classes. Jobs that belong to class j arrive dynamically to the system and the time between following arrivals is a random variable with average λ_j. Class j jobs have random processing times with average μ_j. Let the k-th job that arrives to the production system belong to class j; in that case, its due date d_k satisfies Eq. (1):

$$d_k = a_k + \delta_j \tag{1}$$

In Eq. (1), a_k denotes the arrival time of the k-th job and δ_j is the due date parameter of class j, i.e. a constant that takes on real values. A machine does not need to be setup if two adjacent jobs in the production schedule belong to the same class. Nonetheless, if production switches from some job family to another and the latter is j, then a sequence-independent setup of length σ_j is required.

2.1 Heuristic Priority Rules

A heuristic rule computes the priorities of jobs in the input queue in respect to some machine. The new scheduling data that are made available with a new arrival to the production system are taken into account to update the job priorities. Eight priority rules are examined in this article as follows:

- R1 - highest priority is given to job with minimum arrival time: $\min_l a_l$
- R2 - queueing job with minimum completion time has highest priority: $\min_l (a_l + p_l)$
- R3 - queueing job with shortest cycle time has highest priority: $\min_l (p_l + t_{now} - a_l)$
- R4 – queueing job with smallest setup time has highest priority: $\min_l s_l$
- R5 – queueing job with smallest critical ratio has highest priority: $\min_l ((d_l - t_{now})/p_l)$
- R6 – highest priority is given to job with minimum due date: $\min_l d_l$
- R7 – queueing job with minimum sum of processing and setup times: $\min_l (p_l + s_l)$
- R8 – queueing job with minimum slack time considering processing and setup: $\min_l (d_l - t_{now} - p_l - s_l)$

In the bulleted list above, p_l symbolizes the processing time of the l-th queueing job, t_{now} denotes the current time, s_l is the setup needed if the l-th job is selected and d_l is the due date of the l-th queueing job.

The following job assignment scheme is considered in this research. If there is a single job in the queue and a single machine then, normally, the former is assigned to the latter. If there is only one pending job and more than one idling machines, then the job is assigned to the machine with the smallest required setup; possible ties are broken at random. If there is more than one queueing job and only one idle machine, then the job with highest priority (as calculated by the employed priority rule) is assigned to that machine. The same applies to the case where there are more than one idling machines. In that case, if some job possesses highest priority for more than one machines then it is assigned to the one with smallest setup required (again, potentially ties are broken randomly).

2.2 Objective Functions

We evaluate the alternative priority rules of Sect. 2.1 based on the max cycle time, the mean earliness and the percent of the accepted jobs. Let a_k, d_k and C_k denote the arrival time, due date and completion time of the k-th job that arrived to the manufacturing system. In that case, its cycle time is $C_k - a_k$, its earliness equals $max(0, d_k - C_k)$.

If K is the total number of jobs that arrived to the system over some period of time and e are the jobs accepted by the system, then the max cycle time, the mean earliness and the percent of the accepted jobs is computed by Eqs. (2–4):

$$\max_k(C_k - a_k) \tag{2}$$

$$\frac{1}{K}\sum_{k=1}^{K}\max(0, d_k - C_k) \tag{3}$$

$$e/K \times 100\% \tag{4}$$

3 Results

The behaviour of the system described in Sect. 2 was investigated using the modelling framework of discrete-event simulation (DES). More specifically, the event-oriented approach of DES was adopted in this research. A DES simulation model that is based on the event-oriented approach consists of the state and event sets, the state-event transition function, the clock structure and the DES algorithm. The state-event transition function defines the next system state based on the occurrence of the current simulation event. The clock structure is comprised of the current simulation time, the next occurrence times of all admissible events and of the rules for updating the latter. The DES algorithm mimics the dynamic behaviour of the systems by producing a series of event occurrences, or equivalently, a series of state transitions.

The authors made use of the object-oriented language C + + and of the standard template library (STL) to implement the dynamic simulators of the examined system. The well-established Mersenne Twister random number generator was utilized in the stochastic simulations of this research.

Various source and header files constitute the implementations defining the random number generators together with the various elements that make up the model and execute the DES algorithm to produce the simulation experiment data. The authors used the compiler which is included in the integrated development environment (IDE) MS Visual Studio Community to convert source code files to executables.

A personal computer with 64-bit operating system, 4 GB RAM and 3.4 GHz CPU was used to conduct all numerical experiments of this article. The simulators that were developed for this research by the authors can be made available to the interested readers.

3.1 Design of Experiments

Seven simulation cases are studied in this investigation where each case relates to a production system with arrival and processing times that follow the exponential distribution. The system under consideration consists of a two-jobs capacity queue and three machines with different processing speeds of work: the first one is the fastest, while the third is the slowest and the second maintains an intermediate speed. We implemented a fractional factorial experimental design where we examine the effect of the following factors: the average interarrival times λ_j, the due date parameters δ_j and the setup parameters σ_j. For each factor we considered three levels; the complete description of the seven simulation cases is given in the numbered list below:

1. $n = 2$, $m = 3, f = 2$, $\mu_j = 1$, $\lambda_j = 10$, $\delta_j = 2$, $\sigma_j = 3$ for all j
2. $n = 2$, $m = 3, f = 2$, $\mu_j = 1$, $\lambda_j = 8$, $\delta_j = 2$, $\sigma_j = 3$ for all j
3. $n = 2$, $m = 3, f = 2$, $\mu_j = 1$, $\lambda_j = 6$, $\delta_j = 2$, $\sigma_j = 3$ for all j
4. $n = 2$, $m = 3, f = 2$, $\mu_j = 1$, $\lambda_j = 10$, $\delta_j = 4$, $\sigma_j = 3$ for all j
5. $n = 2$, $m = 3, f = 2$, $\mu_j = 1$, $\lambda_j = 10$, $\delta_j = 6$, $\sigma_j = 3$ for all j
6. $n = 2$, $m = 3, f = 2$, $\mu_j = 1$, $\lambda_j = 10$, $\delta_j = 2$, $\sigma_j = 1$ for all j
7. $n = 2$, $m = 3, f = 2$, $\mu_j = 1$, $\lambda_j = 10$, $\delta_j = 2$, $\sigma_j = 5$ for all j

The base simulation case is scenario (1) and we examine the effect of various levels of mean interarrival times in cases (2), (3). In simulation cases (4), (5) and (6), (7) we study the effect on system performance of various due date and setup parameter levels, respectively. All priority rules elaborated in Sect. 2 are considered in all simulation cases.

Ten independent replications were conducted for every simulation scenario and job priority rule. In order to allow the simulation to reach steady state, all replications were executed up to the completion of 50 thousand manufacturing jobs yielding a total of 7 (simulation cases) $\times$ 8 (priority rules) $\times$ 10 (simulation replications) = 560 experiments.

3.2 Examining the Effect of the Mean Interarrival Times

The max cycle time, the mean earliness and the percent of accepted jobs for each job priority rule and for simulation scenarios 1–3 is shown in Figs. 1, 2 and 3. A positive correlation between the mean time between arrivals and the mean earliness is observed which can be attributed to the resulting workload imposed in the production system.

The dissimilarities between the alternative job priority rules are easier to distinguish in cases with relatively small average times between arrivals. The R7 priority rule outperforms all other heuristics regarding the objective of mean earliness in cases 1–3. When considering the standard deviations of the statistical data, it is inferred that the aforementioned superior performance of R7 is statistically slightly different from the performance of R4 in cases 1–3.

A noteworthy observation from Fig. 1 is the considerable poor performance of job priority heuristics R2, R3 and R7 in terms of the metric of max cycle time.

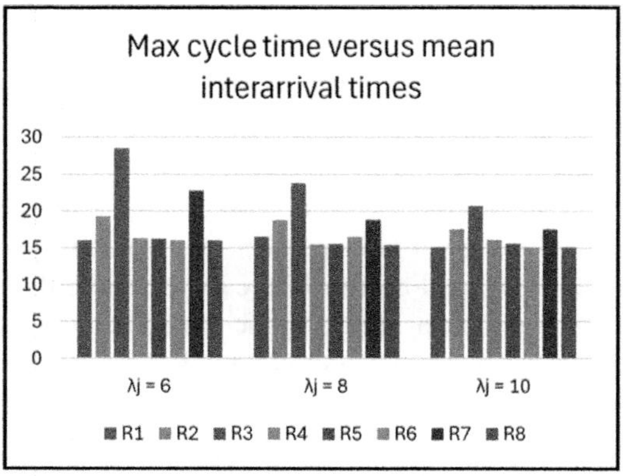

Fig. 1. Max cycle time versus mean interarrival times.

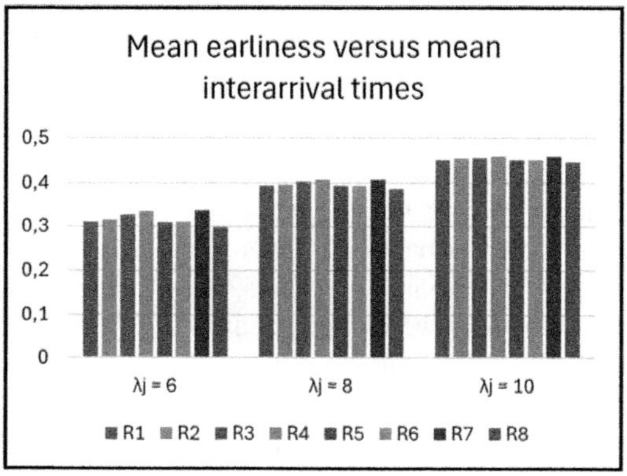

Fig. 2. Mean earliness versus mean interarrival times.

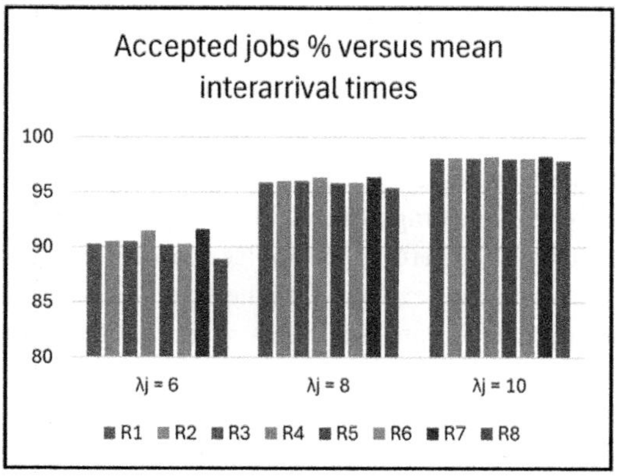

Fig. 3. Accepted jobs % versus mean interarrival times.

3.3 Examining the Effect of the Due Date Parameters

The max cycle time, the mean earliness and the percent of accepted jobs are invariant to changes of the due date parameters for all priority rules except R5, which subtracts the current time from the due date of the l-th queueing job and divides the difference with the processing time of the l-th queueing job.

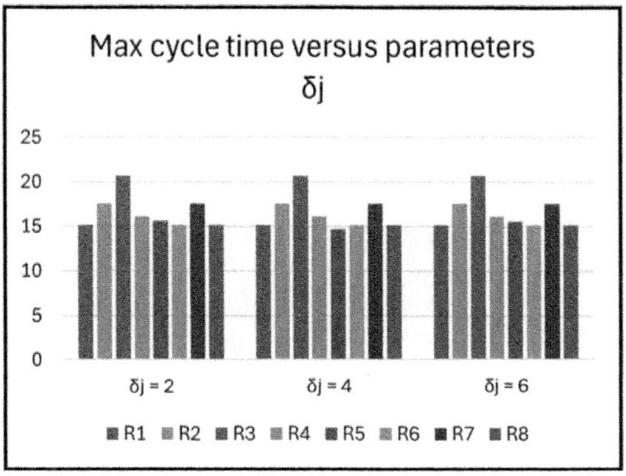

Fig. 4. Max cycle time versus parameters δ_j.

Regarding max cycle time, the R8 heuristic ranks first (mean 15.11, standard deviation 0,02) in two of the simulation cases. Regarding the percent of accepted jobs metric, the R7 heuristic ranks first, as it allows the production system to accept and process the greater number of jobs.

Eventually, regarding the mean earliness metric, R7 heuristic ranks first again; afterwards, the following times for mean earliness are ensured by the R4 and R3 rules for the production system under investigation.

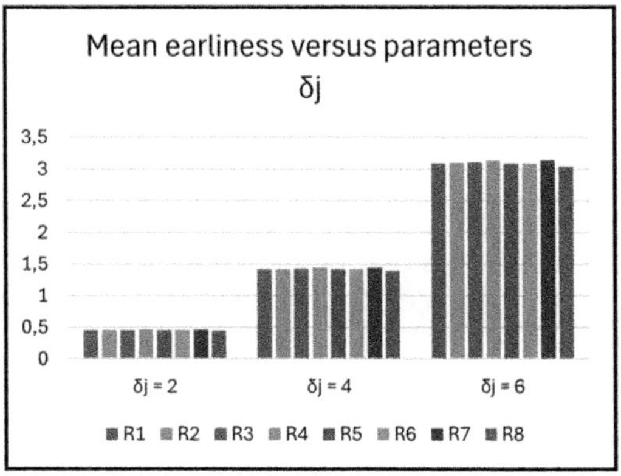

Fig. 5. Mean earliness versus parameters δ_j.

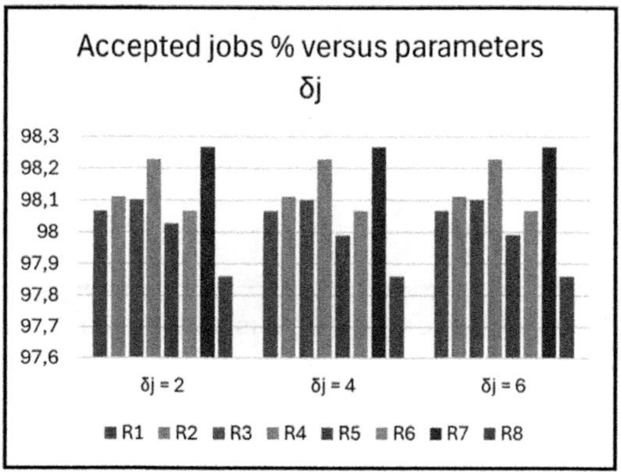

Fig. 6. Accepted jobs % versus parameters δ_j.

3.4 Examining the Effect of the Setup Parameters

The max cycle time, the mean earliness and the percent of accepted jobs of all priority rules for simulation scenarios with varying parameters σ_j, are shown in Figs. 7–9. Parameters σ_j determine the length of the setups; this explains a negative correlation of the setup parameters with mean earliness (refer to Fig. 8). As parameter σ_j gets smaller, the setup times decrease, and this causes the performance differences between the alternative heuristics to become less distinct.

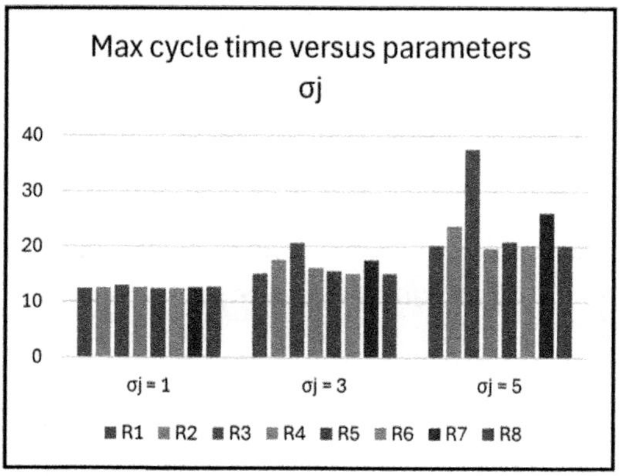

Fig. 7. Max cycle time versus parameters σ_j.

The R7 heuristic ranks first in terms of the mean earliness and the percent of accepted jobs. R7 is a setup-oriented heuristic, however it is noteworthy that the rest of the setup-oriented heuristics, R4 and R8, perform relatively poor regarding mean earliness and the percent of accepted jobs.

The R5 dispatching rule excels in terms of the max cycle time metric for the case with $\sigma_j = 1$, while it is outperformed by R8 in the simulation case with $\sigma_j = 3$. Regarding the case with $\sigma_j = 5$, R4 ensures that the production system achieves the shortest max cycle time. Finally, it is interesting to point out the dramatic performance deterioration of R3 for the metric of the max cycle time, as the setup parameters increase.

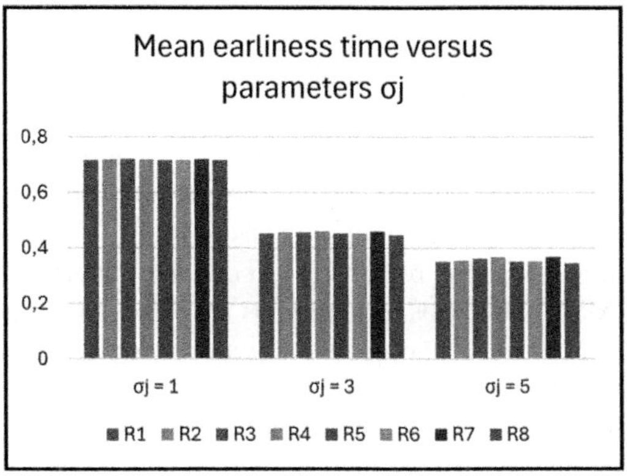

Fig. 8. Mean earliness versus parameters σ_j.

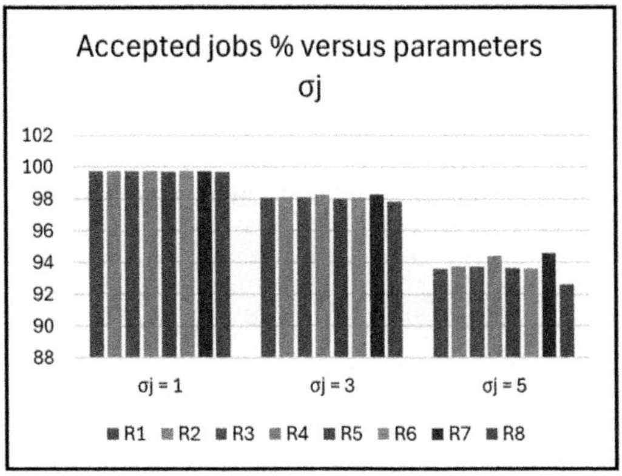

Fig. 9. Accepted jobs % versus parameters σ_j.

4 Discussion and Research Perspectives

In this article we used simulation to compare eight priority rules in a production system with parallel machines and setups. The major findings that can guide managerial decision making in industry are presented as follows.

Firstly, our simulation data indicate that effective production scheduling is primarily advantageous when the plant is subjected to considerable stress, e.g. because of high rate of incoming jobs, prolonged setup times etc. In cases where the workload in the plant is moderate, the differences between the various scheduling heuristics are dimmed and the importance of the overall production scheduling function fades. The numerical results suggest a negative correlation between max cycle time and average earliness.

In general, setup-aware job priority rules perform better than basic heuristics such as first-in-first-out, critical-ratio etc. However, there are some exceptions to that; the R7 and R8 rules were found to perform poorly in respect to the metrics of max cycle time, mean earliness and the percent of accepted jobs respectively.

For minimizing max cycle time it is observed that the setup length when switching production from some job family to another is the primary consideration; the R4, R5 and R8 rules give the best results for this objective function in the three simulation cases. Respectively, for maximizing mean earliness and the percent of accepted jobs, R7 heuristic outperforms in all of the simulation cases.

A plausible extension of this research is to examine alternative production system settings such as flexible job shops, open shops etc. The investigation of different job priority heuristics and/or alternate objective functions would also be of interest. Finally, one could extend this work by considering intelligent computational approaches for priority rule selection based on current system state and/or design and construction of new scheduling heuristics.

Acknowledgments. The project TAEDR-0535864 "Network of Excellence for the Development Dissemination and Application of Digital Transformation Technologies in the Greek Manufacturing Industry" is carried out within the framework of the National Recovery and Resilience Plan Greece 2.0, funded by the European Union - NextGenerationEU.

Disclosure of Interests.. No conflicts of interests are reported for this research.

References

1. Cervenanska, Z., Vazan, P., Juhas, M., Juhasova, B.: Multi-criteria optimization in operations scheduling applying selected priority rules. Appl. Sci. **11**(6), 2783 (2021). https://doi.org/10.3390/app11062783
2. Chien, C.-F., Lan, Y.-B.: Agent-based approach integrating deep reinforcement learning and hybrid genetic algorithm for dynamic scheduling for Industry 35 smart production. Comput. Ind. Eng. **162**, 107782 (2021). https://doi.org/10.1016/j.cie.2021.107782
3. Engenhausen, F., Lodding, H.: Managing sequence-dependent setup times-the target conflict between output rate, WIP and fluctuating throughput times for setup cycles. Prod. Plann. Control **33**(1), 84–100 (2022). https://doi.org/10.1080/09537287.2020.1822642
4. Fan, H., Xiong, H., Goh, M.: Genetic programming-based hyper-heuristic for solving dynamic job shop scheduling problem with extended technical precedence constraints. Comput. Oper. Res. **134**, 105401 (2021). https://doi.org/10.1016/j.cor.2021.105401
5. Li, Y., Gu, W., Yuan, M., Tang, Y.: Real-time data-driven dynamic scheduling for flexible job shop with insufficient transportation resources using hybrid deep Q network. Robot. Comput. Integr. Manuf. **74**, 102283 (2022). https://doi.org/10.1016/j.rcim.2021.102283
6. Liu, R., Piplani, R., Toro, C.: Deep reinforcement learning for dynamic scheduling of a flexible job shop. Int. J. Prod. Res. **60**(13), 4049–4069 (2022). https://doi.org/10.1080/00207543.2022.2058432

7. Sadeghi, P., Rebelo, R.D., Ferreira, J.S.: Using variable neighbourhood descent and genetic algorithms for sequencing mixed-model assembly systems in the footwear industry. Operat. Res. Perspect. **8**, 100193 (2021). https://doi.org/10.1016/j.orp.2021.100193
8. Shady, S., Kaihara, T., Fujii, N., Kokuryo, D.: A novel feature selection for evolving compact dispatching rules using genetic programming for dynamic job shop scheduling. Int. J. Prod. Res. **60**(13), 4025–4048 (2022). https://doi.org/10.1080/00207543.2022.2053603
9. Xanthopoulos, A.S., Koulouriotis, D.E.: Cluster analysis and neural network-based metamodeling of priority rules for dynamic sequencing. J. Intell. Manuf. **29**(1), 69–91 (2018). https://doi.org/10.1007/s10845-015-1090-0
10. Xanthopoulos, A.S., Koulouriotis, D.E.: Simulation study of scheduling heuristics for parallel machines with sequence-independent setups. IFAC-PapersOnLine **55**(10), 526–531 (2022). https://doi.org/10.1016/j.ifacol.2022.09.447
11. Xie, J., Li, X., Gao, L., Gui, L.: A new neighbourhood structure for job shop scheduling problems. Int. J. Prod. Res. (2022). https://doi.org/10.1080/00207543.2022.2060772
12. Zhang, J., Ding, G., Zou, Y., Qin, S., Fu, J.: Review of job shop scheduling research and its new perspectives under Industry 4.0. J. Intell. Manuf. **30**(4), 1809–1830 (2019). https://doi.org/10.1007/s10845-017-1350-2
13. Paraschos, P.D., Xanthopoulos, A.S., Koulinas, G.K., Koulouriotis, D.: Machine learning integrated design and operation management for resilient circular manufacturing systems. Comput. Ind. Eng. **167**, 107971 (2022). https://doi.org/10.1016/j.cie.2022.107971
14. Xanthopoulos, A.S., Chnitidis, G., Koulouriotis, D.E.: Reinforcement learning-based adaptive production control of manufacturing systems. J. Ind. Prod. Eng. **36**(5), 313–323 (2019). https://doi.org/10.1080/21681015.2019.1647301
15. Katsios, D., Xanthopoulos, A.S., Koulouriotis, D.E., Kiatipis, A.: A simulation optimisation tool and its production/inventory control application. Int. J. Simulat. Modell. **17**(2), 257–270 (2018). https://doi.org/10.2507/IJSIMM17(2)425
16. Haned, A., Kerdali, A., Boudhar, M.: Scheduling on identical machines with preemption and setup times. Int. J. Prod. Res. **62**(1–2), 444–459 (2024). https://doi.org/10.1080/00207543.2023.2276825
17. Gebreyesus, G., Fellek, G., Farid, A., Fujimura, S., Yoshie, O.: Gated-Attention model with reinforcement learning for solving dynamic job shop scheduling problem **18**: 932-944 (2023). https://doi.org/10.1002/tee.23788
18. Chen, R., Li, W., Yang, H.: A deep reinforcement learning framework based on an attention mechanism and disjunctive graph embedding for the job-shop scheduling problem. IEEE Trans. Industr. Inf. **19**(2), 1322–1331 (2023). https://doi.org/10.1109/TII.2022.3167380
19. Wang, H., Peng, T., Nassehi, A., Tang, R.: A data-driven simulation-optimization framework for generating priority dispatching rules in dynamic job shop scheduling with uncertainties. J. Manuf. Syst. **70**, 288–308 (2023). https://doi.org/10.1016/j.jmsy.2023.08.001
20. Palombarini, J. A., Barsce, J. C., Martinez, E. C.: Chapter 14- Simulation-based generation of rescheduling knowledge using a cognitive architecture. Designing Smart Manufacturing Systems, 345–397 (2023). https://doi.org/10.1016/B978-0-32-399208-4.00023-4
21. Xiong, H., Wang, H., Shi, S., Chen, K.: Comparison study of dispatching rules and heuristics for online scheduling of single machine scheduling problem with predicted release time jobs. Expert Syst. Appl. **243**, 122752 (2024). https://doi.org/10.1016/j.eswa.2023.122752
22. Zhang, M., Wang, L., Qiu, F., Liu, X.: Dynamic scheduling for flexible job shop with insufficient transportation resources via graph neural network and deep reinforcement learning. Comput. Ind. Eng. **186**, 109718 (2023). https://doi.org/10.1016/j.cie.2023.109718

iWMS: A Warehouse Management System for a Goods-to-Person Warehouse Automation

Dimitra Zotou[1], Stefanos Papadam[1(✉)], Andreas Kargakos[1], Ioannis Kostavelis[1,2], Maria Bliantidou[3], Dimitrios Giakoumis[1], Dimosthenis Ioannidis[1], and Dimitrios Tzovaras[1]

[1] Centre for Research and Technology Hellas, Information Technologies Institute (CERTH/ITI), 6 km Charilaou-Thermi, Thessaloniki, Greece
{dzotou,sgpapadam,akargakos,gkostave,dgiakoum,djoannid, Dimitrios.Tzovaras}@iti.gr

[2] International Hellenic University, P. Kanellopoulou 2, Katerini, Greece
gkostave@ihu.gr

[3] TETTIX - N.MORENOS SINGLE MEMBER PC, Industrial Area of Sindos, Zone C, OT 48A, 57400 Thessaloniki, Greece
info@tettix.info

Abstract. Recently, there has been a surge in the development of advanced warehouse management systems that seamlessly incorporate robotized technologies. These robots have the capability to operate independently or collaborate with human staff to enhance the efficiency of items picking and storage. The paper at hand, introduces an intelligent Warehouse Management System, denoted as iWMS, designed for a goods-to-person warehouse environment. The system is configured to retrieve data of standard format compatible with commercial WMS through an application programming interface (API), while maintaining control over the robotic processes. This work aims to address the development of a software that will analyze incoming and outgoing orders and allocate the task of collecting and distributing bins with an Autonomous Mobile Robot (AMR). The proposed software performs a systematic analysis of incoming orders, linking them with the respective fiducial markers that contain detailed information about the precise location of the relevant bin within the warehouse. Subsequently, the system assigns the task of orders collection to one or more AMRs, taking into account their availability and current positions within the warehouse. This is achieved using an algorithm that maximizes efficiency by optimizing both execution time and travel distances. Additionally, the application consistently updates the stock in the database based on the products identified within the bins, ensuring accurate and real-time stock counting in the warehouse database. The ultimate goal of the iWMS is to provide an easy-to-use tool, allowing the seamless co-existence between the workers and the robotic platforms in a common workplace. This iWMS is part of a robotic warehouse solution currently undergoing testing in simulation.

Keywords: Warehouse Management System · Order picking · Robotics · goods-to-person

I. Kostavelis et al. (Eds.): ICSC 2024, CCIS 2110, pp. 148–160, 2025.
https://doi.org/10.1007/978-3-031-69344-1_11

1 Introduction

With the rise of e-commerce [9] and the increasing complexity of supply chain networks [32], there is a growing demand for innovative technologies that can streamline warehouse processes, improve efficiency, and enhance overall productivity [29]. Traditional warehouse management practices are often labor-intensive and susceptible to human error, leading to inefficiencies in inventory control, order fulfillment, and logistics management [28]. However, advancements in robotics, automation, and artificial intelligence (AI) have paved the way for novel solutions that promise to revolutionize the way warehouses are managed and operated [10], [12].

Technological developments in robotics, automation and artificial intelligence present viable solutions to these problems and can help warehouse operations to achieve new levels of efficiency. In order to decrease the need for manual labour and increase throughput rates, robotic arms [24] and autonomous mobile robots (AMRs) [18] made possible the autonomous material handling, order picking and inventory replenishment.

The goods-to-person systems (G2P) are designed to optimize the distribution of goods within the warehouse by bringing items directly to the human operator, rather than requiring workers to navigate the warehouse floor to locate and retrieve products [19]. By utilizing solutions like robotic arms, conveyors, and automated storage and retrieval systems (AS/RS) [13], goods-to-person systems drastically reduce picking times and minimize human error [31].

In order for the advanced technologies to be integrated into warehouses, a Human-Machine Interaction (HMI) is needed [16], like touchscreens or voice commands, facilitating efficient communication and control between humans and robotic systems. Additionally, real-time monitoring and AR [22] provide operators with actionable insights, while predictive analytics empower decision-making [26].

The contributions of our work are summarized as follows:

- A complete software system designed to optimize workflow efficiency, streamline order fulfillment processes, and facilitate collaboration between human workers and robotic platforms in a goods-to-person warehouse environment.
- Accurate and real-time stock counting by updating the warehouse database.

The rest of this paper is organized as follows: Sect. 2 presents an overview of the current state-of-art methods on warehouse management systems and their cooperation with robots. Section 3 contains a comprehensive description of our proposed architecture and proves the efficiency of our method. Conclusions along with a discussion on future work are drawn in Sect. 4.

2 Related Work

An approach to automate control systems with minimal auxiliary robots and optimized paths for production processes using the EVIN methodology, combining neural networks and ant colony optimization (ACO) is presented in [25].

It introduces an analytical block to predict optimal robot numbers and evaluates the system across three scenarios: i) without the block, ii) with it, and iii) with ACO in different application increments, particularly focusing on mobile robots like assistants and warehouse units, with potential for broader application and future expansions. The improvement of AMRs in intralogistic processes implementation is presented in [27], by addressing programming costs, process requirements, and operator interaction limitations, offering a comprehensive solution through innovative interface design for programming AMR and operator-AMR communication as well as a tool to manage multiple AMRs and operators efficiently, optimizing task allocation and scheduling.

A decentralized Automated Guided Vehicle (AGV) fleet architecture and task allocation method are introduced in [33] to enable dynamic task allocation and reallocation within the fleet. The proposed algorithm allows AGVs to bid for tasks and adjust distribution in response to system changes. This contributes to flexible factory automation, demonstrating collaboration between AGV fleets and other machines in smart factories.

An iWMS was implemented in [14], by using an Xamarin IOT application for exchanging information with end-users, a web application for database communication and a robot for product transportation. The work in [23] suggests an IoT-based WMS coupled with advanced data analytics, in order to address the difficulties of managing complicated and customized customer orders. In order to improve operation, a smart WMS is installed in [35] in a large distribution center that uses optimization algorithms and artificial intelligence. The system encompasses all aspects of the warehouse process, such as order picking, stock planning, and transportation, and uses anomaly detection to increase productivity.

This paper introduces iWMS, an intelligent Warehouse Management System for goods-to-person warehouses. The system utilises an API to retrieve data from commercial inventory management, while maintaining control over robotic operations. The warehouse is strategically divided into two zones. First, robots manage an unattended area, while the second is a collection area where humans retrieve goods transported by robots. Our goal is to create software that analyses orders and assigns bin collection and distribution tasks to an AMR. The software analyses orders and links them to fiducial markers for accurate warehouse bin location information. Next, the system assigns order collection to selected AMRs based on their availability and warehouse location. Our algorithm maximises efficiency by optimising execution time and travel distances. The warehouse database is updated with accurate and real-time stock counts based on products identified in bins. The iWMS simplifies collaboration between workers and robotic platforms in shared workspaces with an easy-to-use tool.

3 Methodology

The primary objective of the purposed architecture is to optimize goods-to-person activities inside a warehouse setting. To achieve this, an intelligent WMS is implemented, i) able to send and retrieve data to an existing WMS; ii) having control of robot operations inside the warehouse iii) analyzing orders, optimizing the collection of them by using the Travel Salesman Problem (TSP); and iv) keeping tack of stock levels in real-time.

3.1 System Architecture

Django [2], renowned for its versatility and scalability, is an open-source web framework written in Python [11]. Its rich set of features, including its built-in administrative interface and robust security measures, make it an ideal choice for constructing complex web applications. In addition, Django provides support for creating application programming interfaces (APIs) through the Django REST Framework [3]. The Django REST Framework is a toolkit that extends the capabilities of Django in order to make the development of web APIs easier. It offers a collection of tools and utilities that can improve the speed and efficiency with which RESTful APIs are constructed. With the help of Django REST Framework, there is the ability to easily serialise Django models into JSON or other formats, define custom endpoints, manage authentication and permissions.

In conjunction with Django, we integrate the MySQL database management system [5] to store and manage our application's data efficiently. MySQL, a widely-used relational database, offers numerous advantages such as reliability, scalability, and excellent performance. The integration with Django is simple, due to Django's built-in support for numerous database engines, including MySQL. [15].

The utilization of MySQL in conjunction with Django also benefits from the user-friendly interface provided by phpMyAdmin [30]. phpMyAdmin, a web-based administration tool written in PHP, simplifies database management tasks by offering a graphical interface for performing operations such as database creation, querying, and administration. This integration streamlines the development process and enhances productivity by providing developers with a convenient environment for database management tasks.

Furthermore, Apache2 serves as web server, facilitating the delivery of web content to users [7]. Apache2 is renowned for its stability, performance, and extensibility. Its seamless integration with Django ensures optimal performance and reliability.

By utilising the aforementioned tools, iWMS is developed, with the exception of robot communication. It is possible to establish a connection between the iWMS and the Robotic Operating System (ROS) [6] by utilising the roslibJS [8] roslib2dJS libraries. These libraries offer the essential tools that facilitate the interconnections and communication between the various modules and the primary nodes of the application. These libraries communicate with Rosbridge via WebSocket and allows publishing, subscribing, service calls, and other ROS functions [21]. The architecture of the system is shown in Fig. 1.

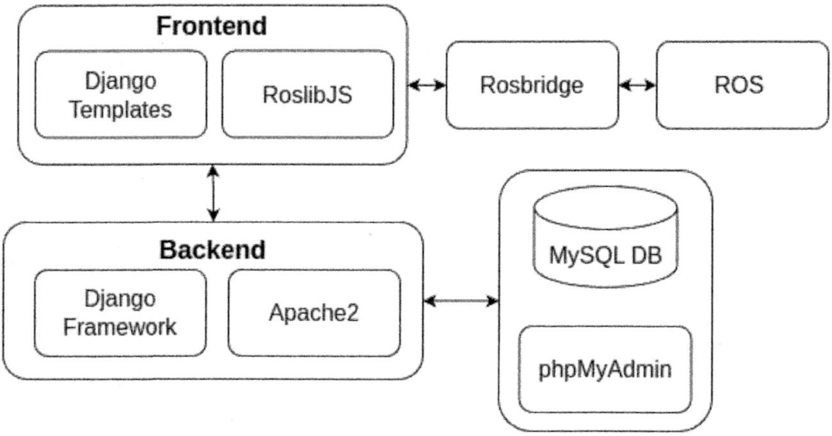

Fig. 1. iWMS architecture

3.2 Warehouse Configuration

The designed warehouse is divided into two zones. The first is an unattended area run entirely by robots, while the second is a collection area where human workers receive bins brought by robots. The equipment for the warehouse was designed using the Blender software [1]. Initially, shelves were constructed. These shelves were of the dexion kind, with a width of 2000 mm and a height of 4500 mm. Each dexion unit contains 72 bins of items, each with only one type of product inside. The quantity of 108 dexion units were placed in Gazebo simulation environment [4], as shown in Fig. 2. The structure of the warehouse was based on a traditional layout [34].

The collecting orders workstation area is located outside of the shelves and consists of six workstations where human people await delivery bins from the AMR in order to execute incoming orders. When the collecting operation is complete, the AMR picks up the bins and restores them to their original location in the warehouse.

The processes and procedures that take place in a warehouse is the first stage of an automated warehouse system. To establish a foundation for the development of an automated system, it is necessary to enhance a warehouse by assigning code names during the solution's development process, as it is shown in Fig. 3a

- The warehouse we are referring to, as it is possible to have more than one. The warehouse is symbolized with an integer.
- The warehouse floor presented as an integer.
- The warehouse's section symbolized as a letter from the Latin alphabet.
- The dexion's aisle as an integer.
- The rack as two letters from the Latin alphabet.

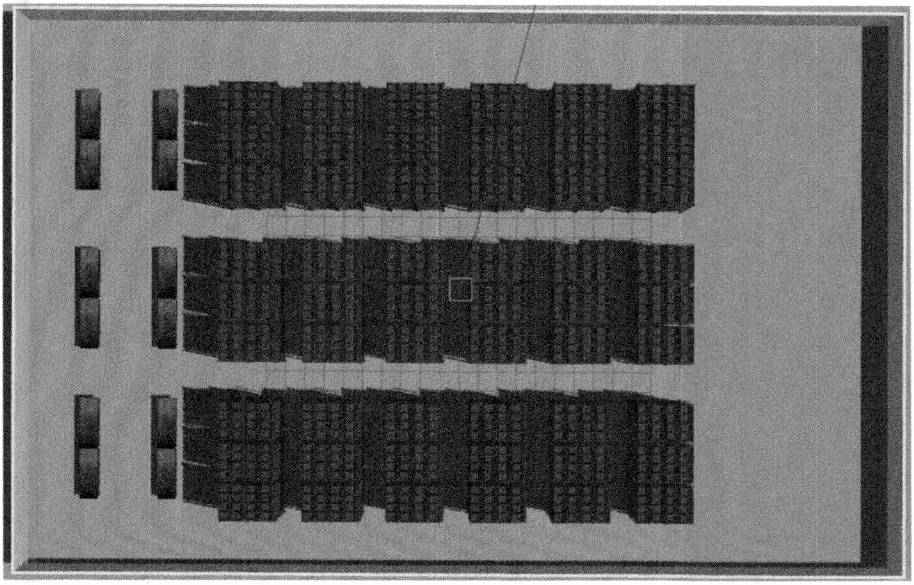

Fig. 2. Warehouse layout in simulation

Besides the shelves, code names should, also, be assigned to bins. Each bin is labelled with dexion's code name, the floor number (numbered 1 through 9) and its specific location front or back, indicated by positions 1 to 4, labelled as F1–F4 or B1–B4), as shown in Fig. 3b.

As illustrated in Fig. 4, each bin features a grid of fiducial markers, specifically ArUco markers [17], along with a barcode on the front side. The barcode indicates the type of product that will be inside the bin, a piece of information stored in the database. Employees at the workstation use this information to verify if the bin contains the requested product. The grid of ArUco markers is intended to assist the robot with the pick-and-place operation. In addition to the bins, each shelf of the dexion is also equipped with ArUco markers. Essentially, four grids of markers are placed, one for each bin row, so that in case a bin is missing, the AMR will have a reference of the bin's location. Lastly, an ArUco marker is placed on the floor in front of every column of bins, allowing the AMR to know where to go when the iWMS sends the request for collection/return.

3.3 iWMS Database

The iWMS database was build in phpMyAdmin, based on the architecture described in Sect. 3.1. The database has been meticulously planned and executed in order to fulfil the precise demands of our intelligent warehouse management system. The system functions as a centralised repository for all data pertaining to employee records, supplier information, stock levels and order processing. The utilisation of this extensive database empowers the system to execute staff

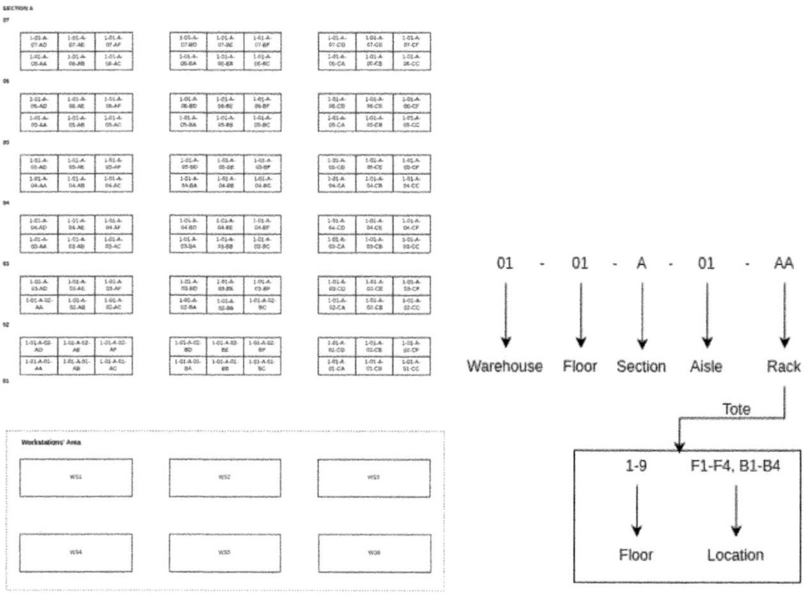

(a) Warehouse configuration (b) Dexion configuration example

Fig. 3. Warehouse classification

administration, order processing and inventory monitoring with precision and adaptability. In order to optimise data organisation and storage, the database incorporates a number of crucial tables. Figure 5 displays the key information contained within the database, along with its corresponding relationships.

Users have the option to add data to the iWMS manually, one-by-one. Nevertheless, to ensure smooth operation of the integrated iWMS, data acquisition can be done either by uploading a CSV file directly to the database or by establishing communication with an existing WMS. The first method is straightforward: data is organized into CSV files for each database class and uploaded using a graphical user interface (GUI). However, the second method poses more challenges.

The aforementioned Django REST framework (Sect. 3.1), provides an API to enable communication with external systems, making it a robust solution for incorporating additional functionality and data into web applications. This integration process involves several key steps. First, some required libraries, such as "requests" or "http.client", must be installed to facilitate the communication with the external API. Next, a serializer is created within Django REST framework to define the structure of the data that will be received from the external API. Subsequently, a custom Django REST framework view is developed to: handle HTTP requests to the external API, process the responses, and serialize the data for facilitation within the Django application. This view is then mapped to a URL within the Django application's URL routing configuration.

Fig. 4. Bin with fiducial markers and barcode in the warehouse

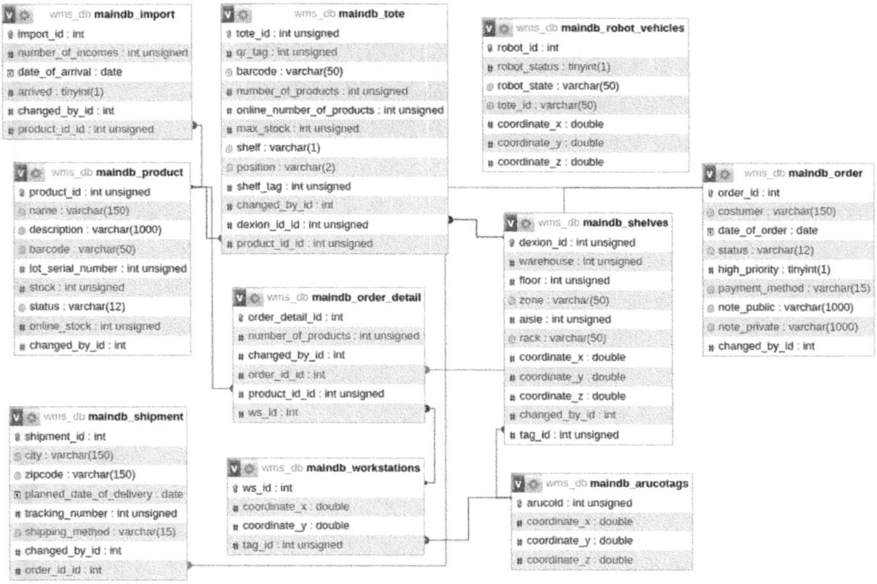

Fig. 5. Database important tables.

Throughout this process, thorough testing is essential to ensure the integration of the functions as intended, with appropriate error handling and consideration for edge cases.

The home page of the iWMS on desktop is depicted in Fig. 6 after the database has been provided with the necessary information. In addition to the desktop computer, the iWMS can also be utilised from a tablet or a smartphone. The login page of iWMS for smartphone is shown in Fig. 7.

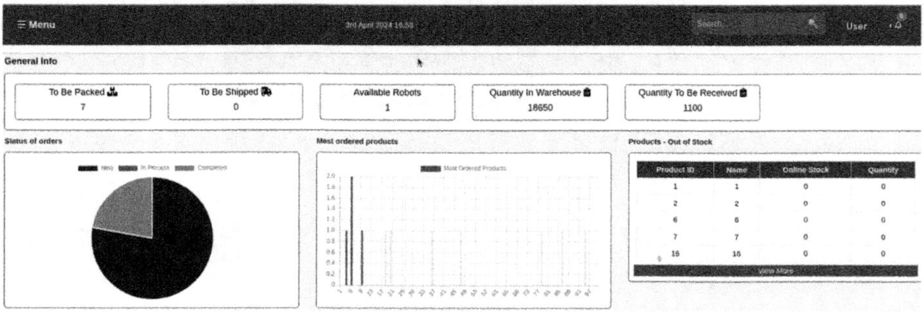

Fig. 6. iWMS

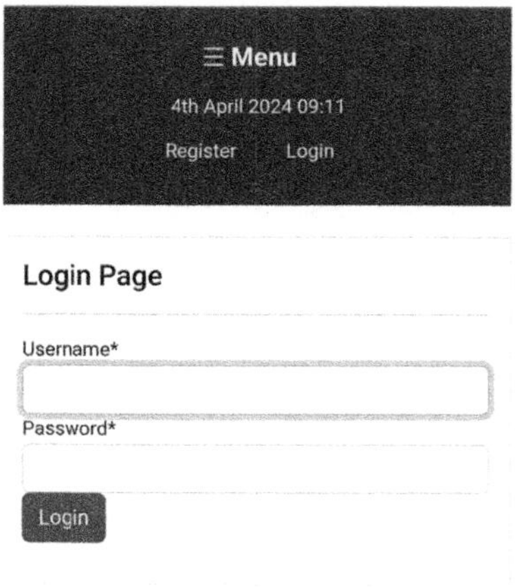

Fig. 7. Login page from smartphone

3.4 AMR's Mission Planning

The iWMS establishes communication with ROS using the roslibJS and roslib2dJS libraries. This allows it to transmit information about the bins that the AMR needs to collect. The AMR will provide feedback to the workers to ensure they are kept informed about its operations during this time period. An illustration of the procedure that is depicted can be found in Fig. 8. The AMR provides iWMS with details about its precise location and its current operation. When the AMR retrieves a bin, the database is promptly updated to reflect the fact that the bin is no longer situated at the location where it was initially placed.

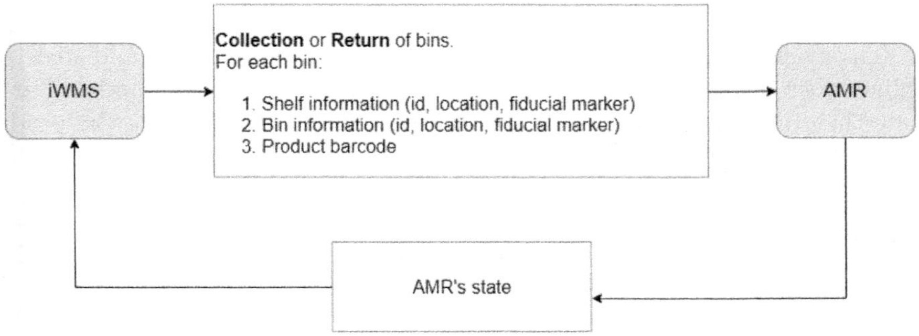

Fig. 8. Communication between iWMS and AMR

When the AMR has collected all of the requested bins, the iWMS displays a pop-up question to the user, asking whether the AMR should proceed to the workstation or remain in its position to receive another request, as shown in Fig. 9. In the first option, when the AMR arrives at the workstation, it locates the bins on the requested workstation for the picker to collect the quantity. After that, the AMR retrieves the bins again and returns them to their original position. When the AMR has completed its task, it notifies the iWMS that it is ready for the next task.

3.5 Real-Time Stock Monitoring

Before iWMS sends a request for tote collection, the user collects all of the orders that need to be carried out. In case a product is requested more than once, the algorithm will treat it as a single item, with the exception of situations in which the bin does not contain the required quantity of products that have been requested. Then, the iWMS checks the availability of the AMR, its initial position, and the bins' position, utilizing the Traveling Salesman Problem (TSP) [20], in order to optimize the order the bins will be collected, minimizing execution time and distance.

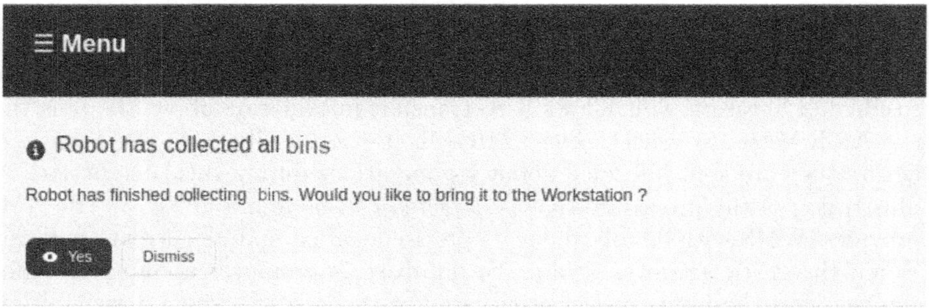

Fig. 9. System notification when the AMR has finished collecting bins

The available stock of each product is clarified as *online stock* and *stock*. The online stock of the products that have been requested has been updated at the time that the request is sent, removing the requested quantity of the product. This is important, because the system needs to be aware of whether or not there is sufficient stock in case other request is made while the previous one is still being processed. When the pickers receive the requested bins and remove the necessary quantity of a product, they update the *stock*, confirming the updated online stock.

4 Conclusion

In this paper, we present iWMS, an intelligent Warehouse Management System tailored for goods-to-person warehouse environments. With the possibility of integration with commercial WMS and having control over robotic operations, iWMS offers a comprehensive solution for efficient warehouse management. By strategically dividing the warehouse into two zones and employing the suggested architecture, iWMS optimizes task assignment, enhances order processing, and ensures real-time stock management.

The development of iWMS represents a significant step towards streamlining warehouse operations and facilitating seamless collaboration between human workers and robotic platforms. The system's user-friendly interface and emphasis on efficiency make it a valuable asset for modern warehouse environments seeking to enhance productivity and reduce operational costs.

In the near future, we are planning to conduct real-world testing and validation of the iWMS in different warehouse environments to assess its performance, scalability, and usability.

Acknowledgments. This research was carried out as part of the project "BUTLER" (Project code: KMP6-0234159) under the framework of the Action "Investment Plans of Innovation" of the Operational Program "Central Macedonia 2014-2020", that is co-funded by the European Regional Development Fund and Greece.

References

1. Blender 4.0. http://www.blender.org/, accessed: 2024-03-15
2. Django. http://www.djangoproject.com/, accessed: 2024-03-15
3. Django rest framework. https://www.django-rest-framework.org/, accessed: 2024-03-15
4. Gazebo. https://gazebosim.org/, accessed: 2024-03-15
5. Mysql database management system. https://www.mysql.com/, accessed: 2024-03-15
6. Ros - robot operating system. https://www.ros.org/, accessed: 2024-03-15
7. Beginning PHP, Apache, MySQL Web Development. John Wiley & Sons (2004)
8. Alisher, K., Alexander, K., Alexandr, B.: Control of the mobile robots with ros in robotics courses. Proc. Eng. **100**, 1475–1484 (2015). https://doi.org/10.1016/j.proeng.2015.01.519
9. Balaska, V., Tsiakas, K., Giakoumis, D., Kostavelis, I., Folinas, D., Gasteratos, A., Tzovaras, D.: A viewpoint on the challenges and solutions for driverless last-mile delivery. Machines **10**, 1059 (2022). https://doi.org/10.3390/machines10111059
10. Bogue, R.: Warehouse robot market boosted by covid pandemic and technological innovations. Ind. Robot Int. J. Robot. Res. Appl. **49**(2), 181–186 (2022)
11. Dauzon, S., Bendoraitis, A., Ravindran, A.: Django: web development with Python. Packt Publishing Ltd (2016)
12. Dhaliwal, A.: The Rise of Automation and Robotics in Warehouse Management, pp. 63–72 (10 2020). https://doi.org/10.1201/9781003032410-5
13. Dhaliwal, A.: The rise of automation and robotics in warehouse management. In: Transforming Management Using Artificial Intelligence Techniques, pp. 63–72. CRC Press (2020)
14. Dhouioui, M., Frikha, T.: Intelligent warehouse management system. In: 2020 IEEE International Conference on Design & Test of Integrated Micro & Nano-Systems (DTS). pp. 1–5. IEEE (2020)
15. DuBois, P.: MySQL. Addison-Wesley (2013)
16. Fabian Lorson, A.F., Hübner, A.: New team mates in the warehouse: human interactions with automated and robotized systems. IISE Trans. **55**(5), 536–553 (2023). https://doi.org/10.1080/24725854.2022.2072545
17. Garrido-Jurado, S., Muñoz-Salinas, R., Madrid-Cuevas, F., Marńn-Jiménez, M.: Automatic generation and detection of highly reliable fiducial markers under occlusion. Pattern Recogn. **47**(6), 2280–2292 (2014) 10.1016/j.patcog.2014.01.005, https://www.sciencedirect.com/science/article/pii/S0031320314000235
18. Ghelichi, Z., Kilaru, S.: Analytical models for collaborative autonomous mobile robot solutions in fulfillment centers. Appl. Math. Model. **91**, 438–457 (2021)
19. Hameed, H.M., Rashid, A.T., Al Amry, K.A.: Automatic storage and retrieval system using the optimal path algorithm. In: The 3rd Scientific Conf. of Electrical and Electronic Engineering Researches (SCEEER). pp. 15–16 (2020)
20. Hoffman, K.L., Padberg, M., Rinaldi, G., et al.: Traveling salesman problem. Encyclop. Operat. Res. Manag. Sci. **1**, 1573–1578 (2013)
21. Islam, M.T., Hameem, I.R., Saha, S., Chowdhury, M.J.R., Deowan, M.E.: A simulation of a robot operating system based autonomous wheelchair with web based hmi using rosbridge. In: 2023 3rd International Conference on Robotics, Electrical and Signal Processing Techniques (ICREST). pp. 175–180 (2023). https://doi.org/10.1109/ICREST57604.2023.10070046

22. Konstantinidis, F.K., Kansizoglou, I., Santavas, N., Mouroutsos, S.G., Gasteratos, A.: Marma: a mobile augmented reality maintenance assistant for fast-track repair procedures in the context of industry 4.0. Machines **8**(4), 88 (2020). https://doi.org/10.3390/machines8040088
23. Lee, C., Lv, Y., Ng, K., Ho, W., Choy, K.: Design and application of internet of things-based warehouse management system for smart logistics. Int. J. Prod. Res. **56**(8), 2753–2768 (2018). https://doi.org/10.1080/00207543.2017.1394592
24. Liang, C., et al.: Automated robot picking system for e-commerce fulfillment warehouse application. In: The 14th IFToMM World Congress. vol. 1 (2015)
25. Likhouzova, T., Demianova, Y.: Robot path optimization in warehouse management system. Evol. Intel. **15**(4), 2589–2595 (2022)
26. Lodgaard, E., Dransfeld, S.: Organizational aspects for successful integration of human-machine interaction in the industry 4.0 era. Procedia CIRP **88**, 218–222 (2020). https://doi.org/10.1016/j.procir.2020.05.039, https://www.sciencedirect.com/science/article/pii/S2212827120303541, 13th CIRP Conference on Intelligent Computation in Manufacturing Engineering, 17-19 July 2019, Gulf of Naples, Italy
27. Niermann, D., Petzoldt, C., Freitag, M.: Intuitive and flexible process control for autonomous mobile robots: A case study in a large logistics enterprise. Procedia CIRP **120**, 153–158 (2023) 10.1016/j.procir.2023.08.028, https://www.sciencedirect.com/science/article/pii/S2212827123006996, 56th CIRP International Conference on Manufacturing Systems 2023
28. Pujawan, N., Vanany, I., Dewa, P.: Human errors in warehouse operations: an improvement model. Int. J. Logist. Syst. Manag. **27**, 298 (2017). https://doi.org/10.1504/IJLSM.2017.10005117
29. Redżeb, K.: Innovative methods in warehouse management a comprehensive review. In: Alareeni, B., Hamdan, A. (eds.) Technology: Toward Business Sustainability, pp. 365–379. Springer Nature Switzerland, Cham (2024)
30. Stobart, S., Vassileiou, M., Stobart, S., Vassileiou, M.: Mysql database and phpmyadmin installation (2004)
31. Tubis, A.A., Rohman, J., Smok, A., Dopart, D.: Analysis of human errors in the traditional and automated order-picking system. In: International Conference on Intelligent Systems in Production Engineering and Maintenance. pp. 406–419. Springer (2023)
32. Wiedmer, R., Griffis, S.E.: Structural characteristics of complex supply chain networks. J. Bus. Logist. **42**(2), 264–290 (2021)
33. Xia, W., Goh, J., Cortes, C.A., Lu, Y., Xu, X.: Decentralized coordination of autonomous agvs for flexible factory automation in the context of industry 4.0. In: 2020 IEEE 16th International Conference on Automation Science and Engineering (CASE). pp. 488–493 (2020). https://doi.org/10.1109/CASE48305.2020.9216961
34. Yang, X., Liu, X., Feng, L., Zhang, J., Qi, M.: Non-traditional layout design for robotic mobile fulfillment system with multiple workstations. Algorithms **14**(7) (2021). https://doi.org/10.3390/a14070203, https://www.mdpi.com/1999-4893/14/7/203
35. Žunić, E., Delalić, S., Hodžić, K., Beširević, A., Hindija, H.: Smart warehouse management system concept with implementation. In: 2018 14th Symposium on Neural Networks and Applications (NEUREL). pp. 1–5 (2018). https://doi.org/10.1109/NEUREL.2018.8587004

Harnessing IoT and Robotics for Comprehensive Human Activity Recognition in Smart Buildings

Petros Toupas(✉), Georgios Tsamis(✉), Dimitra Zotou, Dimitrios Giakoumis, Konstantinos Votis, and Dimitrios Tzovaras

Centre for Research and Technology Hellas, Information Technologies Institute, Thessaloniki, Greece
{ptoupas,gtsamis,dzotou,dgiakoum,kvotis,Dimitrios.Tzovaras}@iti.gr

Abstract. The incorporation of Internet of Things (IoT) devices and robotics into smart building environments has introduced new opportunities for human activity recognition (HAR). The paper introduces an innovative approach that combines IoT sensors and robotic data to create a complete dataset for Human Activity Recognition (HAR) in smart building settings. The system utilises a synchronised data collection technique to gather information from fixed IoT sensors, wearables, and smart devices, as well as from mobile robots. The dataset obtained includes a wide variety of sensor modalities, such as accelerometers, gyroscopes, microphones, motion sensors, smart plugs, and cameras (thermal, RGB-D). A proposed strategy is presented to tackle the difficulties of multi-modal data fusion and classification by fusing all sensor data into a single machine learning model. This study lays the groundwork for future works into Human Activity Recognition (HAR) systems, which involve the integration of multi-sensor settings, sophisticated data fusion algorithms, context-sensitive identification, and tailored support for individuals working or residing in smart environments. The setup of the sensors and use cases of this study were conducted in a smart home environment. Nevertheless, the integrated system can be tailored to suit the requirements of any smart building.

Keywords: Multi-Sensor Fusion · Data Collection · Robotics

1 Introduction

In recent years, the concept of smart buildings has undergone a revolution as a result of the proliferation of Internet of Things (IoT) devices and advancements in robotics [1,21]. Through the integration of a wide range of sensors, actuators, and intelligent systems, these technologically advanced environments provide unprecedented levels of automation, efficiency, and comfort [6,13]. Human

P. Toupas, G. Tsamis and D. Zotou—Equal contribution.

I. Kostavelis et al. (Eds.): ICSC 2024, CCIS 2110, pp. 161–173, 2025.
https://doi.org/10.1007/978-3-031-69344-1_12

Activity Recognition (HAR) stands out as an essential component for optimising building operations [16] and promoting safety and security [7] among the numerous applications that have been made possible by the combination of all of these technologies.

In addition, the ongoing development of HAR algorithms and machine learning techniques has made it possible to create systems that are more advanced and accurate, and that are able to recognise a wide variety of human activities with a notable degree of precision [15]. These developments have opened up new avenues for applications that go beyond traditional building management. Some examples of these applications include healthcare monitoring [17], elder care assistance [14], and retail industry [10].

The paper presents a novel approach that leverages the integration of Internet of Things (IoT) devices and robotics for comprehensive human activity recognition (HAR) in smart building environments. The main contribution of our work is summarised as follows:

- Introduced an innovative methodology that seamlessly combines IoT sensors and robotic data enabling comprehensive and holistic human activity recognition (HAR) within smart building environments.
- Proposed a strategy that tackles multi-modal data fusion and classification challenges by consolidating all sensor data into a single machine learning model. When necessary, the system intelligently leverages the robotic platform through a heuristic model for enhanced data fusion.

The rest of this paper is organised as follows: Section 2 presents an overview of the current state-of-art methods and relative work on fusion models in smart environments and HAR implementation. Section 3 contains a comprehensive description of our proposed architecture and Sect. 4 presents the use case scenario our method was tested. Conclusions along with a discussion on future work are drawn in Sect. 5.

2 Background

In Industry 4.0, multiple sensors monitor machines and workers to enhance processes and safety. Data fusion techniques combine heterogeneous sensor data, improving monitoring system performance [18]. Real-time visibility and traceability within smart factories have been achieved in [23], by leveraging IoT devices such as RFID readers and tags. These devices turn everyday manufacturing resources into smart manufacturing objects (SMOs) for real-time production process communication. Innovative laser scanners in smart factories allow SMO movements to be observed and captured. Image and video processing algorithms create a 3D real-time visualisation model for visibility and traceability. A comprehensive multi-AGV tracking system using advanced technologies is proposed in [22] to improve tracking accuracy and efficiency. The system uses AprilTag, a multi-AGV scheduling system, improved YOLOv5 with OBB, extended Kalman filtering (EKF), and global vision to accurately calculate AGV coordinates and heading angles inside a warehouse. An unmanned forklift-based logistics pallet segmentation for smart logistics is introduced in [3]. The Multi-Feature Fusion-Guided Multiscale Bidirectional Attention (MFMBA) neural network extracts and fuses multiple features and uses a multiscale architecture to account for pallet appearance variations. A bidirectional attention mechanism assigns weights from both horizontal and vertical directions, improving segmentation accuracy.

Sensor technology and data fusion techniques in the field of Human Activity Recognition (HAR) have enabled the development of novel frameworks for improving urban environments [12]. A framework for HAR in smart cities is provided in [9], by fusing smartphones and IoT, utilising raw sensor data, including accelerometer, gyroscope, magnetometer, and Google Fit activity tracking module readings, in order to promote healthier lifestyles. According to the authors, by employing deep recurrent neural networks (DRNN), the framework achieves impressive accuracy in recognising human activities, surpassing previous studies with an accuracy rate of 99.43%. A multimodal deep learning approach for group activity recognition in office environments is introduced in [8]. Audio and visual data from videos are integrated, capturing complex interactions among individuals. By training the fusion network on the AMI Corpus dataset, the approach extracts joint audio–visual features and considers temporal dependencies to improve classification accuracy.

A sensor fusion-based HAR classifier is developed in [2], studying warehouse activities, which can cause workplace hazards and musculoskeletal disorders. Three IMUs record body movement during warehouse tasks. For each sensor, Deep Learning (DL) algorithms model raw time series data. An architecture for robust people detection in smart environments by fusing infrared and visible video streams using the INT-Horus framework is presented in [4]. It covers acquisition, segmentation, fusion, identification, and tracking levels, improving detection accuracy with heterogeneous camera data.

The ExtraSensory dataset [19,20] presents a comprehensive collection of annotated data acquired from smartphones and wearable devices. In this dataset, 60 participants were engaged in performing daily activities within natural settings, without specific task instructions. The dataset encompasses a diverse range of primary activities representing human body states, as well as secondary activities such as sleeping, eating, and toileting, providing a comprehensive representation of human behaviour in real-world scenarios. The Opportunity dataset [5] offers a unique perspective by incorporating annotated measurements recorded from both on-body and object sensors. The data collection process involved four participants performing a predetermined set of activities within a controlled, monitored environment. Similar to the ExtraSensory dataset, the data from body-worn sensors in the Opportunity dataset was utilised to address the multi-label classification problem.

These datasets, encompassing diverse data acquisition methodologies, sensor modalities, and activity annotation schemes, provide researchers with valuable resources for exploring and evaluating human activity recognition techniques in both naturalistic and controlled settings. The complementary nature of these datasets facilitates a comprehensive understanding of the challenges and opportunities associated with real-world applications of human activity recognition systems.

This work presents a comprehensive and innovative approach for human activity recognition (HAR) in smart buildings by seamlessly integrating IoT devices and mobile robotic platforms. It enables fusion of multi-modal data from diverse sensors - fixed IoT sensors, wearables, smart devices, and robots with cameras/depth sensors - facilitating a holistic understanding of activities. The novel integration of mobile robot data as an additional sensing modality provides supplementary video/depth sensing to enhance recognition. The synchronised data collection technique captures heterogeneous sensor data simultaneously, allowing temporal correlation across modalities. A key innovation is the unified deep learning fusion model that consolidates all sensor data, remaining robust even with variable sensor availability. When the fusion model faces uncertainty, a heuristic model intelligently guides the mobile robot to reposition itself for enhanced data collection and improved accuracy. The modular design allows customising and deploying the system for diverse smart building environments like homes, offices, and warehouses.

3 System Architecture

The proposed system architecture, as depicted in Fig. 1, exhibits a high degree of adaptability and reconfigurability by design. It can seamlessly integrate with the existing sensor infrastructure and smart building components of the targeted implementation environment. This architectural flexibility allows for efficient deployment across a diverse range of systems and applications. One of the primary objectives of the proposed system extends beyond mere accuracy in human activity recognition, seeking the effective management of the uncertainty through the deployment of flexible models and algorithms. This approach aims to enhance the system's robustness and reliability in handling the inherent complexities and uncertainties associated with real-world data.

The fusion of multimodal data streams from various sensor modalities is facilitated through the incorporation of unimodal components. These unimodal components can be executed in a distributed manner across discrete Raspberry Pi devices or centralised on a server infrastructure, depending on the specific requirements and constraints of the deployment scenario. The fusion process involves the harmonious convergence of audio data with information gathered from wearable devices. This fusion is accomplished through the collaborative efforts of corresponding unimodal components, which process the respective data streams and provide input to the central fusion model.

<u>Data Collection Mode</u>
The proposed system architecture employs a centralised server to orchestrate the data collection process, synchronising inputs from various sources and sensors. The data collector, an integral component of the server, establishes connections with the sensing modalities attached to the Raspberry Pi modules via

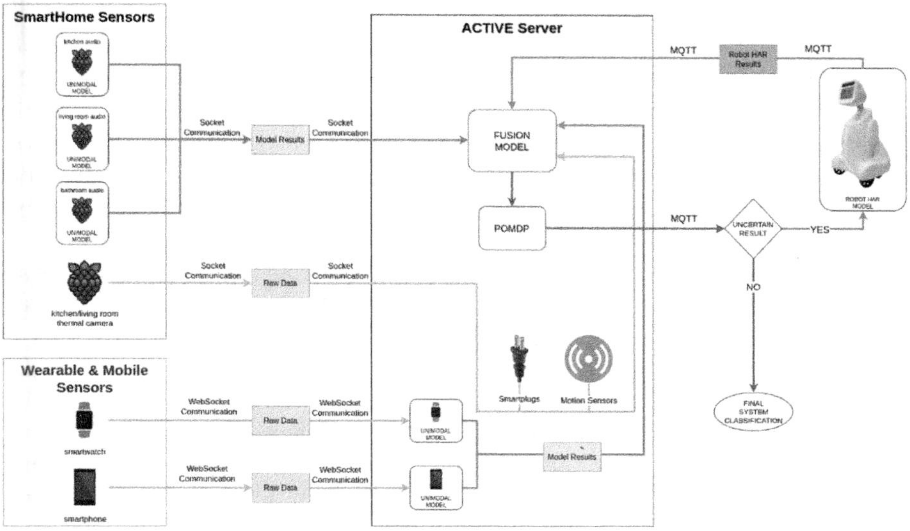

Fig. 1. System Architecture During Live Monitoring

socket communication, and with smart devices (smartwatches and smartphones) through WebSocket communication, enabling the reception of raw data. Acting as a centralised mediator, the data collector facilitates seamless data transfer between the server and the smart devices. The InfluxDB database, another essential component of the server infrastructure, serves as the central repository for all collected data. This centralised structure ensures data consistency and enables comprehensive analysis across multiple modalities.

The proposed solution presents an integrated approach to data collection and monitoring, leveraging the server to manage the overall system operation, while delegating specific data collection tasks to Raspberry Pi modules and smart devices. The incorporation of triggering mechanisms and communication protocols ensures efficient data flow and synchronization, contributing to the system's overall adaptability and suitability for various monitoring needs, including audio, thermal imaging, and smart device data collection.

The data collection process is initiated when the server transmits a "start" trigger signal. Upon receipt of this signal, sensors and smart devices commence synchronised data collection. Conversely, when the server issues a 'stop' trigger signal, sensors and smart devices cease data collection and proceed to store the acquired data. The Raspberry Pi units store the recorded data locally, while all other sensors store the data on the server. Once a session is completed, all devices import the recorded session, including necessary metadata, into the InfluxDB database on the server, facilitating centralised data management and analysis.

Live Monitoring Mode

The results obtained from the fusion model serve as inputs to a Partially Observable Markov Decision Process (POMDP) model, as described in [11]. The POMDP plays a crucial role in the decision-making process, determining whether the robot of the system should take action or maintain its current state based on the uncertain results from the fusion model. This decision-making process forms the foundation for controlling the autonomous behaviour of the robot, enabling it to adapt and respond to the dynamic environment effectively.

In a subsequent step, the combined information from the robot's outputs and the predictions generated by the fusion model undergoes enhancement through a heuristic model. This additional processing stage is designed to augment the certainty of the system, providing a comprehensive and unified understanding of the environment. By leveraging the strengths of various models and data sources, the system achieves a higher level of confidence in its predictions and situational awareness. Once the system attains a sufficient level of certainty, and the POMDP determines that the robot's intervention is no longer required, a command is issued to transition the robot to an idle state. This intelligent control mechanism ensures efficient resource utilisation and minimises unnecessary interventions, contributing to the overall system's effectiveness and energy efficiency.

The proposed system presents a holistic and integrated approach, leveraging the power of multimodal data fusion. By seamlessly integrating various types of sensors and employing advanced machine learning models, the system achieves accurate and robust understanding of the environment. This capability is further enhanced by the incorporation of decision-making processes and heuristic models, ensuring a comprehensive understanding of the environment and enabling appropriate system interventions when necessary.

3.1 Algorithms and Processing Modalities

The proposed system architecture exhibits a modular and flexible design, enabling the seamless integration of diverse sensing modalities for data collection and live monitoring applications. One of the key advantages of deep learning (DL) neural networks, a core component of this architecture, lies in their capability to automatically extract intricate features and uncover useful patterns directly from raw data attained from the installed sensors. Although the system is not restricted to these specific modalities, the following sections detail the sensing modalities and accompanying algorithms that have been integrated into the proposed architecture.

- **Unimodal DNN models:** In this study, a DL approach was also used to generate a high-level feature mapping from wearable and mobile sensors. The human activity recognition (HAR) problem is formulated as a multi-label learning task, in which the data of an activity represents multiple categories at the same time, in order to understand more complex human behavioural

patterns. To address the challenge of handling multiple categories and learning to capture the dependencies of human activity categories, a two-branch architecture was developed. This approach has the advantage of dealing symmetrically with body states and daily activities based on the analysis of the data attained from the wearable and mobile sensors. The goal of this approach is to first identify the patterns in each of the learning objects of body states and daily activity separately and then create a semantic mapping between them.
Microphone arrays consisting of four linearly arranged microphones were used to automatically extract features from sensors of the Internet of Things. The main objective was to detect human activity in a home environment based on the audio signals recorded by the microphones. The common representation found in the literature for classifying environmental sounds is the spectrogram. A spectrogram could present linear frequencies (STFT), "Mel" frequencies or "Gammatone" frequencies. The mel frequency spectrogram is a time-frequency representation, but is tailored to the way sound is perceived by the human auditory system. The "Gammatone" spectrogram is a time-frequency representation based on a fast Fourier transform (FFT) approach to "Gammatone" subband filters, for which the bandwidth increases with increasing centre frequency. The aforementioned three types of representation of different sizes, extracted from raw audio: STFT, Mel (the same representation, the only difference being that the frequency axis is scaled to the Mel scale using overlapping triangular filters) and Gammatone spectrograms (using overlapping gamma distribution filters).
- **Heuristic Model** A heuristic model is an approach that uses practical rules or strategies to solve problems. Within the context of this system, the heuristic model serves two primary purposes: (1) to facilitate the final decision regarding the recognition of human activity by the system, and (2) to guide the robot's subsequent movements or actions. The robot's capability to recognise human activity provides valuable information to the system. By integrating this probability information with inputs from IoT sensors (such as smart plugs and motion sensors) and thermal camera data, the heuristic model enhances the system's decision-making process. It can refine the predictions or adjust the confidence levels associated with recognising human activities, leveraging the robot's visual perception of human activity as an additional factor.
- **Robotic Platform** To enable the robot to recognise human activities, an integrated system was developed, designed to operate entirely on the robotic platform in near real-time. This system comprises three key subsystems: (a) the detection and localisation of humans within the spatial environment, (b) the recognition and tracking of the user, and (c) the recognition of the user's specific activity. The concept of human-aware navigation is a crucial aspect of this system, aimed at guiding the robotic platform through its environment in a safe and unobtrusive manner, minimising any potential discomfort or annoyance to humans present. To model and differentiate human presence from static obstacles, the proxemics theory is employed. According to this

theory, the human personal space is defined as a circular area surrounding the human's centre. To maximise human comfort and ensure reliable coexistence between humans and robots within the shared environment, the system considers only the area outside the defined personal space as a potential movement area for the robot.
- **Fusion DNN model:** A novel method has been devised for feature fusion, resulting a paradigm shift in data integration by offering a fusion mechanism that operates seamlessly regardless of the quantity or diversity of sensors in use. This innovative approach not only streamlines the fusion process but also eliminates the challenging task of reconfiguring the fusion model when faced with fewer sensors, opting instead for a sophisticated data augmentation strategy. By strategically leveraging subsets of sensor data for each observation, this methodology consolidates and enriches the aggregated data Through the seamless integration of a diverse array of sensor combinations, it exponentially augments the volume of available data, thereby significantly enhancing the accuracy and robustness of the system in identifying and classifying human activities, even when confronted with constraints such as limited sensor availability or variability in sensor types.
- **POMDP** The Partially Observable Markov Decision Process (POMDP) method is formulated with the objective of determining optimal robot actions to augment and reinforce a Human Activity Recognition (HAR) system within the context of a smart home environment. This HAR system leverages a diverse array of sensors, including wearables, microphones, cameras, smart plugs, as well as temperature and humidity sensors. The data from these heterogeneous sensors is optimally fused to enhance the accuracy of activity classification. In scenarios where the HAR system's outcomes exhibit uncertainty, the robot intervenes by approaching the individual, conducting its own recognition process, and supplementing the HAR system with additional visual and auditory data captured by its on-board sensors. The POMDP model incorporates the precision of the HAR system, assigning higher probabilities to state transitions that are deemed more likely to occur, thereby enhancing the overall decision-making process.

3.2 Communication Protocols and Messaging

The microcontrollers establish communication with the central server through the exchange of messages facilitated by network sockets. This message exchange serves as the mechanism for initiating or terminating data logging operations on the respective microcontroller or sensor device. The communication protocol employed in this process leverages UTF-8 encoded messages transmitted over socket connections, enabling seamless data transfer across devices. Adherence to a structured message format is a characteristic feature of this protocol, ensuring consistent and reliable communication. Each message conforms to a specific format: `host sensor trigger_action session_id session_label`, where the constituent elements provide essential information for coordinating the data logging process.

- `host`: Identifies the device sending the message, ensuring the routing and context of the message.
- `sensor`: Identifies the specific sensor or device generating the data, providing context for the collected data.
- `trigger_action`: Indicates the trigger signal related to the data reception. This value may be either 'start' or 'stop'.
- `session_id`: Uniquely identifies the current data collection session, allowing data correlation.
- `session_label`: Provides the label related to the categorisation of data based on the activity the user is performing.

Establishing reliable communication channels is a fundamental prerequisite for seamless data exchange and coordination among the various devices and components of the proposed system. Before initiating message exchanges, the Raspberry Pi devices must establish a host connection via the TCP protocol through Socket communication, which ensures reliable data transfer and robust error handling, consequently safeguarding the integrity of the communication channel.

The data collector, residing on the central server, communicates with smart devices (smartwatches and smartphones) through WebSocket communication. This involves establishing a persistent WebSocket connection with the smartwatch and smartphone, facilitating real-time, bidirectional data exchange. The WebSocket connection creates a two-way data channel, enabling the data collector to receive raw data from the smart devices while simultaneously sending commands or trigger events as required.

Furthermore, the robotic platform maintains communication with the central server over the MQTT protocol. This protocol enables the transmission of event triggers and facilitates the real-time transfer of data generated by the robot's heterogeneous array of sensors, ensuring seamless integration and synchronisation between the robotic platform and the central server.

The InfluxDB database, a critical component of the system, provides a communication protocol via a RESTful API, allowing for seamless integration with various devices and platforms. By leveraging this REST API, external devices can establish connections with the InfluxDB database, enabling them to import, retrieve, or edit data as needed. This integration facilitates real-time access and manipulation of data across various applications and scripts, fostering a collaborative and interoperable ecosystem.

4 Smart House Use Case

The described architecture was utilised and validated in the ITI Smart House, which is a rapid prototyping and novel technologies demonstration infrastructure at the premises of CERTH. The sensing modalities that were selected are shown in Fig. 2. They consist of all the modalities currently supported by the proposed framework and provided a plethora of heterogeneous data.

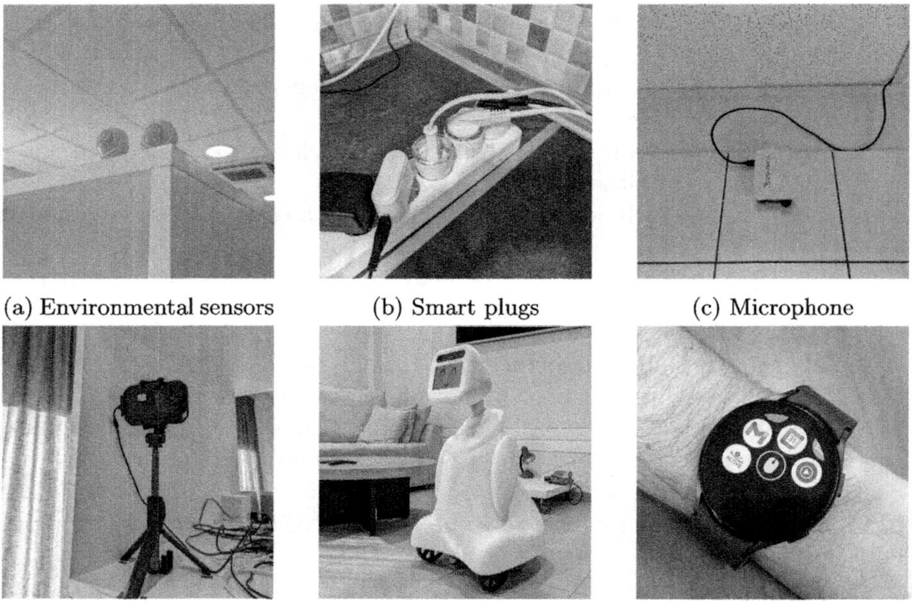

(a) Environmental sensors (b) Smart plugs (c) Microphone

(d) Thermal camera (e) Robotic Platform (f) Wearable

Fig. 2. Sensing Modalities of the installed system in a Smart House Infrastructure

Data collection sessions were carried out following the ensuing protocol; users were asked to conduct various household activities in the ITI Smart House, where sensors were installed as shown in Fig. 3. This setup allowed for an effective coverage of all the significant living spaces in a home. The participants were informed that the sensors will detect movements, sounds etc. and using the algorithms illustrated in 3.1, identify human activities. They also knew that if the decision algorithm is not sure about the current activity, it calls the robot, which, using a camera, confirms the movements. The robot navigated unobtrusively, without disturbing the activities going on in the area.

The use case involved 15 people, aged between 25 and 40 years old, with an average age of 30 years. In addition to their daily habits, and given that the overall system is mainly for elderly people, they were asked to simulate the existence of scheduled medication, as well as the possibility of an emergency, in order to confirm the correct functioning of the whole system, even in critical times. During the use case, data related to various human activities were stored into the central server. The participants performed each activity a certain number of times. The information that was stored concerned the raw data from the sensors, along with the context, i.e. the room and the current activity, in order to improve the unimodal models' performance and thus the overall accuracy of the system.

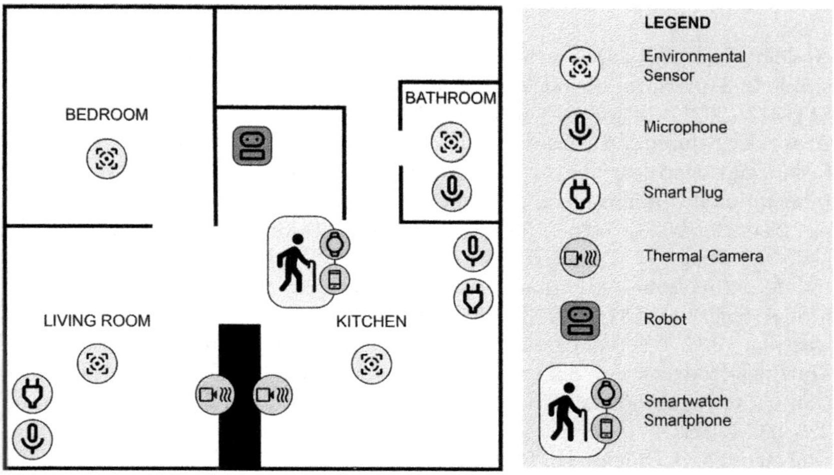

Fig. 3. System and Sensor Topology in a Smart House Infrastructure

5 Conclusion

This study presents a pioneering approach harnessing IoT devices and robotic platforms within smart buildings for human activity recognition (HAR). The proposed system introduces an innovative synchronised data collection technique integrating fixed IoT sensors, wearables, smart devices, and mobile robots, resulting in a comprehensive multimodal dataset. The fusion of these data streams is facilitated through distributed unimodal components collaborating to provide input to a central fusion model. This holistic approach tackles multi-modal data fusion and classification challenges, laying a foundation for future advancements in HAR systems. By integrating multi-sensor settings, sophisticated algorithms, context-sensitive identification, and tailored smart environment support, this study paves the way for refined, personalised HAR systems. While implemented in a smart home, the integrated system's modular design allows adaptation to any smart building requirements, underscoring its versatility and scalability.

Acknowledgement. The research work was supported by the Hellenic Foundation for Research and Innovation (H.F.R.I.) under the "First Call for H.F.R.I. Research Projects to support Faculty members and Researchers and the procurement of high-cost research equipment grant" (Project Name: ACTIVE, Project Number: HFRI-FM17-2271.

References

1. Abdelouahid, R.A., Debauche, O., Marzak, A.: Internet of things: a new interoperable IOT platform. Application to a smart building. Procedia Comput. Sci. **191**, 511–517 (2021). https://doi.org/10.1016/j.procs.2021.07.066
2. Arab, A., Schmidt, A., Aufderheide, D.: Human activity recognition using sensor fusion and deep learning for ergonomics in logistics applications. In: 2023 IEEE International Conference on Internet of Things and Intelligence Systems (IoTaIS), pp. 254–260 (2023). https://doi.org/10.1109/IoTaIS60147.2023.10346052
3. Cai, W., Song, Y., Duan, H., Xia, Z., Wei, Z.: Multi-feature fusion-guided multiscale bidirectional attention networks for logistics pallet segmentation. Comput. Model. Eng. Sci. **131**(3), 1539–1555 (2022)
4. Castillo, J.C., Fernández-Caballero, A., Serrano-Cuerda, J., López, M.T., Martínez-Rodrigo, A.: Smart environment architecture for robust people detection by infrared and visible video fusion. J. Ambient. Intell. Humaniz. Comput. **8**, 223–237 (2017)
5. Chavarriaga, R., Sagha, H., Calatroni, A., Digumarti, S.T., Tröster, G., del Millán, J.R., Roggen, D.: The opportunity challenge: a benchmark database for on-body sensor-based activity recognition. Pattern Recogn. Lett. **34**(15), 2033–2042 (2013). https://doi.org/10.1016/j.patrec.2012.12.014
6. Demrozi, F., Pravadelli, G., Bihorac, A., Rashidi, P.: Human activity recognition using inertial, physiological and environmental sensors: a comprehensive survey. IEEE Access **8**, 210816–210836 (2020). https://doi.org/10.1109/ACCESS.2020.3037715
7. Fereidoonian, F., Firouzi, F., Farahani, B.: Human activity recognition: From sensors to applications. In: 2020 International Conference on Omni-layer Intelligent Systems (COINS), pp. 1–8 (2020). https://doi.org/10.1109/COINS49042.2020.9191417
8. Florea, G.A., Mihailescu, R.C.: Multimodal deep learning for group activity recognition in smart office environments. Future Internet **12**(8), 133 (2020). https://doi.org/10.3390/fi12080133
9. Javed, A.R., Faheem, R., Asim, M., Baker, T., Beg, M.O.: A smartphone sensors-based personalized human activity recognition system for sustainable smart cities. Sustain. Urban Areas **71**, 102970 (2021). https://doi.org/10.1016/j.scs.2021.102970
10. Joy Rakesh, Y., Kavitha, R., Julian, J.: Human activity recognition using wearable sensors. In: Satapathy, S.C., Zhang, Y.D., Bhateja, V., Majhi, R. (eds.) Intelligent Data Engineering and Analytics, pp. 527–538. Springer Singapore, Singapore (2021). https://doi.org/10.1007/978-981-99-6706-3
11. Kurniawati, H.: Partially observable Markov decision processes and robotics. Ann. Rev. Control Robot. Auton. Syst. **5**, 253–277 (2022)
12. Minh Dang, L., Min, K., Wang, H., Jalil Piran, M., Hee Lee, C., Moon, H.: Sensor-based and vision-based human activity recognition: a comprehensive survey. Pattern Recogn. **108**, 107561 (2020). https://doi.org/10.1016/j.patcog.2020.107561
13. Ramanujam, E., Perumal, T., Padmavathi, S.: Human activity recognition with smartphone and wearable sensors using deep learning techniques: a review. IEEE Sens. J. **21**(12), 13029–13040 (2021). https://doi.org/10.1109/JSEN.2021.3069927
14. Schrader, L., Vargas Toro, A., Konietzny, S., Rüping, S., Schäpers, B., Steinböck, M., Krewer, C., Müller, F., Güttler, J., Bock, T.: Advanced sensing and human activity recognition in early intervention and rehabilitation of elderly people. J. Popul. Ageing **13**, 139–165 (2020)

stationary robot arm. Compared to dealing with the risk of stationary robots, ensuring safety around mobile robots presents unique challenges. First, setting safeguards [12] around the mobile robots is challenging because they work in wide working areas. Second, as robots move around, they encounter potential interactions with various types of surrounding objects, which complicates the hazard scenario. Therefore, the risk management approach needs to be specified based on the specific characteristics of robots.

Risk management in the design phase is significant for eliminating hazards before assembling and implementing devices. This involves identifying hazards and integrating safety measures into designed functions. However, one drawback of risk management in the design phase is that no physical devices have been implemented yet, which means the analysis can only be conducted based on the expert's prior knowledge. Traditional checklists suggested by ISO standards are applied in hazard identification and risk analysis steps. For example, methods such as "Failure Modes and Effects Analysis"(FMEA) and "Hazard and Operability Analysis" (HAZOP) [2,3] are commonly used for hazard identification. These approaches alone, however, are insufficient for HRC system risk management, especially in the mobile robot scenario. This is because the investigation relies heavily on personal experience, and the suggested checklist is mainly designed for processing engineering, not suitable for autonomous machinery involved in complicated risk situations.

To tackle the above challenges, we propose a dedicated approach to design phase risk assessment for the workspace involving autonomous mobile robots and human collaboration. First, we use a function-centric hazard identification form, called F-CHIA [4], designed for safety analysis on the autonomous system. The form starts with breaking down a general task into several functions and their realizations, then searching potential hazards based on each realization, and summarizing the key properties and proposing new functional requirements. Though the F-CHIA form is designed for autonomous systems, it is still human experience-based. Simulation, however, is expected to be used as a supplement to the form-based methods, helping with hazard identification and hazard validation. The simulation tool will be built as a digital reflection of the physical system, according to the system's prior knowledge in the early design phase, such as human positions, room layout, and device dimensions.

Assisting by simulations, simulated data can be acquired before the construction of the real system. This enables a numerical risk estimation algorithm. In contrast to the traditional risk estimation method, which relies on predefined matrices and is often generic and not tailored to specific tasks, the new risk estimation algorithm is designed and validated using simulated data [5]. The algorithm is expected to produce continuous predictions of the probability of the risk. Figure 1 shows the working diagram of implementing simulation in the risk management on an autonomous system.

To demonstrate the proposed method, a specific use case is designed as an example. We focus on the delivery process in the logistics task, by assuming the case that human operators and small-size mobile robots collaborate in a factory operation room. In the following chapters, we will provide a systemic description of the use case. The F-CHIA form will be applied to the selected system, followed by modelling the scenario in a 3D simulator called Coppeliasim (V-REP). The simulation is used to search for potential hazards. As collision is identified as the most common risk in the use case, a risk estimation algorithm is developed to compute the collision probability by using predicted trajectories and uncertainties from the Kalman Filter (KF). In the experiment part, the method is investigated and demonstrated in the simulation.

In summary, this paper not only underscores the safety challenges posed by human-robot collaboration (HRC) but also presents practical solutions. Through the utilization of F-CHIA for hazard identification and the introduction of a continuous collision risk estimation algorithm based on the KF, the study contributes valuable methodologies for enhancing safety functions during the design phase of mobile robot applications and offers a robust approach to real-time prediction and mitigation of collision risks in dynamic environments.

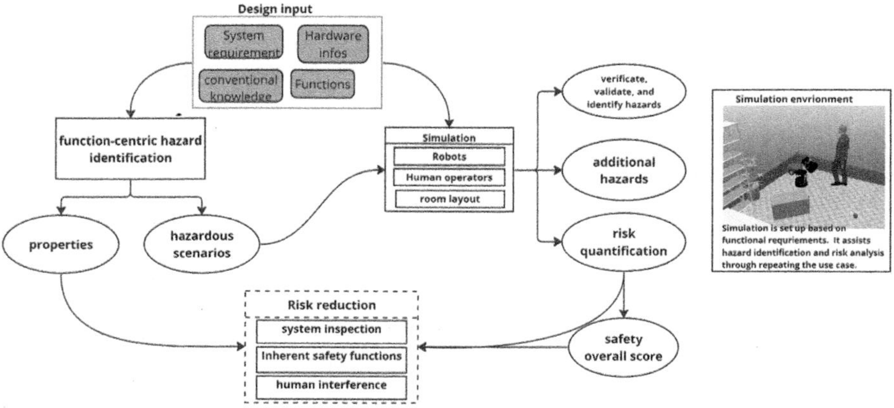

Fig. 1. The illustration of implementing simulation in the safety analysis process of an HRC autonomous system. The simulation is built based on the design input, and takes hazard identification results as input to demonstrate hazards and search for additional hazards. It is also used as a platform to test risk estimation algorithms.

2 Related Works

The high development of manufacturing automation requires more dedicated safety assessments for autonomous systems. Several existing standards provide instructions for risk assessment on autonomous systems. Standards ISO 10218 [8] and ISO/TS 15066 [7] specify the safety requirements of industrial robotics interaction. [7] provides risk reduction measurements for reducing human injuries when collaborating with robots. The standard also states technical guidance for collaborative industrial robotics and work environment. However, it is challenging to define the severity of harm when conducting risk assessment, especially in the early design phase. When it comes to autonomous driving devices, standards such as ISO 3691-4:2020 [9] are available for testing the safety functions of industrial tractors interacting with humans.

It is inadequate to ensure the safety of a specific autonomous system depending on the standards alone [10], as the instructions are usually at a general level to be applied on machines. Studies targeting mobile robots implemented in manufacturing for delivery tasks are in demand. Researches such as [13–15] focused on the safety analysis of mobile robots in various applications. Specifically, [14,15] used simulation tools to demonstrate the risk assessment process. Commonly, the risk levels are estimated by the pre-defined safety regions around the object, but in our project, we use the Kalman Filter to predict the dynamic safety regions based on the current positions of the moving agent.

3 Simulation Setup

The simulation tools can provide a supplement platform for searching, validating, and verifying hazardous scenarios by constructing a virtual environment based on the design concepts. Additionally, in the design phase, it can be utilized to provide simulated data to the risk estimation algorithm. To set up the simulator, the models and their actions, the use case need to be defined. In our project, we take the collision-free navigation task as an example. The models of mobile robots, humans, and factory furniture are imported according to the design requirements. The virtual room is set with a dimension of 5*5 meters. Turtlebot2 is implemented as the robot worker in the environment. A walking 'Bill' and a working 'Bill' are launched as the human operators in the factory. The actions of each model will be modified based on the specifications of the testing scene. Table 1 lists the basic information of dynamic models and corre-

Fig. 2. The overview of the simulation environment, including a monitor system, two human workers, three robots, and office layout.

sponding scenarios in simulation. The overall view of the virtual testing space is shown in Fig. 2.

Table 1. Design information of models launched in simulation

Model	Task	Capability	Scenario
Robot1	Product delivery	Autonomous navigation	Assume the robot has reliable autonomous driving ability, which supports it in conducting product delivery tasks.
Robot2	Product delivery	Autonomous navigation	Assume the robot has reliable autonomous driving ability, which supports it conducting product delivery tasks.
Human1	Lab maintenance	Walking ability	The human operator walks around the room when robots are conducting their tasks. The human walks at normal speed and is able to aware of changes in surroundings.
Human2	Conduct work	Move around the desk	The human works with the equipment on the desk.
Selected robot	Sample delivery	Unstable collision avoidance ability	This is to mimic the case when sensor or software fault occur.
		Invisible by surroundings	This is to mimic the case when faults occur to other robots, or the human is not aware of the robot.
		Sudden turns during navigation	This is to mimic the case when the robot fails to plan the route, or errors exist in the control system.

4 Function-Centric Hazard Identification

The function-centric hazard identification form from [4] is used in this section to identify hazards in the autonomous factory room. The form divides one entire autonomous task into several functions and relevant realizations. By considering the realization of individual function as a 'process', we narrow down the guide word to three: no, part of, and other than, and use the idea from HAZOP to search the deviations, causes and consequences for each realization. Then, a simulation is implemented to search for hidden hazards. To clarify the definitions, 'hazards' means the event that can cause harm to the system, while 'risk' is the probability of a hazard. The risks are determined by the properties of causes, consequences, and severity. Therefore the system is required to apply different risk reduction strategies when facing the hazard with various risks. For example, the robot is expected to select different collision avoidance strategies when seeing humans and robots respectively.

One key output from the form is relevant properties in function realization. These properties are expected to be monitored during system working, for estimating the level of risks. Figure 3 indicates the working framework of the hazard analysis process.

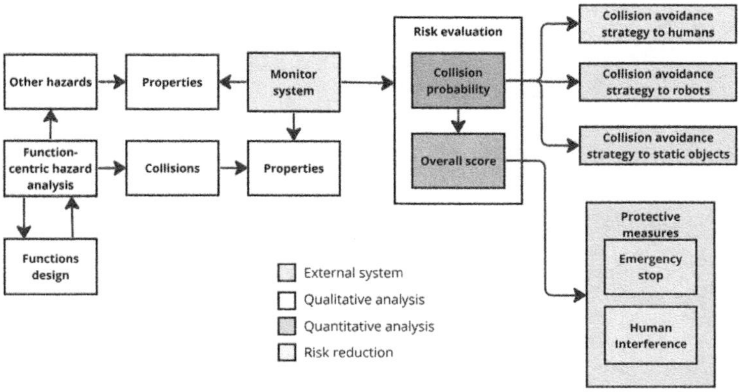

Fig. 3. The designed working pipeline of hazard identification and risk management in the collision scenario.

Table 2 presents the hazard identification process. Note that the items with a star sign were identified during the simulation, which is shown in Fig. 4. The hazards due to component failures are not considered in this study, while only system-level hazards are identified through the given method. Not surprisingly, the biggest hazard is seen as the robot colliding with its surroundings, and the severity of different colliders is illustrated through simulation. To address this typical issue, we propose various risk reduction strategies and investigate risk quantification in the next section. The corresponding properties of this hazard are determined as {robot pose, robot speed, object type, object pose}, which will be implemented for risk analysis in collisions.

5 Risk Analysis for the Collision Scenario

In the above section, hazard identification recognizes collision as one of the most common hazards. Various colliding scenarios and severity levels make the collision complicated. A proper risk analysis of collision will provide a good reference for future risk reduction. In this chapter, we will estimate the risk by calculating the collision probability between the selected robot and surrounding objects. Kalman filter (KF), as a classic state estimation algorithm, is implemented to predict the trajectories of each object.

Assume the properties could be collected through an external monitor system, in the current time T, the properties are

$$\mathbb{P}\left[R_p, R_v, O_{t1}, \ldots, O_{tn}, O_{p1}, \ldots, O_{pn}\right] \tag{1}$$

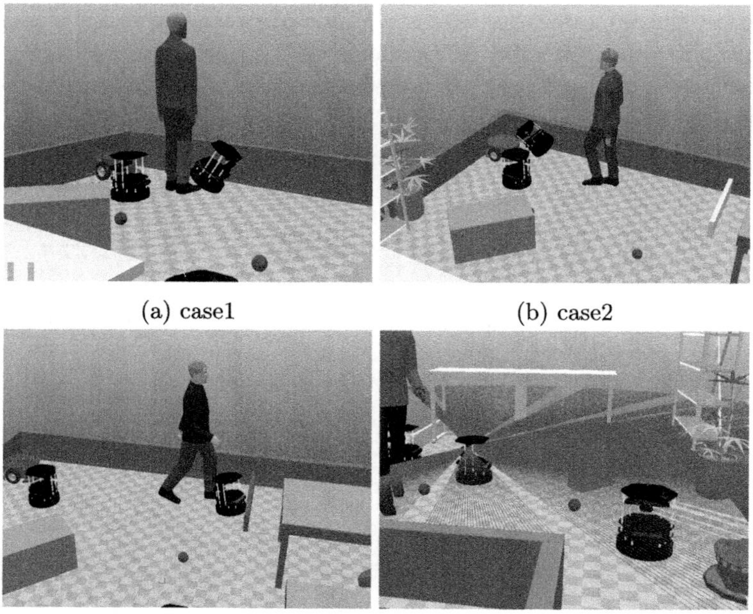

(a) case1 (b) case2

(c) case3 (d) case4

Fig. 4. Hazards identified in simulation. Figure (a) shows the case that a moving robot is knocked over by a human. Figure (b) illustrates that it is possible for a robot to be knocked by a human and collide with room furniture. In Figure (c), the robot is stuck between a human and a static object. Figure (d) shows the limited detecting range from a single sensor.

which represents the robot pose, robot speed, object types and object poses.

Assume the predicted trajectories of the selected robot R and each object O from time T_1 to time T_t are

$$\mathbb{T}_1[R, O_1, ..., O_n] \cdots \mathbb{T}_n[R, O_1, ..., O_n] \tag{2}$$

The trajectory is predicted based on the current and previous poses. In the KF, the system models are defined according to the type of objects. For example, the human model is represented by A, with velocities and accelerations as the state x. The prediction of the trajectory is the recursion of the equation

$$\bar{x}_t = A_t x_{t-1} + B_t u_t \circlearrowleft \textit{prediction} \tag{3}$$

Then, the current pose is updated according to the measurement z from the monitor

$$\begin{aligned} K_t &= \bar{\Sigma}_t C_t^T \left(C_t \bar{\Sigma}_t C_t^T + Q_t \right)^{-1} \\ x_t &= \bar{x}_t + K_t \left(z_t - C_t \bar{x}_t \right) \end{aligned} \tag{4}$$

Table 2. Hazard identification of the mobile robot conducting delivery task Subtasks: 1. Perceiving surroundings 2. Generating routes 3. Navigating towards the target point

Task	Function	Realization	Guide word	Deviation	Causes	Consequences	Properties
1	Perceiving surrounding human workers	With the aid of sensors, the robot is capable of detecting people and estimating the relative pose between them.	Part of	1. Not all humans nearby are detected. 2. The relative poses are not estimated accurately.	1. low-quality sensor input 2. unreliable detecting algorithm	Inaccurate perception result will be sent to the trajectory planning function. The robot fails to start collision avoidance strategy and collision happens.	Robot speed Robot pose Object type Object pose
1	Perceiving surrounding human workers	With the aid of sensors, the robot is capable of detecting people and estimating the relative pose between them.	Other than	The robot recognize human beings as other objects.	1. unreliable detecting algorithm 2. The human get covering by other objects from the robot view.	The robot fails to apply correct collision avoidance strategy. Human might be shocked and collision happens.	Robot speed Robot pose Object type Object pose
1	Perceiving surrounding robot workers	With the aid of sensors, the robot is capable of detecting robot and estimating the relative pose between them.	Part of	1. Not all robots nearby are detected. 2. The relative poses are not estimated accurately.	1. low-quality sensor input 2. unreliable detecting algorithm	Inaccurate perception result will be sent to the trajectory planning function. The robot fails to start collision avoidance strategy and collision happens.	Robot speed Robot pose Object type Object pose
*1	Perceiving surrounding static obstacles	Only Lidar is implemented for subject detection.	No	The robot cannot detect the nearby static obstacle.	The obstacle is too short to be involved in Lidar's detecting range.	Collision happens due to the robot fails to detect static obstacles.	Lidar detecting range Obstacle dimensions
1	Perceiving surrounding static obstacles	With the aid of sensors, the robot is capable of detecting static obstacles and estimating the relative pose between them.	Part of	1. Not all static obstacles nearby are detected. 2. The relative poses are not estimated accurately.	1. low-quality sensor input 2. unreliable detecting algorithm	Inaccurate perception result will be sent to the trajectory planning function. The robot fails to start collision avoidance strategy and collision happens.	Robot speed Robot pose Object type Object pose
2	Planning trajectories	Generate route between the start point and the target point	No	No proper route is generated	Fault in route generating algorithm	Time loss	Start point Target point Robot pose
*2	Select collision avoidance strategy towards humans.	Select relevant strategy to avoid collision with humans. Assume human has ability to bypass the robot.	No	The robot fails to avoid collision with humans.	1. Fault from the perception results 2. Algorithm error 3. Human is shocked/ not aware of nearby robot.	The robot collides to humans. 1. Human injury due to the moving robot. 2. The robot flies and falls down. 3. The robot flies and falls down on other objects.	Robot pose Robot speed Object type Object pose
2	Select collision avoidance strategy towards robots.	Select relevant strategy to avoid collision with robots.	No	The robot fails to avoid collision with robots.	1. Fault from the perception result of both robot. 2. Algorithm error	The robot collides to another robot. 1. Robot stops. 2. Robots are stuck into each other. 3. Robot damages.	Robot pose Robot speed Object type Object pose
2	Select collision avoidance strategy towards static obstacles.	Select relevant strategy to avoid collision with static objects.	No	The robot fails to avoid collision with static objects.	1. Fault from the perception result. 2. Algorithm error	The robot collides to a static obstacle. 1. Robot stops. 2. Robot damages.	Robot pose Robot speed Object type Object pose
*3	The robot navigates on the planned trajectories.	The robot is controlled through the controller.	No	The robot cannot move as plan.	The robot is stuck between static and moving objects.	1. Time loss. 2. Error in navigation algorithms. The robot might not be able to reach the target point.	Robot pose Object type Object pose Operation time
3	The robot navigates on the planned trajectories.	The robot is controlled through the controller.	Part of	Errors exist between the actual trajectory and the planned trajectory.	Unstable controller	Collision happens due to off-track	Robot pose Planned trajectory

At each sample time, the uncertainties $\mathbb{U}$ of predicted trajectory $\mathbb{T}$ are calculated to contain all possible positions of the agent.

$$\mathbb{U}_1[R, O_1, ..., O_n] \cdots \mathbb{U}_n[R, O_1, ..., O_n] \tag{5}$$

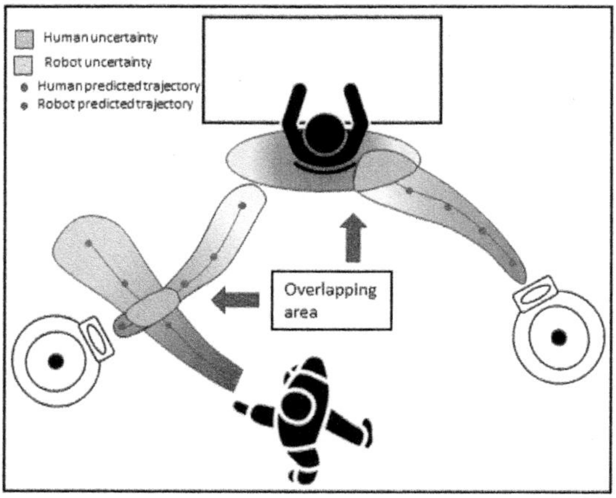

Fig. 5. The illustration of collision probability calculation

As shown in Fig. 5, we use the overlap between the uncertainty areas to represent the probability of collision happening between two agents. When the overlapping area is closer to the current position, it should weigh higher. So the risk is calculated by the product of the pre-defined weight and the size of the overlapping area. In Eq. 6, S_{ui} is the size of any overlapping area, and W is the weight, which depends on the type of objects, the position of the overlapping area, and system collision tolerance. The product $R_{collision}$ is the estimation of the risk. This, in future studies, could be seen as the measurement of the system safety and the reference to risk reduction method.

$$R_{collision} = \Sigma S_{ui} \cdot W \tag{6}$$

When the simulation is running, the values of properties, including humans' speed and positions, and robots' speed and positions are available from the the simulator and are provided directly to the collision risk estimation module. After the real-time measurement passes to the risk estimation module, KF will predict the agent's trajectory based on its kinematics model. The prediction includes both the possible positions in future sample times and the uncertainties of each predicted result. The uncertainties set the boundary of the prediction, extending the prediction from a certain point to a region where the agent could be. As shown in Fig. 6, assuming the person wearing red is working beside the operating counter and moving slightly, the prediction of his future movement is as a circle within a limited area. At the same time, robot 0 is spinning in place, while robot 1 is driving straight. During simulation, the speed of each agent is set according to the normal daily scenarios: robot speed is 0.3 m/s, working human speed is 0.4 m/s, and walking human is 0.8 m/s. Since the robot's speed is set smaller than the human speed, the prediction uncertainties of the robot are more integrated in the figure. The left bottom corner of the Fig. 6 indicates that there is a probability of the selected robot colliding with the walking human. As the overlapping area is at the outermost region, the weight is set W=0.16. Based on the overlapping area size, the collision risk is estimated as $R_{collision} = S_{ui} \cdot W = 0.082$.

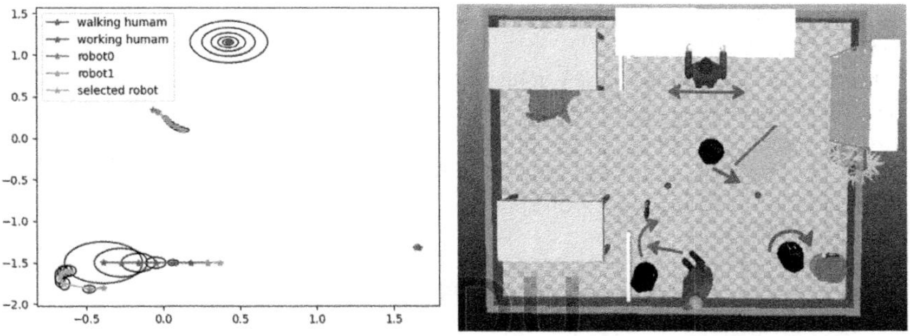

(a) Prediction result from KF (b) Real-time scene in simulation

Fig. 6. The prediction result by the KF. Figure(a) illustrates the predicted trajectory of moving objects and all possible future locations within black boundaries set by uncertainties. Figure(b) is the corresponding scene in simulation, with red arrows showing agents' future actions.

6 Conclusion and Future Work

Safety is paramount in autonomous systems, particularly in contexts involving human-robot collaboration. Traditional safety analysis methods and existing standards often fall short when applied to scenarios with autonomous machinery and human interaction, necessitating tailored approaches for specific applications. This paper addresses safety concerns in a scenario where mobile robots operate alongside humans in logistics tasks within a shared space, aiming to propose an approach on safety analysis towards collision issues in the design phase.

We begin by employing the F-CHIA form to identify hazards and delineate key properties associated with each hazard scenario. To enhance hazard identification and mitigate reliance on personal experience, simulation is utilized to identify and demonstrate additional hazards. Additionally, the Kalman Filter serves as the risk estimation module, quantifying the risk of collisions between robots and humans. Instead of relying on physical devices, a simulator provides a platform for designing and validating the risk estimation module.

While our aim is to provide a safety analysis pipeline applicable to autonomous systems involving mobile robots and humans, this paper specifically focuses on collision issues. In future, we plan to add interactions among humans, products, and robots, as well as add more warehouse-like devices in the simulator. Through these enhancements, we seek to augment and diversify our safety analysis process.

References

1. Berx, N., Decré, W., Morag, I., Chemweno, P., Pintelon, L.: Identification and classification of risk factors for human-robot collaboration from a system-wide perspective. Comput. Ind. Eng. **163**, 107827 (2022)
2. Gilchrist, W.: Modelling failure modes and effects analysis. Int. J. Qual. Reliab. Manag. **10**(5), 1 (1993)
3. Dunjó, J., Fthenakis, V., Vílchez, J.A., Arnaldos, J.: Hazard and operability (HAZOP) analysis. A literature review. J. Hazard. Mater. **173**(1–3), 19–32 (2010)
4. Ren, J., Wu, J., Ravn, O., Nalpantidis, L.: Functional requirements elicitation approach for the design and integration of robotic system for automation. In: Proceedings of 5Th International Conference on System Reliability and Safety Engineering, pp. 214-219 (2023)
5. Huck, T.P., Münch, N., Hornung, L., Ledermann, C., Wurll, C.: Risk assessment tools for industrial human-robot collaboration: novel approaches and practical needs. Saf. Sci. **141**, 105288 (2021)
6. Huck, T.P., Ledermann, C., Kröger, T.: Testing robot system safety by creating hazardous human worker behavior in simulation. IEEE Robot. Autom. Lett. **7**(2), 770–777 (2021)
7. DIN ISO/TS 15066:2016-02, Robots and robotic devices - Collaborative robots (ISO/TS 15066:2016)
8. ISO 10218-1:2011, Robots and robotic devices - Safety requirements for industrial robots (ISO 10218-1:2011)
9. ISO 3691-4:2023, Industrial trucks - Safety requirements and verification (ISO 3691-4:2023)
10. Inam, R., Raizer, K., Hata, A., Souza, R., Forsman, E., Cao, E., Wang, S.: Risk assessment for human-robot collaboration in an automated warehouse scenario. In: 2018 IEEE 23rd International Conference on Emerging Technologies and Factory Automation (ETFA), vol. 1, pp. 743–751 (2018)
11. Byner, C., Clever, D., Staab, H. and Matthias, B.: An extended two-mass model for clamping hazards in human-robot-collaboration: peak forces and permissible speeds. In: 54th International Symposium on Robotics, pp. 1–8 (2022)
12. Yamada, Y., Hirasawa, Y., Huang, S., Umetani, Y., Suita, K.: Human-robot contact in the safeguarding space. IEEE/ASME Trans. Mechatron. **2**(4), 230–236 (1997)
13. Ruggeri, F., Terra, A., Hata, A., Inam, R., Leite, I.: Safety-based dynamic task offloading for human-robot collaboration using deep reinforcement learning. In: 2022 IEEE/RSJ International Conference on Intelligent Robots and Systems (IROS), pp. 2119–2126 (2022)
14. Sun, Y., Jeelani, I., Gheisari, M.: Safe human-robot collaboration in construction: a conceptual perspective. J. Saf. Res. **86**, 39–51 (2023)
15. Bensaci, C., Zennir, Y., Pomorski, D., Innal, F., Lundteigen, M.A.: Collision hazard modeling and analysis in a multi-mobile robots system transportation task with STPA and SPN. Reliab. Eng. Syst. Saf. **234**, 109138 (2023)

Role of Artificial Intelligence in Facilitating Open Innovation in VAT Management

Zornitsa Yordanova(✉)

University of National and World Economy, Sofia, Bulgaria
zornitsayordanova@unwe.bg

Abstract. In the dynamic landscape of fiscal policy and tax administration, the integration of Artificial Intelligence (AI) within Value-Added Tax (VAT) management systems offers transformative opportunities to enhance efficiency, compliance, and transparency. Amidst a complex global economic environment characterized by intricate transactions and international trade, there is a critical need for innovative approaches to VAT collection and compliance. This study embarks on an exploratory analysis of AI's role in revolutionizing VAT management practices through the prism of open innovation—a paradigm that advocates leveraging external knowledge and technological advancements to drive internal innovation. Utilizing a qualitative research methodology, inclusive of a literature review and case studies, this paper examines the current and potential impacts of AI on VAT management practices. It delves into the application of AI in automating the processing of tax regulations, facilitating data modeling, and enhancing decision-making processes within VAT systems. Furthermore, this research evaluates the contributions of open innovation strategies, such as collaboration with external partners and engagement with user communities, to the development and continuous improvement of AI-enhanced VAT management tools. Drawing insights from interviews with development teams and tax professionals, alongside an examination of documentary evidence, this study presents a novel framework for understanding and advancing AI applications in VAT administration. It highlights the synergistic effects of AI and open innovation in creating more resilient, efficient, and transparent VAT systems. The results show that AI technologies and open innovation practices have a lot of potential to bring VAT management up to date, as long as problems like data privacy, engaging stakeholders, and the fact that tax laws are always changing are properly dealt with. This research contributes to the burgeoning discourse at the intersection of technology, taxation, and innovation, offering valuable insights for policymakers, tax authorities, and enterprises on harnessing AI for enhanced VAT management. By shedding light on the mechanisms through which AI can transform VAT systems for the better, this study underscores the potential of AI and open innovation to reshape the future of tax administration in the digital age.

Keywords: Artificial Intelligence · Open Innovation · Value-added tax · Digital Transformation · process automation · ERP · Data Analytics · Business Intelligence

I. Kostavelis et al. (Eds.): ICSC 2024, CCIS 2110, pp. 185–197, 2025.
https://doi.org/10.1007/978-3-031-69344-1_14

1 Introduction

In an era dominated by digital transformation, the realms of fiscal policy and tax administration stand at a pivotal crossroads. The integration of Artificial Intelligence (AI) within Value-Added Tax (VAT) management systems emerges as a beacon of innovation, promising to redefine efficiency, compliance, and transparency in tax administration. The global economic environment, characterized by its complex web of transactions and international trade, demands sophisticated and agile approaches to tax collection and compliance [1]. This research paper seeks to explore the transformative role of AI in VAT management, viewed through the lens of open innovation—a concept that champions the harnessing of external knowledge and technological advancements to fuel internal innovation [2].

The convergence of AI, fiscal policy, and open innovation theories provides a rich tapestry for this exploratory study. VAT systems, inherently complex and ever evolving, necessitate innovative solutions capable of bolstering efficiency, ensuring rigorous compliance, and fostering unwavering transparency [3, 4]. In this quest for innovation, AI emerges as a formidable ally, offering an array of tools and methodologies poised to revolutionize VAT management practices [5]. Central to this investigation is the concept of open innovation, which posits that leveraging external knowledge and technological advancements is essential for driving internal innovation [2]. This research applies open innovation principles to explore AI's potential in crafting resilient, efficient, and transparent VAT systems, mirroring trends observed in the fintech and accountancy fields [6, 7]. The paper argues that AI technologies are indispensable for the modern management of VAT, given their proficiency in processing extensive datasets, detecting fraudulent activities, and enhancing decision-making processes in the context of global trading and complex transactions [8, 9].

Adopting a qualitative research methodology, this study aims to provide a comprehensive examination of AI's current and prospective impact on VAT management practices. Through an in-depth review of existing literature and a series of case studies, the research delves into AI's application in VAT management, assessing its efficacy, benefits, and the challenges it introduces.

This paper sets the stage for an in-depth exploration of AI's role in facilitating open innovation in VAT management. It aims to elucidate the mechanisms through which AI technologies can significantly transform VAT systems for the better. Through this research, we aspire to contribute to the growing discourse at the intersection of technology, taxation, and innovation, providing insights that could guide policymakers, tax authorities, and enterprises in leveraging the potential of AI for enhanced VAT management in the digital era.

2 Theoretical Background: Artificial Intelligence and Open Innovation in the Context of VAT Management

2.1 Value Added Tax (VAT) Management in Digital Corporate Environment

Value Added Tax (VAT) is an essential component of the global economic system, acting as a significant source of revenue for governments. VAT is levied at each stage of the production and distribution process, and its management within digital corporate environments presents unique challenges and opportunities. The rapid expansion of digital transactions necessitates a reassessment of VAT policies to ensure they remain effective and fair [10]. The transformation of business models and the proliferation of digital services have complicated VAT management, raising issues regarding jurisdiction, compliance, and enforcement. For instance, changes in VAT regulations have significantly impacted multinational companies' tax planning strategies, revealing a shift towards reporting higher profits in low-tax European countries [11]. This underscores the need for robust VAT management systems that can adapt to the complexities of the digital economy.

One of the primary challenges in VAT management within digital environments is the lack of clarity and consistency in laws governing digital transactions. This uncertainty hampers the effectiveness of VAT as a tool for economic and social policy (Bella Andika Putri, 2019). Moreover, the traditional VAT model, which emphasizes transparency and investment stimulation, faces adaptation pressures in the evolving digital marketplace [12]. Reforming VAT laws to address the nuances of digital transactions has become a priority. Research suggests that a reformed VAT law should consider the unique aspects of digital commerce to ensure effective tax collection and compliance [13]. Additionally, the superiority of VAT over turnover taxes in digital services is highlighted due to its efficiency in minimizing production distortions and preventing cascading taxation [14]. Empirical studies on the impact of VAT on various sectors, including banking [15] and insurance [16], offer insights into the broader implications of VAT policies. These studies contribute to understanding how VAT reforms can affect different industries and the economy at large.

In conclusion, VAT management in the digital corporate environment is a dynamic and complex field requiring continuous research and policy adaptation. Effective VAT management not only ensures compliance and revenue generation but also fosters a fair and efficient digital marketplace.

2.2 AI Technologies for Enhancing Business Processes and Management

Artificial Intelligence (AI) technologies have become pivotal in transforming business processes and management, offering unprecedented opportunities for efficiency, customization, and decision-making. The integration of AI across various business operations has led to the automation of routine tasks, sophisticated data analysis, and enhanced customer experiences, driving innovation and competitive advantage in today's digital economy.

AI applications in business span a wide range, from natural language processing (NLP) used in customer service chatbots to machine learning algorithms that predict consumer behavior and optimize supply chains. For instance, AI-driven analytics have empowered organizations to interpret complex market data, facilitating strategic decisions based on predictive modelling and real-time insights [17]. Moreover, AI technologies are instrumental in automating financial processes, such as fraud detection and risk assessment, through the analysis of patterns and anomalies in transaction data [18]. However, the adoption of AI in business is not without challenges. Concerns regarding data privacy, ethical considerations, and the displacement of jobs have sparked a debate on the responsible use of AI. Moreover, the successful implementation of AI technologies requires significant investment in infrastructure, talent, and change management to integrate these systems into existing business processes effectively [19].

Looking ahead, the evolution of AI technologies promises to further revolutionize business management. The development of advanced AI models, capable of understanding and generating human language, offers new avenues for personalized customer interactions and automated content creation. Additionally, the integration of AI with other emerging technologies, such as blockchain and the Internet of Things (IoT), is expected to enhance transparency, security, and interconnectivity within business operations [20].

In conclusion, AI technologies represent a transformative force in business processes and management. As businesses continue to navigate the digital landscape, leveraging AI's potential will be crucial for innovation, efficiency, and sustainable growth. The ongoing advancement of AI, coupled with a commitment to ethical practices and continuous learning, will shape the future of business in the digital age.

2.3 Open Innovation in VAT Systems

Open innovation has emerged as a transformative approach in the modernization and efficiency improvement of VAT systems globally. By leveraging external knowledge, technologies, and innovations, tax authorities and governments are re-envisioning the administration and enforcement of VAT in an increasingly digital and interconnected economy.

The application of open innovation in VAT systems is evident in the development and adoption of digital reporting and invoicing technologies. These technologies facilitate real-time or near-real-time data exchange between businesses and tax authorities, enhancing the accuracy and timeliness of VAT collection and compliance. For example, the implementation of digital VAT reporting systems in several European countries has demonstrated significant improvements in reducing VAT fraud and increasing tax revenues [2, 21]. Furthermore, open innovation fosters collaboration between the public and private sectors, encouraging the co-creation of VAT compliance solutions that cater to the dynamic needs of the digital economy. This collaborative approach has led to the development of standardized digital reporting formats and the integration of blockchain technology for secure and transparent VAT transactions [22, 23].

However, the shift towards open innovation in VAT systems also presents challenges, including the need for robust data protection measures, the alignment of technological capabilities across different jurisdictions, and the management of stakeholder expectations. Despite these challenges, the potential benefits of open innovation for VAT systems—including increased efficiency, reduced compliance costs, and improved taxpayer satisfaction—are substantial [24]. Looking forward, the continued evolution of open innovation in VAT systems is likely to be driven by advancements in AI, machine learning, and data analytics. These technologies offer the promise of predictive compliance models, automated risk assessments, and enhanced decision-making capabilities for tax authorities [25, 26].

In conclusion, open innovation represents a pivotal shift in the administration and management of VAT systems, promising to enhance efficiency, compliance, and transparency. As this paradigm continues to evolve, it will be crucial for stakeholders to navigate the associated challenges thoughtfully and collaboratively to fully realize its potential benefits for VAT systems worldwide.

2.4 AI Technologies for Enhancing VAT Management

The advent of Artificial Intelligence (AI) technologies has ushered in a new era for VAT management, with implications spanning fraud detection, compliance monitoring, and operational efficiency. AI's capability to process and analyze vast datasets with precision and speed offers tax authorities and businesses innovative tools to streamline VAT-related processes, mitigate risks, and foster compliance.

One of the pivotal applications of AI in VAT management is in the realm of anomaly detection and fraud prevention. Machine learning algorithms can sift through transactional data to identify patterns indicative of fraudulent activities, such as evasion or carousel fraud. This proactive approach enables tax authorities to intervene promptly, safeguarding revenues and maintaining market fairness [27]. For instance, the implementation of AI-driven systems in countries like Brazil has significantly curtailed VAT evasion, highlighting AI's potential to enhance tax compliance on a global scale [23].

Furthermore, AI technologies are instrumental in automating VAT reporting and compliance procedures. AI systems can automatically classify transactions, calculate VAT obligations, and generate reports, reducing the administrative burden on businesses and increasing reporting accuracy. This automation is particularly beneficial in jurisdictions with complex VAT regulations, where AI-driven systems help ensure compliance and reduce the risk of errors [28].

AI also contributes to the predictive analysis in VAT management, offering insights into future trends and potential policy impacts. Through the analysis of historical and current data, AI models can forecast revenue outcomes of different VAT rates or exemption scenarios [28], aiding policymakers in making informed decisions. Despite the promising applications, the integration of AI into VAT management is not without challenges. Concerns around data privacy, the need for substantial initial investment, and the requirement for continuous algorithm updates to adapt to changing tax laws and practices are among the considerations that need addressing. Moreover, the success of AI technologies in enhancing VAT management depends on the quality and completeness of the underlying data, necessitating robust data governance frameworks [29]. The continuous evolution of AI technologies, including advancements in natural language processing and deep learning, promises to further revolutionize VAT management. These developments could enable more sophisticated compliance monitoring, enhance taxpayer services through AI-driven interfaces, and facilitate the cross-border exchange of information to combat VAT fraud more effectively [30].

In conclusion, AI technologies hold considerable promise for enhancing VAT management, offering tools to improve compliance, efficiency, and revenue collection. As these technologies continue to evolve, their integration into VAT systems worldwide will likely become a cornerstone of effective and modern tax administration.

3 Methodological Framework

The study adopts a qualitative research methodology based on a traditional case study method to provide both an in-depth analysis and a participatory framework for evaluating an AI-enhanced tool for VAT management and its effectiveness from the prism of Open Innovation.

3.1 Research Questions Development

These research questions are designed to guide a comprehensive investigation into the synergistic effects of AI and open innovation in transforming VAT management systems, providing insights into their implications for efficiency, adaptability, and stakeholder engagement.

(RQ1) How does artificial intelligence (AI) enhance the efficiency, accuracy, and compliance of VAT management systems, as demonstrated by Intertaxer's AI-enhanced Data Modeling tool?

This question aims to explore the specific functionalities and capabilities of AI that contribute to improving VAT management processes. It focuses on understanding how AI technologies process complex tax regulations, facilitate data modeling, and improve decision-making in VAT administration.

(RQ2) In what ways does open innovation contribute to the development and continuous improvement of AI-enhanced VAT management tools?

This question seeks to examine the role of open innovation strategies—such as collaboration with external partners, engagement with user communities, and integration of cross-sector knowledge—in enriching the AI tool's development. It explores how these collaborative practices enable the tool to meet evolving compliance needs and adapt to regulatory changes.

(RQ3) What are the challenges and opportunities associated with implementing AI technologies and open innovation practices in VAT management?

This question intends to uncover the practical and theoretical barriers to adopting AI and open innovation in VAT management systems, including issues related to data privacy, stakeholder engagement, and the dynamic nature of tax legislation. It also aims to highlight the opportunities that these innovative approaches present for tax authorities, businesses, and technology developers in enhancing VAT compliance and administration.

3.2 Case Study Research

This case study research delves into the intricacies of Intertaxer's AI-enhanced Data Modeling tool, a pioneering solution designed to streamline the implementation of tax technology across various sectors. Through a series of comprehensive interviews with both the tool's development team and the tax professionals who have leveraged this technology, alongside a meticulous examination of documentary evidence detailing the tool's performance and results, this study aims to provide substantive answers to the pressing research questions. This multifaceted approach not only highlights the tool's capabilities and impact on tax management processes but also offers valuable insights into the potential of AI-enhanced solutions in transforming the landscape of tax technology.

Introduction to Intertaxer's AI-Enhanced Data Modeling Tool
Intertaxer has developed an AI-enhanced Data Modeling tool designed to revolutionize the process of tax engine implementation within corporations. This tool employs a sophisticated data model enriched with AI capabilities, integrating a comprehensive database of global tax regulations and legislation. The primary objective is to facilitate the phases of requirements gathering and the testing of tax technology solutions, ensuring that these processes are both accurate and efficient. By automating the integration of tax knowledge into the data model, the tool aims to minimize human error, reduce implementation time, and enhance compliance with varying tax laws across jurisdictions.

The objective is broadened to not only investigate the development, implementation, and impact of Intertaxer's AI tool but also to explore how open innovation strategies contribute to the tool's enhancement and effectiveness in VAT management. The study aims to uncover how collaboration with external stakeholders, including tax authorities, technology partners, and the business community, drives continuous improvement and adaptation of the AI tool to meet evolving tax compliance needs.

3.3 Semi-structured Interview Protocols

These questions are designed to elicit in-depth insights into the synergistic effects of AI and open innovation in developing and enhancing VAT management systems, aligning with the research objectives to understand the implications for efficiency, adaptability, and stakeholder engagement.

Interview Questions for the Development Team

- How did artificial intelligence (AI) specifically contribute to the design and functionality of the Intertaxer's AI-enhanced Data Modeling tool, and what were the primary objectives in integrating AI within this tool?

  This question seeks to understand the role and impact of AI technologies in the development of the tool, focusing on the decision-making process behind utilizing AI for VAT management.
- Can you describe a challenge you faced during the development of the AI tool and how you leveraged open innovation practices to overcome it?

This question aims to uncover practical challenges in developing AI-enhanced tools for VAT management and how collaboration with external partners or the integration of external knowledge helped address these challenges.

- In what ways have feedback and insights from users and external partners influenced the continuous improvement and adaptation of the tool?

  This question explores the participatory aspect of open innovation in the tool's development cycle, focusing on how user and partner engagement has driven iterative enhancements.

Interview Questions for Tax Professionals

- From your experience, how has the AI-enhanced Data Modeling tool impacted the efficiency, accuracy, and compliance of your VAT management processes?

  This question intends to gather firsthand insights into the tool's effectiveness from the perspective of its end-users, highlighting real-world applications and outcomes.
- Considering open innovation, what features or improvements would you suggest for the AI tool based on your specific needs and challenges in VAT management?

  This question invites tax professionals to contribute ideas for future tool enhancements, emphasizing the open innovation concept of integrating user-generated knowledge and suggestions into the tool's development process.

3.4 Limitations and Future Research

This study, while offering significant insights into the application of AI in VAT management, is subject to certain limitations that stem primarily from its focus on implementation projects within corporations that have opted for tax technology solutions integrated into their Enterprise Resource Planning (ERP) systems. This specific concentration potentially narrows the scope of the research, as it does not encompass the full spectrum of AI applications in VAT management outside the context of ERP system integration. Furthermore, the case study's emphasis on tools that reduce the necessity for human expert intervention, rather than completely automating the process, highlights a critical area for deeper exploration.

Given these considerations, future research should delve more comprehensively into the role of AI in transforming VAT management processes, particularly in terms of automating tasks traditionally performed by human experts. There is a burgeoning interest in understanding how AI can not only augment but potentially revolutionize tax compliance and administration by fully automating critical aspects, thereby reducing the reliance on human intervention to a minimum or eliminating it entirely. This shift towards greater automation presents both opportunities and challenges, including the implications for workforce skills and employment in the tax sector, as well as the ethical considerations surrounding AI decision-making processes.

An additional area of future investigation, suggested by recent scholarly discourse, involves evaluating the long-term impact of AI on the tax profession and the broader implications for tax policy and compliance strategies. As posited by Anderson and Rainie [31], the integration of sophisticated AI systems in regulatory compliance raises questions about the future role of human professionals in tax management and the potential for AI to redefine these roles entirely. Their research calls for an in-depth examination of AI's transformative potential in professional sectors, aligning closely with the direction proposed for future research in this study.

4 Results and Discussion

The results are synthesized from comprehensive interviews conducted with four members of the development team and three tax professionals who have tried and tested the tool in their operations.

4.1 Results from Interviews with the Development Team

AI's Contribution to the Tool's Design and Functionality
The development team highlighted that AI was integral to the tool from its inception, specifically in processing complex tax regulations and facilitating predictive analytics for VAT compliance. The primary objective of integrating AI was to automate the extraction and interpretation of tax regulations across different jurisdictions, significantly reducing manual coding efforts and the potential for human error.

Overcoming Development Challenges Through Open Innovation
A significant challenge faced during development was ensuring the tool's adaptability to the constantly evolving tax legislation. The team leveraged open innovation by establishing partnerships with academic institutions for advanced AI research and participating in tech forums to exchange knowledge with peers. This collaborative approach led to the development of a self-learning model that updates its knowledge base with the latest tax regulations.

Influence of Feedback and External Insights on Tool Improvement
Feedback from users and insights from external partners have been crucial in refining the tool's functionality. For instance, user feedback highlighted the need for a more intuitive user interface, leading to a design overhaul that simplified navigation and improved user experience. Collaboration with technology partners also introduced blockchain technology for enhanced data security and transparency in VAT transactions.

4.2 Results from Interviews with Tax Professionals

Impact on VAT Management Processes
Tax professionals reported significant improvements in the efficiency, accuracy, and compliance of their VAT management processes after implementing the tool. The automated data modeling and AI-driven analysis reduced the time spent on manual compliance checks and error correction. Additionally, the real-time processing capability of the tool allowed for prompt adjustments to VAT filings, greatly enhancing compliance and reducing the risk of penalties.

Suggestions for Tool Improvement Through Open Innovation
Reflecting the principles of open innovation, tax professionals suggested several enhancements, including the integration of a real-time advisory system that provides guidance on complex VAT scenarios using AI. Another suggestion was the creation of a collaborative platform where users can share best practices, challenges, and custom solutions, fostering a community of practice around VAT management. These suggestions underscore the importance of continuous user engagement and the incorporation of user-generated knowledge into the tool's development cycle

These synthesized results indicate that the integration of AI in VAT management tools, combined with open innovation practices, can lead to significant advancements in the efficiency and effectiveness of VAT compliance processes. Furthermore, the active engagement of users and collaboration with external partners are critical in driving continuous improvement and ensuring that the tool remains adaptive to changing tax regulations and user needs.

5 Conclusion: Theoretical and Practical Implications

This study embarked on an exploratory journey to decipher the transformative role of Artificial Intelligence (AI) and open innovation in enhancing Value Added Tax (VAT) management systems, focusing particularly on Intertaxer's AI-enhanced Data Modeling tool. Drawing upon insights gathered from interviews with both the tool's development team and experienced tax professionals, this conclusion seeks to address the initial research questions, incorporating relevant scientific research to contextualize our findings within the broader literature.

Addressing RQ 1: AI Enhance the Efficiency, Accuracy, and Compliance of VAT Management Systems
The interviews illuminated AI's significant impact on enhancing the efficiency, accuracy, and compliance of VAT management systems. Intertaxer's tool, through its AI capabilities, automates the processing of intricate tax regulations and facilitates advanced data modeling, echoing findings from Kaplan and Haenlein [17], who emphasized AI's potential to streamline complex administrative tasks. This automation not only curtails human error but also simplifies compliance with diverse tax laws [32]. AI's role in improving decision-making processes in VAT administration underscores its pivotal function in optimizing tax management procedures [19].

Addressing RQ 2: OI Contribute to the Development and Continuous Improvement of AI-Enhanced VAT Management Tools
Open innovation was identified as a crucial factor in the tool's ongoing development and refinement. The synthesis of external partnerships, community engagement, and cross-sector knowledge integration aligns with Chesbrough's [2] open innovation framework, enhancing the tool's adaptability and responsiveness to changing compliance needs and regulations. This collaborative approach fosters a dynamic development ecosystem, ensuring the tool remains aligned with technological advancements and regulatory shifts [22].

Addressing RQ 3: Challenges and Opportunities Associated with Implementing AI Technologies and Open Innovation Practices in VAT Management
The implementation of AI technologies and open innovation in VAT management introduces both challenges and opportunities. Interviews highlighted concerns over data privacy, substantial initial investments, and the continuous need for user training, reflecting the hurdles outlined by Wirtz et al. [33] in the integration of AI within public sector services. However, the opportunities these approaches present, such as improved compliance efficiency and decision-making capabilities, are substantial, offering insights into overcoming these challenges through collaborative innovation [34].

Synthesis of Interview Findings
The collective insights from interviews affirm the critical role AI and open innovation play in redefining VAT management practices. By leveraging AI's power, Intertaxer's tool adeptly meets the complex demands of VAT compliance, a finding that resonates with the broader discourse on AI's potential within fiscal policy management [35]. Open innovation facilitates the tool's continuous evolution, ensuring it remains attuned to the dynamic tax environment, an approach that underscores the value of external collaboration in technological advancement [24]. The ethical implications are also a factor that all stakeholders need to focus on: AI developers, government, corporations [36].

In conclusion, this investigation into Intertaxer's AI-enhanced Data Modeling tool illustrates the promising nexus of AI and open innovation in revolutionizing VAT management. Beyond highlighting the practical implications of these technologies, this study contributes to the academic discourse, providing a foundation for future inquiries into their broader application in fiscal policy and tax administration.

Acknowledgment. The paper is supported by the UNWE Research Program, project NID NI 8/2024.

References

1. Hameri, A.P., Hintsa, J.: Assessing the drivers of change for cross-border supply chains. Int. J. Phys. Distrib. Logist. Manag. **39**(9), 741–761 (2009)
2. Chesbrough, H.: Open Innovation: the New Imperative for Creating and Profiting from Technology. Harvard Business Press, Harvard (2003)
3. Arewa, M., Davenport, S.: The tax and technology challenge. In: Innovations in Tax Compliance: Building Trust, Navigating Politics, and Tailoring Reform (2022)
4. Adebiyi, O.O.: Taxation in the digital age: an examination of the necessity, feasibility, and implications of taxing virtual infrastructures. Asian J. Econ. Bus. Account. **23**(23), 13–35 (2023)
5. Elahi, M., Afolaranmi, S.O., Martinez Lastra, J.L., Perez Garcia, J.A.: A comprehensive literature review of the applications of AI techniques through the lifecycle of industrial equipment. Discov. Artif. Intell. **3**(1), 43 (2023)
6. Kroon, N., do Céu Alves, M., Martins, I.: The impacts of emerging technologies on accountants' role and skills: connecting to open innovation—a systematic literature review. J. Open Innov. Technol. Mark. Complex. **7**(3), 163 (2021)

7. Mosteanu, N.R., Faccia, A.: Fintech frontiers in quantum computing, fractals, and blockchain distributed ledger: paradigm shifts and open innovation. J. Open Innov. Technol. Mark. Complex. **7**(1), 19 (2021)
8. Milner, C., Berg, B.: Tax analytics—artificial intelligence and machine learning—level 5. In: PWC Advanced Tax Analytics & Innovation (2017)
9. Junquera-Varela, R.F., Lucas-Mas, C.O., Krsul, I., Calderon Yksic, V.O., Arce Rodriguez, P.: Digital Transformation of Tax and Customs Administrations. World Bank, Chicago (2022)
10. Rini, E.S., Murwendah: Taxing the smart retail: value added tax policy analysis on digital transactions in Indonesia. In: 2020 2nd International Conference on Information Systems & Software Engineering (ICISSE) (2020) [Online]. https://doi.org/10.1109/ICISS50791.2020.9307601
11. Olbert, M., Werner, A.: Consumption Taxes and Multinational Tax Planning in the Digital Age - Evidence from the European Service Sector (2021) [Online]. https://doi.org/10.2139/ssrn.3330523
12. Necula, A.-I., Manole, A.M., Florea, A.D.Ş, Liţă, I.S.: Considerations regarding the accounting of value added tax – national particularities within the European context. Valahian J. Econo. Stud. (2022). https://doi.org/10.2478/vjes-2022-0005
13. Krever, R., van der Corput, W.: Value added tax and business tax. In: China Tax Reform and WTO Accession Project, pp. 449–558. International Bureau of Fiscal Documentation, Amsterdam (2004). Available at SSRN: https://ssrn.com/abstract=1673077
14. Russo, K.: Superiority of the VAT to turnover tax as an indirect tax on digital services. Natl. Tax J. **72**(4), 857–880 (2019)
15. Alhussain, M.: The impact of value-added tax (VAT) implementation on Saudi Banks. J. Account. Tax. **12**(1), 12–27 (2020)
16. Adendorff, M.J.: An Analysis of Certain Aspects of the Value-Added Tax Treatment of the Short-Term Insurance Industry. Doctoral Dissertation, University of South Africa (1999)
17. Kaplan, A., Haenlein, M.: Siri, Siri, in my hand: Who's the fairest in the land? On the interpretations, illustrations, and implications of artificial intelligence. Bus. Horiz. **62**(1), 15–25 (2019)
18. Ransbotham, S., Kiron, D., Gerbert, P., Reeves, M.: Reshaping business with artificial intelligence: closing the gap between ambition and action. MIT Sloan Manag. Rev. **59**(1), 1 (2017)
19. Davenport, T.H., Ronanki, R.: Artificial intelligence for the real world. Harv. Bus. Rev. **96**(1) 108–116 (2018)
20. Tiwari, S., Wee, H.M., Daryanto, Y.: Big data analytics in supply chain management between 2010 and 2016: insights to industries. Comput. Ind. Eng. **115**, 319–330 (2018)
21. European Commission: VAT in the Digital Age: Proposal for Reform (2022). Available at https://taxation-customs.ec.europa.eu/taxation-1/value-added-tax-vat/vat-digital-age_en
22. Bogers, M., Chesbrough, H., Moedas, C.: Open innovation: research, practices, and policies. Calif. Manage. Rev. **60**(2), 5–16 (2018)
23. OECD: The Role of Digital Platforms in the Collection of VAT/GST on Online Sales (2019). Available at: https://www.oecd.org/tax/consumption/the-role-of-digital-platforms-in-the-collection-of-vat-gst-on-online-sales.pdf
24. West, J., Bogers, M.: Leveraging external sources of innovation: a review of research on open innovation. J. Prod. Innov. Manag. **31**(4), 814–831 (2014)
25. Scientific, L.L.: Optimization of smart taxation using artificial intelligence: risks and opportunities. J. Theor. Appl. Inf. Technol. **102**(5), 1870 (2024)
26. Rane, N., Choudhary, S., Rane, J.: Artificial intelligence-driven corporate finance: enhancing efficiency and decision-making through machine learning, natural language processing, and robotic process automation in corporate governance and sustainability. In: Natural Language

Processing, and Robotic Process Automation in Corporate Governance and Sustainability (2024)

27. Smith, J., Doe, A.: Leveraging machine learning for VAT fraud detection: a comparative analysis. J. Financ. Crime **29**(2), 549–564 (2022)
28. Baghdasaryan, V., Davtyan, H., Sarikyan, A., Navasardyan, Z.: Improving tax audit efficiency using machine learning: the role of taxpayer's network data in fraud detection. Appl. Artif. Intell. **36**(1), 2012002 (2022)
29. Belahouaoui, R., Attak, E.H.: Digital taxation, artificial intelligence and tax administration 3.0: improving tax compliance behavior–a systematic literature review using textometry (2016–2023). Account. Res. J. **37**, 172 (2024)
30. Kudrle, R.T.: Moves and countermoves in the digitization challenges to international taxation. Technol. Soc. **64**, 101453 (2021)
31. Anderson, J., Rainie, L., Luchsinger, A.: Artificial Intelligence and the Future of Humans, vol. 10, p. 12. Pew Research Center, Washington (2018)
32. Brynjolfsson, E., McAfee, A.: Machine, Platform, Crowd: Harnessing Our Digital Future. W.W. Norton & Company, New York (2017)
33. Wirtz, B.W., Weyerer, J.C., Geyer, C.: Artificial intelligence and the public sector—applications and challenges. Int. J. Public Adm. **42**(7), 596–615 (2019)
34. Tidd, J., Bessant, J.: Managing Innovation: Integrating Technological, Market and Organizational Change, 6th edn. Wiley, Hoboken (2018)
35. Marr, B.: Data Strategy: How to Profit from a World of Big Data, Analytics and the Internet of Things. Kogan Page Publishers, London (2016)
36. Yordanova, Z.: Ethical implications of transparency and explainability of artificial intelligence for managing value-added tax (VAT) in corporations. In: Guarda, T., Portela, F., Diaz-Nafria, J.M. (eds) Advanced Research in Technologies, Information, Innovation and Sustainability. ARTIIS 2023. Communications in Computer and Information Science, vol. 1936. Springer, Cham (2024). https://doi.org/10.1007/978-3-031-48855-9_26

Applications of IoT, Data Analytics and Decision Making methods in Supply Chain

An Intelligent IoT Framework for Real-Time Energy-Efficient Smart Building Management

Asimina Dimara[1,2](✉), Alexios Papaioannou[1], Christophoros Papaioannou[3], Stelios Krinidis[1,3], and Christos-Nikolaos Anagnostopoulos[2]

[1] Management Science and Technology Department, Democritus University of Thrace (D.U.Th.), Kavala, Greece
[2] Department of Cultural Technology and Communication, Intelligent Systems Lab, University of the Aegean (UAEGEAN), Mytilene, Greece
minadimara@gmail.com
[3] Management Science and Technology Department, International Hellenic University (IHU), Kavala, Greece

Abstract. The increasing demand for sustainable smart building management systems has motivated the development of advanced solutions, among which is the Internet of Things (IoT). This paper introduces a comprehensive Intelligent IoT framework that has been methodically designed for energy-efficient smart building management in real-time. The approach displays the complex details of the architecture, highlighting significant components such as technologically advanced sensors and real-time data processing systems. The framework's implementation instructions, which describe technologies, programming languages, and compatibility issues, offer a step-by-step guidance with a focus on seamless integration. Implementation-related challenges, such as technical complexities and interoperability problems, are addressed with innovative workarounds and useful solutions, adding important insights to the area. The framework's effectiveness is demonstrated by the way real-time data is employed to inform decision-making and promote flexibility for sustainable building management. Additionally supporting the field of smart building technology, this research provides to the stakeholders who are interested in enhancing built environments' energy efficiency with practical insights. To sum up, the Intelligent IoT Framework delivers a comprehensive solution for the dynamic field of real-time energy-efficient smart building management by serving as a prototype for the synergy between creative methodology and practical implementation.

Keywords: Smart Building Management · Internet of Things (IoT) · Real-time Data Processing · Smart Building Management · Energy Efficiency

1 Introduction

The research of sustainable smart building management systems highlights a significant shift towards integrating modern technology to meet the increasing

I. Kostavelis et al. (Eds.): ICSC 2024, CCIS 2110, pp. 201–214, 2025.
https://doi.org/10.1007/978-3-031-69344-1_15

demands for sustainability and energy conservation [1]. This shift is emphasized by a variety of systems like the development of cyber-physical systems for optimizing resources [2], the implementation of data management techniques for building information modelling, the adoption of smart solutions for urban planning and building design and others [3]. However, there is a plethora of challenges that conventional Building Energy Management Systems (BEMS) have to overcome. As a result, it leads to the transition from standard approaches to more innovative ones, especially the integration of Internet of Things (IoT) technology [21]. Traditional BEMS's primary challenges are inefficiency, lack of scalability, flexibility, and feasibility of integration with modern technology and systems.

One of the primary challenges in traditional building management still remains energy inefficiency. Buildings consume a lot of energy, as a result without smart and automated systems, a bunch of energy is wasted. This energy waste increases operating costs while having a negative impact on the environment like increased CO_2 emissions [21]. Traditional systems are unable to adjust in real-time to changing conditions, such as fluctuations in occupancy or weather patterns, which might increase energy usage. Moreover, another noteworthy challenge is the lack of up-to-date data, information, and analytics. Conventional BEMS mostly operate in distinct blocks and have limited resources for collecting and/or analyzing data. This limitation makes it more difficult to adopt proactive maintenance strategies and make well-informed decisions. This limitation in adapting proactive and smart decision-making strategies increases repair costs and downtime [5].

It has been observed that a building's demands change gradually, as a result, issues with scalability and adaptation arise [6]. Traditional ones can be inflexible, and challenging to modify or improve while needing an extensive cost and time delay for performing modifications. Moreover, it can be challenging to integrate modern technology or adapt to the evolving requirements of management and occupants because of this inflexibility. The motivation to deploy the Internet of Things (IoT) in BEMS arises from the aforementioned challenges. Intelligent systems, interconnected architecture and IoT technologies provide an opportunity to overcome the limitations of conventional BEMS [21]. Massive amounts of real-time data may be gathered and analyzed from a variety of sensors and devices inside the building due to the IoT. This ability enables better efficiency in operations, predictive maintenance, and better-informed decision-making.

Within this context, this paper introduces a holistic solution for an Intelligent IoT framework (IIF) tailored for energy-efficient smart building management. The suggested framework integrates real-time data processing systems and advanced sensors while monitoring and optimizing the building process in real time. Moreover, comprehensive suggestions for the suggested framework and implementation are included while solutions for interoperability problems and technological difficulties are addressed. This research aims to represent an example of creative building management solutions while providing useful insights to improve sustainability and energy efficiency in built environments. One of the main objectives is to fill the knowledge gap in the dynamic field of sustainable building management by addressing the disparity between theoretical concepts and actual applications.

The remainder of the paper is structured as follows: Sect. 2 addressed the methodology to design the IoT framework including the system design and architecture. Section 3 presents the details for the implementation like hardware and software requirements, and challenges faced. Finally, the conclusions are presented in the last section.

2 Methodology

This section addresses the development of an IIF for energy-efficient building management. It highlights the key components, data collection and how the data is utilized.

2.1 System Design

Several vital components are required for the development of the IIF for energy-efficient smart building management for it to function and be effective. The following are characterized as the system's primary components:

i Sensor Network. A network and a set of advanced sensors and equipment are installed in the building to collect real-time data on various indoor conditions, like temperature, humidity, occupancy, and energy consumption. These sensors when integrated represent the nodes of the IoT network and serve as the primary source of data input for the framework.

ii Data Processing System. The data received by the sensor network is processed using real-time data processing systems. This processing is exploited to extract useful insights and identify patterns. It may include several sub-components depending on the system's complexity like the pre-processing Module, feature extraction module, analytics engine and others.

iii Middleware. Middleware is the communication system and is established to facilitate the seamless transmission of information among the system's numerous components. It may include several sub-components depending on the system's complexity like network protocols, data transmission and messaging (e.g., MQTT [7]) and security mechanisms.

iv AI Layer. An AI layer is integrated into the framework, exploiting AI algorithms to enhance energy management, predict energy generation from renewable sources, and mitigate energy while optimizing thermal comfort within the building [1].

v Decision Support system (DSS). The DSS is embedded within the framework to enable data analytics, fault detection, and optimization algorithms. Within this framework, other main sub-components may be integrated like a recommendation system and a control (actuation) system.

vi User Interface (UI). The UI is provided to the users to interact with the framework. This UI allows building stakeholders to monitor building performance, adjust settings, access relevant information and receive any information and notifications.

The primary components and sub-components described above form the building blocks for the suggested IoT framework depicted in Fig. 1. Such a framework provides a flexible, layered and scalable system design that can be easily adjusted and updated over time.

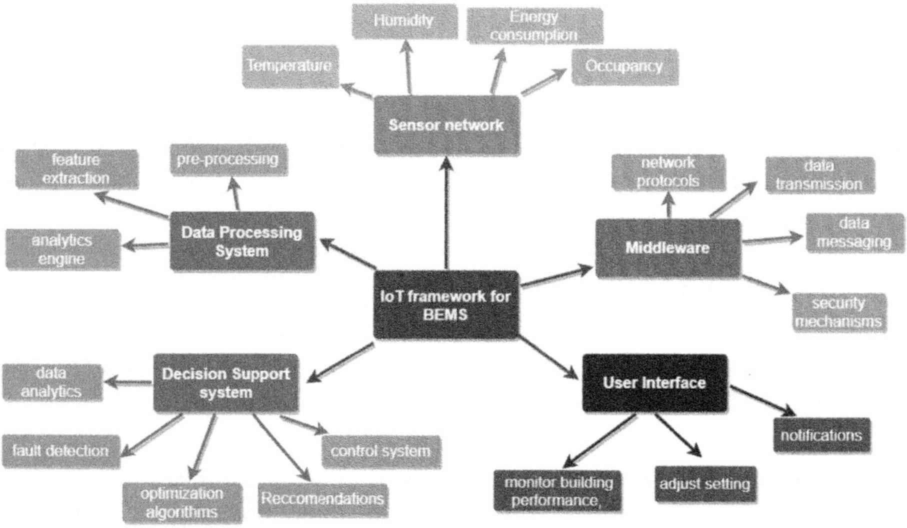

Fig. 1. System design: Main components of the IoT Frameworks

2.2 Architecture and Components

Based on the above system design and analysis of the key components the architectural framework is breakdown into a bottom-up layered architecture as follows:

i Physical Layer. The primary functions of this layer are summarized as:
   - Comprises all the physical sensors and devices installed throughout the building.
   - Retrieves real-time data from the indoor conditions and energy consumed within the building.
   - Starting point for data retrieval and acquisition.

ii Communication Layer. The primary functions of this layer are summarized:
   - Seamless transmission of data streams between the physical layer and higher layers of the system.
   - Encompasses the protocols, middleware, and networking infrastructure necessary for reliable and efficient data exchange.
   - Data pushed to the processing layer for further analysis and decision-making.

iii Data Processing Layer. The primary functions of this layer are summarized as
  - Receives all the data pushed from the physical layer and processes it to identify patterns.
  - Feature extraction and data analytics.
  - Transforming raw sensor data into readable information for the AI and UI layer.

iv AI and Decision Support Layer. The primary functions of this layer are summarized as
  - Integrates AI algorithms for energy management, predictive analytics, and optimization.
  - Decision support functionalities, including fault detection, recommendation systems, and control mechanisms.
  - Leveraging advanced algorithms to optimize energy usage and enhance building performance.

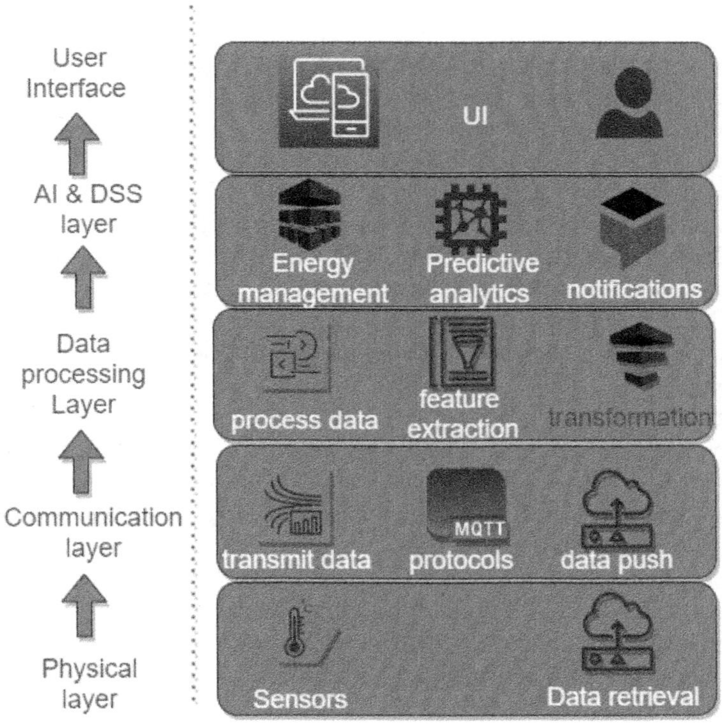

Fig. 2. Architecture and Components

v User Interface (UI). The primary functions of this layer are summarized as
  - Provides stakeholders with a user-friendly interface to interact with the system.

- Monitor building performance, adjust settings, access relevant information, and receive notifications through the UI.
- Engagement and management with the intelligent IoT system.

In summary, the Intelligent IoT system's architectural framework (Fig. 2) is organized bottom-up, starting with the physical layer, which serves as the system's foundation. Continuing up higher levels manage user interface, process data communication, and AI integration. The implementation of a layered approach ensures a methodical and structured design that handles the complex issues of energy-efficient smart building management.

2.3 Data Collection Methods and Sensors

Within the suggested IoT framework for energy-efficient smart building management, various methods are deployed for data collection to ensure comprehensive monitoring of indoor conditions and energy consumption. These methods include:

1. Sensor networks are strategically installed throughout the building environment. These sensors are designed to capture real-time data like temperature humidity, occupancy, lighting levels, CO_2, and energy consumption. The sensors are distributed across different areas of the building to ensure a wide coverage while enabling detailed monitoring of indoor conditions. Specifically, multisensors can be utilized to capture multiple parameters simultaneously [12]. Installing multisensors offers both cost efficiency (one sensor instead of multiple) and space efficiency (consolidating multiple sensors into one unit) [12]. This consolidation reduces installation costs, and minimizes the physical footprint of sensors within the building, while simplifying maintenance efforts.
2. Energy meters or energy analyzers or smart meters are employed to monitor energy consumption levels within the building. These meters are installed at the central electrical panels of the facility to measure electricity, water, gas, or other utility usage. By collecting data on energy consumption energy usage patterns are identified while providing opportunities for energy optimization.
3. Data logging systems are utilized to record and store all data collected by the sensors. The collected data is then stored in databases, either locally or on a cloud server. By exploiting databases, the data is efficiently organized and readily accessible for analysis and algorithm training. Additionally, this data is used for visualization data at the UI level.

2.4 Data Processing

To manage the various real-time data streams effectively complicated algorithms, methods, and technologies are developed for data processing [10]. These include various methodologies like predictive analytics, data aggregation strategies for combining information from various sensors, and machine learning algorithms for pattern recognition and anomaly detection. Energy-efficient smart building management is made possible by real-time data processing, which makes immediate insights and proactive recommendations possible.

2.5 Utilization of Data for Energy-Efficient Building Management

Processed real-time data is required for energy-efficient building management. Data is used for decision-making actions and a set of optimization actions and actions that can maximize resource utilisation. The utilization of this data involves the following key components:

i Dynamic Optimization of Building Systems. BEMS can dynamically optimize building systems through the processing of real-time data. The main objective of such systems is to mitigate energy waste by identifying current demand and performing real-time adjustments to Heating and Cooling settings, lighting levels, and other building services while regulating a neutral thermal comfort sensation [1].

ii Data-Driven Decision Making. Data-driven processes for making decisions are supported by real-time data analysis. BEMS analyze any potential for energy efficiency and evaluates strategies to accomplish energy savings by using insights obtained from processed data.

iii Adaptive Control Strategies. To enhance energy efficiency dynamically, the system incorporates AI-based and automated feedback channels and adaptive control strategies. Through constant real-time data monitoring and comparison with pre-established targets, the BEMS automatically modify control strategies in response to changing indoor conditions.

iv Continuous Monitoring and Optimization. Real-time data processing enables continuous monitoring while optimizing building performance.

3 System Implementation

This section provides an overview of the main steps, requirements, and methodologies adopted in the deployment of the suggested framework. It encompasses the detailed hardware and software specifications necessary for the system's operation and presents the challenges encountered during the development phase, along with the solutions that were implemented to overcome these obstacles.

3.1 Implementation Details

The implementation details of the IIF for real-time energy-efficient smart building management follows a comprehensive approach integrating various technologies, protocols, and tools. The main procedure followed for this framework is described in Fig. 3.

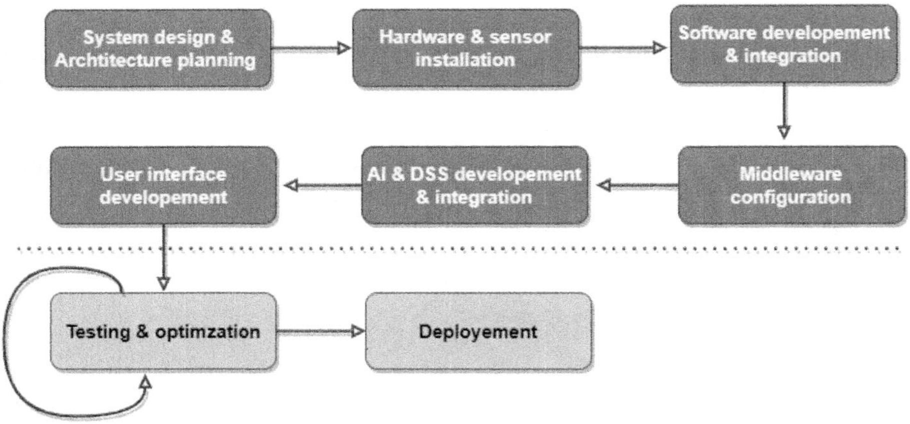

Fig. 3. Implementation flow chart

3.2 Hardware and Software Requirements

For the suggested framework the requirements encompassing hardware components are presented in Table 1 for software dependencies, libraries, and platforms are presented in Table 2. Finally, UI requirements are presented in Table 3.

Table 1. Hardware Components

Component	Description
Raspberry Pi 4 (8 GB RAM) [11]	Acts as the central processing unit of the system, handling data processing, hosting the middleware, and running the AI models
Multisensor Fibaro (Z-Wave Compatible) [12]	Used for collecting various indoor environmental data such as temperature, humidity, occupancy, and lighting levels
Energy Meter Qubino (Z-Wave Compatible) [13]	A Z-Wave compatible smart meter for monitoring energy consumption within the building

3.3 Challenges Faced and Solutions

During the implementation phase of the framework, several challenges were faced, ranging from technical complexities to integration issues. The summary of these challenges and the solutions are summarized in Table 4.

4 Experimental Results

This section presents the empirical findings from the IIF testing during a two-month experimental period. The objective is to control indoor conditions to

Table 2. Software dependencies, libraries, and platforms

Component	Description
zwave2mqtt [14]	A bridge software that connects Z-Wave devices to MQTT
Python [15]	The primary programming language used for developing the system's backend services, including data processing algorithms and the user interface
MQTT [16]	A lightweight messaging protocol for small sensors and mobile devices, optimized for high-latency or unreliable networks
AI Libraries (TensorFlow) [7]	These libraries are used for developing and running machine learning models for predictive analytics and optimization within the system

Table 3. UI requirements

Component	Type/Framework/Technology	Purpose/Use
Database [17]	RDBMS and NoSQL (PostgreSQL, MongoDB)	To store and manage sensor data, user settings, energy consumption records, AI model predictions, and system logs
Front-End [18]	JavaScript Frameworks (React.js, Angular)	For developing the client-side application, creating a dynamic and responsive UI
Back-End [19]	Web Application Framework (Django)	For developing the server-side application, managing database interactions, and handling business logic

Table 4. Challenges Faced and Solutions

Challenge	Solution
Integration with Existing BEMS	Developed custom adapters and API gateways for interoperability
Scalability and Data Volume Management	Designed a layered architecture using microservices and selected databases
Real-time Data Processing and Analysis	Integrated processing technologies and o ptimized AI models for real-time analysis
Security and Privacy Concerns	Implemented security measures including encrypted transmission and secure MQTT
UI Usability and Accessibility	Adopted user-centered design principles and conducted extensive user testing for UI
Energy Meter and Sensor Integration	Developed a flexible integration layer using zwave2mqtt for unified device communication

enable a comparison of energy consumption, processing efficiency, and thermal comfort, both with and without the smart system's intervention.

4.1 Experimental Setup

The IIF was deployed and tested within a residential apartment spanning 75 square meters. This type of apartment was chosen for its typical size and energy usage patterns, representative of urban living spaces. The environment was equipped with a carefully selected array of IoT devices to monitor various parameters and control energy consumption effectively. A floor plan of the selected residence and the installation points are depicted in Fig. 4. The IIF equipment is as described in Table 1 with the addition of a Zwave-compatible smart Thermostat (Heatit Z-Temp 2 [20]).

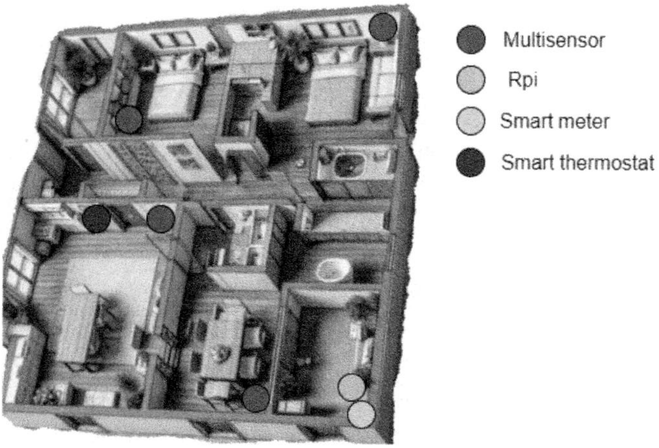

Fig. 4. Sensors and equipment installation

An overview of the key features and utilities of the house, including its orientation, location within the building, size, power type, energy consumption, and heating system details are presented in Table 5.

Table 5. characteristics of the house

Characteristic	Details
Orientation	South-East
Floor	1st
Size	75 square meters
Type of Power	Electricity
Average Electricity Consumption	265 kWh/month
Heating System	Electrical radiators (1 per room) with gas
Cooling System	3 Aircondition 12000 BTU (living room and bedrooms)

4.2 Data Collection and Monitoring

The process for data collection was designed to ensure an accurate assessment of the apartment's energy and environmental status. This was made possible by the IIF network devices. The methodology depended on the continuous operation of IoT devices that allowed real-time data acquisition and transmission of data to a central processing unit for analysis. Table 3 summarizes the methodology and types of data gathered during the data collection phase for the IIF.

Table 6. Data information

Data Category	Description
Environmental Conditions	From the multisensors (mls) placed throughout the apartment
Temperature (mls)	To monitor indoor temperature fluctuations
Humidity (mls)	To assess moisture levels within the living spaces
Occupancy (mls)	To detect presence in rooms, enabling smart energy management
Energy Consumption	Detailed measurements of electricity usage in real-time by Qubino smart meter
Heating System Operation	Operation times and setting temperature data

An indicative set of data collected from a day with 15-min sgranularity is depicted in 5. It presents the indoor temperature in Celsius, humidity percentage, and PMV index, which is an established measure of thermal comfort that predicts the mean vote of a large group of people on the 7-point thermal sensation scale. The average temperature over the presented day is approximately 19.73°C, with humidity averaging at around 56.78%. The PMV index averages at about -0.51, suggesting a slight tendency towards cooler conditions. The relatively consistent PMV values, predominantly in the slightly cool range, suggest that the heating system could be adjusted to bring the PMV closer to zero, which corresponds to a neutral thermal comfort.

4.3 Evaluation Metrics

Table 7 structures the key performance indicators that will be used to assess the framework's impact on energy efficiency, operational cost savings, occupant comfort, and environmental sustainability. Each metric provides insight into different aspects of the system's effectiveness and contributes to an overall evaluation of its performance.

4.4 Methodology and Results

The experiments were performed over two months, from January 1, 2024, to February 29, 2024. This interval included days with active IIF control measures

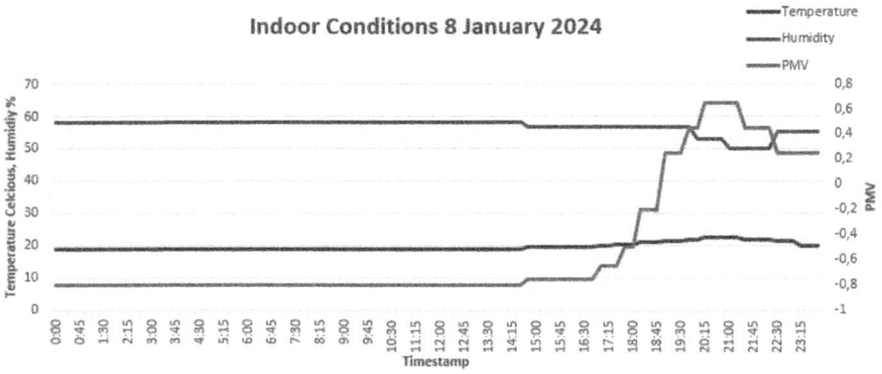

Fig. 5. Monitored Indoor conditions

Table 7. key performance indicators to assess the IIF

Metric	Description
Energy Savings	The percentage reduction in energy consumption after implementing the IoT system compared to the baseline period
Data Processing Efficiency (Latency)	The latency of the system, reflecting the speed of data processing
Data Processing Efficiency (Throughput)	The throughput of the system, reflecting the amount of data processed over time
Thermal Comfort (PMV)	The enhancement of PMV index
Cost Efficiency	The return on investment calculated by comparing the cost savings from energy efficiency against the implementation and operational costs
Environmental Impact	Quantification of the reduced carbon footprint due to energy savings

as well as days without, alternating between them. Such an approach allowed for a controlled comparison under similar indoor and outdoor conditions. By conducting the experiments in this manner, the influence of external variables on the building's energy efficiency and thermal comfort could be minimized, therefore ensuring that any observed differences in performance metrics could be attributed with greater confidence to the operation of the IIF.

The results of the performance metrics evaluation for the IIF are summarized in Table 8. The IIF resulted in energy savings and CO_2 emission reductions while having improvements in data handling capabilities. Overall, the system demonstrates a good return on investment, which could be improved during summer when the Air conditions are used.

Table 8. IIF results

Description	Results
Energy Savings	9% reduction
Data Processing Efficiency (Latency)	Significant reduction in latency, improved by 30%
Data Processing Efficiency (Throughput)	Throughput increased by 40%, indicating faster processing and response times
Thermal Comfort (PMV)	PMV improvement from −0.8 to −0.4, nearing the neutral comfort zone
Cost Efficiency	ROI observed to be 7 year
Environmental Impact	Estimated 15% reduction in CO_2 emissions

5 Conclusions

To briefly sum up, the current paper has successfully demonstrated and evaluated an Intelligent IoT Framework (IIF) intended for real-time energy-efficient smart building management. A set of controlled experiments conducted over two months, from January 1 to February 29, 2024, verified the framework's capability to enhance energy savings by 9% and improve data processing efficiency while significantly improving occupants' thermal comfort. The system is expected to be reimbursed over seven years. The environmental impact assessment additionally proposes a 15% decrease in CO_2 emissions while demonstrating the framework's potential to support sustainability. Overall, the results offer an excellent basis for how the IIF has contributed to smart building technologies and addressed the growing need for energy conservation and management in modern built environments.

Acknowledgement. This work is partially supported by the FLEdge project F-DUT-2022-0337. FLEdge project has been funded by the General Secretariat of Research & Innovation goals (GSRI) under the Driving Urban Transitions (DUT) Partnership, which has been co-funded by the European Union.

References

1. Dimara, A., Vasilopoulos, V.G., Krinidis, S., Tzovaras, D.: NRG4-U: a novel home energy management system for a unique loadprofile. Energy Sour. Part A Recov. Util. Environ. Effects **44**(1), 353–378 (2022)
2. Barroso, S., Bustos, P., Núñez, P.: Towards a cyber-physical system for sustainable and smart building: a use case for optimising water consumption on a smartcampus. J. Ambient. Intell. Humaniz. Comput. **14**(5), 6379–6399 (2023)
3. Ferrari, S., Zoghi, M., Paganin, G., Dall'O', G.: A practical review to support the implementation of smart solutions within neighbourhood building stock. Energies **16**(15), 5701 (2023)
4. Dimara, A., et al.: BEMS in the era of internet of energy: a review. In: Artificial Intelligence Applications and Innovations: 17th IFIP WG 12.5 International Conference, AIAI 2021, Hersonissos, Crete, Greece, June 25-27, 2021, Proceedings 17. Springer International Publishing, Cham (2021). https://doi.org/10.1007/978-3-030-79150-6_37

5. Tushar, W., Yuen, C., Saha, T.K., Morstyn, T., Chapman, A.C., Alam, M.J.E., Poor, H.V.: Peer-to-peer energy systems for connected communities: a review of recent advances and emerging challenges. Appl. Energy **282**, 116131 (2021)
6. Mariano-Hernández, D., Hernández-Callejo, L., Zorita-Lamadrid, A., Duque-Pérez, O., García, F.S.: A review of strategies for building energy management system: model predictive control, demand side management, optimization, and fault detect & diagnosis. J. Build. Eng. **33**, 101692 (2021)
7. MQTT: The Standard for IoT Messaging. https://mqtt.org/. Accessed 29 Mar 2024
8. What is a Multisensor? https://frient.com/the-friently-blog/what-is-a-multisensor/. Accessed 28 Mar 2024
9. What are Smart Meters? https://www.ibm.com/topics/smart-meter. Accessed 28 Mar 2024
10. Stefanopoulou, A., et al.: Ensuring reliability in smart building IoT operations through real-time holistic data treatment. In: IFIP International Conference on Artificial Intelligence Applications and Innovations. Springer Nature Switzerland, Cham (2023). https://doi.org/10.1007/978-3-031-34171-7_16
11. Raspberry Pi 4 - Model B - 8GB. https://grobotronics.com/raspberry-pi-4-model-b-8gb.html. Accessed 30 Mar 2024
12. Fibaro Multisensor. https://www.fibaro.com/en/products/motion-sensor/. Accessed 30 Mar 2024
13. Smart meter Qubino. https://qubino.com/products/smart-meter/. Accessed 30 Mar 2024
14. OpenZWave/Zwave2Mqtt. https://github.com/OpenZWave/Zwave2Mqtt. Accessed 30 Mar 2024
15. Python. https://www.python.org/. Accessed 30 Mar 2024
16. Tensor Flow. https://www.tensorflow.org/. Accessed 30 Mar 2024
17. MongoDB. https://www.mongodb.com. Accessed 30 Mar 2024
18. https://angular.io/. Accessed 30 Mar 2024
19. https://www.djangoproject.com/. Accessed 30 Mar 2024
20. Heatit Z-Temp 2. https://www.z-wave.com/shop-z-wave-smart-home-products/heatit-z-temp-2. Accessed 30 Mar 2024
21. Rossmann, J., Heinze, F.: Modeling and simulation of malfunctions in automation systems. In: 2010 IEEE 15th Conference on Emerging Technologies & Factory Automation (ETFA 2010). IEEE (2010)

Supporting Digitalization of ERP (SAP) Value-Added Tax Management Through Data Analytics Tools

Zornitsa Yordanova(✉)

University of National and World Economy, Sofia, Bulgaria
zornitsayordanova@unwe.bg

Abstract. This study investigates the function of data analytics tools in facilitating the digitalization of the Value-Added Tax (VAT) component within SAP, an Enterprise Resource Planning (ERP) system. The theoretical framework incorporates concepts from digital transformation theories and ERP system integration, with a specific emphasis on the utilization of data analytics in ERP settings such as SAP to enhance VAT management procedures. The hypothesis posits that the incorporation of data analytics technologies improves the efficiency, accuracy, and strategic compliance management of Value Added Tax (VAT), resulting in substantial enhancements compared to traditional VAT handling methods in Enterprise Resource Planning (ERP) systems. The research employs a case study methodology, complemented with a cross-sectional survey. The objective is to analyze the utilization of data analytics technologies in firms that use SAP for VAT administration, with a focus on understanding the integration, application, and resulting outcomes. The case study technique offers comprehensive insights into the practical uses and difficulties of adopting data analytics in SAP for VAT reasons, while the survey collects more extensive empirical data on the effectiveness and user satisfaction of such integrations across various industries. The research technique entails gathering qualitative data by conducting interviews with finance and IT specialists from specific firms. The purpose is to chronicle their firsthand experiences using SAP and data analytics in the context of VAT management. The results suggest that the incorporation of data analytics tools into SAP has a substantial positive impact on VAT administration. This is achieved through the automation of data collection and analysis, leading to a reduction in errors and an improvement in compliance with intricate tax regulations. Respondents have reported a significant improvement in operational efficiency, which includes faster processing times and enhanced accuracy in VAT computations. Nevertheless, the study also highlights obstacles to successful integration, including the requirement for specialized expertise to effectively utilize data analytics capabilities and difficulties in aligning these tools with current SAP configurations. Notwithstanding these difficulties, the general attitude towards incorporating data analytics tools into SAP for VAT purposes is optimistic, emphasizing its capacity to revolutionize VAT administration procedures in enterprises.

Keywords: project management · digitalization · technology management · digital transformation

I. Kostavelis et al. (Eds.): ICSC 2024, CCIS 2110, pp. 215–227, 2025.
https://doi.org/10.1007/978-3-031-69344-1_16

1 Introduction

The development of value added tax (VAT) management processes in enterprise resource planning (ERP) systems such as SAP and Microsoft Dynamics has undergone significant changes over the past two decades [1]. For the optimal functioning of these processes, however, there are still significant obstacles that hinder its ability to work efficiently and fully comply with regulations, especially when transactions affect many countries at the same time (triangulations) or complicated tax treatment. The main challenges stem from the constantly changing legislation and VAT treatment, making it difficult for any of the ERPs to efficiently and cost-effectively handle these updates [2]. The integration of Artificial Intelligence and Data Analytics solutions offers numerous opportunities to overcome these limitations, harnessing the power of data to revolutionize VAT administration processes without the expensive modifications to ERP logic. This research employs significant articles in the field to illustrate how the incorporation of data analytics into ERP systems could catalyze a novel era of VAT administration. Furthermore, it presents a case study of a data analytics tool that can provide efficient help in these areas.

Data analytics offers a great opportunity to improve the efficiency of tax administration. Studies have shown that it is effective in improving tax collection and compliance methods. Atayah and Alshater's [3] study on the use of machine learning and advanced analytics in detecting tax fraud emphasizes the ability of analytics to utilize operational data for strategic advantages, indicating a way towards more advanced tax administration systems [3]. Escap [4] proposes the use of Big Data in tax administration, advocating for a change in how tax authorities handle and oversee taxation data. The incorporation of Data Analytics into ERP systems for VAT management offers distinct benefits. The difficulty in handling VAT in conventional ERP configurations generally arises from constraints in data processing and analysis capabilities. Research conducted by Bandara et al. [5] and Janchai and Poonpool [6] highlights the significance of data analytics in addressing these constraints and facilitating a more adaptable and proactive approach to managing tax data within ERP systems [5, 6]. Moreover, the strategic utilization of data analytics tools in VAT management enables a shift from a responsive to a proactive approach in tax administration. Through the utilization of predictive analytics and decision support systems, tax authorities and businesses can foresee tax obligations and adherence problems in advance.

Furthermore, integrating data analytics into SAP ERP systems for VAT reasons is in line with the wider objectives of digital transformation [7]. This integration streamlines tax compliance and promotes a culture of innovation and ongoing enhancement in tax administration processes. The literature has not adequately highlighted the significant impact of data analytics on tax operations. Experiments have been conducted on closed statements to evaluate their suitability for digital transformation, specifically in terms of data security [8]. Additionally, the importance of big data and data analytics in shaping the future of accountancy and accountant education has been recognized [9].

The integration of Data Analytics tools into ERP systems for VAT management is a significant achievement in tax administration. It fills a distinct need in both research literature and corporate practices. This strategy has the potential to address existing challenges in VAT administration and also has the ability to generate opportunities for enhanced efficiency, compliance with regulations, and well-informed strategic decision-making. This paper examines the utilization of data analytical tools to effectively tackle the present difficulties encountered by corporations in VAT management. It investigates a case study of an IT company that develops such solutions. The goal of these solutions is to verify tax-related information, analyze VAT treatments and historical transactions in relation to the legal framework, and ensure that transactions are in line with various VAT scenarios.

2 Theoretical Background

2.1 Digital Transformation and ERP Systems Integration for VAT

Berlinski, Elise, and Morales [10] highlighted the rigidity of classical ERP systems in the face of rapidly advancing digital technologies, a sentiment echoed also by Koumas, M., Dossou, P.E., and Didier [11] who pointed out the critical role of ERP modernization in digital transformation. However, both discussions tend to oversimplify the complexities involved in integrating new digital technologies with existing ERP frameworks [12], often overlooking the nuanced challenges such as data privacy concerns, legacy system interoperability, and the varied capabilities of ERP systems across different organizational contexts.

The theoretical landscape of digital transformation is richly contoured by models that assess digital maturity and provide frameworks for integrating digital technologies into ERP systems [13]. These models offer valuable conceptual tools for understanding digital transformation but frequently fall short in addressing the specificities of VAT management within ERP systems. They often neglect the operational realities of tax compliance and the practical implications of digitalization for tax professionals and accountants, thereby highlighting a gap in the literature that requires further exploration [14].

The advent of Industry 4.0 has ushered in a new era for ERP systems, with technologies such as AI, IoT, and Big Data offering transformative potentials [15]. These studies provide crucial insights into the technological advancements shaping ERP systems. However, they tend to underestimate the challenges of ERP adaptation in the context of Industry 4.0, particularly around issues of workforce training, data governance, and the scalability of such technologies within ERP systems tailored for VAT management [14]. The role of digital transformation in enhancing VAT management processes within ERP systems is a burgeoning area of research. Some rare studies delved into how digital technologies can automate and streamline VAT-related processes, offering promising perspectives but these focused mostly on the ethical perspectives [16]. Nevertheless, there is a lack of empirical research on the actual implementation challenges, the effectiveness of these technologies in different regulatory environments, and their impact on VAT compliance and auditing practices.

In summary, the existing literature on digital transformation and ERP systems integration offers insufficient insights into the challenges and opportunities presented by the digital era, particularly in relation to VAT management. Thus, there are significant gaps, particularly in operationalizing theoretical models, addressing the specifics of VAT management in a digitally transforming environment, and understanding the practical challenges of integrating Industry 4.0 technologies into ERP systems. These areas represent fertile ground for future research, promising to deepen our understanding of digital transformation's implications for ERP systems and VAT management.

2.2 Data Analytics and Business Intelligence Tools for VAT Management

The integration of Data Analytics into ERP systems represents a transformative shift in the approach to VAT management [17]. This segment of the literature review critically examines the contributions, methodologies, and implications of recent research on the use of Data Analytics within ERP frameworks to enhance VAT management processes. The discussion aims to highlight the potential benefits, identify operational challenges, and point out gaps in the current body of knowledge that could guide future research directions.

The application of Data Analytics in ERP systems offers unprecedented opportunities to improve VAT management's efficiency and accuracy [18]. However, the literature tends to generalize the benefits of Data Analytics without delving into the complexities of VAT compliance across different jurisdictions or industries, potentially oversimplifying the challenges involved in adapting Data Analytics solutions to the diverse needs of VAT management [6]. The potential of predictive analytics in forecasting VAT liabilities and compliance issues is a topic of burgeoning interest. While Filom, Amiri, and Razavi [19] underscore the significance of automation in reducing decision-making errors, their research could benefit from a more critical examination of the predictive models' accuracy and their adaptability to the dynamic nature of data regulations. The reliance on historical data for predictions may not always account for sudden regulatory changes or novel tax avoidance schemes, underscoring the need for ongoing refinement of predictive models [20].

The role of Data Analytics in enhancing regulatory compliance is highlighted by Oguejiofor et al. [21]. They advocate for an integrated approach to digital transformation, implicating the utilization of Data Analytics for more robust compliance frameworks. However, the discussion often overlooks the practical challenges in aligning Data Analytics outputs with the diverse and evolving tax compliance frameworks globally, suggesting a gap in research focused on the interoperability of Data Analytics tools with various regulatory environments. A critical overview of the literature reveals a significant gap in addressing the operational challenges and implementation hurdles of integrating Data Analytics into ERP systems for VAT management. While theoretical benefits are discussed somehow, empirical research is scarce on the actual deployment of these systems within organizations, the training required for tax professionals, and the real-world effectiveness of Data Analytics in detecting and preventing VAT-related frauds and errors.

In conclusion, while the integration of Data Analytics into ERP systems for enhanced VAT management is poised to offer significant advantages in terms of efficiency, accuracy, and compliance, the literature review exposes a need for more nuanced research. Future studies should aim to bridge the gap between theoretical potential and practical implementation, focusing on specific challenges related to VAT compliance, the adaptability of predictive models to changing tax landscapes, and the operational realities of deploying Data Analytics solutions within diverse organizational and regulatory contexts.

3 Research Design

3.1 Methodological Framework

The research design is structured to evaluate the benefits of data analytics tools developed by an IT consulting firm called Intertaxer, specifically within the scope of tax engine implementation projects in SAP ERP systems. Emphasizing a qualitative case study method, the study aims to uncover the nuanced impacts of these tools on enhancing Value-Added Tax (VAT) management processes. This approach allows for a deep dive into the practical applications, challenges, and outcomes of integrating data analytics into ERP VAT management.

3.2 Case Study Analysis

The focal point of this research is a detailed case study of the IT consulting company Intertaxer which has developed and implemented a suite of data analytics tools for VAT management in SAP ERP systems. The case study is designed to offer comprehensive insights into:

- Development and Design: Understanding the rationale, objectives, and technological underpinnings of the data analytics tools developed by the IT consulting firm for addressing Tax Engine implementation projects.
- Implementation Process: Examining the methodologies and strategies employed in the integration of these tools into tax engine implementation projects, highlighting the collaborative efforts between the consulting firm and client organizations.
- Benefits Realization: Analyzing the tangible and intangible benefits observed post-implementation, such as enhanced efficiency, accuracy in VAT processing, and improved compliance with tax regulations.
- User Experience and Challenges: Gathering feedback from both the consulting team and client-side users on their experiences, including ease of use, challenges encountered, and the support provided throughout the implementation process.

Data collection for the case study will involve:

- In-depth Interviews: Conduct semi-structured interviews with project team members, including developers, project managers, and consultants, as well as key stakeholders from client organizations.
- Project Documentation Review: Analyzing project reports, design documents, and performance data to quantify the impact and effectiveness of the data analytics tools.
- Observational Studies: Where possible, observing the implementation process and the operational use of the tools in real-time to gather firsthand insights.

3.3 Data Analysis

Qualitative data from interviews, documents, and observations will undergo thematic analysis to identify key themes related to the implementation and use of data analytics tools in VAT management. This analysis will highlight the benefits, challenges, and practical implications of deploying these tools in tax engine projects.

3.4 Expected Outcomes

The case study is anticipated to provide a rich, detailed understanding of how data analytics tools facilitate the digitalization and optimization of VAT management in ERP systems, specifically within the context of tax engine implementation projects. Expected outcomes include:

- Strategic Insights: Offering strategic insights into the integration of data analytics tools in VAT management, supporting the digital transformation efforts of enterprises.
- Best Practices and Lessons Learned: Identifying best practices and lessons learned during the implementation of these tools, contributing to the body of knowledge for future projects.
- Recommendations for Improvement: Providing actionable recommendations for IT consulting firms and client organizations to maximize the benefits of data analytics in ERP VAT management.

This research design aims to illuminate the complex dynamics of implementing data analytics tools in tax engine projects, contributing valuable insights to both academic research and practical applications in ERP system enhancement.

4 Results and Discussion

The results section is structured to provide a comprehensive overview of our findings from the tax technology implementation projects. It encompasses three key areas:

- Client and Implementing Company Dynamics: This section delves into how clients and implementing companies align on needs and identify gaps during the tax technology project lifecycle.
- Data Analytics Tools and Innovation: Here, we explore the utilization of Data Analytics tools throughout the implementation process, highlighting innovations brought forth by the analyzed IT company.
- Benefits, Challenges, and Customer Experiences: A summary that encapsulates the benefits and challenges encountered, alongside insights into customer experiences with the tax technology solutions.

Each section aims to present a detailed analysis to foster a deeper understanding of the intricate dynamics involved in tax technology projects.

4.1 Unrevealing Clients and Implementing Companies' Needs

In Table 1, we demonstrate the accumulative insights on the needs and insufficient experience of clients during tax technology implementation projects.

Table 1. Clients' unmet needs during tax technology projects based on interviews

Core need	Explanation
Efficiency in implementation	Superior quality, accelerated delivery, Resource Optimization, massively tested, AI-powered for précised fit
Budget constraints	Limitations for tax projects no matter their priorities are regulative requirements mostly (but sometimes they are considered as automation)
Human resources involved	Highly valued employees with extensive knowledge required for such projects are overloaded with day-to-day business to participate in requirements gathering and testing
IT resources involved	No available highly experienced and certified IT staff
Project Management Complexity	Lack of experienced project managers; Poor communication channels within big organizations; Lack of project management tools
Data issues and insufficiencies	Not enough data for testing on the Testing environment (SAP and ERP in general)
Predictability of TO-BE processes	No flexibility in engaged employees in looking into the TO-BE processes

In Table 2, we demonstrate the accumulative insights on the needs and insufficient experience of vendors or consultants, who execute tax technology projects.

Table 2. Implementing companies' needs during tax technology projects based on interviews

Core need	Explanation
Client expertise and experts' involvement into projects	Streamlined access to comprehensive Expertise in Taxation, IT, and Product Specifics
Budget constraints	Inconsistency between budget limitations and requirements
IT resources involved	Not enough available IT resources (people-related)
Time-consuming approvals and alignments	Accelerated implementation and quicker launch timeframes
Project Management Complexity	Lack of internal project management knowledge and experience for the complexity level of such projects

(*continued*)

Table 2. (*continued*)

Core need	Explanation
Data issues and insufficiencies	There is not enough data for testing purposes, plus data does not cover all tax scenarios possible for the company's complexity in transactions
Lack of quality and extensive testing	Underestimation of testing once the tax technology solution is implemented, before go-live
Inefficiency in decision-making for TO BE processes	Slow decision-making and lack of procedures to follow smooth and quick decision-making flow
Many customization needs	Early detection of project discrepancies Extensive Testing for Robust Validation Leveraging AI Tools to complement consultant proficiency

Analyzing the insights from interviews on the unmet needs and challenges faced by clients and implementing companies during tax technology projects allows us to match corresponding challenges and needs, highlighting areas for mutual focus and improvement. Here, we group and match these challenges to propose targeted solutions that benefit both parties.

Matched Needs and Challenges

- Efficiency and Resource Optimization

  Clients seek: Efficiency in implementation, emphasizing superior quality, accelerated delivery, and resource optimization, possibly through AI.

  Vendors need: Streamlined access to client expertise, highlighting the importance of tapping into client-specific knowledge to drive efficient implementations.

  Match Point: Both parties can benefit from leveraging AI and other technologies to optimize resources and implementation processes. Collaborative efforts in sharing expertise and employing technology-driven solutions can bridge this gap.
- Budget Constraints and Cost Management

  Clients face: Budget constraints, necessitating prioritization even among projects with regulatory requirements.

  Vendors confront: Inconsistencies between budget limitations and project requirements, stressing the need for efficient cost management.

  Match Point: Transparent and upfront discussions on budget allocations and project requirements can help both clients and vendors align their expectations and explore cost-effective solutions.
- Human and IT Resources Challenges

  Clients report: Overloaded key employees and a lack of available, experienced IT staff.

  Vendors indicate: Not enough available IT resources and a need for client expertise and expert involvement.

Match Point: Addressing this mutual challenge requires a strategy focused on effective workload management, including potentially outsourcing certain tasks to alleviate the burden on key staff and exploring partnerships for IT support.

- Project Management Complexity

  Clients identify: A lack of experienced project managers and poor communication channels.

  Vendors acknowledge: A deficiency in internal project management knowledge and experience.

  Match Point: Both groups can benefit from investing in project management training and tools, improving communication strategies, and possibly hiring or contracting experienced project managers to guide complex projects.
- Data Issues and Testing Insufficiencies

  Clients highlight: Insufficient data for testing and challenges with predictability in "TO-BE" processes.

  Vendors emphasize: Data inadequacies for comprehensive testing and the underestimation of extensive testing needs.

  Match Point: Collaborative efforts to ensure comprehensive data availability and a shared approach to extensive, rigorous testing can help mitigate these challenges. This includes setting realistic expectations for the "TO-BE" processes and engaging in early detection of discrepancies.
- Decision-making and Customization Needs

  Clients mention: Challenges with predictability and flexibility in process envisioning.

  Vendors note: Inefficiencies in decision-making and the need for early discrepancy detection and customization.

  Match Point: Streamlining decision-making processes and adopting flexible, agile methodologies can benefit both parties. Joint workshops and continuous feedback loops can facilitate smoother decision-making and customization efforts.

By closely examining and matching the challenges and needs of clients and vendors, it's clear that many of these issues are interrelated and can be addressed through enhanced collaboration, better communication, and shared strategies for resource optimization, project management, and comprehensive testing. Identifying these matched challenges and needs is a crucial step toward developing targeted solutions that address the complexities of tax technology projects for both clients and implementing companies.

4.2 Data Analytics Tools During the Implementation Process

The Data Analytics applications of Intetaxer are the following, covering the described needs and functionalities, ordered within the implementation phases of an ordinary project management cycle.

Requirement Gathering stage

IT-DC: Data Analytics for Tax Insight

IT-DC is a sophisticated data analytics tool that methodically examines both transactional and master data from clients. It provides comprehensive insights into tax scenarios and drivers, enhancing the tax technology implementation process.

Tax Explorer: AI-Enhanced Data Modeling
Tax Explorer utilizes a data model enhanced by AI, incorporating extensive tax knowledge. It facilitates a more efficient requirements-gathering process by identifying gaps, summarizing tax information, and crafting targeted questions for stakeholder interviews during the tax technology implementation.

Solution Design Stage
IT-DC pinpoints every tax-related data field required for the solution's design.

IT-DC delivers a comprehensive, data-driven overview of tax processes across the entire organization.

Tax Explorer provides an in-depth understanding of tax knowledge, integrating it with the client's specific process requirements.

Build and Development Stage
MTT automates unit testing within the tax technology solutions, evaluating all potential tax scenario combinations, tax drivers, and their current configurations.

MMM is an AI-powered Taxability Driver Mapping tool that accurately associates specific customer material data with standard tax categories.

IT-DC generates detailed test cases to enhance build quality before UAT, supplying the necessary data for their creation.

Testing Stage
MTT is a mass transaction tester tool that automates unit testing in the implemented solution for all possible combinations of tax scenarios with their tax drivers.

IT-DC provides test cases all together with the required data needed for their generation.

Go-Live Stage
MTT streamlines regression testing in the implemented solution by automating the evaluation of all conceivable combinations of tax scenarios and their drivers.

Tax Explorer provides actionable guidance and recommendations for post-go-live modifications, drawing on comprehensive content.

4.3 Benefits Realization

KPIs for IT-DC and Tax Explorer

- IT-DC significantly boosts the visibility of tax scenarios, including tax drivers, by over 80%, ensuring comprehensive oversight.
- IT-DC captures the full spectrum of an organization's tax scenarios with 99% precision.
- Tax Explorer streamlines the Vertex O Series implementation process, reducing both the time and specialized knowledge required across various countries.

- IT-DC cuts down the time required to identify necessary tax data fields by over 85%.
- Tax Explorer significantly streamlines the process of discerning specific tax categories and their effects across various countries, achieving a 90% optimization in time and expertise.
- MTT boosts build and unit testing efficiency by 99%.
- MMM cuts down the time and expertise required for taxability driver mapping by 95%.
- MMM improves the precision of taxability driver mapping by 80%.
- IT-DC slashes test case generation time by 85%.
- MTT, a comprehensive transaction testing tool, automates unit tests within the solution, covering every possible combination of tax scenarios and their respective tax drivers.
- IT-DC supplies complete test cases, accompanied by all necessary data required for their generation.
- MTT achieves a 99% automation rate in regression testing.
- Tax Explorer enhances the efficiency of implementing changes by 60%.

5 Conclusion

This investigation elucidates the multifaceted benefits and challenges inherent in digitalizing VAT processes within SAP ERP systems through Data Analytics technologies. It provides a nuanced understanding of the transformative potential of these tools, not just from a theoretical perspective but grounded in empirical research and practical application. The study underscores a significant leap forward in managing VAT complexities through Data Analytics, manifesting in enhanced efficiency, precision in tax computations, and compliance management. These improvements are pivotal, offering enterprises a robust framework to navigate the intricate labyrinth of tax regulations with agility and confidence. The empirical data, gathered from interviews with finance and IT specialists, paint a vivid picture of the operational upliftment experienced by firms adopting these technologies. They report marked enhancements in processing speeds, accuracy, and overall operational efficiency, underscoring the tangible impact of Data Analytics on VAT administration.

However, this journey is not devoid of challenges. The research candidly highlights the hurdles in integrating Data Analytics tools into existing SAP configurations, spotlighting the need for specialized expertise and addressing the complexities of aligning new technologies with legacy systems. These challenges, although significant, do not diminish the optimism surrounding the adoption of Data Analytics in ERP systems for VAT management. Instead, they provide valuable insights into the areas requiring attention and further innovation, setting the stage for continuous improvement and adaptation.

The matched needs and challenges between clients and implementing companies, as derived from the study, reveal a shared path towards overcoming operational inefficiencies, budget constraints, resource limitations, and project management complexities. This alignment is crucial, as it fosters a collaborative environment where both parties can leverage their strengths, share knowledge, and work towards common goals. The study's findings advocate for a partnership approach, emphasizing the importance of shared strategies for resource optimization, effective communication, and embracing agile methodologies to navigate the complexities of tax technology projects.

The case study of Intertaxer and the deployment of Data Analytics tools like IT-DC and Tax Explorer further illustrate the practical application and benefits of these technologies in real-world settings. These tools have demonstrated their ability to significantly improve visibility, accuracy, and efficiency in VAT management processes, marking a significant advancement in tax technology solutions.

In conclusion, this paper not only contributes to the academic discourse on digital transformation and ERP system enhancement for VAT management but also serves as a beacon for corporations and IT consulting firms navigating the digitalization of tax processes. It lays the groundwork for future research, encouraging a deeper exploration into the integration challenges, while also highlighting the immense potential of Data Analytics to revolutionize VAT management in the era of digital transformation. The path forward is clear: embracing innovation, fostering collaboration, and continuously adapting to overcome the challenges of digitalization in tax administration.

Acknowledgment. This work was financially supported by the UNWE Research Programme NID NI 4/2023.

References

1. Shygun, M.M., Zhuravel, A.: Global trends in transformation of decision support systems: case with VAT in SAP. In: Grima, S., Sood, K., Özen, E. (eds.) Contemporary Studies of Risks in Emerging Technology, Part B, pp. 183–206. Emerald Publishing Limited, Bradford (2023). https://doi.org/10.1108/978-1-80455-566-820231009
2. Lang, M., Risse, R. (eds.): Tax Law and Digitization: how to Combine Legal Tech and Tax Tech. Kluwer Law International BV, Alphen Aan Den Rijn (2022)
3. Atayah, O.F., Alshater, M.M.: Audit and tax in the context of emerging technologies: a retrospective analysis, current trends, and future opportunities. Int. J. Digit. Account. Res. **21**, 95 (2021)
4. ESCAP, U.: The Digitalization of Tax Administrations in Asia and the Pacific: a Manual for Practitioners (2022)
5. Bandara, F., Jayawickrama, U., Subasinghage, M., Olan, F., Alamoudi, H., Alharthi, M.: Enhancing ERP responsiveness through big data technologies: an empirical investigation. Inf. Syst. Front. **26**(1), 251–275 (2024)
6. Janchai, S., Poonpool, N.: (2020) Audit Data Analytics Capability and Tax Performance: An Empirical Evidence from Tax Departments in Thailand. Doctoral Dissertation, Mahasarakham University
7. Gao, J.: Research on financial informatization construction of business and finance integration. Int. J. Sci. Res. (IJSR) **11**(7), 354–358 (2022)
8. Saeed, S., Altamimi, S.A., Alkayyal, N.A., Alshehri, E., Alabbad, D.A.: Digital transformation and cybersecurity challenges for businesses resilience: issues and recommendations. Sensors **23**(15), 6666 (2023)
9. Theuri, P., Campbell, R., Owens-Jackson, L.: A literature review of technology-related research in accounting education: 2010–2020. Account. Perspect. **23**(1), 79–114 (2024)
10. Berlinski, E., Morales, J.: Digital technologies and accounting quantification: the emergence of two divergent knowledge templates. Crit. Perspect. Account. **98**, 102697 (2024)

11. Koumas, M., Dossou, P.E., Didier, J.Y.: Digital transformation of small and medium sized enterprises production manufacturing. J. Softw. Eng. Appl. **14**(12), 607–630 (2021)
12. Zhao, X., Chen, Q.A., Zhang, H., Chen, P., Chen, S.: A study on the influencing factors of corporate digital transformation: empirical evidence from Chinese listed companies. Sci. Rep. **14**(1), 6243 (2024)
13. Aslanova, I.V., Kulichkina, A.I.: Digital maturity: definition and model. In: Advances in Economics, Business and Management Research (2020). [online]. https://doi.org/10.2991/aebmr.k.200502.073
14. Solbach, M.C.: International Business Transactions and Taxation: Practical Guidance and Framework for Executives. Springer Nature, Cham (2023). https://doi.org/10.1007/978-3-031-39240-5
15. Adebanjo, D., Laosirihongthong, T., Samaranayake, P., Teh, P.L.: Key enablers of industry 4.0 development at firm level: findings from an emerging economy. IEEE Trans. Eng. Manag. **70**(2), 400–416 (2021)
16. Yordanova, Z.: Ethical implications of transparency and explainability of artificial intelligence for managing value-added tax (VAT) in corporations. In: 3rd International Conference on Advanced Research in Technologies, Information, Innovation and Sustainability, ARTIIS 2023, vol. 1936, pp. 344–353. Springer Nature Switzerland, Cham (2024)
17. Zakharkina, L., Rubanov, P., Alibekova, B., Zakharkin, O., Moldashbayeva, L.: The impact of digital transformation in the accounting system of fuel and energy complex enterprises (international experience). Int. J. Energy Econ. Policy **12**(5), 152–161 (2022)
18. Aletrino, A.: Vat detection on incoming invoices using ERP data: a machine learning approach. Doctoral Dissertation, Tilburg University
19. Filom, S., Amiri, A.M., Razavi, S.: Applications of machine learning methods in port operations–A systematic literature review. Transp. Res. Part E Logist. Transp. Rev. **161**, 102722 (2022)
20. Hassan, M., Aziz, L.A.R., Andriansyah, Y.: The role artificial intelligence in modern banking: an exploration of AI-driven approaches for enhanced fraud prevention, risk management, and regulatory compliance. Rev. Contemp. Bus. Anal. **6**(1), 110–132 (2023)
21. Oguejiofor, B.B., et al.: A review on data-driven regulatory compliance in Nigeria. Int. J. Appl. Res. Soc. Sci. **5**(8), 231–243 (2023)

Decision Making in the Intelligent Distribution Centers of the Industry 4.0 Era: A Structural Approach

Orestis Efthymiou and Stavros T. Ponis(✉)

School of Mechanical Engineering, National Technical University Athens, Heroon Polytechniou 9, 15780 Athens, Greece
staponis@central.ntua.gr

Abstract. Nowadays, the growing need for retailers to compete with their products across cost, quality and service dimensions on international markets has given rise to the need of developing more efficient and sustainable warehousing management strategies and processes. Traditional warehouses were designed to serve mainly one type of customers, usually stores, and at specific times during the day, while contemporary Distribution Centers (DCs) need to be able to serve all types of retail channels, such as e-commerce, stores and click-and-collect orders, that are received continuously within the day and have to be handled as soon as possible. Even though the topic of warehouse management and performance has attracted significant attention during the past decades, literature is mainly focused on facility location problems, inventory control and warehouse process design and management, with the emphasis being put on the load/material routing and order picking processes in the warehouse, due to them being demanding, labor intensive and costly. When it comes to decision making in DCs, be that operational or administrative, literature is rather limited. This paper provides the necessary focus on all the day-to-day issues that a DC director needs to come to terms with, in order to run DC operations successfully. In addition, these issues are addressed in the context of Industry 4.0, taking under consideration the managerial changes and organizational transformations that the emerging Industry 5.0 dictates or requires from contemporary DC management, which have the employee and the environment at the epicenter. The principal research question addressed in this paper, is how DC management can cope with these changes and effectively support the decision-making process with a structured set of planning, controlling, operational and administrative decisions. In that direction, this paper attempts to provide a set of guidelines and a proposed road map for DC management, which will effectively support the decision-making process in the warehouse of the Industry 4.0 era.

Keywords: management decision support · distribution centers · warehouse management · Industry 4.0 · Industry 5.0

I. Kostavelis et al. (Eds.): ICSC 2024, CCIS 2110, pp. 228–247, 2025.
https://doi.org/10.1007/978-3-031-69344-1_17

1 Introduction

Distribution Centers (DCs) perform an essential role within each supply chain by gathering materials from different suppliers, fulfilling customer orders and performing various value-added activities (Baker, 2007). The detailed function of each DC, strongly depends on the supply chain strategy of each corporation, which derives from the business model that it follows, i.e. on whether it is demand or supply-driven (ibid). Thus, an efficient DC design is needed in order to provide improved material flow and reduce the logistics costs of facilities (Dotoli et al., 2015). Designing operations within a DC, needs to take into consideration the elements of distribution strategy, internal activities, and the distribution operations' attributes (Vidal Vieira et al., 2017). Distribution strategy dictates whether the focus of the company is on supply or demand. When focusing on demand, the DC mostly aims at being agile and having quick response operations with a high level of precision. On the other hand, when focusing on supply, the DC aims at being lean and trying to reduce high inventory levels, waste in resources and long lead times. The internal activities of a DC include all the different operations that occur within the DC, such as receiving, put-away, picking, marshalling and dispatching (ibid). These activities tend to be similar in almost all DCs, but the way they are structured depends mostly on distribution operations' attributes, such as types and quantity of products, number of orders and order lines, and cost of labor, facilities and equipment (Bartholdi & Hackman, 2011). Another distribution attribute that affects DC focus, are the numerous types of commercial channels that it has to support (Koster et al., 2007). Nowadays, and especially after the COVID-19 pandemic, orders within a DC tend to be massively different in terms of size and speed of execution, when store orders, e-commerce orders, Omni-channel orders, click-and-collect and many more, have to be prepared under the same roof and with highly different demand patterns. Configuration of the DC is therefore a vital component of logistics for offering the Omni-channel experience to customers (Kembro et al., 2018) but also critical since it affects both logistical costs and service standards (Faber et al., 2017). Thus, complexity has significantly increased on numerous procedures within a DC, may that be a Warehouse Management System (WMS) that has to be setup correctly for every single process, or an automation system that has to be organized fittingly to the needs of the business, making it therefore intricate for someone to manage accurately. Therefore, one realizes that DC management plays a vital role in the success or failure of any organization, within today's super competitive environment.

However, even though the topic of warehouse management and performance has attracted significant attention during the past decades, literature is primarily focused on network design problems such as facility location analysis and size and material/product related problems such as inventory management, order picking and material handling. When it comes to a holistic approach of operational and administrative decision making in the DC, literature is scarce. This paper studies the operational and administrative decision-making portfolio of the DC manager, which is necessary for the successful management of the facility in both strategic and operational levels. The research question that will try to be answered, is how DC management can be organized in order to fulfill today's challenges, as a collection of planning and controlling, operational and administrative decisions and procedures. In Sect. 2, the existing literature on this specific field is studied and research areas with significant potential for useful results are identified, but also current research shortcomings. Furthermore, the above-mentioned issues are addressed in the context of Industry 4.0, since the objective of this paper is to contribute to improving knowledge of DC operational and administrative decisions, in relation to available Industry 4.0 technologies. This paper is organized in four discrete sections. The current one introduces the basic concepts and states the research objectives. Section 2 describes the methodology used for the literature review process utilized in this paper and presents an analysis of the collected material. Section 3 describes and determines an extensive range of operational and administrative decisions that have to be taken for a DC in order to run both day-to-day business and strategic topics successfully, and Sect. 4 concludes the works of this paper with a summary, and by presenting the research contributions, limitations, future research perspective and potential of this study.

2 Literature Review

This section is dedicated in reviewing the literature related to decision making in DCs operating and competing in the Industry 4.0, post-pandemic era. To illustrate the whole picture of the current business environment, a brief overview of Industry 4.0 and its impact on material handling and contemporary warehouses/DCs will be presented to provide the necessary theoretical background for the discussion of the next section.

The methodology used for this review is quite straightforward. Four searches were performed, all of them on the well-known SCOPUS academic database. For all searches, the language was set to English and all accessible records, such as reviews, journals and conference papers with no time constraints were included in the search space. The main keywords chosen for the searches were "managerial decisions" and "operational decisions", in relation to either "warehouse" or "distribution center". The first search was made by applying search string: TITLE-ABS-KEY ("managerial decisions" AND "warehouse") AND (LIMIT-TO (LANGUAGE, "English")). The search returned twenty-three (23) papers. After reading their titles, just five (5) papers were found to be related to Logistics and Supply Chain and the rest were associated with "data warehouses" within the field of Information Technology (IT), and therefore were deemed as irrelevant. The second search was made by applying search string: TITLE-ABS-KEY ("managerial decisions" AND "distribution center") AND (LIMIT-TO (LANGUAGE, "English")). By replacing the word "warehouse" with "distribution center" on the second search, authors wanted to ensure that all available papers would get included, since it's quite often that these two terms are interrelated, and thus, one is used instead of the other within bibliography. Indeed, it proved to be right, since this second search returned sixty-seven (67) papers. Following reading of their titles, forty-three (43) were spotted to be related to Logistics and Supply Chain and twenty-four (24) were associated with environmental, medical or planning issues, and therefore were judged as inapt. The third search was made by applying search string: TITLE-ABS-KEY ("operational decisions" AND "distribution center") AND (LIMIT-TO (LANGUAGE, "English")). The search returned two hundred eighty-seven (287) papers. Once again, all their titles were read by the authors and one hundred twenty (120) papers found to be unrelated, since they were mostly associated to medicine, meteorology and energy, but also few were addressing issues about computing, call centers and maintenance. On the contrary, one hundred and sixty-seven (167) papers were related to Logistics and Supply Chain and therefore were chosen for further reading of their abstracts. Finally, the fourth search was made by applying search string: TITLE-ABS-KEY ("operational decisions" AND "warehouse") AND (LIMIT-TO (LANGUAGE, "English")). As noted earlier, once more we chose to replace the word "distribution center" with "warehouse" on the fourth search, in order to ensure that papers related to the same topic are not excluded. It proved to be a correct decision, since five hundred and seventy-one (571) papers were returned. Following reading of all their titles, two hundred thirty-four (234) were related to Logistics and Supply Chain and three hundred thirty-seven (337) were irrelevant, as they were all addressing "data warehouses" associated to various sectors, such as medicine and healthcare, geography and the environment. Following the initial rejection process of papers, described in the previous step, the abstracts of the four hundred forty-nine (449) identified papers were closely examined in order to determine whether they were appropriate for addressing the research question set in Sect. 1. As a result, a screening procedure was imposed based on the following exclusion criteria, i.e. a) duplicate articles, such as conference papers that have subsequently been upgraded into journals, b) contributions that despite having the requested keyword string in their text, were not directly relevant to the studied subject, and c) papers that focused on DC related issues such as building location analysis, inventory management, picking and routing concepts among other, but not on warehouse management and decision making processes that a DC director needs to come to terms with on a day-to-day basis in order to run operations successfully. In other words, a typology of managerial decisions that a DC director faces on a daily basis, analyzed and organized within a single source. The authors judiciously discussed each paper and then either omitted it from the final sample or retained it for further review. A large number of papers fell within category 2 of the exclusion criteria, but the greatest majority was within category 3, where almost all out of which were focusing mainly on designing of specific operations, such as picking & packing concepts and equipment, and not on broadly discussing about running a DC by debating and showing what is required in terms of operational and administrative decisions. Consequently, eighteen (18) papers were chosen for the final step of full text, in-depth assessment due to this process. An additional set of seven (7) papers, were also added to the list for in-depth assessment. These were found through reading the initial eighteen papers and researching their bibliographic references.

Following thorough assessment of all twenty-five (25) papers, fifteen (15) papers were found to be straying from the main analysis topic, as they were focusing mainly on warehouse design issues and not operational decisions. Therefore, even though their abstracts had shown differently, once fully read, it was decided by the authors to exclude them from the list representing the existing literature that analyzes warehouse operational decisions. Basic information about the chosen ten (10) papers is shown in Table 1.

Table 1. Existing papers analyzing warehouse operational decisions.

Authors and Year	Title	Source	# of Citations*	Focus of the Study
Faber et al., (2013)	Organizing warehouse management	Journal Paper	138	This study examines how warehouse management, which is comprehended as a collection of planning and control decisions and procedures, is organized and steered by task complexity and market dynamics
Khan et al., (2016)	Fuzzy-AHP approach for warehouse performance measurement	Conference Proceedings	15	This study discusses short- and long-term warehouse management decisions and develops an integrated approach that links operational and strategic decisions to an overall warehouse performance measurement system
Khanzode & Shah (2017)	A comprehensive review of warehouse operational issues	Journal Paper	30	This study explores the existing warehousing literature on various activities that take place within a warehouse. It also addresses the research gap on operational issues through a taxonomy that combines all related warehouse operations
Vidal Vieira et al., (2017)	An AHP-based framework for logistics operations in distribution centres	Journal Paper	33	This study proposes a framework for designing operations in DCs based on a combined study of the elements of distribution strategy, internal activities and characteristics of distribution operations
Binos et al., (2020)	Decision Support Research in Warehousing and Distribution: A Systematic Literature Review	Journal Paper	2	This study investigates literature on decision support in warehousing and distribution operations and tries to comprehend how this decision support research can support operational decision makers in managing the daily volume of work in the warehouse

(continued)

Table 1. (*continued*)

Authors and Year	Title	Source	# of Citations*	Focus of the Study
Gu et al., (2007)	Research on warehouse operation: A comprehensive review	Journal Paper	1161	This study analyzes decisions that have to be taken regarding warehouse operation. Additionally, an extensive review on warehouse operation planning problems is presented
Koster et al., (2007)	Design and control of warehouse order picking: A literature review	Journal Paper	2101	This study gives feedback about decisions on design and control of order picking and discusses about common decisions at tactical and operational level
Kembro et al., (2018)	Adapting warehouse operations and design to omni-channel logistics	Journal Paper	64	This study investigates how warehouse operations are affected by the move toward integrated omni-channels
Staudt et al., (2015)	Warehouse performance measurement: a literature review	Journal Paper	129	This study focuses on operational warehouse performance measurement and presents various metrics and definitions for direct & indirect warehouse performance measurement indicators
Davarzani & Norrman, (2015)	Toward a relevant agenda for warehousing research: literature review and practitioners' input	Journal Paper	120	This study discusses about warehouse operational issues and decisions both from literature and practitioners' point of view. Topics include operations, human resources and technology among others

*retrieved from SCOPUS & Google Scholar

According to Binos et al. (2020), there has been a significant amount of study on strategic decision support in geographic location, warehouse and distribution center design and sizing, as well as demand planning and forecasting to date, but the literature on decision assistance for daily warehousing operations is, however, fragmented and underdeveloped. Furthermore, it is mentioned that due to the rising complexity of daily warehouse operations, decision support systems will need to become more sophisticated and intelligent in order to provide real-time assistance to decision makers. Finally, the absence of research into human–machine collaboration in adaptive decision support systems to aid warehouse operational decision makers is highlighted. In the works of Gu et al. (2007), a review on warehouse operation planning problems and decisions is presented, which are classified according to the various functions within the warehouse, i.e. storage, picking, receiving and shipping. These problems require quite frequently decisions to be taken, which are typically of a short duration and localized, since they are at the operational level. Furthermore, another result of the operational nature that these decisions have is that they should be viewed dynamically, with new information about the operating environments being regularly included. According to Koster et al. (2007), feedback about decisions on design and control of order picking is given, and also discussion about common decisions at tactical and operational levels is made. More specifically, the paper mentions that common decisions at these levels usually relate to layout design and dimensioning of the storage system, assignment of SKUs (Stock Keeping Unit) to storage locations, assignment of picking orders and grouping aisles into work zones, routing of order picking activities, and sorting of picked units. The paper of Kembro et al. (2018) investigates how warehouse operations are affected by the move toward integrated omni-channels and exhibits a record of operational changes that take place, which in turn trigger decisions at operational and administrative level to be taken. The paper mentions that even though warehouse operation segments such as receipts, storage and shipping may look as if they remain the same, fundamental decisions should be made for internal changes. These include decisions on aisle reconfiguration, lane depth and stacking height, material handling equipment for put-away and picking, changes on WMS routines for various activities, and changes on scheduling, rotation and shifts of warehouse staff. According to Staudt et al. (2015) the number and variety of objects to be handled; the amount of daily workload to be completed; and the number, nature, and variety of procedures required to meet the needs and demands of customers and suppliers, determine the complexity of warehouse activities. In order to measure performance of the operational and administrative decisions taken regarding these activities, there are various quantitative and qualitative indicators. These are presented in the paper as direct and indirect indicators. Direct warehouse performance indicators include the dimensions of time, quality, cost and productivity, where literally hundreds of aspects can be measured within the warehouse activities, through data produced constantly throughout the operation. Indirect warehouse performance indicators on the other hand are not so easily computable and require structured mathematical tools to evaluate different kinds of information and extract correlations and performances from various databases. Such indicators are customer perception, flexibility, maintenance and staff performance. The paper of Davarzani & Norrman (2015), discusses about warehouse operational issues and decisions both from literature and practitioners' point of view. It presents various examples of decisions regarding storage & picking operations, human resources and technology. According to Khanzode & Shah (2017) and the structured literature review that they wrote on warehouse operational issues, all previous reviews are primarily concentrating on warehouse design and they are overlooking overall productivity. Out of the 186 publications that they critically reviewed regarding warehouse operational considerations, 127 concerned picking concepts and equipment and 25 talked about routing concepts. The remaining was evenly spread on sorting, layout, slotting and replenishment. According to Faber et al. (2013), systematic research into the factors of warehouse planning and control structure appears to be missing, and that in the current warehouse management literature an analysis-oriented research on isolated sub problems is prevailing. It is clearly mentioned in their paper that there was hardly any literature up to that time that explicitly captured warehouse management as a coherent entity. Therefore, we see that existing literature mainly offers scattered material as far as managerial decisions regarding administrative and operational issues and the topic is not organized holistically, in a way that academics and practitioners could obtain insights, let alone combining and addressing it under the umbrella of the Fourth Industrial Revolution and the changes that its technologies have brought during the recent years.

Industry 4.0's first wave of transformation has started almost a decade ago and has greatly impacted Logistics and the field of material handling and intralogistics so far. According to Efthymiou & Ponis (2019) key technologies of Industry 4.0, are Internet of Things (IoT) including Industrial Wireless Networks (IWN) that are able to sense, communicate, identify and process, Cloud Computing, Cyber Physical Systems (CPSs), Advanced Robotics, Artificial Intelligence (AI) and Machine Learning, Augmented Reality (AR), Big Data analytics, Digital Twins and Simulation, and 3D Printing. Via advances in materials and information, robotics and cloud technology, RFID (Radio Frequency Identification), Autonomous Guided Vehicles (AGVs) and autonomous decisions of material handling systems, Industry 4.0 will cause impressive changes in material handling and in-house logistics. Future warehouses and factories will have all their components embodied in the cloud as individual agents, and all systems, such as AGVs, industrial robots and operators, will be interconnected and will also have the potential to make their own decisions. Technologies such as big data analytics, simulation and digital twins will greatly impact managerial and strategic planning of material handling. Since nowadays it is common that insufficient amount of information to be gathered for tasks such as production, logistics and services, when data will be created automatically and continuously by the various entities within these systems without any human intervention, then sharing and organizing their produced data will create a digital shadow of the real world. Therefore, by using analytics for sensor data, not only imminent problems, but potentially dangerous changes can be predicted well in advance. As time progresses, therefore, logistics decisions will become more data-based, allowing continuous process development and ensuring the efficiency of these data-based decisions through the systematic use of Information Technology (IT) and systems (Efthymiou & Ponis, 2019). Müller et al. (2016), present in their paper that Industry 4.0 technologies could help in material handling to reduce throughput losses in case of equipment failure. Based on technological advances, like intelligent industrial robots and M2M (Machine-to-Machine) communication, systems have become intelligent enough in order to reconfigure themselves automatically in case they detect a failure in the overall system, or report an unusual situation before it becomes problematic for the operation. Therefore, preventive or predictive preventive maintenance is another key use case of IoT, once data analytics is involved, and this is particularly critical in a warehouse or factory environment, since it can have significant consequences in terms of OEE (Overall Equipment Effectiveness), a main metric of production productivity. Finally, with hundreds of dozens different products having the need to be stored in an average warehouse, space needs to be optimally utilized in order to guarantee that products and orders can be retrieved, processed and shipped as quickly as possible. Industry 4.0 assures a technology-driven, high-speed setting that allows warehouse executives to know what happens almost anywhere inside the vast warehouse space at a specified time, ranging from machine performance, temperature conditions, energy consumption, stock status or material flow. Key technology for this is indisputably the RFID, which can present precise localization of mobile devices in indoor environments by using active and passive readers. In unison, sensors can also be fitted into the infrastructure of the warehouse building itself such as racking that could report their status, or within the various utilities, including connected lights and ventilation systems in order to optimize energy consumption, which in turn results in lower costs and lower carbon footprint of the facility.

3 Operational and Administrative Decisions in Intelligent DCs

During the last few years DCs have become the main supply chain engine, since order fulfillment has become extremely vital, most importantly due to fast growth of e-commerce. DCs perform a critical intermediate function between supply chain members, shaping both supply chain costs and service towards the customers. The more DCs grow in size, the greater is the diversity of their customer needs, and the more complex their internal processes become. Therefore, managing complex DCs in an effective and efficient way has become a demanding and challenging task. Thus, the principal question is how DC management can be organized in order to fulfill today's challenges, as a collection of planning and controlling operational and administrative decisions and procedures.

According to Frazelle (2016), warehouse processes that require planning and controlling include among others: inbound handling, receiving, storage, picking location allocation, order batching and release, order picking and packing, value-adding activities, preparing for dispatch and document creation. According to Slack et al. (2015), warehouse management includes all planning and control procedures and decisions for operating a warehouse. The end goal of planning and control is to satisfy customer demand by ensuring that operations run effectively. Planning is proactive, since it entails determining of what should be done and how, while control is to safeguard that the desired plan is followed through. Within planning, there are strategic, tactical and operational decision levels. The horizon of strategic decision level is usually counted in years since it represents the long-term goals and plans, while tactical decision planning is usually months and operational is represented in days. However, for many DCs the tactical planning horizon can only be days or weeks, due to the highly dynamic environment (ibid). Khan et al. (2016), mention that DC management can be divided into long- and short-term decisions. Long term decisions are related to warehouse size and location, inventory management as far as count accuracy is concerned, customer service and capital investment. On the other hand, short term decisions are related to order management, transportation management and inventory management as far as inventory turnover ratio is concerned. According to Faber et al. (2013), capacity planning for equipment and personnel, stock planning, transport planning and storage location assignment planning are the most important tactical decisions in DCs. Capacity planning for equipment, personnel and transport decide on the needed amount within each category that should be available daily in order for the DC to operate effectively. Stock planning determines the number of products that should be on stock at each time, and therefore influences the goods receipt cycles. Finally, storage location assignment planning determines the type of location that products will have within the DC (i.e. pallet, box, block stacking, VNA, etc.) and the different zones that will exist within these types of storage locations. This last part is particularly important, since it can reduce or increase the warehouse space needed and time it takes for order picking or storage and retrieval. Operational decisions of DCs, which as previously mentioned represent the day-to-day planning and are mainly based on actual data, rather than historic (van den BERG, 1999), usually deal with the storage, retrieval and order picking operations and all the scheduling, routing and sequencing they require. For this type of decisions, various Industry 4.0 technologies have greatly assisted in making them more automated, but also less time consuming for managers. Incorporation of technologies such as Mobile and IoT contribute effectively to connecting systems or machines through distributed logistics and supply chain processes to improve operational and efficiency related solutions. Such solutions make goods and services 'smart', which in turn release humans from unnecessary labor. Planning and supervising numerous logistics activities is not needed anymore due to various automation solutions and systems that are able to plan and execute their workflow without human involvement or assistance (Ponis & Efthymiou, 2020). This is however not the case in most DCs up to date, therefore, controlling is a principal part of warehouse management since things do not always come about as supposed to when plans are implemented. Control is the process of monitoring, analyzing, reporting, and taking action through intervention when adjustments are necessary in order to allow operations to achieve the objectives that were placed in the original plan (Slack et al. 2015). For successful control, the speed of information is essential. Information is created by various generated data in the work floor of the DC, and the speed at which data can be transformed into information by the control system is the most important element of control. Speed of data transformation into information may be critical, but the more sophisticated a control system is, the higher the cost to establish such a system becomes. Therefore, management in each DC should make a detailed analysis of the actual needs before proceeding to implementation of a control system to be justified economically. This in turn means that there is no single way of designing a control system for a DC, and each time it must be assembled according to the specific operational and organizational needs that it's constructed for (Faber et al. 2013). Medina et al. (2009), present an application of Simulation for Predictive Control (SimPC) as a tool for decision making in non-automated DCs. This application incorporates stochastic features for a realistic representation of operations, by using real-time data management capabilities, to create more comprehensive and customizable performance metrics and operational parameters adjustments.

Within the context of DC and warehouse management, "administrative decision making" can be described as the act of formulating general rules, company policies, major objectives and laying down broad projects that relate to the DC or warehouse. In other words, it decides "what" is to be done and "when" it is to be done and is about guiding, leading, and controlling the efforts of the various groups within a company towards some common goals. On the other hand, "operational decision making" entails formulating, initiating, and bringing together the various elements towards some pre-determined goals. It involves coordinating, actuating and integrating the diverse organizational components while sustaining the viability of the organization. Videlicet, it is the "how" of the organization, and tries to get things done through and with the people of formally structured groups to manage day to day business Weihrich et al., 1988). For the remaining of this chapter, these two groups of decision making will be studied, and further split into smaller clusters and various examples will be provided. Before we analyze the different groups of decisions, it must be noted that some of the decisions mentioned below, are generally managerial and not specific to logistics or warehousing. This is because a DC could belong to a Third-Party Logistics (3PL) company and be a stand-alone entity both as a warehouse and a company. This implies that some of the decisions will have to concern typical operational and administrative issues outside the sphere of logistics and material handling. Therefore, a Managing Director (MD) of a 3PL company will need to not only be able to make supply chain decisions, but also purely managerial regarding the administration and operation of the company. As seen in Fig. 1, administrative decisions have been categorized by the authors in ten groups. These are: vision, finance, regulations, benchmarking, upkeep, market, procedures, policy, people and various, which is a group of single other decisions not related to any other category.

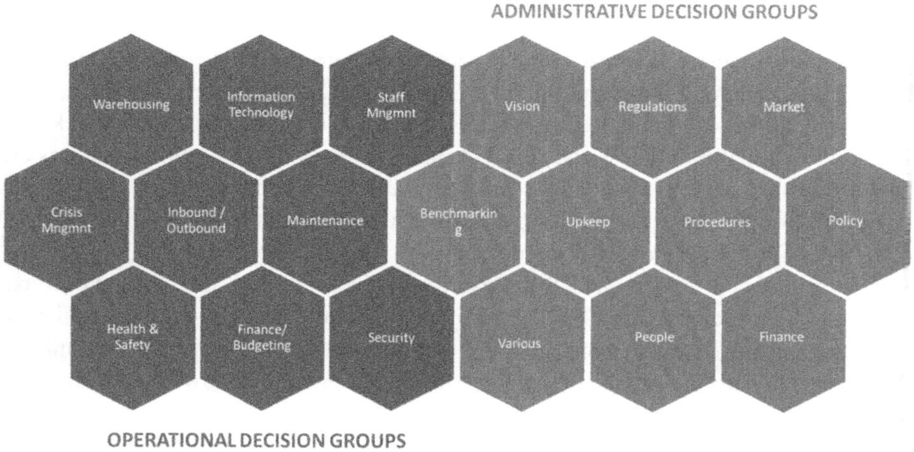

Fig. 1. Decision groups

Regarding vision and long term goals, the MD of a 3PL company or a DC director, should be able to set and ensure strategic guidance and direction for the upcoming years, take investment decisions that can alter the structure of the company/DC such as size of warehouse and location, or the level of digitization in processes, or the use of automation for various warehouse processes like picking/packing/dispatching, etc. Furthermore, preparing and implementing comprehensive business plans to facilitate achievement by planning cost-effective operations and market development activities is also needed. Financial mission includes the entire gamut of financial management decisions that is divided into investment, financing and dividend decisions (Sudhindra Bhat, 2008). Thus, management is responsible for forecasting expected events in business and perceiving their financial implications. They should also be able to set and ensure that the company achieves its financial mission by finding new customers and new sources of revenue, or by programming strategic funds and projecting baseline. As far as regulations are concerned, management is responsible for making the required decisions so that the company/DC meets and follows all legal and local regulations and requirements. Complying with warehousing, material handling, and shipping requirements by studying existing and new legislation is important, and so is enforcing adherence to these requirements. Benchmarking is another group of administrative decisions. Management should use industry best practices and benchmarking to set-up company service standards, to decide and frame Service Level Agreements (SLAs) with clients. Management should also take decisions on trying to reach a low-price/high-value offering to their clients, whether they are internal or external, but in the same time strive for lowest possible operating expenses, while offering the highest possible quality. According to Gu et al. (2010), other than benchmarking, analytic models and simulations can also be an approach for performance evaluation within a DC. Analytic performance models can be either aisle-based models that focus on single storage systems and tackle service & travel time, or integrated models that deal with multiple storage systems and combine travel time analysis and service quality criteria with various other performance measures such as operational cost and storage capacity. As far as human resources, management is responsible for taking high-level decisions regarding company staff. Ensuring labor relations, compensation and benefits related issues, recruitment and selection of management team, job designing, general training & development and career guidance. Deciding and setting annual MBO (Management by Objectives) targets for management team is also another task that needs to be performed. According to Davarzani & Norrman (2015), ergonomics of warehouse jobs, is also of top importance at the administrative level human resource management. Furthermore, exploring how repetitive picking work during a whole shift influences performance of workers is another topic of significance, since this may have direct impact on warehouse Key Performance Indicators (KPIs). Based on Wu & Hou (2009) if DC managers could apprehend the substantial increase or decrease of employee performance over time, and then use the appropriate employee management strategies such as training or rewards, based on their performance, then operational efficiency of DCs can effectively be improved. Such models, which are based on employee performance estimation and employee performance trend analysis, can methodically and accurately analyze performance of employees and thus assist managers to take the most fitting decisions. The upkeep of premises requires a substantial number of decisions to be taken regularly. According to Staudt et al. (2015), Facility management is defined as a) warehouse facility maintenance and repair, b) collaboration with various facilities-related departments, c) construction of new building infrastructure, and d) fire protection equipment. After people management, facility management has the second biggest impact on warehouse capability, according to the study. Management is responsible for deciding on implementation of strategic plans regarding maintenance of equipment and systems. For example, if implementing a predictive preventive maintenance system through IoT technologies on current automation systems is a viable option or not.

Process efficiency is another important group of administrative decisions. DC management should be constantly reviewing efficiency of existing processes & procedures and taking actions towards improvement. At the administrative level, this implies a high-level design and not minor details of sub processes within the DC. Management should also regularly check market trends and technological changes regarding DCs and warehousing. Maintain professional and technical knowledge by attending educational workshops, review professional publications, establish personal networks and participate in professional societies and EXPOs in order to be informed about upcoming changes. Based on Davarzani & Norrman (2015), decisions related to technology and equipment include selection of automation level, choosing of appropriate warehouse equipment, selection of suitable warehouse management system, and planning and application of those technologies and equipment. Market and suppliers for new technologies should be regularly observed to be able to take decisions on whether they could be useful for the company. For example, use of AR and VR (Virtual Reality) technologies within the warehouses was something that nobody could imagine two decades ago. VR technology, commercialized originally by video games, has since grown to be used in supply chains. Logistics companies can take informed decisions to improve product flows and monitor processes by letting users to simulate and analyze 3D environments. For example, DHL deployed a vision picking system with customer Ricoh that caused a 25% increase in performance of order picking when using smart glasses (DHL InMotion, 2018). Another example is AI and Machine Learning. Cognitive development and improvement in logistics tasks, through the development of technologies such as AI and advanced robotics, have a vast positive impact on the industry (Wang, Wan, Li, & Zhang, 2016). It will not be far away into the future, when we will be able to see DCs operating with autonomous lift trucks that will be able to arrange and communicate their own schedule, charging and "resting" time according to warehouse receiving and dispatch timetable.

Finally, the MD of a 3PL company or a DC director should ensure company policies and guidelines are communicated all the way from the top down in the company and that they are always followed. Furthermore, management should be communicating and maintaining trust relationships with shareholders, business partners and authorities, and liaising with transport companies, suppliers, and clients. Moreover, should be providing strategic advice regarding logistics & supply chain to the board and chairperson. Additionally, should be acting as the public speaker and public relations representative of the DC (or company in case of 3PL) in ways that strengthen its profile.

As far as operational decisions are concerned, the authors have classified them in nine groups as seen in Fig. 1. These concern inbound/outbound operations, warehousing operations, Information Technology, maintenance, staff, crisis management, health & safety, finance, and security.

Inbound/Outbound operations represent a major share of DC processes. Inbound logistics include the processes and procedures regarding delivery of goods and/or raw materials from suppliers to the DC. Key operational challenges for inbound logistics processes lie in identifying trustworthy and consistent suppliers, balancing inbound and outbound flows, and managing on-time shipments. Outbound logistics include the processes and procedures regarding preparing the goods for dispatch, issuing all necessary documents, working with reliable 3PL partners, implementing reverse logistics, making route optimization and risk management regarding transportation, and keeping track of the cargo during the entire process from DC to the end customer, whether this is a store (B2B operation) or a person (B2C operation). Decisions also include the assignment of inbound and outbound carriers to warehouse docks, the schedule of the service of carriers at each dock, and the allocation and dispatching of material handling equipment and staff (Gu et al., 2007). Thus, operational decisions that relate to this group must address all the above-mentioned tasks daily. Hence, management should ensure that receiving and dispatch operations are running smooth, through initiating, coordinating, and enforcing all needed policies and procedures. Based on Binos et al. (2020), as the years go by, planning, predicting, and scheduling in real-time will become more important due to elements of uncertainty. Therefore, it will be vital to extract information and real-time features from the environment in order to enhance employees' decision ability for managing and operating warehouses. According to Kagermann (2014), for transportation, Industry 4.0 technologies will allow for systems to be capable of recording events and statuses in real-time by using Auto-ID and sensor technology. This will permit instant detection and location of any disruption to the system, thereby enabling a rapid response. IoT technology, through RFID for example, can also improve inbound & outbound operations, by allowing for almost instant counting and recognizing of products inside a box or pallet.

Warehousing operations represent the biggest portion of activities within a DC as far as cost and staff is concerned. Warehousing procedures usually include the activities of storage, picking, consolidation, deconsolidation, sorting, merging SKUs, co-packing, assembling, moving materials within warehouse space, buffering, labeling, stock handling, stock-taking and quality control checking (Kłodawski et al., 2017). The reason that warehousing processes exist, is to add new value to materials through production processes and buffering/smoothing material flows by storing excessive flows and making reserves. At the same timeall these processes should be designed, planned and executed in a sustainable manner, which implies adopting environmentally responsible practices and strategies to minimize the environmental impact of warehouse operations while maintaining efficiency and cost-effectiveness. By doing that, businesses can reduce their ecological footprint, lower operational costs, enhance their corporate social responsibility, and contribute to a more environmentally sustainable supply chain and logistics industry.

In that context, management should be responsible for maintaining warehousing operations by taking decisions for all above mentioned activities and procedures, but also ensure daily that quality objectives and deadlines are met. Based on Kovac & Djurdjevic (2020), the process of order picking is the most labor intensive within a DC, and therefore its efficiency is exceptionally important for maintaining low operating costs. Therefore, operational level decisions that correspond to order picking, such as order picking routing, storage assignment, job assignment and order picking method selection, should be carefully organized in order to reduce daily operating costs. According to Gu et al. (2007), three of the fundamental decisions that need to be taken within the warehousing function are the inventory levels per SKU that should be kept, the frequency of replenishment per SKU, and where should the SKU be stored within the premises. As far as this final decision is concerned, further criteria and constraints influence the outcome, such as storage space capacity and efficiency, picker capacity and efficiency based on picker cycle time, compatibility between storage locations and products, response time, and item retrieval policy (e.g., first-in, first-out, etc.). Working on new needs of existing customers and designing and implementing new processes is also included in the tactical operational decisions. Each of the above-mentioned activities can be from plain simple to extremely complicated, according to the way it has been designed and the systems that are used each time. Stock handling for example requires several decisions to be taken, such as deciding on the volume that will be stocked, the type of locations, the type of lift truck equipment that will be used, the stock turnover rate, etc. Or as another example, control of inventory levels and accuracy, requires to organize physical counts (i.e. stocktaking), deciding on when these will take place in order not to interfere with daily picking and replenishment of locations, arranging necessary staff and equipment for doing this work (e.g. lift platforms), reconciling results with WMS, etc. Within this field, Industry 4.0 technologies can be particularly helpful in the coming years. In the context of warehousing, Cyber Physical Systems will be the central originator of change. Warehouses implementing Industry 4.0 technologies will use smart machines and systems that benefit from the end-to-end incorporation of Information and Communication Technology (ICT) on almost all processes. In the smart warehouse of the future, devices, people, and resources will all interact with each other conveniently and constantly, which basically means that traditional warehousing operations will change completely, as goods will be individually recognizable and located at all times, aware of their past, current status and alternate routes to reach their target state. Autonomous robots and warehousing systems will be able to monitor and configure themselves in accordance with the needs of the current situation, cooperate with each other to decide who has spare capacity at any given time, and take the final decision to operate on their own to achieve the best possible output (Kagermann, 2014). Thus, we see that exciting times are coming for DCs and intralogistics systems that will radically change the way operational decisions are taken.

Information Technology is an integral part of every DC these days, with the WMS being the "heart" of the warehouse. DCs use WMS to assist warehouse operations in various ways. A WMS principally aims to manage movement of goods within a DC and process the related transactions, which mainly include shipping, receiving, put-away and picking. The WMS is a database driven application that maintains the inventory and records almost all warehouse transactions. WMS can be classified into three Tiers. This categorization is based on the built-in functionality and flexibility of the WMS product and the higher the Tier, the greater is possible to handle business complexity and product capability. Generally, a WMS accelerates order handling time, manages warehouse areas, improves inventory accuracy, offers instant order status information, and augments labor productivity (Andiyappillai, 2019). In general, the WMS must have tools and functions to support all main steps and logistic processes of the DC. WMS also helps with recording user data, and therefore being able to set KPIs to meet SLAs with the customers. Therefore, management should be very careful when deciding with which WMS software provider to partner with, because once selected, it's very difficult to change. Another IT related operational duty within a DC, which in turn creates several decisions to be made, include managing RF scanners. Scanners are usually the main accessory for doing all work within a DC, like picking, receiving, storing, etc. Scanners require Wi-Fi network, linkage and parameterization to the WMS and of course maintenance, due to the mistreatment that they get from users within the harsh warehouse environment. For all these actions, daily decisions should be taken by warehouse IT management. Finally, operational decisions should also be taken regarding ordering and stock levels of IT consumables, like labels for products, boxes and pallets, ribbons, paper for delivery notes, etc.

Maintenance represents another category of operational decisions within a DC. Management should maintain physical condition of the DC by inspecting equipment, systems & building, and issuing work orders for repair and requisitions for replacement. DCs are places where dozens of lift trucks operate. They require specific preventive maintenance checks, but also repairs due to mechanical errors. Decisions and actions for maintenance of these machines are a daily issue and a significant responsibility since they are vital for accomplishing daily work within the warehouse. Complex automation systems, when available, are also in much need of upkeep. For such systems, usually contracts exist regarding regular preventive maintenance and specific stock of important spare parts is kept and constantly refreshed once parts are used, to ensure uninterrupted operation. For such systems, usually an emergency Hotline also exists, that additional software related help can be received remotely. All these points and features need to be constantly supervised and commanded by experts. Finally, warehouses are huge buildings, so regular maintenance scheduling requires a lot of effort if one ponders that there are hundreds (if not thousands) of lighting fixtures within the building, dozens of restrooms, electrical sockets, windows, ventilation, and air conditioning systems that need almost constant daily care.

People are an integral part of the operation within a DC, and they are usually great in numbers, because most work is manual (counting, picking, packing, etc.), therefore operational decisions regarding staff are essential for effective operation. Usually around 90% of staff within a warehouse is blue collar workers and therefore shift supervisors are needed to bridge the gap with management. Operational actions and decisions that need to be taken regarding staff include scheduling and assigning employees according to daily needs, maintaining DC staff by recruiting, selecting, orienting and training employees, delegating responsibilities and supervising the work of subordinates, maintaining warehouse staff job results by coaching, counseling and disciplining employees, and finally, planning, following up/monitoring and appraising job results in order to drive maximum performance. Crisis Management is another category of operational decisions. Executives should have strong crisis management skills and act swift in times of need by taking the correct decisions. Logistics is all about constant changes in normal flows due to unexpected events within the supply chain, so managers need to make decisions continuously. COVID-19 pandemic is an excellent example. DCs had to radically change the way they operate due to the pandemic, and management had to make many operational decisions to keep staff safe and comply with new legislations. Working from home (teleworking) is not a possibility for manual/physical work that takes place in DCs, so management had to come up with other ideas due to COVID-19 measures. For example, shifts had to be reorganized in a way that staff from one shift doesn't meet colleagues from another. Employees had to stay home for weeks or months due to either being in vulnerable groups or had kids to look after due to school closures. This created a small chaos in preparing daily timetables. Within the premises, staff had to be physically distanced as much as possible, so lunch breaks had to be reorganized to have smaller groups of people within common break areas. The same thing also had to be organized regarding shift start and finish, so that crowding in areas such as clock-in & clock-out is avoided. Management is also responsible for ensuring compliance with health and safety legislation for staff and premises. Meetings should be regular with health & safety inspector and requirements that are asked, should be implemented, and followed. Typical actions that should be decided and acted upon concern among others, promoting awareness about potential safety hazards, providing protective clothing, providing proper training and courses about warehouse safety processes, marking hazardous zones clearly, eliminating potential safety hazards and carrying out regularly fire safety drills. Security is another topic that requires serious attention by the management. DCs are areas where large amount of stock and equipment is gathered, and therefore risk of theft and loss of property is high. Therefore, management is responsible for safeguarding warehouse operations and contents by establishing and monitoring security procedures and protocols. Decisions should be made on what type of CCTV or access control system should be purchased and installed and needs for guarding the premises with a security company should be arranged. Last but not least, management is responsible for achieving financial objectives by preparing an annual budget, scheduling expenditures, analyzing variances and initiating corrective actions. Operational decisions regarding finance, are more day-to-day or tactical and relate more on various purchases and unexpected operating expenditures. As one can see, managing a DC can be highly complex, with decisions taken being related not only within the strict confines of logistics and supply chain, in order to fulfill customer needs.

4 Conclusions

Distribution Centers perform a vital role within each supply chain by collecting materials from various suppliers, preparing customer orders, and performing various value-added activities. The specific function of each DC depends mainly on the supply chain strategy of each corporation, but usually the layout and flow of goods within the premises tend to follow some basic standard rules. The growing need for retailers to compete in international markets with their goods across cost, quality and service dimensions has given rise to the need of developing more effective warehouse management and strategies. Even though the topic of warehouse management and performance has attracted plenty of attention during the last decades, literature is principally focused on operational design, such as picking and routing concepts, building location and size analysis, and inventory management processes. When it comes to operational and administrative decisions that must be taken for a DC in order to run operations successfully, literature is scarce. This paper sought to describe and determine an extensive range of operational and administrative decisions that have to be taken for a DC in order to run both day-to-day business and strategic topics successfully. In addition, these issues are addressed through the lens of Industry 5.0 and the changes that its technologies have generated.

The literature study showed that systematic research into the factors of warehouse planning and control structure appears to be missing and that in the current warehouse management literature an analysis-oriented research on isolated sub problems is predominating. Following the revision of literature, it became obvious that it was difficult to find any literature up to that point that explicitly captured warehouse management as a coherent entity. Therefore, we see that managerial decisions regarding administrative and operational issues are not addressed per se in the existing literature, let alone combining and addressing it within the context of Industry 4.0 and impact of its technologies. The principal question raised in the paper was how DC management can be organized to fulfill today's challenges, as a collection of planning and controlling operational and administrative decisions and procedures. Through the analysis, we showed that administering a DC is a very complicated process that requires both general management knowledge and specific supply chain knowledge. In order for operations in a DC to run smoothly, there are a series of decisions that need to be taken both strategically and tactically/operationally. We separated decision making into administrative and operational. Administrative decision-making addresses what should be done and when this should be done. It relates to vision and long-term goals, general financial management decisions, legal and local regulations and requirements that need to be met and followed, industry best practices and benchmarking according to competition in similar types of business, human resources related issues and policies, process efficiency regarding operation, and market trends and technological advancements within the sector of operation. On the other hand, operational decision-making addresses how things should be done and relates more to managing day-to-day business. It concerns mainly inbound/outbound and warehousing processes and procedures, and IT systems. These three elements are the main constituents of every DC and there are numerous decisions, as explained, that need to be managed. Other than these three elements, operational decision making relates also to upkeep and maintenance of equipment, systems and building, scheduling, and assigning employees, supervising and analyzing job results, coaching and disciplining staff, and complying with health and safety regulations. Taking swift decisions regarding urgent issues is also very critical, since logistics is all about constant changes in normal flows due to unexpected events. Finally, all of the above, where also addressed in the context of Industry 4.0 and the vicissitudes that its technologies have brought during the first wave of transformation, or the expected changes that will take place during the second and third waves in the upcoming years.

Finally, there are some inherent limitations to this analysis. Firstly, it was a very tedious and burdensome method to determine the inclusion/exclusion requirements. Consequently, various valuable publications may be available that have been omitted from the sample. For this, if such an eventuality has happened, the writers apologize to their peers a priori. Secondly, it should be noted that the choice of language restricts the results of our study, as many publications are likely to use a language other than English. Recording and analyzing more facts regarding operational & administrative decisions of DCs is included in the authors' future research agenda. So is also, the development of a technology and process reference model for supporting critical operational & administrative decisions of modern and intelligent DCs.

Acknowledgments. This project is carried out within the framework of the National Recovery and Resilience Plan Greece 2.0, funded by the European Union – NextGenerationEU – Project Code: TAEDR-0535864.

Disclosure of Interests. The authors have no competing interests to declare that are relevant to the content of this article.

References

Andiyappillai, N.: Implementing warehouse management systems (WMS) in logistics: a case study. Int. J. Logist. Syst. Manag. **2**(1), 12–23 (2019). https://doi.org/10.5281/zenodo.2576011

Baker, P.: An exploratory framework of the role of inventory and warehousing in international supply chains. Int. J. Logist. Manag. **18**(1), 64–80 (2007). https://doi.org/10.1108/09574090710748171

Bartholdi, J., Hackman, S.: Warehouse & Distribution Science Release 0.94. The Supply Chain and Logistics Institute, School of Industrial and Systems Engineering, Georgia Institute of Technology (2011). https://www.scl.gatech.edu/sites/default/files/downloads/gtscl-warehouse_science_bartholdi.pdf

Binos, T., Adamopoulos, A., Bruno, V.: Decision support research in warehousing and distribution: a systematic literature review. Int. J. Inf. Technol. Decis. Mak. **19**(03), 653–693 (2020). https://doi.org/10.1142/s0219622020300013

Davarzani, H., Norrman, A.: Toward a relevant agenda for warehousing research: literature review and practitioners' input. Logist. Res. **8**(1), 1 (2015). https://doi.org/10.1007/s12159-014-0120-1

DHL InMotion: DHL rolls out global augmented reality program. DHL InMotion; DHL InMotion (2018). https://inmotion.dhl/en/esports/article/dhl-rolls-out-global-augmented-reality-program

Dotoli, M., Epicoco, N., Falagario, M., Costantino, N., Turchiano, B.: An integrated approach for warehouse analysis and optimization: a case study. Comput. Ind. **70**, 56–69 (2015). https://doi.org/10.1016/j.compind.2014.12.004

Efthymiou, O.K., Ponis, S.T.: Current status of industry 4.0 in material handling automation and in-house logistics. Int. J. Ind. Manuf. Eng. **13**(10), 1370–1374 (2019). https://doi.org/10.5281/zenodo.3566333

Faber, N., de Koster, M.B.M., Smidts, A.: Organizing warehouse management. Int. J. Oper. Prod. Manag. **33**(9), 1230–1256 (2013). https://doi.org/10.1108/ijopm-12-2011-0471

Faber, N., De Koster, R.B.M., Smidts, A.: Survival of the fittest: the impact of fit between warehouse management structure and warehouse context on warehouse performance. Int. J. Prod. Res. **56**(1–2), 120–139 (2017). https://doi.org/10.1080/00207543.2017.1395489

Frazelle, E.: World-Class Warehousing and Material Handling. Mcgraw-Hill Education, New York (2016)

Gu, J., Goetschalckx, M., McGinnis, L.F.: Research on warehouse operation: a comprehensive review. Eur. J. Oper. Res. **177**(1), 1–21 (2007). https://doi.org/10.1016/j.ejor.2006.02.025

Gu, J., Goetschalckx, M., McGinnis, L.F.: Research on warehouse design and performance evaluation: a comprehensive review. Eur. J. Oper. Res. **203**(3), 539–549 (2010). https://doi.org/10.1016/j.ejor.2009.07.031

Weihrich, H., Halff, J., Koontz, H.: Management: a Global Perspective. Study Guide, 2nd edn. Mcgraw-Hill, New York (1988)

Kagermann, H.: Change through digitization—value creation in the age of industry 4.0. In: Management of Permanent Change, pp. 23–45 (2014). https://doi.org/10.1007/978-3-658-05014-6_2

Kembro, J.H., Norrman, A., Eriksson, E.: Adapting warehouse operations and design to omni-channel logistics. Int. J. Phys. Distrib. Logist. Manag. **48**(9), 890–912 (2018). https://doi.org/10.1108/ijpdlm-01-2017-0052

Khan, S.A., Dweiri, F., Chaabane, A.: Fuzzy-AHP approach for warehouse performance measurement. In: 2016 IEEE International Conference on Industrial Engineering and Engineering Management (IEEM) (2016). https://doi.org/10.1109/ieem.2016.7798001

Khanzode, V., Shah, B.: A comprehensive review of warehouse operational issues. Int. J. Logist. Syst. Manag. **26**(3), 346 (2017). https://doi.org/10.1504/ijlsm.2017.10002597

Kłodawski, M., Lewczuk, K., Jacyna-Gołda, I., Żak, J.: Decision making strategies for warehouse operations. Arch. Transp. **41**(1), 43–53 (2017). https://doi.org/10.5604/01.3001.0009.7384

Koster, R., Le-Duc, T., Roodbergen, K.J.: Design and control of warehouse order picking: a literature review. Eur. J. Oper. Res. **182**(2), 481–501 (2007). https://doi.org/10.1016/j.ejor.2006.07.009

Kovac, M., Djurdjevic, D.: Optimization of order-picking systems through tactical and operational decision making. Int. J. Simul. Model. **19**(1), 89–99 (2020). https://doi.org/10.2507/ijsimm19-1-505

Medina, L.A., Bilsel, R.U., Wysk, R.A., Prabhu, V., Ravindran, A.R.: Simulation for Predictive Control of a distribution center. In: Proceedings of the 2009 Winter Simulation Conference (WSC) (2009). https://doi.org/10.1109/wsc.2009.5429694

Müller, C., Grunewald, M., Spengler, T.S.: Redundant configuration of automated flow lines based on "Industry 4.0"-technologies. J. Bus. Econ. **87**(7), 877–898 (2016). https://doi.org/10.1007/s11573-016-0831-7

Ponis, S.T., Efthymiou, O.K.: Cloud and IoT applications in material handling automation and intralogistics. Logistics **4**(3), 22 (2020). https://doi.org/10.3390/logistics4030022

Slack, N., Brandon-Jones, A., Johnston, R.: Operations Management. Pearson, London (2015)

Staudt, F.H., Alpan, G., Di Mascolo, M., Rodriguez, C.M.T.: Warehouse performance measurement: a literature review. Int. J. Prod. Res. **53**(18), 5524–5544 (2015). https://doi.org/10.1080/00207543.2015.1030466

Bhat, S.: Financial Management : Principles and Practice. Excel Books, New Delhi (2008)

van den Berg, J.P.: A literature survey on planning and control of warehousing systems. IIE Trans. **31**(8), 751–762 (1999). https://doi.org/10.1023/a:1007606228790

Vidal Vieira, J.G., Ramos Toso, M., da Silva, J.E.A.R., Cabral Ribeiro, P.C.: An AHP-based framework for logistics operations in distribution centres. Int. J. Prod. Econ. **187**, 246–259 (2017). https://doi.org/10.1016/j.ijpe.2017.03.001

Wang, S., Wan, J., Li, D., Zhang, C.: Implementing smart factory of industrie 4.0: an outlook. Int. J. Distrib. Sensor Netw. **12**(1), 3159805 (2016). https://doi.org/10.1155/2016/3159805

Wu, Y.-J., Hou, J.-L.: A model for employee performance trend analysis of distribution centers. Hum. Factors Ergon. Manuf. **19**(5), 413–437 (2009). https://doi.org/10.1002/hfm.20157

Starting Logistics Centers: An In-depth Analysis of the Greek Legal and Regulatory Framework

Mavridou Sofia, Fragkaki Afroditi, and Folinas Dimitris(✉)

Department of Supply Chain Management, International Hellenic University, 601 00 Katerini, Greece

s.mavridou@pieria.pkm.gov.gr, fragafro@yahoo.gr, folinasd@ihu.gr

Abstract. A logistics center, or hub, comprises a range of organized logistics services and infrastructure related to various modes of transportation. It is established and operated in an area where activities facilitating intermodal transport and storage services are permitted. A key component of such a center is its connection to or inclusion of a railway station, port, or airport. Alternatively, it can be described as a geographical zone where companies engaged in the transport, storage, management, and distribution of goods are situated, providing logistics services that involve interconnecting and transitioning between different modes of transport, assembling, distributing, and consolidating loads, as well as packaging, unpacking, and transferring goods. Additionally, these centers offer value-added services aimed at streamlining load flow, fostering the adoption of information and communication technologies, and implementing telematics systems. The establishment and operation of a logistics center help reduce the cost of transporting goods by shifting the transport flow from road to rail, thus ensuring more environmental, economic, and safety benefits. Our research seeks to examine the organizational and legal dimensions of logistics centers with the objective of fostering sustainable economic development through public and private partnerships. Employing contemporary legal science and advanced research methodologies, we aim to refine the Greek legislative framework governing the provision of transport and logistics services. Our investigation encompassed a thorough review and analysis of current Greek legislation, scrutinizing its implementation by economic entities (both public and private). Through a comprehensive examination of Greek legislation and a doctrinal exploration of logistics services, we undertook a theoretical and practical investigation into existing legal regulations within this domain. In light of our findings, we presented some concluding remarks about Greek law, aiming to highlight and map possible optimizations of the Greek legislative framework governing the provision of transport and logistics services. Furthermore, our research advocates for the implementation of measures involving public administrative interventions aimed directly at controlling organizations offering transport and logistics services. These proposed measures are designed to exert a positive influence on the sustainable development of the transport sector.

Keywords: Logistics centers · Legal and regulatory framework · Greece

I. Kostavelis et al. (Eds.): ICSC 2024, CCIS 2110, pp. 248–255, 2025.
https://doi.org/10.1007/978-3-031-69344-1_18

1 Introduction

The institutional framework for the implementation of the terms of the freight centres (or Logistics Centers - LC) is characterized by the cooperation of several administrative bodies that are part of different ministries, spreading their competences. In the past, when the needs of the time were limited because the mode of transport was at a low level, the legal framework served a completely different transport infrastructure network. With the globalization of the economy, new markets have emerged, transport speeds have increased, and the supply chain industry has evolved to such an extent that it covers a wide range of economic activities, from preparation of production to redistribution and transport. The Greek state, despite its inability to complete the specialized infrastructure for the creation of freight centres, has established an appropriate framework that will allow private initiative to develop independently of the completion of the required infrastructure. The main development objectives of the LCs are:

- The rationalization of the transport system and, more generally, objectives relating to transport policy or environmental protection.
- Regional development by attracting investment.
- Business development.

The modern logistics industry is an important pillar in the expansion of the economy and acts as a crucial factor in development. On the one hand, companies make every effort to reduce the cost of the supply chain by fully utilizing and integrating the resources at their disposal. On the other hand, local governments are vigorously promoting the development of modern logistics industries as an important strategy to support sustainable economic development, improve the investment environment and enhance social and economic benefits (Yingxiu et al., 2017). The contribution of this position paper to the scientific community consists of summarizing the institutional interventions in the development of freight centers, evaluating them, and incorporating them into the policy community for immediate implementation.

2 Defining Logistics Center Paradigm

A Logistics Center refers to an area with intense activity related to the movement of goods. This movement starts at the point of production, passes through many intermediate stations, and finally reaches specific points of sale and consumption.

According to Law 3333/2005 (Fek A'91/12-4-2005): "*A Logistics Center (LC) is an organically integrated set of structures, structured services and infrastructure of different means of transport, established and operating in an area where activities for combined transport services are allowed and which necessarily includes or is linked to a railway station or port or airport*'. It is the physical space in which businesses are established which are either providers (e.g. transport, transit, 3PLs) or users (e.g. distribution centres of commercial and industrial enterprises) of freight transport and logistics services.

A Logistics Center is defined as a hub located in a specific area and where all logistics activities related to the transport, distribution of goods and the logistics process in general take place (Article 1 of Law 3333/2005). The main function of a Logistics Center is to handle and transport freight. Each Logistics Center or terminal is characterized by a specific nominal capacity, i.e. the amount of freight that can be handled within a certain time frame and under normal conditions. The nominal capacity is related to the area of land occupied by the Logistics Center in question and to its level of technological, labor, and administrative capacity. The infrastructure of a Logistics Center must be able to cope with current traffic and future trends, together with technological and logistical changes. Freight centres mainly refer to areas where goods can be stored without the existence of customs duties and value added taxes (explanatory memorandum to Law 3333/2005).

The management of freight transport, the development of synergies between stakeholders and the strengthening of the regional economy are key functions of logistics parks in the transport system. In the context of fierce competition and diversified customer needs, logistics companies are increasingly coordinating with each other within logistics parks (Liu et al. 2007). This connectivity enables them to efficiently share resources such as infrastructure, information, and customer orders, draw knowledge from each other and ultimately evolve the quality of their service offerings, for example by reducing order time and adding more value to the final products (Apeejay, 2022).

The logistics industry in Greece is expected to benefit from significant opportunities soon. Maintaining the country's position as a central interconnection hub in South-Eastern Europe and a link between Western Europe and Asia provides significant growth potential. There is ample scope for investment in areas such as ports, warehouses, island ports and the road and rail network (Strategic Transport Investment Framework 2014–2025). Expanding the sector requires investment in environmentally friendly technologies and digitalization to reduce emissions and increase efficiency. In addition, the development of e-commerce and the efficient use of available investment resources through initiatives such as the National Strategic Research Fund 2021–2027 and Connecting Europe are essential factors for the growth of the sector (Naftemporiki, 2024).

Policy interventions in the logistics industry include subsidies, capital investments, fiscal incentives, strategy formulation, regulations and other tactics aimed at developing logistics parks (Wenwen et al., 2020).

3 Implementation Framework

In our country, there is a complex legislative framework for freight centres, which is characterized by overlaps, reversals of responsibilities and restrictions. The multiplicity of legal provisions causes confusion and makes it difficult to implement them effectively. The lack of coordination between the competent authorities exacerbates this situation. More specifically:

3.1 Law. 3333/2005

H The creation of the regulatory framework started with the Development Law 3299/2004, which offers public and private entities the opportunity to implement logistics infrastructure projects, such as warehouses and freight centres, with low business risk and favorable taxation. This process was completed by Law 3333/2005, which provides for the establishment of freight centres with the aim of promoting and strengthening the operation of combined transport. The design, financing, establishment, construction, and operation of the Freight Centre is undertaken by a company which receives a grant and is made up of natural and legal persons under private and public law.

Law 3333/2005 lays down, inter alia, the requirements concerning the size of a Logistics Center. According to the explanatory memorandum to the law, depending on this area, the Logistics Center must have specific transport infrastructure, such as rail, port and air facilities, or must ensure access to the country's transport network (explanatory memorandum to the draft law: 'Regulation of transport issues'). This measure limits the number of areas that can accommodate a LC, while at the same time creating favorable conditions for areas close to ports and for the Greek ports themselves.

The Law clarifies the legal details for the creation and operation of the center in the form of a public limited company and allows for the possibility of freight centres to be set up in partnership with private companies and public bodies.

The legislator seeks to support the implementation of the National Logistics Strategy with two main objectives:

- Strengthening and modernizing the freight transport and logistics system in the country, with a view to promoting the development of the logistics chain and supporting the development of other sectors of the national economy, such as industry, exports, trade, tourism, agricultural production, etc.
- Promotion of Greece as a competitive and high-quality hub of transit activity in Southeastern Europe, aiming at the efficient utilisation of transit cargo and the development of related value-added services such as storage, repackaging,

Private companies such as transport and transit companies, logistics companies, commercial and investment companies, as well as public bodies such as local and port authorities, railway, and air transport organisations, etc. may also participate in the freight hubs. In addition, the presence of businesses offering support and assistance services, such as post offices, hotels, banks, restaurants, telecommunications, insurance companies, customer services, etc. is necessary and desirable. According to Law 3333/2005, a company wishing to set up a LC may receive a grant depending on the various calls for proposals issued by the Ministry of Transport and Communications and based on the evaluation of specific criteria.

The aim of establishing this legal framework for the operation of logistics companies is to develop appropriate administrative services to ensure the continuous monitoring of these activities. At the same time, a national strategy for the sector is envisaged, with the aim of making Greece an important hub for transit activity. In addition, modern initiatives combining logistics development with environmental protection are promoted.

3.2 Law 3982/2011

In 2011, Law 3333/2005 was repealed because it was considered ineffective and Law 3982/2011 (Government Gazette 143/A/17-6-2011) entitled "Simplification of the licensing of technical professional and manufacturing activities and business parks and other provisions" was passed. According to the provisions of this law, the term "Business Park" was formulated, which is defined as an organizationally integrated set of structures, services and infrastructure and the licensing procedure for storage centres was simplified (explanatory memeorandum on the draft law "New institutional framework for the exercise of economic activity and other provisions"). Although the types of business parks that can be established have been defined (Article 41), however, to date no parks of a special type have been established in accordance with the provisions of the law for the establishment of logistics businesses, but many such activities have been established within the business parks of Law 4458/65 and BPEEs of Law 2545/1997 (Logistics Technical Report, 2021).

3.3 Law 4302/2014

With the enactment of Law 4302/2014, the previous law was amended and the gaps in the operation and implementation of the logistics chain were covered. In essence, the law. 4302/2014 comes to complement and specify the Law 3982/2011 on logistics parks - Logistics. Specifically, logistics issues were regulated, and two new types of Business Parks were identified, the establishment and operation of which will be governed by the provisions of Law no. 3982/2011: National Logistics Business/Freight Parks (HLEP), and Logistics Business Park (Logistics Park).

As stated in the explanatory memorandum of the Law, the legislative framework distinguishes logistics parks into those designated as national parks, which are mainly related to the servicing of transport loads imported or exported from the country (EPEE) and those which are called upon to serve the supply chain within the country (EPEA).

Article 14 defines the National Supply Chain Business/Commodity Park (NSCP) as a new form of Business Park, the development of which requires a minimum area of 300 hectares. However, the approval for the development of the Business Park, its operation, urbanization, etc., shall be in accordance with the provisions of Articles 41 to 64, of Law No. 3982/2011.

Article 15 delimits two areas, one in Attica and one in Thessaloniki, within which Business/Commercial Parks of National Scope (BCPs) may be approved:

- Area of 'Thriassio Field' in Attica.
- Former 'Camp Gonou' in Thessaloniki.

According to the explanatory memorandum of the law, a carbon footprint registration system for businesses is being set up which will be kept at the Ministry of Transport and Networks and will be communicated to all interested parties. By enacting this law, the legislator's ambition for the Greek Supply Chain is aimed at modernizing the freight transport and logistics system in Greece and, secondly, at promoting Greece as a competitive and quality hub in South-Eastern Europe. In this way, Greece will become attractive for attracting transit cargo through its ports, but also through its road and rail infrastructure to the markets of the Balkans and Central Europe.

In essence, the law attempted to remove the rigidities of the previous institutional framework and the uncertainty that investors faced due to ambiguities and shortcomings in the licensing process. In essence, a policy was drawn up which sought to reduce the cost of supply for businesses, while at the same time reducing the cost of consumer goods (Ex-ante evaluation report on the impact on competitiveness of the draft law entitled (Regulation of Supply Chain Issues and other provisions, 2014). In this context, the main objectives of Law 4302/2014 were:

- The definition of the activities of logistics and companies in the sector.
- The protection of the environment and the promotion of green logistics.
- Improving the institutional framework for the establishment and operation of companies.
- The attraction of freight and the creation of value-added services.
- The designation and development of National Business Parks.
- Development of administrative structures for the continuous monitoring of the sector and the development of a national strategy.

Ten months after the implementation of the law, most of the expected measures have been implemented, leading to a lack of specificity on important issues that were foreseen. There was ambiguity on green logistics, as the way to record carbon and methods for routing, loading, recycling, and reducing residues in the product life cycle were not clearly defined (SEV, 2015).

3.4 Law 4759/2020

The Law 4759/2020 "Modernization of Spatial Planning and Urban Planning Legislation and other provisions", mentions in chapter C the regulations for off-plan construction and organized receptors and in article 39 of the same law, entitled: "Organized Receptors of Manufacturing and Business Activities" - (Amendment of para. (amendment of Article 44(4) and Article 44(4) and paragraph (4) of Article 44). 2 of Article 52 of Law No. 52. 3982/2011). Terms and provisions relating to the regulations concerning the area, building conditions, organisation and operation of freight centres were amended.

3.5 Law 4982/2022

Law 4982/2022 (published on 15 October 2022 in the Government Gazette (195/A/15-10-2022) imposes a single legal framework for Business Parks, offering significant incentives for their establishment, mainly aimed at regional development, the development of industrial production and green entrepreneurship. The terms and conditions for the creation, management, development, and operation of Business Parks are defined, as well as the activities that can be carried out within them to enhance investment activities and industrial development.

In essence, it introduces a single legislative framework, with a transitional period of five years for the integration of all existing parks into the new regime. This achieves a single codified legal framework for greater legal certainty, essential for attracting investment, unlike the previous regime with 3 existing laws and each Park subject to a different legal framework. Consequently, the categories and types of Business Parks are simplified and reduced, while the approval and development of a park in two or more distinct geographical areas is allowed, if they form an organic integrated whole within the same wider area, allowing development in areas that do not have other space for parks with more businesses and economies of scale (Mitsios, 2023).

The new law provides additional incentives and simplifications, such as the elimination of the minimum area for establishing a park and the provision for the first time that the cash contribution is exempted as an expense. Business Park categories are simplified and reduced, and more activities are allowed. In addition, mandatory self-management is abolished, and new provisions are introduced regarding the legal entity managing the park. In addition, Business Parks are allowed to be established in different geographical areas when they form an integrated whole within the same wider area (Mitsios, 2023).

Significant benefits are created for the regulation of freight centres, including:

- The consolidation of all existing freight centres into a single set of rules.
- The creation of a favorable environment for attracting investment in the creation of new freight centres.
- Simplifying the authorization procedures for the creation of freight centres.
- Accelerate the development of new freight centres and facilitate the expansion of existing ones.
- Effective management of freight centres.
- Providing incentives for the establishment of businesses in freight centres.

The new law raises high expectations for the restructuring of the Logistics Center institution as it sets the basis for the development of new modernized centres.

4 Conclusions

Therefore, for Greece to increase its attractiveness as an international Logistics Center or as a leading regional logistics hub, it should focus on four priorities:

- Improving interconnectivity with global trade corridors and other hubs, with a particular focus on the Greek maritime ecosystem.
- Upgrading port and supply chain infrastructure, investing in logistics parks, following on from the progress made in port infrastructure.
- Strengthen the financial ecosystem to provide high quality financial and business services.
- Upgrading technological infrastructure, innovation, and human capital to support the development of new business models and the implementation of the required transformation of supply chains.

The location of freight centres should therefore be focused along two lines: serving existing needs (large urban centres, industrial activity) and strategic choice of locations (ports/airports, interconnection of the country with other countries).

References

Apeejay (2022). Global Logistic Parks. https://apeejaygloballogisticspark.com/

Law 3333/2005 Explanatory memorandum to the draft law: "Arrangements on transport issues". https://www.hellenicparliament.gr/userfiles/2f026f42-950c-4efc-b950-340c4fb76a24/r-teme-eis.pdf

Law 3982/2011 Explanatory Report on the draft law "New institutional framework for the exercise of economic activity and other provisions". https://www.hellenicparliament.gr/UserFiles/2f026f42-950c-4efc-b950-340c4fb76a24/n-neoik-eisig-sunolo.pdf

Law. 4302/2014: Explanatory memorandum to the draft law "Regulation of Supply Chain Issues and other provisions". https://www.hellenicparliament.gr/UserFiles/c8827c35-4399-4fbb-8ea6-aebdc768f4f7/8438149.pdf

Ministry of Development & Investment General Secretariat of Industry (GSI) (2021) Technical Report. https://www.ggb.gr/sites/default/files/basic-page-files/%ce%a4%ce%95%ce%a7%ce%9d%ce%99%ce%9a%ce%97%20%ce%95%ce%9a%ce%98%ce%95%ce%a3%ce%97_logistics-2020.pdf

Mitsios, S.: EY, N. 4982/2022: The New Legislative Framework for the Establishment, Development, Management and Operation of Business Parks (2023).

Nauteboriki: (2024) https://www.ey.com/el_gr/tax/tax-alerts/greece-new-law-4982-2022-neo-nomothetiko-plaisio. Survey Mc Kinsey Company https://www.naftemporiki.gr/finance/economy/1585205/

SEV: Report of the ex-ante competitiveness impact assessment of the draft law "Regulation of Supply Chain Issues and other provisions". Business Environment Observatory (2014). https://www.cold.org.gr/library/downloads/Docs

SEV: Together for Development? Together for Growth: 82 Actions in 11 Policy Areas - May 2015, Working Paper. Ministry of Development, Competitiveness, Infrastructure, Transport & Networks, General Secretariat for Transport, Strategic Transport Investment Framework 2014–2025 (2015). https://www.sev.org.gr/ekdoseis/mazi-gia-tin-anaptyxi-82-draseis-se-11-tom/

Tsimitsaki, E.: National School of Public Administration and Local Government, Municipal Administration and Green Supply Chain (Green Logistics) (2015)

Wenwen, J., Shuo, S., Dachuan, D.: Construction and operation of logistics parks: insights from Bremen's experience. IOP Conf. Ser. Earth Environ. Sci. **587**, 012040 (2020). https://doi.org/10.1088/1755-1315/587/1/012040

Qi, Y., Sun, Y., Lang, M.: Evaluating the Performance of the Logistics Parks: A State-of-the-Art Review (2017). https://doi.org/10.1007/978-3-319-69096-4_6

Investigating Consumers and Growers Views on Edible Olive Quality Assurance: A Case Study

Panagiotis Tsarouhas[1(✉)] and Kyriaki Anthopoulou[2]

[1] Department of Computer Science and Biomedical Informatics, University of Thessaly, Papasiopoulou 2-4, Galaneika, 35131 Lamia, Greece
ptsarouhas@uth.gr

[2] Department of Supply Chain Management (Logistics), International Hellenic University, Kanellopoyloy 2, 60100 Katerini, Greece

Abstract. The development and implementation of quality systems contributes to the production of quality products. The quality and safety of food starts with the quality of the raw material produced on the farm. The aim of this study is to investigate the views of consumers and growers regarding quality assurance of edible olives. The study analyses olive cultivation and consumption, focusing on the importance of quality certification (such as ISO 9001) for producers. It examines how demographic variables such as geographical location, gender, education level and income affect cultivation and consumer behavior. The study finds that consumers prefer products with respect for the environment and certified quality. It also points out its methodological limitations, such as the use of convenience sampling and social media for data collection, which may not adequately reflect the wider population of producers and consumers. Finally, future research should use more diverse and representative sampling methods, possibly including qualitative research techniques such as interviews or focus groups, to gain deeper insights into the motivations, challenges and perceptions in the olive growing sector.

Keywords: edible olive · management · quality · customer satisfaction

1 Introduction

This paper presents total quality management and ISO systems, its components and the benefits of the ISO 9001 standard, as well as referring to ISO 9000 certified companies (Brucks et al., 2000; Madu et al., 1995; Rahman, 2019; Suchánek, et al., 2017; Cruz, 2015). In addition, it examines both the process of production and processing of olives and aspects of quality management in this industry (Evans, and Lindsay, 1999; Kenyon, and Sen, 2016). Next, an analysis of the different types of olives is carried out, including natural table olives, processed green olives (Chow and Zhang, 2008; García, et al., 2001; Kotler, and Amstrong, 2012).

Quality certification in the production of edible olive production is an important issue concerning the assurance of the quality and safety of the products consumed by

I. Kostavelis et al. (Eds.): ICSC 2024, CCIS 2110, pp. 256–268, 2025.
https://doi.org/10.1007/978-3-031-69344-1_19

consumers (Jahanshahi, 2011; Kenyon, and Sen, 2016; Dale, and McQuater, 1998; Ahire, et al., 1996). The purpose of this paper is to investigate the opinions of consumers and growers regarding the quality assurance of the edible olive.

Through the questions, cultivation practices used by farmers are analyzed and how they can be improved to increase the quality of the olives. In addition, we explore how farmers' awareness of best practices can be determined and the use of science and technology applications can be promoted. From the consumer side, consumer preferences and trends in the olive market are explored (Ehsani, 2015; Tu, et al., 2013; Razak, et al., 2016; Imami, et al., 2011).

2 Total Quality Management

Total Quality Management (TQM) is examined with three approaches: quality leadership, formal evaluation models, and empirical research. Various experts, such as Deming, Ishikawa, Crosby, and Feigenbaum, present approaches to quality improvement. Although neither approach provides complete solutions, they highlight common themes such as leadership and training. These ideas influenced later research in the field of quality management. Companies use standardized quality models, such as Baldrige, EFQM, and the Deming Applied Award, to evaluate and improve their practices. Research by Anderson et al. (1994) provided a comprehensive analysis, identifying key elements in Deming's approach, including proactive leadership and continuous improvement.

Studies looking at the creation of a reliable measurement tool for Total Quality Management have resulted in significant contributions. This tool can help researchers and managers make quality assessment decisions. The studies focus on both the reliability and applicability of the tool in industrial enterprises. In addition, they consider the use of tools and methodologies, such as those described by Ishikawa and Imai, to facilitate the quality improvement process in firms.

2.1 Total Quality Management and Its Components

Through the analysis carried out, important conclusions regarding Total Quality Management (TQM) emerge. It is noted that various authors have different views, but there are common themes that are repeatedly highlighted. In addition, companies can adopt standardized models as a framework for effectively implementing quality management practices.

A Quality Management System (QMS) includes many elements beyond the basics. These include tools and techniques to improve overall quality. After reviewing the literature, these elements are classified into two dimensions: the management system and the technical system. These dimensions are used to characterize and evaluate the various elements of the Quality Management System.

The technical system, which includes a set of tools and techniques, is necessary for the successful implementation of the QMS. It is important to have the right success factors and approaches, such as process design and the involvement of business members, to ensure the success of TQM.

Applying these elements makes TQM an improvement culture that promotes business improvement over time, rather than just a temporary change. This approach includes the participation of all members of the business, training, work groups and communication systems, which represent important factors for the success of the system.

2.2 Benefits of the ISO 9001 Standard

The study highlights the multiple benefits of the ISO 9001 standard in various aspects of business performance, such as efficiency and customer satisfaction. Top benefits include improved efficiency and customer satisfaction, with profitability and improved systemization following. However, other important benefits such as improved market share and corporate image are also recognized, while others such as improved competitive position have received less research emphasis.

Nield & Kozak (1999) state that the benefits of the ISO standard can be categorized into three main categories: operational benefits, marketing benefits and human resource benefits. These include improved systems, competitive advantage and increased customer satisfaction.

Casadesús & Giménez (2000) distinguish between internal and external benefits. Internal benefits include job satisfaction and reduced staff turnover, while external benefits relate to factors such as customer satisfaction and increased sales.

Finally, other researchers report benefits related to either operational performance or financial performance, showing the complexity and diversity of benefits resulting from ISO adoption.

3 Edible Table Olive

The process of processing table olives includes harvesting at various stages of ripening, washing and grading. The olives are then immersed in salt solutions, where their fermentation takes place due to the action of the microbes present on their surface and in the processing environment. Various factors influence the process, such as the olive variety, microbial species and technological parameters.

The debitterization of olives occurs through processes of diffusion yielding and enzymatic hydrolysis of the bitter compound oleuropein. The growth of microbes, mainly non-spoilage ones, is decisive, while yeasts can positively or negatively influence the process. Fermentations are carried out in various conditions, while the products are usually sold in bags or tanks, usually after pasteurization or with the addition of sorbic acid for preservation.

The commercial preparation of olives is usually done by harvesting them at various stages of ripening and their immediate fermentation in brine. The olives can then be packed and sold or undergo various preservation methods.

4 Research Methodology

The research method used focused on the use of an electronic questionnaire, which was created with Google Forms and distributed through various social networking platforms, such as Facebook, Instagram, Messenger, and Viber. The questionnaire was available for completion for a certain period of time.

The sampling method chosen was convenience sampling, aiming to collect a large sample of responses in a short period of time. Although this method was chosen for ease and speed of data collection, it may not represent all demographic groups in a balanced manner.

However, advantages of the sampling method include low cost and speed of data collection. The disadvantage of the method is the uncertainty regarding whether the sample is representative of the population, with the result that the results can be indicative.

The sample is characterized by undetermined probability, since for any element of the population we do not know in advance the probability that it will be included in the sample.

To achieve the purpose of the work, an electronic questionnaire was created using appropriate digital tools, mainly Google Forms. The questionnaire consists of three categories of questions: list questions, category questions, and rating questions.

List questions provide the respondent with a list of answers from which to choose one. The category questions were designed so that the respondent fit into only one category. Finally, the evaluation questions aim to collect data concerning the respondent's opinion.

The aim through these questions was to assess certain aspects or opinions and gather data that would help to better understand the opinions, preferences or opinions of the participants.

This study aims to examine various aspects related to the cultivation and consumption of edible olives. To analyze the data collected through a questionnaire, he intends to use the chi-square (x^2) test and ANOVA analyses. The chi-square test will be applied to test frequencies between qualitative variables, while ANOVA analysis will be considered to test frequencies between qualitative and quantitative variables.

The structure of the questionnaire consists of three main groups of questions. The first group concerns the demographics of the participants, while the next two groups concern olive growers and consumers respectively.

For growers, issues such as the production process, olive tree safety and quality, as well as market access and awareness of quality assurance practices are addressed.

For consumers, purchasing behavior, preference and knowledge about various aspects of the olive are examined, as well as the influence of factors such as quality, price and brand reputation on their purchasing decisions.

In addition, research questions are formulated that aim to test the connections between various variables, such as geographic location, gender, education level and income, with aspects related to olive cultivation and consumption.

In this way, the study seeks to reveal possible relationships between the various variables, thus providing evidence for understanding the processes of production and consumption of edible olives and the associated purchasing behaviors.

4.1 Correlation Analysis

The variables examined belong both to the category of qualitative and to the category of quantitative variables. The first research questions examine the relationships of qualitative variables, so the chi-square (x^2) test is used. Through this specific test, the statistically significant relationship between the variables under consideration is investigated. The research questions then examine the relationships between qualitative and quantitative variables. ANOVA analysis of variance is used to test the above relationships. Through this specific test, the statistically significant relationship between the variables under consideration is investigated (Table 1).

Table 1. Correlation Geographical Division - Grower or Consumer

	Cases					
	Valid		You were missing		Total	
	N	Rate	N	Rate	N	Rate
Geographical Division × Grower or Consumer	80	100.0%	0	.0%	80	100.0%

Geographical Division × Grower or Consumer

			Grower or Consumer		Total
			Grower	Consumer	
Département	Macedonia	Meter	8	22	30
		Range %	26.7%	73.3%	100.0%
		Column %	20.0%	55.0%	37.5%
		Total %	10.0%	27.5%	37.5%
	Thrace	Meter	8	0	8
		Range %	100.0%	.0%	100.0%
		Column %	20.0%	.0%	10.0%
		Total %	10.0%	.0%	10.0%
	Epirus	Meter	1	0	1
		Range %	100.0%	.0%	100.0%
		Column %	2.5%	.0%	1.3%
		Total %	1.3%	.0%	1.3%
	Peloponnese	Meter	1	0	1
		Range %	100.0%	.0%	100.0%
		Column %	2.5%	.0%	1.3%
		Total %	1.3%	.0%	1.3%
	Central Greece	Meter	15	14	29
		Range %	51.7%	48.3%	100.0%
		Column %	37.5%	35.0%	36.3%
		Total %	18.8%	17.5%	36.3%
	Thessaly	Meter	7	1	8
		Range %	87.5%	12.5%	100.0%
		Column %	17.5%	2.5%	10.0%
		Total %	8.8%	1.3%	10.0%
	Crete	Meter	0	1	1
		Range %	.0%	100.0%	100.0%
		Column %	.0%	2.5%	1.3%

(*continued*)

Table 1. (*continued*)

		Total %	.0%	1.3%	1.3%
	Islands of the Aegean Sea	Meter	0	1	1
		Range %	.0%	100.0%	100.0%
		Column %	.0%	2.5%	1.3%
		Total %	.0%	1.3%	1.3%
	Ionian Sea Islands/Iptanissos	Meter	0	1	1
		Range %	.0%	100.0%	100.0%
		Column %	.0%	2.5%	1.3%
		Total %	.0%	1.3%	1.3%
Total		Meter	40	40	80
		Range %	50.0%	50.0%	100.0%
		Column %	100.0%	100.0%	100.0%
		Total %	50.0%	50.0%	100.0%

Chi-Square Test			
	Value	df	Asympt. Sig (2- sided)
Pearson Chi-Square	24.07	8	,002
Probability Ratio	29.91	8	,000
Linear- by -Linear Assosiation	1.74	1	,187
N of valid Cases	80		

According to the results of the above tables, we notice that the variable "Geographical Area" determines whether the respondent is a "Farmer or Consumer". From the Chi-Square Test table we find the statistically significant relationship between the two variables, as the static significance of the relationship is less than the significance level set at 0.05 ($p = 0.002 < 0.05$) (Table 2).

Table 2. Correlation Geographical Division - Main Cultivation Method

	Cases					
	Valid		You were missing		Total	
	N	Rate	N	Rate	N	Rate
Geographical Division x What is the main method of olive cultivation?	40	50.0%	40	50.0%	80	100.0%

Geographical Division x What is the main method of olive cultivation?				
	What is the main method of olive cultivation?			Total
	Conventional (use of fertilizers and pesticides)	Organic (using natural fertilizers and pesticides)	Both compatible and organic methods	

(*continued*)

Table 2. (*continued*)

Département	Macedonia	Meter	1	7	0	8
		Range %	12.5%	87.5%	.0%	100.0%
		Column %	11.1%	30.4%	.0%	20.0%
		Total %	2.5%	17.5%	.0%	20.0%
	Thrace	Meter	0	8	0	8
		Range %	.0%	100.0%	.0%	100.0%
		Column %	.0%	34.8%	.0%	20.0%
		Total %	.0%	20.0%	.0%	20.0%
	Epirus	Meter	0	0	1	1
		Range %	.0%	.0%	100.0%	100.0%
		Column %	.0%	.0%	12.5%	2.5%
		Total %	.0%	.0%	2.5%	2.5%
	Peloponnese	Meter	1	0	0	1
		Range %	100.0%	.0%	.0%	100.0%
		Column %	11.1%	.0%	.0%	2.5%
		Total %	2.5%	.0%	.0%	2.5%
	Central Greece	Meter	7	8	0	15
		Range %	46.7%	53.3%	.0%	100.0%
		Column %	77.8%	34.8%	.0%	37.5%
		Total %	17.5%	20.0%	.0%	37.5%
	Thessaly	Meter	0	0	7	7
		Range %	.0%	.0%	100.0%	100.0%
		Column %	.0%	.0%	87.5%	17.5%
		Total %	.0%	.0%	17.5%	17.5%
Total		Meter	9	23	8	40
		Range %	22.5%	57.5%	20.0%	100.0%
		Column %	100.0%	100.0%	100.0%	100.0%
		Total %	22.5%	57.5%	20.0%	100.0%

Chi-Square Test

	Value	df	Asympt. Sig (2- sided)
Pearson Chi-Square	51.50	10	,000
Probability Ratio	51.30	10	,000
Linear- by -Linear Assosiation	1.20	1	,272
N of valid Cases	40		

According to the results of the above tables, we observe that the variable "Geographical Region" determines the "Main Cultivation Method". From the Chi-Square Test table we find the statistically significant relationship between the two variables, as the static significance of the relationship is less than the level of significance set at 0.05 ($p = 0.000 < 0.05$) (Table 3).

Table 3. Correlation Geographical Division - Safety and Quality

	Cases					
	Valid		You were missing		Total	
	N	Rate	N	Rate	N	Rate
Geographical Division x How do you ensure the safety and quality of your olive trees	40	50.0%	40	50.0%	80	100.0%

Geographical Division x How do you ensure the safety and quality of your olive trees

			How you ensure the safety and quality of your olive trees			Total
			Regular pest and disease testing	Compliance with industry and government standards and regulations	Both Regular pest and disease testing and Compliance with industry and government standards and regulations	
Département	Macedonia	Meter	8	0	0	8
		Range %	100.0%	.0%	.0%	100.0%
		Column %	34.8%	.0%	.0%	20.0%
		Total %	20.0%	.0%	.0%	20.0%
	Thrace	Meter	7	8	0	8
		Range %	87.5%	12.5%	.0%	100.0%
		Column %	30.4%	11.1%	.0%	20.0%
		Total %	17.5%	2.5%	.0%	20.0%
	Epirus	Meter	0	0	1	1
		Range %	.0%	.0%	100.0%	100.0%
		Column %	.0%	.0%	12.5%	2.5%
		Total %	.0%	.0%	2.5%	2.5%
	Peloponnese	Meter	1	0	0	1
		Range %	100.0%	.0%	.0%	100.0%
		Column %	4.3%	.0%	.0%	2.5%
		Total %	2.5%	.0%	.0%	2.5%
	Central Greece	Meter	7	8	0	15
		Range %	46.7%	53.3%	.0%	100.0%
		Column %	30.4	88.9%	.0%	37.5%
		Total %	17.5%	20.0%	.0%	37.5%
	Thessaly	Meter	0	0	7	7
		Range %	.0%	.0%	100.0%	100.0%
		Column %	.0%	.0%	87.5%	17.5%
		Total %	.0%	.0%	17.5%	17.5%
Total		Meter	23	23	8	40
		Range %	57.5%	22.5%	20.0%	100.0%
		Column %	100.0%	100.0%	100.0%	100.0%

(continued)

Table 3. (*continued*)

	Total %	57.5%	22.5%	20.0%	100.0%

Chi-Square Test

	Value	df	Asympt. Sig (2- sided)
Pearson Chi-Square	51.50	10	,000
Probability Ratio	51.30	10	,000
Linear- by -Linear Assosiation	16.61	1	,000
N of valid Cases	40		

According to the results of the above tables, we observe that the variable "Geographical Region" determines "Safety and Quality". From the Chi-Square Test table we find the statistically significant relationship between the two variables, as the static significance of the relationship is less than the level of significance set at 0.05 ($p = 0.000 < 0.05$) (Table 4).

Table 4. Correlation Gender - Point of Purchase

	Cases					
	Valid		You were missing		Total	
	N	Rate	N	Rate	N	Rate
Gender × Where do you prefer to buy olives?	40	50.0%	40	50.0%	80	100.0%

Gender × Where do you prefer to buy olives?

			Gender × Where do you prefer to buy olives?			Total
			From the public market	From the Super Market	From the producer	
Sex	Man	Meter	8	8	1	17
		Range %	47.1%	47.1%	5.9%	100.0%
		Column %	50.0%	50.0%	12.5%	42.5%
		Total %	20.0%	20.0%	2.5%	42.5%
	Woman	Meter	8	8	7	23
		Range %	34.8%	34.8%	30.4%	100.0%
		Column %	50.0%	50.0%	87.5%	57.5%
		Total %	20.0%	20.0%	17.5%	57.5%
Total		Meter	16	16	8	40
		Range %	40.0%	40.0%	20.0%	100.0%
		Column %	100.0%	100.0%	100.0%	100.0%
		Total %	40.0%	40.0%	20.0%	100.0%

Chi-Square Test

	Value	df	Asympt. Sig (2- sided)
Pearson Chi-Square	3.68	2	,159

(*continued*)

Table 4. (*continued*)

Probability Ratio	4.16	2	,125
Linear- by -Linear Assosiation	2.31	1	,129
N of valid Cases	40		

According to the results of the above tables, we notice that the variable "Gender" does not determine the "Point of Purchase". From the Chi-Square Test table we find that there is no statistically significant relationship between the two variables, as the static significance of the relationship is greater than the significance level set at 0.05 ($p = 0.0159 > 0.05$).

In addition, further analyzes were carried out, but due to the limitation of the length of the paper, we present the following results:

(a) the variable "Geographical Area" determines the "Production Target", from the Chi-Square Test we find the statistically significant relationship between the two variables, as the static significance of the relationship is less than the level of significance set at 0.05 (p-value $= 0.000 < 0.05$).
(b) The variable "Education Level" determines the "Opinion of maintaining high quality standards", from the Chi-Square Test we find the statistically significant relationship between the two variables (p-value $= 0.003 < 0.05$).
(c) The "Annual Income" variable does not determine the "Quality" factor in terms of buying olives, from the ANOVA analysis we find that there is no statistically significant relationship between the two variables (p-value $= 0.406 > 0.05$).
(d) The variable "Age" determines the factor "Sustainability" in terms of buying olives, from the ANOVA table we find that there is no statistically significant relationship between the two variables (p-value $= 0.136 > 0.05$).

5 Results and Discussion

The research provides an important and detailed picture of olive cultivation and consumption, highlighting producer practices and consumer preferences. However, despite the most complete analysis it presents, there are some issues that deserve further consideration.

One of the main issues arising from the research is the reliance on convenience sampling and social media platforms for data collection. This may limit the representativeness and scope of the research, as it may not fully reflect the diversity of less digitally engaged populations.

Therefore, a more balanced approach could include the use of both qualitative and quantitative methods for data collection. This would help create a more complete picture of the global olive industry and enhance the credibility of the results.

Furthermore, despite the success in highlighting the correlations between various variables, such as geographical compartment and preferences of producers and consumers, geographical and cultural diversity should be taken into account. Practices and preferences can vary significantly between different regions and cultures, so generalizing conclusions to other regions should be done with caution.

Future research should therefore focus on a more diversified methodological approach, expand geographical coverage and combine qualitative and quantitative methods. This would help create a more comprehensive picture of the global olive industry and provide important clues on the interaction between consumer preferences, agricultural practices and market dynamics in the olive industry.

In the context of the international literature, the relationship between consumers and green food is a topic that has been significantly influenced by many factors, such as health, environmental awareness and food quality. Zhou et al. (2013) study highlights the significant influence of these factors on consumers' green food purchasing behavior. At the same time, research by Gao et al . (2013) highlights similar trends in the Chinese market.

These surveys reveal that consumers are looking for food that does not threaten their health and respects the environment. In addition, the quality and authenticity of the products are important factors when making purchasing decisions. The implementation of practices such as the HACCP plan contributes not only to ensuring high quality products but also to the economic well-being of the country, as found by the research of Rejeb & Keogh (2019).

In addition, geographic region significantly influences consumer production and consumption preferences and practices. Regions with a large number of producers, such as Macedonia, Thrace, and Central Greece, play an important role in the green food market.

Overall, comparing the results of this report with the international literature reveals significant similarities and differences in consumer attitudes towards green food. This understanding can be a valuable tool for improving production practices and developing green food markets that meet consumer needs and preferences.

6 Conclusions

Quality certification in the production of edible olives requires the implementation of quality systems at all stages of the production process. These systems include procedures for selecting, harvesting, cleaning, processing and packaging the olives. Manufacturers can adopt quality standards such as ISO 9001 to ensure consistency and reliability of production processes. Quality criteria include the size, color, flavor and creaminess of the olives, while certification may also include environmental standards. Transparency about product quality is also important, while the research presented reveals significant correlations and influences on various aspects of olive consumption and production, such as geographic location, gender, education and income level.

The research could be a useful tool for policy makers to develop regulations and support systems that encourage sustainable and profitable olive cultivation, taking into account factors such as production methods and quality assurance practices. The contribution of the study is valuable because of: (i) deepens the understanding of the dynamics of the olive industry, (ii) provides data-based information for stakeholders and gives specific directions for further research, and (iii) helps to define practices for policy making.

The study carried out on olive cultivation offers important indications for the improvement of production techniques in the sector. In particular, findings on cultivation methods, tree health and quality assurance practices can guide olive growers in the direction of improvement. In addition, understanding consumer preferences and buying behavior provides strategic direction for businesses in the industry and can influence policy making. The research framework also highlights potential limitations and weaknesses, such as sampling methodology and geographic limitation. Suggestions for future studies include using more representative sampling methods and incorporating qualitative research methods for a more holistic understanding.

References

Ahire, S.L., Golhar, D.Y., Waller, M.A.: Development and validation of TQM implementation constructs. Decis. Sci. **27**(1), 23–56 (1996)

Anderson, J.C., Rungtusanatham, M., Schroeder, R.G.: A theory of quality management underlying the Deming management method. Acad. Manag. Rev. **19**(3), 472–509 (1994)

Brucks, M., Zeithaml, V.A., Naylor, G.: Price and brand name as indicators of quality dimensions for consumer durables. J. Acad. Mark. Sci. **28**, 359–374 (2000)

Casadesús, M., Giménez, G.: The benefits of the implementation of the ISO 9000 standard: empirical research in 288 Spanish companies. TQM Mag. **12**(6), 432–441 (2000)

Chow, C.S., Zhang, L.L.: Measuring consumer satisfaction and dissatisfaction intensities to identify satisfiers and dissatisfiers. J. Consum. Satisf. Dissatisf. Complain. Behav. **21**, 66–79 (2008)

Cruz, AV.: Relationship Between Product Quality And Customer Satisfaction. Walden University, Minneapolis (2015)

Dale, B., McQuater, R.: Managing Business Improvement and Quality: Implementing Key Tools and Techniques. Blackwell Business, Oxford (1998)

Ehsani, Z., Ehsani, M.H.: Effect of quality and price on customer satisfaction and commitment in Iran auto industry. Int. J. Serv. Sci. Manag. Eng. **1**(5), 52–56 (2015)

Evans, J.R., Lindsay, W.M.: The Management and Control of Quality. South-Western College Publishing, Cincinnati (1999)

García, P., Brenes, M., Romero, C., Garrido, A.: Colour fixation in ripe olives. Effect of the type of iron salt and other processing factors. J. Sci. Food Agric. **81**, 1364–1370 (2001)

Imami, D., Zhillima, E., Skreli, E., Canavari, M., Rama, M.: Consumer preferences for olive oil in Tirana, Albania. Int. Food Agribus. Manage. Assoc. **13**(3) (2011)

Jahanshahi, A.A., Gashti, M.A.H., Mirdamadi, S.A., Nawaser, K., Khaksar, S.M.S.: Study of effects of customer service and product quality on customer satisfaction and loyalty. Int. J. Humanit. Soc. Sci. **1**(7), 253–260 (2011)

Kenyon, G.N., Sen, K.C.: Perception of Quality. Springer, London (2016)

Kotler, P., Amstrong, G.: Principle of Marketing, 14th edn. Prentice Hall, New Jersey (2012)

Madu, C.N., Kuei, C.H., Lin, C.: A comparative analysis of quality practice in manufacturing firms in the US and Taiwan. Decis. Sci. **26**(5), 621–635 (1995)

Nield, K., Kozak, M.: Quality certification in the hospitality industry: analyzing the benefits of ISO 9000. Cornell Hotel Restaur. Adm. Q. **40**, 40–45 (1999)

Rahman, S.U.: Leadership styles and TQM: an empirical study of Turkish manufacturing companies. Total Qual. Manag. Bus. Excell. **30**(3–4), 274–287 (2019)

Razak, I, Nirwanto, N., Triatmanto, B.: The impact of product quality and price on customer satisfaction with the mediator of customer value. J. Market. Cons. Res. **30**, 59–68 (2016)

Rejeb, A, Keogh, J.G.: Applying HACCP in the Tunisian olive oil industry: a theoretical background. J. Bus. Manage. Econ. Res. **3**(4), 1–18 (2019)
Suchánek, P., Richter, J., Králová, M.: Customer satisfaction with quality of products of food business. Prague Econ. Papers **26**(1), 19–35 (2017)
Tu, Y.T., Li, M.L., Chih, H.C.: An empirical study of corporate brand image, customer perceived value and satisfaction on loyalty in shoes industry. J. Econ. Behav. Stud. **5**(7), 469–483 (2013)
Zhou, Y., Thøgersen, J., Ruan, Y., Huang, G.: The moderating role of humanvalues in planned behavior: the case of Chinese consumers' intention to buy organic food. J. Consum. Mark. **30**(4), 335–344 (2013)

Manufacturing-as-a-Service: A Systematic Review of the Literature

Anastasia Karamanli[1](✉), Alexandros Xanthopoulos[1], Antonios Gasteratos[1], and Dimitrios Koulouriotis[2]

[1] Department of Production and Management Engineering, School of Engineering, Democritus University of Thrace, V. Sofias 12, 67100 Xanthi, Greece
{ankarama,axanthop,agaster}@pme.duth.gr

[2] School of Mechanical Engineering, National Technical University of Athens, Heroon Polytechniou 9, 15772 Athens, Greece
jimk@pme.duth.gr

Abstract. The Manufacturing-as-a-Service (MaaS) paradigm has received considerable attention in the research and business community over the past few years. MaaS provides manufacturing resources and capabilities as service, available for utilization by organizations via a digital thread, allowing them to concentrate in their significant competencies. This literature review enriched with bibliometrics, aims to examine the current state of MaaS by analyzing selected and contemporary references from Scopus database. The analysis was conducted with the help of specialized bibliometrics software, and the quantitative results include annual trends, leading publications, journals and organizations, citation distributions, co-occurrence of keywords, and journal co-citations. In addition, the publications have been classified according to the methodologies implemented for the data collection and analysis, their objectives, the results obtained, as well as their contribution to the field of manufacturing. This study sheds light on the status and trends in the field of MaaS and has the potential to aid researchers in forming their research agenda and advancing their work on this topic.

Keywords: Manufacturing-as-a-Service · Smart Manufacturing · Industry 4.0 · Cloud Manufacturing · Literature Review · Bibliometric Analysis

1 Introduction

Manufacturing as a Service [1] is an innovative approach to industrial production that is revolutionizing the traditional manufacturing landscape. With the rise of digital technologies [2–5] and the advent of the Internet of Things [6], MaaS offers a paradigm shift by providing on-demand manufacturing capabilities to businesses and individuals [7]. In this model, manufacturing processes, equipment, and expertise are made accessible through a service-based platform [8, 9], enabling customers to access production resources without the need for heavy capital investments or extensive infrastructure [10, 11]. MaaS opens up new possibilities for customization, rapid prototyping [12–14], and decentralized manufacturing [15], empowering organizations to streamline their supply

I. Kostavelis et al. (Eds.): ICSC 2024, CCIS 2110, pp. 269–281, 2025.
https://doi.org/10.1007/978-3-031-69344-1_20

chains [16], accelerate time to market, and meet the dynamic demands of today's market [17, 18].

In this paper, we present a bibliometric analysis and a literature review of selected, contemporary publications on MaaS. Bibliometrics [19] is a multidisciplinary field that employs mathematical and statistical methods to quantitatively analyze scholarly publications. The contribution of this research is that it provides a starting point for tracking the advancement and progression of MaaS and provides insights on the structure and dynamics of this scientific field. Section 2 outlines the data source and the methods employed for this study. In Sect. 3, we provide a comprehensive presentation of statistical data, including current state and trends of MaaS research. Additionally, research focal points, and co-citation trends are analyzed, while the corresponding diagrams representing the networks of findings are given. A more detailed review of the selected sources is presented in Sect. 4, where an overview of each publication is presented. Publications are classified according to their purpose in three categories: "Theoretical MaaS background", "MaaS mechanisms" and "Data management solutions". Section 5 finally, offers a summary of the findings along with indicative directions for future research.

2 Methods

The publications that were included in this study were retrieved from the Scopus database, a widely recognized source for scholarly literature. The Scopus database contains a plethora of scientifically credible and influential publications and provides enriched metadata such as citation information etc.

We searched for the term "manufacturing as a service" in the fields "article title", "abstract", and "keywords" of the Scopus database. The date range for the search was the last 20 years and no constraints were set regarding the attributes of the documents apart from the language, which had to be English. The database query retrieved 77 documents but only 44 papers were ultimately included in this study due to their relevancy and due to space considerations. The selected publications belonged to 3 categories. The most prevalent document type was proceedings paper, accounting for 22 publications, which corresponds to 50% of the total. The second most common document type was article, with 20 publications, representing 45% of the total. The third document type was letter with two occurrences in the query results.

Science mapping plays a crucial role in bibliometrics, offering insights into the state and progression of a discipline. Several software tools are available for bibliometric analysis such as VOSviewer, CiteSpace, and GraphPad Prism. In this study, we utilized VOSviewer [19] because of its user-friendly GUI and advanced functionalities pertaining to co-occurrence and co-citation analysis, among others. The VOSviewer software was employed to construct co-citation and keyword co-occurrence networks.

3 Statistical Data Analysis

3.1 Annual Trends in MaaS and Top Institutions with Related Publications

The annual trends in MaaS-related publications are depicted in Fig. 1(a). Since the first papers that were published in 2012 [20–22], MaaS-related research has grown at a relatively modest pace during the next 10 years. Especially after 2020, an increasing number of publications on this topic appear in the literature. This growing trend can be attributed, among others, to the overall advent of servitization in the global business ecosystem.

Figure 1(b) shows the top 5 institutions; the North Carolina State University has the most publications in this topic, with a total of 5 papers [1, 6, 8, 23, 24], accounting for 11.36% of all publications in this category. The Georgia Institute of Technology comes in second with 4 publications, followed by the Beihang University, the Fraunhofer IPA, and the Texas A & M University. It is noted that the publications that were analyzed in this research were contributed by more than 40 institutions in total; over 80% of the contributing organizations had no more than one paper.

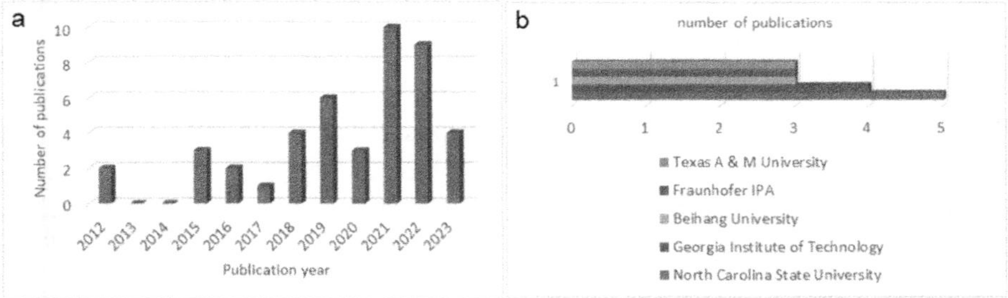

Fig. 1. (a) Annual trends in MaaS-related publications; (b) The top 5 institutions with MaaS-related publications.

3.2 Distribution of Sources and Citation Analysis

The 44 papers of our study were published in more than 20 sources, including journals and conference proceedings. Circa 80% of the examined research outlets published only one paper on MaaS. Figure 2(a) depicts the top 5 journals that published the most papers; note that this figure includes two titles that publish conference papers (Procedia CIRP and Procedia Manufacturing) and one title that publishes letters. With a total of 6 papers, the journal with the most publications is Procedia CIRP.

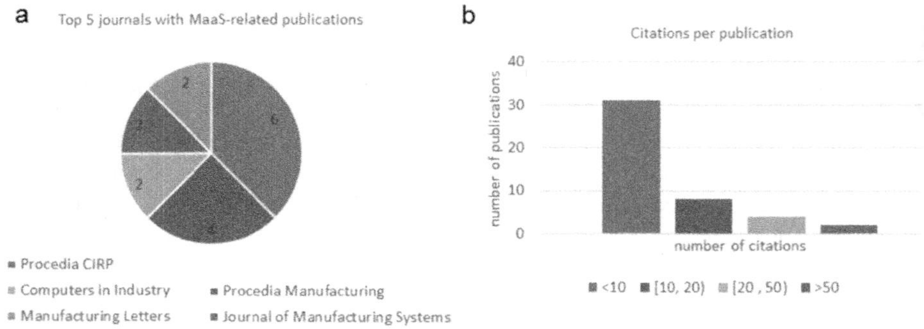

Fig. 2. (a) Top 5 journals with MaaS-related publications; (b) Distribution of citations per publication.

The 44 publications of our bibliometric analysis received a total of 612 citations; on average each paper is cited approximately 14 times. Nonetheless, in Fig. 2(b) we see that the distribution of citations per paper is skewed, and the majority of publications have less than 10 citations. An important factor that contributes to this phenomenon is that MaaS is a contemporary field and most papers have been published very recently. The top cited papers are shown in Table 1 [1, 15, 22, 24, 26].

Table 1. Top highly cited papers related to MaaS.

Paper title	Source	Author names	Publication year	Citations
New IT driven service-oriented smart manufacturing: Framework and characteristics	IEEE Transactions on Systems, Man, and Cybernetics: Systems	Tao, F., Qi, Q	2019	250
Decentralized cloud manufacturing-as-a-service (CMaaS) platform architecture with configurable digital assets	Journal of Manufacturing Systems	Hasan, M., Starly, B	2020	57
Scheduling of manufacturers based on chaos optimization algorithm in cloud manufacturing	Robotics and Computer Integrated Manufacturing	Hu, Y., Zhu, F., Zhang, L., Lui, Y., Wang, Z	2019	45
Using manufacturing service descriptions for flexible integration of production facilities to manufacturing clouds	Proceedings of the 18th International Conference on Engineering, Technology and Innovation, ICE 2012	Rauschecker, U., Stöhr, M	2012	25
Interoperability as a Key Enabler for Manufacturing in the Cloud	Procedia CIRP	Mourad, M., Nassehi, A., Schaefer, D	2016	24

3.3 Keyword Analysis and Focal Points of MaaS Research

The co-occurrence of index terms can serve as a reliable indicator of the current areas of interest in an academic discipline, such as MaaS. In the 44 MaaS-related publications covered in this study, a total of 498 keywords were identified. About 2.2% of the keywords had at least 5 occurrences in the examined pool of papers.

The VOSviewer software was utilized to construct the keyword co-occurrence network in the context of this research (refer to Fig. 3). The sizes of the nodes in Fig. 3 correspond to the weights assigned to them; larger nodes indicate higher weights. The distance between two nodes signifies the strength of their relationship; shorter distances indicate stronger connections. A connecting line between two keywords indicates their co-occurrence, with thicker lines indicating a higher frequency of co-occurrence. The nodes sharing the same color belong to a specific cluster, in Fig. 3 we see 3 clusters of keywords. Keywords with notable frequencies include "manufacture" and "cloud manufacturing".

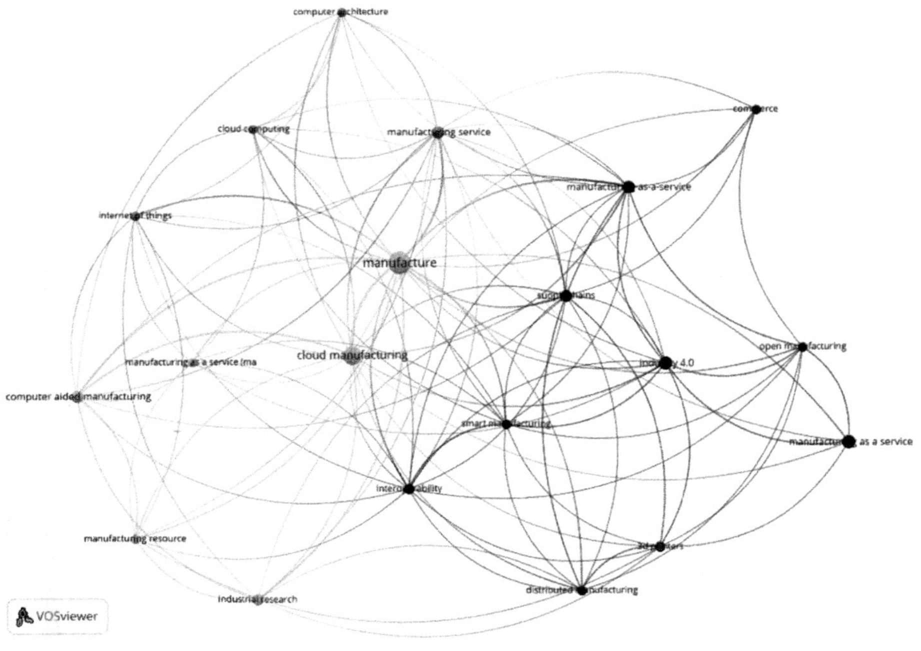

Fig. 3. Keywords co-occurrence network of MaaS-related literature.

3.4 Analysis of Journal Co-citations

The analysis of co-citations among journals is an effective method for studying the structure and characteristics of the underlying field as well as of individual source titles. Figure 4 displays the co-citation network, which was constructed with the use of the VOSviewer software. The size of each node represents the activity level of the journal, including the number of published papers. The smaller the distance between nodes is, the higher the frequency of citations becomes. In Fig. 4, we can discern three distinct journal clusters which are identified by a unique color.

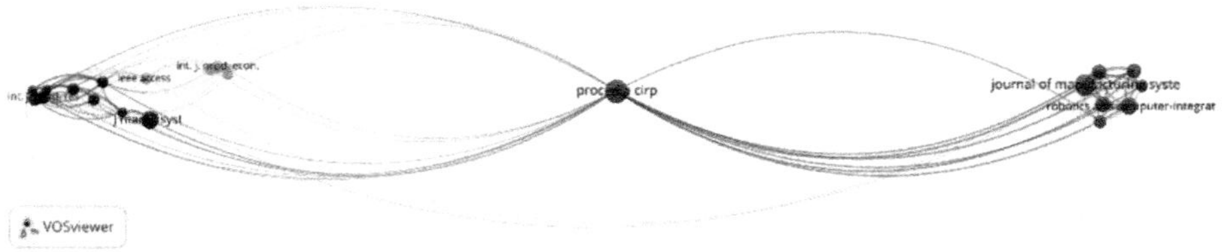

Fig. 4. Journal co-citation network of MaaS-related literature.

4 Literature Review

A deeper analysis of the content of the sources reveals their actual contribution to the manufacturing sector. MaaS aims the automated pairing of requests and applicable manufacturing assets through algorithms [10], and such concepts still lack sufficient standards for an unhindered integration in an industrial environment. To overcome this insufficiency, each of the publications under investigation contributes in either a theoretical or functional way. In this context, the objectives of the sources could be classified into three main categories: "Theoretical MaaS background", "MaaS mechanisms", "Data management solutions". For example, the work of Kusiak [27] aims to discuss the six enablers which will empower the concept of universal manufacturing, by providing flexibility and affinity. Therefore, it is proposed that the implementation of contemporary industrial strategies, such us digitization or open manufacturing, will fulfill production needs of any type and magnitude, allowing the optimization of the enterprises regardless of various constraints concerning the market, the environment, and natural or human caused failures. All those sources that cover the manufacturing-as-a-service topic from a theoretical and conceptual view are listed in Table 2.

On the other hand, a considerable part of the sources, aims to propose specific mechanisms, the implementation of which cultivates trust [6] and immediacy [8] between the different stakeholders on a manufacturing digital thread, as it is formed through the servitization [28] of MaaS. A mechanism design approach for instance, is proposed by Pahwa, Starly and Gohen [8]. More specifically, it is suggested that the final consumer names his own price, and the procedure tracks down service providers who are willing to take over the production of the part under the stated price. Publications which suggest a particular mechanism for the smooth adoption of MaaS by the manufacturing sector, are listed in Table 3. Most of the sources, however, focus on the proposal of data management software solutions, needed for such digitization and democratization [29], MaaS implies. Hasan and Starly [1] report the development of such a software architecture, which aims to connect clients with manufacturing service providers directly, assuring transparency, data integrity, data origin and maintaining data ownership to its creators. Publications related to data management solutions can be found in Table 4 below.

Regarding now the methodologies implied in the sources under investigation, a great number of them propose an architecture for the incorporation of the MaaS into the contemporary industry. Such architectures may represent the sequence of a production flow and the data disposition [31] including various stakeholders, until the final client and are formed with the help of computer aided programs [32]. Other architectures propose a decision learning and making [30] model which utilizes provided data to facilitate the operation of enterprises applying MaaS. Pahwa, Starly and Gohen [8] simulate a service marketplace, to examine the impact of various factors, such as pricing. Respectively, Tessaro, Vick and Krüger [20], conducted simulations and laboratory experiments to evaluate an on-demand service model in terms of stability, readiness etc. Additionally, some alternative methods detected among the literature, consist of the development of a statistical model [12], resolution of objective functions [33] and optimization algorithms [15].

Under the perspective of the industry 4.0, a significant percentage of the publications investigate the role of data collection, processing, and preservation technologies. Wang [29], installed sensors in a sequence of machines to extract data from a manufacturing process and calculate various metrics out of them. Other contemporary data management technologies have been examined combined with the MaaS prototype: blockchain architectures [23], or cloud manufacturing [15, 16, 26]. Moreover, the literature review indicated that 14 out of 44 papers involve various case studies. For instance, Tedaldi and Miragliota [16], present an analysis of 6 various cases of manufacturing platforms. Also, the publication of Liu, Gong and Jiao [33], examines the implementation of their proposed system in an enterprise which constructs custom kitchens.

Finally, the results obtained by the publications included in the present literature review prove the contribution of each research in the manufacturing field. More specifically, Rauschecker [22] concludes that his proposed system, not only coordinates manufacturing of complicated configurable products, but also enables the limitations and capabilities of the production network clarity available during the specific product process. Regarding the data management technologies, remarkable results have also arisen from the studies under investigation. On the other hand, Ordienes-Meré [34] expresses that information capabilities such as cloud manufacturing, can be reinforced with more layers, which will provide increased levels of trust and interoperability. Some of the publications even provide calculated numerical data. For example, Chaudhuri [17] conducts an economic analysis about the profits a supplier could achieve through a MaaS process. However, the papers with a theoretical background, express more general conclusions around the development of the MaaS strategy. For instance, through an extended discussion about contemporary manufacturing techniques, Kusiak [27] concludes that universal manufacturing is going to facilitate the operation of enterprises regardless of their size, by empowering their capabilities and preventing various disasters.

Table 2. Theoretical MaaS background

References	Overview
[7]	Discussion of the five significant elements of Cyber-Physical Production Systems, also known as Industry 4.0: smart design, smart machining, smart monitoring, smart control, smart scheduling
[9]	Presentation of a summary of the requirements needed for the supply-chain operations on a digital B2B platform. Discussion of the goals and the advantages of this multi-sided platform
[10]	Analysis of the operation of prototype manufacturing enterprises and proposal of a gridline relevant to how SMEs should get prepared for MaaS
[13]	Interview of 15 companies about additive manufacturing in a supply chain context, investigating various subcases
[21]	Paradigms of manufacturing systems and evaluation of key system-of-systems factors: autonomy, belonging, connectivity, diversity and emergence
[27]	Discussion on digitization, open manufacturing, service orientation, shared manufacturing, sustainability and resilience
[28]	Presentation of the implementation of the Digital Platform Model in manufacturing services in European enterprises
[35]	Presentation of the challenges MaaS and cyberphysical system face to create an effective, flexible structure
[36]	Investigation of the upcoming cloud computing technologies through 3,697 related studies

Table 3. MaaS mechanisms

References	Overview
[6]	Proposal of an authentication framework "Witness Box Protocol" which trustfully verifies an online manufacturing machine identity with its physical condition
[8]	Proposal of a mechanism design approach which improves the accessibility of prototyping services suppliers, while leverages their excess capacity
[12]	Presentation of an approach lean on embedding custom anti-counterfeiting signatures in the design files, which aims to protect against counterfeiting attacks
[17]	Development of optimal prices which a MaaS platform can charge to maximize both its own and its supplier profit
[24]	The sequential decision-making problem is represented as a Markov decision process, and it is solved by using Deep Reinforcement Learning (DRL)
[30]	Presentation of the collaborative contracting for MaaS fulfillments and its importance. Through collaborative contracting, tournament-based crowdsourcing requires evaluation and selection of manufacturing service providers, as a best-matching problem of multi-criteria decision making
[31]	Description of a MaaS platform which includes a virtual marketplace and with the selection of various parameters aims an optimized production demand satisfaction
[33]	Proposal of a framework which supports decision-making in low-carbon Product Family Planning and Manufacturer Loading Balancing
[37]	Introduction of the Product Generation Module (PGM) and evaluation of the co-production of external products to achieve optimization of workload and efficiency in a Matrix Production System
[38]	Proposal of a strategy which combines crowdsourcing technologies with production planning to achieve MaaS functional goals

(*continued*)

Table 3. (*continued*)

References	Overview
[39]	Description of a flexible autonomous production system, based on a grid and agents
[40]	Proposal of a production method which combines the opportunities of injection molding regarding manufacturing efficiency and precision with those of 3D printing regarding least possible waste and high flexibility. The system is to be applied in the production of combined material bilayer tensile specimens

Table 4. Data management solutions

References	Overview
[1]	Proposal of middleware architecture solutions for CMaaS platforms
[11]	Cloud Manufacturing platforms and MaaS under a business perspective
[14]	Overview of the AM supply chains, presentation of the "Additive Manufacturing-as-a-Service" and identification of important research challenges regarding the market design, control algorithms and security
[15]	Research of the task of scheduling in the cloud manufacturing environment and analysis of the factors which have an impact on scheduling
[16]	Development of a case study based on a metal processing enterprise in Europe, which regards the cloud manufacturing project
[18]	Review of the combination of collaborative e-Manufacturing and Service-Oriented Architecture to form a new manufacturing paradigm which includes cloud of services that enable the concept of MaaS
[20]	A universal strategy of identification and closed-loop control of manufacturing resources, delivered through web services
[22]	A concept of how to interconnect factory-IT systems in flexible production networks
[23]	Report of the design and implementation of middleware software architectures that allow specific CMaaS platforms to take advantage of the secure asset models for the Ethereum ecosystem and the consistent big data storage capabilities
[25]	Proposal of a framework which combines new information technology and services: New IT driven service-oriented smart manufacturing (SoSM)
[26]	Interoperability is recognized as a key enabler for cloud manufacturing. Proposal of a framework for implementation of interoperability across heterogenous computer aided manufacturing systems
[29]	Report of an open-source strategy which aims to embed sensors both into manufacturing resources and into hardware
[32]	Proposition of a model which uses cloud services to arrange effectively the production functionality by using computer aided solutions, such us CAD or ERP
[34]	Thorough analysis of practical aspects of cloud manufacturing and proposal of a mechanism which extracts KPIs, based on the processes in a trustworthy way
[41]	Description of the technological perspective for a cloud service-based control approach and its implementation and proposal of a multi-layer control approach
[42]	Aim of the research is the development of a sustainable framework which evaluates cloud-based distributed manufacturing systems
[43]	Presentation of the implementation of DevOps by embedding industry 4.0 methods to achieve collaboration and sustainability in supply chains. A blockchain-based information system is combined with a cloud manufacturing system to form a supply chain management system for a railcar manufacturer
[44]	Study of systems which optimize and evaluate cloud manufacturing system

(*continued*)

Table 4. (*continued*)

References	Overview
[45]	Investigation into Reference Architectures and Digital Twins and how they contribute to the development of cloud-based applications
[46]	Presentation of how crowdsourcing cyber platform technologies contribute in the MaaS implementation through intelligent decision support systems
[47]	Presentation of the implementation of Distributed Ledger Technologies in the manufacturing field. Proposal of a shared- manufacturing concept which examines the efficiency of the technology presented regarding the communication and computation, in resource-limited IoT networks
[48]	Presentation of a manufacturing framework which simulates a MaaS system for the satisfaction of remote production orders. In the system presented, Asset Administration Shell functions and International Data Space Connectors are implied
[49]	Description of enabling technologies for the transformation of vertical sectors, and the emergence of 6G Internet of Verticals. Examination of examples regarding cloud manufacturing, MaaS, smart energy grids and Internet of Robotics

5 Conclusions and Indicative Extensions

This study presented a bibliometric analysis of selected publications related to MaaS. The findings of this analysis can be summarized as follows.

It is observed that there is a growing trend in the number of papers relevant to MaaS. The North Carolina State University had the highest number of publications, and the top institutions, in terms of scientific output, come from US, China, and EU. The journal Procedia CIRP ranked first among the MaaS-related journals.

The most frequently cited work in the MaaS field is the work of Tao and Qi [25]. On average, the papers on MaaS receive a substantial number of citations, nonetheless the distribution of citations per paper is notably skewed. The keyword co-occurrence analysis revealed major areas of interest within the MaaS realm as well as the interconnections between them. Collaboration among multiple authors is common in the MaaS domain; all the top 5 publications with the highest number of citations involved more than one author. The journal co-citation analysis identified the Procedia CIRP and the Journal of Manufacturing Systems to hold great influence in the MaaS field.

Regarding now the literature review, it is apparent that each of the publications constitutes a unique contribution to the manufacturing sector. With a quick glance at the table presented, one can perceive the specific subject of each research, under the general concept of MaaS, thus helping many more outcoming research about it. The main thematic categories addressed in the sources, relate to the theoretical background for the emerging industrial technologies, to the mechanisms for the MaaS implementation and to solutions for the data management along the entire supply chain of a manufacturer.

A straightforward way to extend this research is to consider additional papers as well as an enhanced analysis of the publications by constructing co-authorship and keyword density maps, among others. A major extension of this study would be a full-scale literature review including detailed classification of the papers according to the specific methodologies implied in each of them, or the results obtained, conceptual or numerical and proposal of new directions for future research.

Acknowledgments. The project TAEDR-0535864 "Network of Excellence for the Development, Dissemination and Application of Digital Transformation Technologies in the Greek Manufacturing Industry" is carried out within the framework of the National Recovery and Resilience Plan Greece 2.0, funded by the European Union – NextGenerationEU.

References

1. Hasan, M., Starly, B.: Decentralized cloud manufacturing-as-a-service (CMaaS) platform architecture with configurable digital assets. J. Manuf. Syst. **56**, 157–174 (2020)
2. Xanthopoulos, A.S., Chnitidis, G., Koulouriotis, E.D.: Reinforcement Learning-based adaptive production control of pull manufacturing systems. J. Ind. Prod. Eng. **36**(5), 313–323 (2019)
3. Xanthopoulos, A.S., Koulouriotis, E.D.: Cluster analysis and neural network-based metamodeling of priority rules for dynamic sequencing. J. Intell. Manuf. **29**(1), 69–91 (2018)
4. Paraschos, P.D., Xanthopoulos, A.S., Koulinas, G.E., Koulouriotis, E.D.: Machine learning integrated design and operation management for resilient circular manufacturing systems. Comput. Ind. Eng. **167**, 107971 (2022)
5. Katsios, D., Xanthopoulos, A.S., Koulouriotis, E.D., Kiatipis, A.: A simulation optimization tool and its production/inventory control application. Int. J. Simul. Model **17**(2), 257–270 (2018)
6. Mehdi, N., Starly, B.: Witness box protocol: automatic machine identification and authentication in industry 4.0. Comput. Ind. **123**, 103340 (2020)
7. Namjoshi, J., Rawat, M.: Role of smart manufacturing in industry 4.0. Mater. Today **63**, 457–478 (2022)
8. Pahwa, D., Starly, B., Cohen, P.: Reverse auction mechanism design for the acquisition of prototyping services in a manufacturing-as-a-service marketplace. J. Manuf. Syst. **48**, 134–143 (2018)
9. Mourtzis, D., Angelopoulos, J., Panopoulos, N.: A survey of digital B2B platforms and marketplaces for purchasing industrial product service systems: a conceptual framework. Procedia CIRP **97**, 331–336 (2020)
10. Bulut, S., Wende, M., Wagner, C., Anderl, R.: Impact of Manufacturing-as-a-Service: business model adaption for enterprises. Procedia CIRP **104**, 1286–1291 (2021)
11. Tedaldi, G., Miragliotta, G.: Early adopters of Manufacturing-as-a-Service (MaaS): state-of-the-art and deployment models. J. Manuf. Technol. Manag. **34**(4), 580–600 (2023)
12. Tiwari, A., Villasenor, E.J., Gupta, N., Reddy, N., Karri, R., Bukkapatnam, S.T.S.: Protection against counterfeiting attacks in 3D printing by streaming signature-embedded manufacturing process instructions. In: Proceedings of AMSec'21, November Virtual Event, Republic of Korea, pp. 11–21 (2021)
13. Engelseth, P., Salman, M., Mushtaq, W., Awaleh, F., Kozlowski, R., Glavee-Geo, R.: Additive manufacturing: currently a disruptive supply chain innovation? Oper. Supply Chain Manag. **14**(4), 410–422 (2021)
14. Salinas, S.A., Monroy, P.L., Fang, Y., Loparo, K.A.: Blockchain-empowered distributed additive manufacturing-as-a-service: an architectural perspective. IEEE Netwo. **37**(5), 114–121 (2023). https://doi.org/10.1109/MNET.129.2200459
15. Hu, Y., Zhu, F., Zhang, L., Lui, Y., Wang, Z.: Scheduling of manufacturers based on chaos optimization algorithm in cloud manufacturing. Robot Comput. Integr. Manuf. **58**, 13–20 (2019)

16. Tedaldi, G., Miragliotta, G.: The role of engineering-to-order machinery manufacturers in future cloud manufacturing supply chains: a business case and a strategic perspective. Prod. Plan. Control **33**(9–10), 1011–1023 (2021)
17. Chaudhuri, A., Datta, P.P., Fernandes, K.J., Xiong Y.: Optimal pricing strategies for manufacturing-as-a service platforms to ensure business sustainability. Int. J. Prod. Econ. **234**, 108065 (2021)
18. Moghaddam, M., Silva, J.R., Nof, S.Y.: Manufacturing-as-a-service-from e-work and service-oriented architecture to the cloud manufacturing paradigm. IFAC-PapersOnLine **48**(3), 828–833 (2015)
19. Liao, H., Tang, M., Luo, L., Li, C., Chiclana, F., Zeng, X.J.: A bibliometric analysis and visualization of medical big data research. Sustainability **10**, 166 (2018)
20. Tessaro, V., Vick, A., Kruger, J.: Universal identification and control of industrial manufacturing equipment as a service. Proc. Est. Acad. Sci. **70**(4), 444–452 (2021)
21. Ford, S., Rauschecker, U., Athanassopoulou, N.: System-of-system approaches and challenges for multi-site manufacturing. In: Proceedings of the 2012 7th International Conference on System of Systems Engineering, Genoa, Italy, 16–19 July, 543–548 (2012)
22. Rauschecker, U., Stohr, M.: Using manufacturing service descriptions for flexible integration of production facilities to manufacturing clouds. In: Proceedings of the 2012 18th International Conference on Engineering, Technology and Innovation, 6297693 (2012)
23. Hasan, M., Ogan, K., Starly, B.: Hybrid blockchain architecture for cloud manufacturing-as-a-service (CMaaS) platforms with improved data storage and transaction efficiency. Proc. Manuf. **53**, 594–605 (2021)
24. Pahwa, D., Starly, B.: Dynamic matching with deep reinforcement learning for a two-sided Manufacturing-as-a-Service (MaaS) marketplace. Manuf. Lett. **29**, 11–14 (2021)
25. Tao, F., Qi, Q.: New IT driven service-oriented smart manufacturing: framework and characteristics. IEEE Trans. Syst. Man Cyber. **49**(1), 81–91 (2019)
26. Mourad, M., Nassehi, A., Schaefer, D.: Interoperability as a key enabler for manufacturing in the cloud. Procedia CIRP **52**, 30–34 (2016)
27. Kusiak, A.: Universal manufacturing: enablers, properties, and models. Int. J. Prod. Res. **60**(8), 2497–2513 (2021)
28. Bettoni, A., Barni, A., Sorlini, M., Menato, S., Giorgetti, P., Landolfi, G.: Multi-sided digital manufacturing platform supporting exchange of unused company potential. In: IEEE International Conference on Engineering Technology and Innovation (2018)
29. Wang, K., Dave, P., Hanchate, A., Sagapuram, D., Natarajan, G., Bukkapatnam, S.T.S.: Implementing an open-source sensor data ingestion, fusion, and analysis capabilities for smart manufacturing. Manuf. Lett. **33**, 893–901 (2022). https://doi.org/10.1016/j.mfglet.2022.07.109
30. Gong, X., Wang, S., Jiao, R.J., Gebraeel, N.Z.: Collaborative contracting for Manufacturing-as-a-Service (MaaS) by information content measurement and decision tree learning. Adv. Eng. Inform. **56**, 101911 (2023)
31. Landolfi, G., Barni, A., Izzo, G., Fontana, A., Bettoni, A.: A MaaS platform architecture supporting data sovereignty in sustainability assessment of manufacturing systems. Procedia Manuf. **38**, 548–555 (2019)
32. Wang, J., Qiao, L., Qie, Y.: Process planning service model design for cloud manufacturing. In: 2017 13th IEEE Conference on Automation Science and Engineering (2017)
33. Liu, X., Gong, X., Jiao, R.J.: Low-carbon product family planning for manufacturing as a service (MaaS): bilevel optimization with linear physical programming. Sustainability **14**, 12566 (2022)
34. Ordienes-Mere, J., Villalba-Diez, J., Zheng, X.: Challenges and opportunities for publishing IIoT data in manufacturing as a service business. Procedia Manuf. **39**, 185–193 (2019)

35. Iquebal, A.S., et al.: Towards realizing cybermanufacturing kiosks: quality assurance challenges and opportunities. Procedia Manuf. **26**, 1296–1306 (2018)
36. Hung, Y.-H.: Investigating how the cloud computing transforms the development of industries. IEEE Access **7**, 181505–181517 (2019)
37. May, M.C., Schmidt, S., Kuhnle, A., Stricker, N., Lanza, G.: Product generation module: automated production planning for optimized workload and increased efficiency in matrix production systems. Procedia CIRP **96**, 45–50 (2021)
38. Gong, X., Jiao, R., Jariwala, A., Morkos, B.: Crowdsourced manufacturing for delivery of manufacturing as a service. In: Proceedings of the 2021 IEEE IEEM (2021)
39. Moergestel, L., Puik, E., Telgen, D.: Implementation of an agent-based manufacturing grid. In: IEEE Twelfth International Symposium on Autonomous Decentralized Systems (2015)
40. Gong, K., Xu, H., Liu, H., Cao, Z., Fuenmayor, E., Major, I.: Hybrid manufacturing of mixed-material bilayer parts via injection molding and material extrusion three-dimensional printing. J. Appl. Polymer Sci. **140,** 53972 (2023)
41. Adamson, G., Holm, M., Moore, P., Wang, L.: A cloud service control approach for distributed and adaptive equipment control in cloud environments. Procedia CIRP **41**, 644–649 (2016)
42. Nagarajan, H.P.N., Raman, A.S., Haapala, K.R.: A sustainability assessment framework for dynamic cloud-based distributed manufacturing. Procedia CIRP **69**, 136–141 (2018)
43. Matenga, A.E., Mpofu, K.: Blockchain-based cloud manufacturing SCM system for collaborative enterprise manufacturing: a case study of transport manufacturing. Appl. Sci. **12**, 8664 (2022)
44. Xianxian, C., Yuan, M., Zhou, Z., Sun, C.: Research on optimal selection of services and optimal allocation of resources in cloud manufacturing environment. J. Phys. Conf. Ser. **1314**, 012167 (2019)
45. Marosi, A.C., et al.: Interoperable data analytics reference architectures empowering digital-twin-aided manufacturing. Future Internet **14**, 114 (2022)
46. Gong, X., Jiao, R., Jariwala, A., Morkos, B.: Crowdsourced manufacturing cyber platform and intelligent cognitive assistants for delivery of manufacturing as a service: fundamental issues and outlook. Int. J. Adv. Manuf. Technol. **117**, 1997–2007 (2021)
47. Nguyen, L.D., Broring, A., Pizzol, M., Papovski, P.: Analysis of distributed ledger technologies for industrial manufacturing. Sci. Rep. **12**, 18055 (2022)
48. Inigo, M.A., Legaristi, J., Perez Javier Cuenca, A., Kremer, B., Montejo, E.: Towards standardized manufacturing as a service through asset administration shell and international data spaces connectors. In: 48th Annual Conference of the IEEE Industrial Electronics Society (2022)
49. Nekovee, M.: Transformation from 5G for verticals towards a 6G-enabled internet of verticals. In: 14th International Conference on COMunication Systems & NETworks, pp. 905–910 (2022)

Socio-Economic Framework, Standards and Novel Practices in Logistics

Studying the Buyer Abusive Behavior Towards Truck Owners

Margarita I. Zarogianni(✉) and Costas Assimakopoulos

International Hellenic University, 57009 Sindos, Greece
margaritazarogianni@yahoo.gr

Abstract. Investigating the contemporary dynamics of stakeholder relations, this study delves into the escalating pressures faced by truck owner-operators, specifically addressing instances of abusive behavior from buyers (BAB). This paper seeks to elucidate the factors that influence the prevalence and manifestation of buyer abuse across diverse business contexts. This approach not only extends the current academic discourse but also contributes to practical implications for truck owner-operators and policy makers alike. The findings derived from this research, guided by multiple authoritative sources, provide a robust analytical framework for navigating the intricate interplay between stakeholder pressures, contractual arrangements, and other factors (Kim et al., 2022; Johnson, 2021). It is noteworthy that the correlations between Buyer Abusive Behavior (BAB) with and without a contract are based on insights derived from a supplementary analysis within Kim's seminal paper, adding a layer of specificity to the study's methodology. Drawing insights from a sample of 122 owner-operation drivers in Germany, the research systematically investigates both contractual and non-contractual manifestations of BAB through a rigorous methodology using the cluster sampling method and questionnaires. This additional detail enhances the depth and reliability of our analytical approach. Built upon the Korean study model, this research's preliminary results deviate from the first research model, revealing nuanced distinctions inherent to the German truck-owner-operators.

Keywords: Buyer Abusive Behavior · Truck Owner · Supplier Performance and Safety

1 Introduction

The evolution of buyer-supplier dynamics across successive decades has exhibited a discernible trend of heightened buyer influence, elucidating a paradigm shift in market dynamics with discernable impacts on supplier-customer relationships. Smith and Jones (2019) emphasize the pervasive impact of buyer power on supplier vulnerability and welfare. This study delves into the intricate landscape of buyer abusive behavior (BAB) targeting truck owners within the contemporary transportation industry. Rooted in the foundational insights provided by Kim's article, published in 2022, our research endeavors to illuminate the nuanced challenges faced by truck owners in response to exploitative buyer practices.

I. Kostavelis et al. (Eds.): ICSC 2024, CCIS 2110, pp. 285–294, 2025.
https://doi.org/10.1007/978-3-031-69344-1_21

Complementing Kim's pivotal insights, our study aims to discern patterns and manifestations of buyer abuse within the contractual relationships forged between truck owners and buyers. A meticulous examination of instances both with and without formal contracts allows us to gauge the variations in abusive behavior and its repercussions on the operational and financial well-being of truck owners.

To contextualize our exploration, we interweave additional references highlighting the broader dynamics of buyers' power over their suppliers. Smith and Jones (2019) emphasize the profound impact of this power dynamic on supplier vulnerability and overall supplier welfare. Moreover, Miller and Wagner (2021) contribute valuable insights into strategies wielded by buyers to exert power over suppliers and the ensuing challenges confronted by suppliers within these relationships.

As we scrutinize the multifaceted dimensions of buyer abuse, we shed light on the adverse consequences faced by truck owners, encompassing unjust contractual terms, delayed payments, and arbitrary demands. The comparative analysis of scenarios involving formal contracts and those without enables a nuanced examination of the role of contractual agreements in either mitigating or exacerbating abusive behavior. In this study we examine buyers' abusive behavior (BAB) and supplier welfare in truck owner operators in Germany in terms of two dimensions. First dimension: contract related BAB, second dimension: contract unrelated BAB. In addition, we examine BABs exerted by the buyers of trucking services against truck owner-operators as their suppliers.

2 Methodology

The methodology employed in composing a scientific paper adheres rigorously to systematic procedures. Initially, the process entails the implementation of cluster sampling techniques to acquire data, thereby ensuring the representative inclusion of diverse population subsets. Subsequent data analysis is facilitated through the utilization of SPSS software affording a robust framework for comprehensive examination and interpretation.

Noteworthy challenges encountered during the study encompass the precise identification and inclusion of exclusively truck owner driver operators. The data collection phase spanned a duration of four months, during which rigorous efforts were concentrated on recruiting participants solely from the demographic of truck owners who are actively engaged in professional activities within Germany.

The study encompasses a sample of 122 truck owners operating within the distinctive context of the contemporary trucking industry in Germany, ensuring a holistic representation of experiences and challenges faced by drivers in their engagements with buyers. According to Eurostat, almost three quarters of the total goods transported by land in Germany (73.6% in 2021) and this share is expected to increase in the coming years. In addition, more than half of the cabotage in the EU in 2022 was performed in Germany (51.7%).

Our unit of analysis is the supplier: an individual truck owner–operator. We verified that they were owner–operators before asking them to participate and we used a face-to-face survey to collect the data. We use the questionnaire as a tool. Finally, the original questionnaire was written both in Greek and English.

3 Theoretical Framework

In recent years buyers' power over their suppliers has been frequent subject of study. From bibliography they arise both the positive and the negative impacts of buyer power on supplier welfare. Research findings reveal that when buyers have more bargaining power, suppliers face various kinds of difficulties. On the other hand, if suppliers can expand their own bargaining power (e.g., through size or market share) and therefore increase interdependence, buyers' greater market share could prove beneficial for the suppliers. (Hofer, 2012, Huang, 2012). In addition, if a supplier is weak and has no bargaining power to build interdependence, byer can exploit this supplier for short-term gains (Anderson & Jap, 2005).

According to Douglas and Swartz (2017), the trucking industry plays a crucial role in both national and global economies. Trucks are essential for the functioning of European society as they transport a wide range of goods to consumers and provide vital transportation services to businesses. In the EU, trucks handle nearly 80% of land freight transport, with 6.5 million trucks currently operating in the region and over half a million manufactured within the EU in 2022. The average age of trucks is 14.2 years, and approximately 3.74 million trucks were registered in Germany, making it a suitable location for further research.

Examining working conditions in the trucking industry, it is evident that truck drivers now work longer hours for lower real wages compared to the past. They suffer the indignity of being forced to wait for hours to get loaded or unloaded while people whose time is more highly valued are taken care of first. Their work and pay structure often call for them to forego compensation for their time in trade for the opportunity to put in extra hours to run extra miles every week, often keeping them away from home for weeks at a time (Michael H. Belzer, 2000). Multiple research studies have confirmed that the trucking industry is highly competitive and challenging, with conditions becoming more demanding than in previous years, exacerbated by newcomers entering the field and working for minimal compensation. As noted by Viscelli (2016), buyers within the trucking sector have introduced novel labor supply and management tactics that transfer potential risks and costs onto suppliers.

On the topic of power, the concept has been fundamental in social exchange theory since its early stages of development (Blau, 1964). Emerson (1962) examined power dynamics in relational settings, focusing on one actor's dependence on another. Building upon this framework, Emerson (1972) later defined power within exchange relations. In this context, exchange relations are viewed as temporal sequences comprising opportunities for exchange, leading to initiations and subsequent transactions. An exchange network consists of actors interconnected directly or indirectly through such exchange relations, with each actor serving as a convergence point for multiple exchanges. Within an exchange relation between actors A and B, the power of A over B in the Ax:By exchange scenario (where x and y denote valuable resources) rises relative to the value of y to A and declines in proportion to y's availability to A from alternative sources apart from B. This dependence-based power dynamic, posited by Emerson, underscores that A's power over B escalates as B's reliance on A increases.

Expanding upon this notion, Viscelli (2016) observes prevalent exploitative behaviors by buyers in the trucking industry, where suppliers' bargaining power is notably feeble due to their reliance on buyers. Literature suggests that buyers' coercive power can lead to abusive treatment of suppliers, particularly when buyers exploit less autonomous suppliers to gain greater value at their expense (Marshall, 2019; Schleper, 2017).

As elucidated by Hoskisson et al. (2017), prospect theory serves as a framework for understanding individual risk-taking behavior, predicting decision-making choices aimed at maximizing gains while facing risks and uncertainties. Concurrently, Christian (2009) highlights that workers who engage in frequent and riskier behaviors are more prone to accidents. Over decades, scholars across various disciplines, as noted by Barberis (2013) and Holmes et al. (2011), have investigated decisions involving gain versus loss. Pertinent to our inquiry, Miller et al. (2017) and Miller and Saldanha (2016) find that operational performance in the trucking industry positively impacts safety. However, safety outcomes are influenced by various factors within the sociotechnical system, as indicated by Brown et al. (2000), among which individuals' risk-taking behaviors play a significant role, as emphasized by Christian et al. (2009). Furthermore, several driver-related factors contributing to safety performance have been identified. For instance, years of occupational driving experience were positively associated with higher levels of traffic safety (Li, 2013).

Studies suggest that occupational truck drivers should be provided with safety-oriented work schedules and conditions to effectively manage workload and receive training not only for technical skills but also for safety-related attitudes and behaviors (Li, 2013).

4 Hypothesis Development

Over passed decades, a plethora of academic literature has explored and analyzed the positive and negative effects of buyer power on supplier welfare. This body of research has delved into the complex interplay between buyers and suppliers, offering valuable insights into their economic relationships. It is noteworthy that stronger buyers have economic incentives to exploit their power over weaker suppliers (Cox, 2001; Schleper et al., 2017; Weil, 2014). In the trucking industry, buyers streamline their schedules by compelling truck owner-operators to accept assigned loads, even if some are not profitable for the operators (Viscelli, 2016). Belzer (2000) notes that buyers often subject owner-operators to long waiting times for loading or unloading without compensation. Despite being self-employed, owner-operators can refuse loads; however, doing so may lead buyers to terminate their business relationships due to low switching costs (Crook & Combs, 2007). Consequently, owner-operators often feel pressured to accept every assignment, even if it jeopardizes their safety (Agnew, 1992), potentially resulting in violations like exceeding work hour limits (Scott & Nyaga, 2019). Moreover, in the trucking industry, contractual arrangements seldom benefit both drivers and carriers financially (Viscelli, 2016). Finally, Santoe (2022) finds that both contract-related and unrelated Buyer Abusive Behaviors (BABs) are negatively associated with supplier performance. This thorough literature review leads us to formulate our initial hypotheses;

H1(a) Contract-related and (b) contract-unrelated BABs are negatively associated with supplier performance.

H2(a) Contract-related and (b) contract-unrelated BABs are negatively associated with supplier safety.

Typical cases of contract-related BAB pertain to payment and ordering such as buyer's unfair subcontract price decision or coercive freight service contract and BAB unrelated to contracts, undue interference in management seems to be commonplace.

We propose that both contract-related and contract-unrelated Buyer Abusive Behaviors (BAB) are detrimental to supplier welfare that consists of performance and safety. Furthermore, we contend that BAB has a moderating impact on the relationship between supplier performance and safety.

H3 Supplier performance is positively associated with supplier safety.

According to Santoe (2022), supplier (owner–operator) performance is positively associated with their safety. This position is significantly strengthened by Miller et al. (2017) who claims that strong performance generates the resources that suppliers like owner–operators need to invest in safety. Britto et al. (2010), Miller & Saldanha (2016) note that there is always a trade-off between performance and safety, as the costs of ensuring safety at work tend to be high. In addition, we assume and expect drivers owner–operators behavior to follow the general prediction of prospect theory, which posits that individuals become more risk-seeking in the face of potential losses (Kahneman & Tversky, 1979). Thus, we posit the previous three hypothesis which illustrated schematically in Fig. 1.

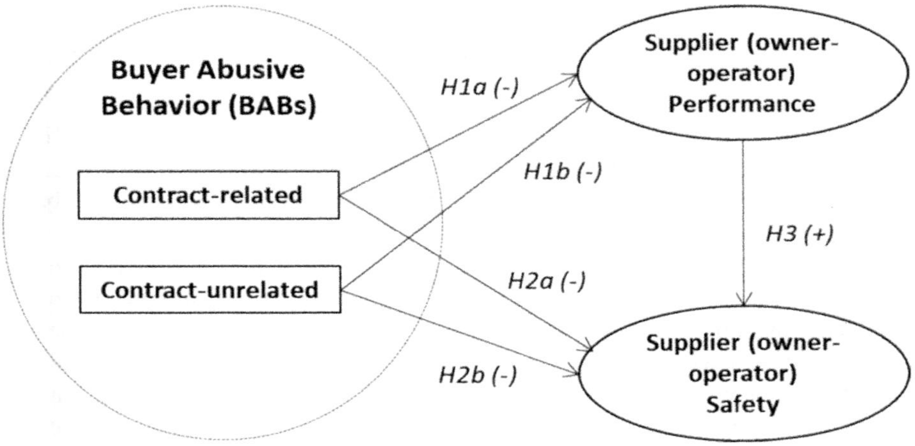

Fig. 1. BAB correlations (Kim et al., 2022)

5 Analysis and Results

Our research involved 122 truck owner-operators. The analysis of the data reveals that 121 (99.18%) were men while there was only one woman (0.82%). According to this sample, this is a male dominated field in Germany. Moreover, 12 persons (9.84%) are aged between 21–30 years old. The 33.61%, 41 truck owner operators aged between 41–50 years old. 39 of 122 aged between 31–40 years old (31.97%), in addition 21 operators aged between 51–60 years old (17.21%) and only the 7.37%, 9 persons are over 61 years old. As a result, the majority of the sample (65.58%) aged between 31–50 years old. As far as education level is concerned, our data reveal the following elements; the vast majority 95,08%, 116 operators are High School graduates, only 3 from 122 have a university degree (2.46%) and 3 of them are graduates from post-secondary education (Table 1).

Table 1. Demographics

		Value Label	N	%
Sex of supplier	1,00	Male	121	99.18%
	2,00	Female	1	0.82%
Age of supplier	1,00	21–30	12	9.84%
	2,00	31–40	39	31.97%
	3,00	41–50	41	33.61%
	4,00	51–60	21	17.21%
	5,00	61 and over	9	7.37%
Educational Level	2,00	High School graduate	116	95.08%
	3,00	Post-secondary education	3	2.46%
	4,00	University graduate	3	2.46%

The analysis was conducted using SPSS software, and the results are presented below. The hypothesis (H1a) posits that buyer's abusive behavior with contract is negatively associated with supplier performance. Pearson correlation coefficient (r) between buyer's abusive behavior with contract and supplier performance was found to be −0.115, indicating a weak negative correlation between the two variables. The significance value (p-value) for this correlation was 0.205, which is greater than the conventional threshold of 0.05. This implies that as buyer's abusive behavior increases, supplier performance slightly tends to decrease. However, the significance level of 0.205 indicates that this correlation is not statistically significant, meaning that the observed relationship could be due to random chance rather than a true underlying effect, the lack of statistical significance suggests that we cannot confidently assert that this relationship exists in the population. Therefore, hypothesis H1(a) is rejected.

The hypothesis (H1b) assumes that buyer's abusive behavior is negatively associated with supplier performance. The Pearson correlation coefficient (r) between buyer's abusive behavior and supplier performance was found to be −0.282. This indicates a negative correlation between the two variables. The significance value (p-value) for this correlation was 0.002, which is less than the conventional threshold of 0.05. The results suggest a moderate inverse relationship between buyer's abusive behavior and supplier performance. This means that as buyer's abusive behavior increases, supplier performance tends to decrease. The significance level of 0.002 indicates that this correlation is statistically significant, thus providing strong evidence to support the hypothesis H1(b) as expected.

H2(a) hypothesis posits that buyer's abusive behavior with contract is negatively associated with supplier safety. The Pearson correlation coefficient (r) between buyer's abusive behavior with contract and supplier safety was found to be 0.054, indicating a very weak positive correlation between the two variables. The significance value (*p*-value) for this correlation was 0.555, which is greater than the conventional threshold of 0.05. However, the lack of statistical significance (*p*-value = 0.555) suggests that this relationship is not meaningful in a statistical sense. Consequently, the hypothesis that buyer's abusive behavior with a contract is negatively associated with supplier safety is not supported by the data. These findings imply that buyer's abusive behavior with a contract does not have a significant impact on supplier safety. Those findings rejected hypothesis H2(a).

H2(b) hypothesis explores the relationship between buyer's abusive behavior without a contract and supplier safety. The Pearson correlation coefficient (r) between buyer's abusive behavior without a contract and supplier safety was found to be −0.038, indicating a very weak negative correlation between the two variables, but he significance value (*p*-value) for this correlation was 0.677, which is greater than the conventional threshold of 0.05. Therefor this relationship is not statistically significant and the hypothesis H2(b) is not confirmed.

Finally, H3 hypothesis posits that supplier performance is positively associated with supplier safety. The Pearson correlation coefficient (r) between supplier performance and supplier safety was found to be 0.020, indicating a very weak positive correlation between the two variables. The significance value (*p*-value) for this correlation was 0.825, which is greater than the conventional threshold of 0.05. Consequently, those findings indicate that hypothesis H3 is not statistically significant and not confirmed (Tables 2, 3).

Table 2. Summary of the results

Hypothesis	Correlations results	Verified/non-verified
H1(a) Contract-related BAB is negatively associated with supplier performance	$p = 0.205$ (>0.05) $r = -0.115$	Non-verified
H1(b) Contract-unrelated BAB is negatively associated with supplier performance	$p = 0.002$ $r = -0.282^{**}$	Verified
H2(a) Contract-related BAB is negatively associated with supplier safety	$p = 0.555$ $r = 0.054$	Non-verified
H2(b) Contract-unrelated BAB is negatively associated with supplier safety	$p = 0.677$ $r = -0.038$	Non-verified
H3 Supplier performance is positively associated with supplier safety	$p = 0.825$ $r = 0.020$	Non-verified

Table 3. *p*-values for Hypothesis testing

		safety	BAB with contract	BAB without contract	performance
safety	Pearson correlation	1			
	Sig. (2-tailed)				
	N	122			
BAB with contract	Pearson Correlation	0.054	1		
	Sig. (2-tailed)	0.555			
	N	122	122		
BAB without contract	Pearson correlation	−0.038	0.270(**)	1	
	Sig. (2-tailed)	0.677	0.003		
	N	122	122	122	
performance	Pearson Correlation	0.020	−0.115	−0.282(**)	1
	Sig. (2-tailed)	0.825	0.205	0.002	
	N	122	122	122	122

** Correlation is significant at the 0.01 level (2-tailed)
* Correlation is significant at the 0.05 level (2-tailed).

6 Conclusions

In this study we examined BAB in the context of trucking operations in Germany. Based on face-to-face survey data collected from truck owner–operators. BAB occurs when a buyer illegally uses its power advantage to force its weaker suppliers. We examine BABs exerted by buyers of trucking services against truck owner–operators as their suppliers. We focused on testing the correlations of BAB with and BAB without contract with suppliers' safety and performance. There have been various limitations to research concerning the limited literature on the subject.

Our findings have far-reaching implications for the field and for decent work in supply chains, because of the fact that trucking operations play an important role in both national and global supply chain operations. We found differences between our finds and the findings of previous researches and we assume that differences are due to different mentality.

We expect our research to trigger a more in-depth study of this topic in the future, with a larger sample of respondents in more countries in Europe and global.

Considering the pervasive influence of social media in contemporary society, as social media "took" personal relationships and "placed" them on the Internet, it is intriguing to explore how buyer reviews affect supplier reputation and, consequently, their sustainability. Future studies could delve into the extent to which social media impacts consumer decision-making processes, essentially transferring traditional word-of-mouth dynamics onto online platforms.

References

Agnew, R.: Foundation for a general strain theory of crime and delinquency. Criminology **30**(1), 47–88 (1992)

Anderson, E., Jap, S.D.: The dark side of close relationships. MIT Sloan Manag. Rev. **46**(3), 75–82 (2005)

Barberis, N.C.: Thirty years of prospect theory in economics: a review and assessment. J. Econ. Persp. **27**(1), 173–195 (2013)

Belzer, M. H.: Sweatshop on Wheels: Winners and Losers in Trucking Deregulation. Oxford University Press, Oxford (2000)

Blau, P. M.: Justice in social exchange. Sociol. Inquir **34**(2) (1964)

Britto, R.A., Corsi, T.M., Grimm, C.M.: The relationship between motor carrier financial performance and safety performance. Transp. J. **49**(4), 42–51 (2010)

Brown, K.A., Willis, P.G., Prussia, G.E.: Predicting safe employee behavior in the steel industry: development and test of a sociotechnical model. J. Oper. Manag. **18**(4), 445–465 (2000)

Sutton-Brady, C., Kamvounias, P., Taylor, T.: A model of supplier–retailer power asymmetry in the Australian retail industry. Ind. Mark. Manage. **51**, 122–130 (2015)

Christian, M.S., Bradley, J.C., Wallace, J.C., Burke, M.J.: Workplace safety: a meta-analysis of the roles of person and situation factors. J. Appl. Psychol. **94**(5), 1103–1127 (2009)

Crook, T.R., Combs, J.G.: Sources and consequences of bargaining power in supply chains. J. Oper. Manag. **25**(2), 546–555 (2007)

Douglas, M.A., Swartz, S.M.: Knights of the road: safety, ethics, and the professional truck driver. J. Bus. Ethics **142**(3), 567–588 (2017)

Emerson, R.M.: Power-dependence relations. Am. Sociol. Rev. **27**(1), 31–41 (1962)

Holmes, R.M., Bromiley, P., Devers, C.E., Holcomb, T.R., McGuire, J.B.: Management theory applications of prospect theory: accomplishments, challenges, and opportunities. J. Manag. **37**(4), 1069–1107 (2011)

Hofer, C., Jin, H., Swanson, R.D., Waller, M.A., Williams, B.D.: The impact of key retail accounts on supplier performance: a collaborative perspective of resource dependency theory. J. Retail. **88**(3), 412–420 (2012)

Hoskisson, R.E., Chirico, F., Zyung, J.Y., Gambeta, E.: Managerial risk taking: a multitheoretical review and future research agenda. J. Manag. **43**(1), 137–169 (2017)

Huang, Q.Y., Nijs, V.R., Hansen, K., Anderson, E.T.: Wal-Mart's impact on supplier profits. J. Mark. Res. **49**(2), 131–143 (2012)

Jones, T.M., Harrison, J.S.: Sustainable wealth creation: applying instrumental theory to the improvement of social welfare. In: Harrison, J.S., Barney, B., Edward Freeman, R., Phillips, R.A. (eds.) The Cambridge Handbook of Stakeholder Theory, pp. 72–91. Oxford University Press, Oxford (2019)

Kim, S., Chae, S., Wagner, S.M., Miller, J.W.: Buyer abusive behavior and supplier welfare: an empirical study of truck owner–operators. J. Supply Chain Manag. **58**(4), 90–111 (2022)

Lu, G., Ding, X., Peng, D.X., Chuang, H.H.C.: Addressing endogeneity in operations management research: recent developments, common problems, and directions for future research. J. Oper. Manag. **64**, 53–64 (2018)

Miller, J.W., Saldanha, J.P.: A new look at the longitudinal relationship between motor carrier financial performance and safety. J. Bus. Logist. **37**(3), 284–306 (2016)

Miller, J.W., Saldanha, J.P., Rungtusanatham, M., Knemeyer, M.: How does driver turnover affect motor carrier safety performance and what can managers do about it? J. Bus. Logist. **38**(3), 197–216 (2017)

Miller, J.W., Golicic, S.L., Fugate, B.S.: Reconciling alternative theories for the safety of owner–operators. J. Bus. Logist. **39**(2), 101–122 (2018)

Nyaga, G.N., Lynch, D.F., Marshall, D., Ambrose, E.: Power asymmetry, adaptation and collaboration in dyadic relationships involving a powerful partner. J. Supply Chain Manag. **49**(3), 42–65 (2013)

Pagell, M., Gobeli, D.: How plant managers' experiences and attitudes toward sustainability relate to operational performance. Prod. Oper. Manag. **18**(3), 278–299 (2009)

Pagell, M., Wiengarten, F., Fan, D., Humphreys, P., Lo, C.K.: Managerial time horizons and the decision to put operational workers at risk: the role of debt. Decis. Sci. **50**(3), 582–611 (2019)

Pagell, M., et al.: The tension between worker safety and organization survival. Manage. Sci. **66**(10), 4863–4878 (2020)

Pagell, M., Parkinson, M., Veltri, A.: Putting worker safety at the heart of supply chain management. In: Sarkis, J. (eds.) The Palgrave Handbook of Supply Chain Management. Palgrave Macmillan, Cham (2023)

Patatoukas, P.N.: Customer-base concentration: implications for firm performance and capital markets. Account. Rev. **87**(2), 363–392 (2012)

Saldanha, J.P., Hunt, C.S., Mello, J.E.: Driver management that drives carrier performance. J. Bus Logist. **34**(1), 15–32 (2013)

Schleper, M.C., Blome, C., Wuttke, D.A.: The dark side of buyer power: Supplier exploitation and the role of ethical climates. J. Bus. Ethics **140**(1), 97–114 (2017)

Scott, A., Nyaga, G.N.: The effect of firm size, asset ownership, and market prices on regulatory violations. J. Oper. Manag. **65**(7), 685–709 (2019)

Smith, K.T., Jones, A., Johnson, L., Smith, L.M.: Examination of cybercrime and its effects on corporate stock value. J. Inf. Commun. Ethics Soc. **17**(1), 42–60 (2019)

Viscelli, S.: The Big Rig: Trucking and the Decline of the American Dream. University of California Press (2016)

Wagner, S.M., Rau, C., Lindemann, E.: Multiple informant methodology: a critical review and recommendations. Sociol. Methods Res. **38**(4), 582–618 (2010)

Wagner, S.M., Coley, L.S., Lindemann, E.: Effects of suppliers' reputation on the future of buyer-supplier relationships: the mediating roles of outcome fairness and trust. J. Supply Chain Manag. **47**(2), 29–48 (2011)

Weil, D.: The Fissured Workplace: Why Work Became So Bad for So Many and What Can Be Done to Improve It. Harvard University Press (2014)

Weil, D.: Gig Economy is No Excuse For Lax Protections For American Workers. The Hill (2018)

Zhao, X., Huo, B., Flynn, B.B., Yeung, J.H.Y.: The impact of power and relationship commitment on the integration between manufacturers and customers in a supply chain. J. Oper. Manag. **26**(3), 368–388 (2008)

Using the National Integrated Specimen Referral Network as a Vehicle to Reach the 3rd 95 in Nigeria in FY22

Faruna Theophilus[1], Ekeh Nelson[1], Obianeri Victor[2], Omolara Emmanuel[3], and Dimitris Folinas[4](✉)

[1] Chemonics, USAID/GHSC-PSM, Abuja, Nigeria
[2] USAID, Abuja, Nigeria
[3] Federal Ministry of Health, NASCP, Abuja, Nigeria
[4] International Hellenic University, Thessaloniki, Greece
folinasd@ihu.gr

Abstract. Laboratory investigations are vital in preventive, diagnostic, therapeutic, and referral services. Efficient delivery of medical laboratory testing services at all levels and locations of healthcare services, especially in rural and poor populations, is essential. Nigeria's diagnostic landscape was plagued with underutilization of medical laboratory equipment, and a formal structure for referral and transport of diagnostic specimens to facilitate rapid diagnosis and laboratory confirmation needed to be revised. To provide quality medical laboratory testing services equitably and cost-effectively, Nigeria needed an integrated, multi-level specimen referral system. The National Integrated Specimen Referral Network (NiSRN) became operational in March 2018. This study examines the NiSRN operations' impact on attaining the third 95 of UNAIDS 95-95-95 targets. Descriptive methodologies were used to assess the viral load (HIV-VL) testing in Nigeria before NiSRN began. Between 2018 and 2022, annual volumes of VL and EID samples transported across the 36 states and the Federal Capital Territory (FCT) and assayed by the Polymerase Chain Reaction (PCR) laboratories were measured. VL suppression was reviewed. Using NiSRN, specimen backlogs were identified and relocated to laboratories that could promptly be analyzed. Eight hundred ninety-nine thousand nine hundred twelve specimens were transported in 2019, rising to 2,001,184 in 2022. VL coverage was 55% in 2018 and steadily rose to 95% in 2022. VL suppression rate was 78% in 2020 and rose to 96% in 2022, exceeding the UNAIDS' third 95 target. The NiSRN, operated by the Federal Government of Nigeria with support from PEPFAR and the Global Fund, has helped to exceed the UNAIDS' third 95 target. As evidenced by these results, PEPFAR and Global Fund teams in Nigeria should continue to support the NiSRN. Nigeria's Government must devise means of continuous sustainability with innovations. Other countries struggling to meet the UNAIDS third 95 can learn from Nigeria's experience.

Keywords: UNAIDS 95-95-95 · viral load suppression · third-party logistics · optimized specimen referral

I. Kostavelis et al. (Eds.): ICSC 2024, CCIS 2110, pp. 295–308, 2025.
https://doi.org/10.1007/978-3-031-69344-1_22

1 Introduction

1.1 Combatting the HIV Surge in Nigeria

The world has been battling with the Human Immunodeficiency Virus (HIV) and the associated illnesses of Acquired Immune Deficiency Syndromes (AIDS) since the outbreak in the early 80s. In Nigeria, Balogun (2014), Entonu & Agwale (2007), and Okoroiwu et al. (2022) reported that the first two cases of HIV in Nigeria were reported in 1986 at an international conference by the Federal Ministry of Health, identifying a sexually active 13-year-old girl and a female commercial sex worker from a neighboring West African country as the victims. Several strategies were adopted to bring the world's attention to the ravaging epidemics, curb the inferno, and permanently stem the tide of tragedy of monumental proportions upon the world. Knowing the enormity of this challenge, the United Nations on AIDS (UNAIDS) provides slogans each year to arouse the world's consciousness. On December 1, World AIDS Day, people celebrate globally. People come together from all around the world to honor individuals who have died from diseases associated with AIDS and to express support for those who are living with HIV. (UNAIDS, n.d). Here are a few examples of the slogans from 2011 to 2023. 2011: Getting to Zero, 2012: Together We Will End Aids, 2013: Zero Discrimination, 2014: Close the Gap, 2015: On the Fast-Track to End Aids, 2016: Hands Up for HIV Prevention, 2017: My Health, My Right, 2018: Know Your Status, 2019: Communities Make the Difference, 2020: Global Solidarity, Shared Responsibility, 2021: End Inequalities. End AIDS. End Pandemics, 2022: Equalize and 2023: Let Communities Lead.

Nigeria, with the support of funding partners, has keyed into every effort that has been made by the world to ensure that the spread of the virus is curbed in the country and to put in place mechanisms for the treatment of those who have been infected by the virus and prevent mother-to-child transmission (PMTCT). The prevalence of HIV in Nigeria rose to a peak of 5.8% in 2001 before it steadily declined to about 3.4% in 2013. The result of the first sentinel survey carried out in Nigeria put the prevalence at 1.8%; in 1993, it was 3.8%, and in 1996, it was 4.5%. The subsequent survey of 1999 gave the figure of 5.4, but in 2003, it started receding to 5.0% and 4.4% in 2005, while the 2010 figure was 4.1% while the latest survey of 2021 put the prevalence rate at 1.3% (NACA, nd). According to Boyd, Jahun, Dirlikov, Greby, Odafe, Abdulkadir, et al. (2020), Of the estimated 1.9 million PLHIV in Nigeria, about 1.4 million are receiving antiretroviral therapy. However, according to Onovo, Adeyemi, Onime, Kalnoky, Kagniniwa, Dessie, and Lee (2023), among adults in Nigeria aged 15 to 49, the estimated national HIV prevalence was 2.1% (95% CI: 1.5–2.7%), or about 2 million people living with HIV. This contrasts earlier estimates of 1.4% from the 2018 NAIIS and UNAIDS estimation and projection package PLHIV estimation of 1.8 million in 2022.

The country's effort to ensure people living with HIV/AIDS (PLWHA) receive adequate care and treatment encompasses the capacity to keep an eye on the results of antiretroviral treatment (ART), viral load suppression, and resistance to ARV drugs. According to Ofem (2012), Nigeria has a vast land mass and population of 140 million people and a total landmass of 923,768. With limited resources, it is impossible to have the required laboratory setting to provide services to all the PLWHA in the country. The alternative is establishing an effective and efficient specimen referral network for the country for the viral load, EID specimen, and any other clinical specimen of interest. As rightly posited by Faruna, Ezekiel, and Odelola (2019), specimen transportation was a challenge in most resource-limited countries like Nigeria. Before 2018, Nigeria had no standardized specimen transportation system, which was identified as a critical causative factor for in-country laboratory capacity underutilization.

Through the supportive visits to healthcare facilities, it was discovered that the diagnostic landscape is characterized by multiple models of clinical sample transfer mechanisms with resultant inefficiencies such as inflated costs, long turnaround time (TAT) for results, and disproportionate testing burden on labs, among others. Remote and hard-to-reach terrains continue to pose a severe threat to the success of scale-up efforts.

In Nigeria, transport was conducted through non-standard, parallel systems, leading to long turnaround times and a need for more visibility. The lack of a standardized sample referral network led to the setting up of a National Integrated Specimen Referral Network (NISRN) – established by the Nigeria Ministry of Health with donor support – it is a cost-effective system currently being implemented by GHSC-PSM using third-party logistics (3PLs) providers to transport specimens from collection centers to testing laboratories.

Integrated Specimen Referral Network (ISRN): Transporting clinical specimens combines different samples (viral load, early infant diagnosis, tuberculosis, malaria testing specimen). The transportation combines from the facilities or hubs where the tests cannot be done to the facilities where the samples are tested, and the results are returned to the facilities where the specimen originated. Kebede, Fonjungo, Tibesso, Shrivastava, Nkengasong, Kenyon, and Ayana (2016), in their study of referral networks in Angola, said that health management authority mapped out all specimen-referring sites, specimen types, and linkages to laboratories where tests would be performed. This was primarily along regional boundaries, and the mapping was crucial in establishing a memorandum of understanding with all stakeholders. The appointed third party (instead of laboratory personnel) transported all samples and results to referring facilities enrolled in the program.

The vision of NISRN is to support the establishment of a cost-effective, efficient, safe, and secure specimen referral and storage system that enables patients to access quality laboratory testing, irrespective of their location in Nigeria. Implementing these lofty ideals is managed through an organization guiding third-party logistics (3PL) vendors with the necessary training, tools, and personnel to gather and provide diagnostic clinical samples from health facilities to various testing laboratories across Nigeria. The responsibility of the 3PL includes the return of results from testing laboratories to the originating health facilities where hardcopy results are needed. However, in the last nine months, hardcopy results returned have reduced to about 25%, where 75% of the viral load results are now returned electronically through the remote sample login (RSL) system. The advantage of this is the quick TAT of results and cutting the cost of operating an integrated specimen referral network.

According to the African Society of Laboratory Medicine (2016), with a well-functioning specimen transportation system, the following trends should be apparent when reviewing the national ART program indicators:

- An increased volume of specimens was collected and tested over time.
- A shorter turnaround time (TAT) returns to the collecting facility for results.

- Fewer specimen rejections at laboratories, as specimens are transported appropriately and promptly.
- More health centers were offering antiretroviral therapy (ART) services because an efficient specimen transportation system encourages decentralization of services.
- Faster ART initiation for patients, as results are returned quickly and consistently.
- A reduced loss to follow-up.

According to Kiyaga, Sendagire, Joseph, McConnell, Grosz, Narayan, and Musinguzi (2013), Uganda attempted to scale up the uptake of early infants' diagnosis (EID) samples from which only 35% of samples were assayed due to sample transportation challenges which varied from facility to facility because of the different transportation methods that were used. A pilot study carried out showed that by using a hub network system, there was an increase from 35% to 51% for sample analysis, and the cost was reduced by 62% while turnaround time was reduced by 47% (Kiyaga et al., … & Musinguzi, 2013). The reduced TAT is in line with the report of the evaluation carried out by the Health, Economics, Finance, and Development Consortium (HEFDC, 2020) of Kenya, contracted by the Global Fund to evaluate the performance of NiSRN in 2020, which had this to say:

Put differently, the average sample referral cost in a non-NISRN-covered facility is approximately 4.5 times that of a NISRN-covered facility.

In establishing a referral network for CD4 clinical samples in Haiti, several facilities accessing CD4 testing for the patients increased from 27 to 113 (315%), the testing volume also improved by an average of 76%, and an increase in the number of people placed on antiretroviral therapy increased to about 182% (Louis et al., … & Balajee, 2015). Samples transfer network design resembles supply chain network design (SCND). The supply chain network design decides the structure of the chain and the accompanying cost and its performance (Farahani et al., 2014). Various decisions, such as the number, size, and location of facilities in the supply chain, are essential to the network design. Again, Simchi-Levi and Kaminsky (2004) considered SCND the primary and essential step for decreasing or increasing the costs and profits of the chains. Strategic, tactical, and operational decisions are involved in designing an efficient supply chain network.

Nigeria's non-existence of a standardized referral system for clinical samples has been identified as a critical causative factor for in-country laboratory capacity underutilization. The diagnostic landscape was characterized by multiple models of clinical sample transfer mechanisms with resultant inefficiencies such as high costs, long turnaround time (TAT) for results, and disproportionate testing burden on labs. Remote and hard-to-reach terrains severely threatened the success of scale-up efforts. The conventional supply chain network design has an operational decision to fulfill customers' demands, price, and provide services. The tactical decisions are hinged on the amount of flow, transportation among the SC's facilities, transportation mode among the SC's facilities, inventory volume and type in SC's facilities, amount, and type of purchase from contracted providers, and the information technology for knowledge management.

1.2 Providing Care and Treatment Services to Clients Identified as Infected with HIV

After South Africa and India, Nigeria has the third-largest number of people living with HIV/AIDS (PLWHA) in the world (2 to 3.2 million) (National Agency for the Control of AIDS, n.d.). The World Health Organization (WHO) 2016 updated its guidelines, which recommended that ART be started for all persons living with HIV at any CD4 cell level and regardless of WHO clinical stage. Nigerian authorities followed these recommendations for adults and adolescents. (strong recommendation, moderate-quality evidence). The strategy ensures that more people living with HIV have access to ART and can live a meaningful life as the disease is kept in check by the treatment.

While on treatment, Nigeria also follows the laboratory guideline in the monitoring of patients that routine viral load monitoring can be carried out at six months, at the 12-month mark, and then, if the patient is stable on ART, every 12-month mark after that to align with regular monitoring and evaluation reporting. (WHO, 2016). The overarching objective is that with treatment progressing well, viral suppression should be achieved for less than 1000 copies/ml. When failure occurs, a change of regimen would be contemplated.

1.3 Partnering with Third-Party Logistics Vendors to Transport Specimens

The services of third-party logistics (3PL) vendors in business setups have become crucial for the success of many organizations because of their cascading benefits. Managers are often overwhelmed with other essential services within the organizations that make 3PL very useful and helpful to the overall achievement of such institutions. They need to take care of the employees, the management of finance, marketing strategies, and ensuring the satisfaction of customers as their primary concerns. These have made such organizations engage the services of 3PLs for logistics services. For this study, the 3PL definition will be the one provided by Evangelista (2014, p. 66) that:

> *Transportation is the minimum activity included in third-party logistics, which are managed by a logistics service provider on behalf of a shipper. Furthermore, additional services like inventory management and storage can be incorporated within the offering, as well as information-related activities like tracking and tracing and value-added supply chain activities, including secondary assembly and product installation.*

The analysis carried out by Aguezzoul (2014) using 67 published between 1994–2013 reveals that the selection of third-party logistics vendors is crucial, and this depends on the region or country, industrial sector, the logistics activity to be outsourced, and the cost implication. As regards their selection, 11 key components were identified, but the cost criterion is the most widely influencing factor, followed by relationship services and the quality of services provided. These factors equally played out during the selection of the 3PLs engaged in operating the specimen referral network in Nigeria that started on March 1, 2018. Maloni and Carter (2006) studied three critical indicators for engaging 3PL services and other outsourcing needs. These are service improvement, cost reduction, and the organization's desire to focus on the core service area. Leuschner, Carter,

Goldsby, and Rogers (2014) said that enhancing performance can be accomplished by setting up a collaborative and relational structure.

The UNAIDS 95-95-95 strategy indicates that by the year 2030, 95% of people should be able to know their HIV status through testing; 95% of people who know their HIV-positive status should be placed on antiretroviral (ARV) drugs, and the 95% of those placed on treatment should have viral load suppression with less than 1000copies per ml (UNAIDS, 2020). Sample transport is now conducted through a standardized system organized by the Government of Nigeria, supported by the PEPFAR and the Global Fund and managed by the Global Health Supply Chain Procurement Supply Management (GHSC-PSM) and works closely with key stakeholders in Nigeria to carry out clinical samples from about 3000 sample collection centers referred to as spokes.

This study aims to evaluate the impact of NiSRN on achieving the third 95 of UNAIDS' 95-95-95 targets in Nigeria.

2 Methodology

The study employed descriptive methodologies to assess HIV viral load testing in Nigeria before NiSRN was implemented. Data on the annual volumes of viral load and early infant diagnosis (EID) samples transported across the 36 states and the Federal Capital Territory from 2018 to 2022 were collected. The samples were assayed at Polymerase Chain Reaction (PCR) laboratories, and viral load suppression rates were reviewed.

The NiSRN Information Management System (NiMS) collects information about the samples transported daily from the healthcare facilities to the hubs or the PCR laboratories (Fig. 1). All the PCR laboratories are linked to the National Laboratory Information Management System (LIMS), where all data regarding the volume of samples analyzed

Fig. 1. NiSRN Information Management System (NiMS) Dashboard

the viral load suppression rate, and the failed assays (Fig. 2). Information gathered from these two platforms is analyzed using the Microsoft Excel tool to arrive at the outcome reported in the result section. Graphs were plotted using the data to lead into the discussion segment of the study.

Fig. 2. The National Laboratory Information Management System (LIMS) Dashboard

3 Result

The number of specimens transported increased from 782,077 viral load samples in FY19 to 975,704 in FY20, 1,396,170 in FY21, and 1,761,060 in FY22, as provided visually in Fig. 3.

The viral load coverage and the suppression rate show a remarkable increase in trend, where coverage was 63% in FY19 and rose steadily to 97% in FY22. Similarly, the suppression rate of 85% in FY19 progressed steadily to 96% in FY22, as seen in Fig. 4 below.

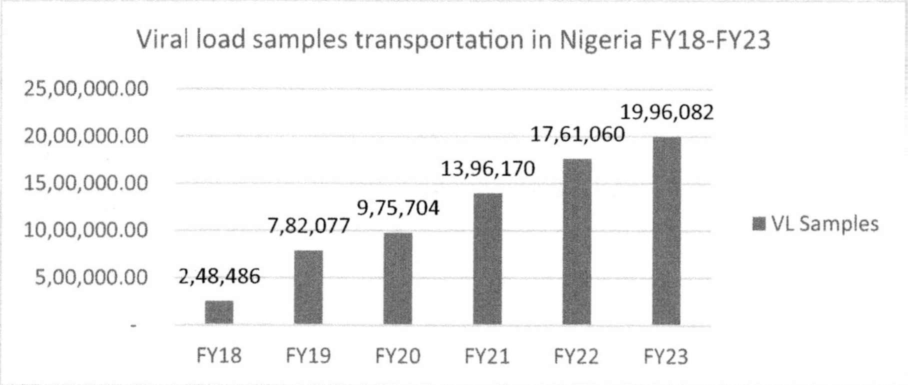

Fig. 3. Viral Load Samples Transportation in Nigeria 2018–2023

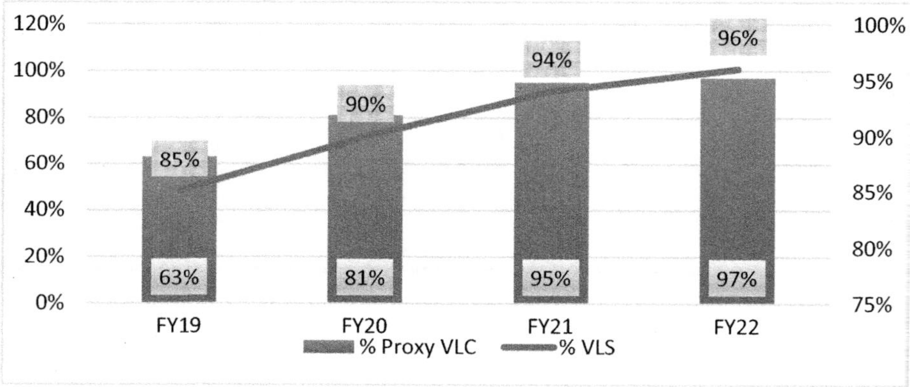

Fig. 4. Improvement in the viral load suppression Rate

4 Discussion

4.1 The Number of Viral Load Specimens Transported for Analysis

In line with the UNAIDS 95-95-95, it is expected that people who are placed on treatment must have their viral low count done at the basement (when placed on ART) and six months after that before an annual viral load analysis to determine if the client is responding to treatment or not. With the implementation of NiSRN, many healthcare facilities found it easy to collect specimens from clients on ART for their viral load assessment, which was easier with NiSRN. This implies that fewer specimens get to the PCR laboratories for analysis, and with the analysis, it is possible to know the viral load level. Consequently, viral load suppression needs to be accounted for. NiSRN identified an unassayed backlog of specimens and relocated them to laboratories capable of prompt analysis.

The NiSRN system provided the platform the implementing partners used to send all the collected specimens from healthcare facilities to the testing laboratories. There is a visible increase in the number of available specimens because there is an avenue to send them to the testing labs, which, in many instances, are far away from the location of the collection.

4.2 Viral Load Coverage for Nigeria

Onotu, Odafe, Abiri, Debem, Dalhatu, et al. (2017) state that the Nigerian antiretroviral therapy (ART) program began in 2004 and is currently one of the biggest in Africa. The study showed that monitoring plasma viral load (VL) is the recommended method for keeping track of an ART patient's response and strengthening adherence. The ART guideline in Nigeria is based on the WHO recommendations adopted by the Federal Ministry of Health (WHO, 2004; FMOH, 2014). According to the UNAIDS country fact sheet, Nigeria has the fourth largest HIV epidemic in the world, with about 1.8 million people living with HIV (UNAIDS, 2020). The target for the country is to get viral load tests done for 95% of these 1.8 million clients. The country has been struggling to get to this target since 2018. In Fig. 4 above, the trend was 63% in fiscal year 19 (FY19), 81% in FY20, 95% in FY21 and 97% in FY22. The NiSRN operation started in fiscal year 19 (March 2018). The deployment of the integrated specimen referral network with a high focus on plasma viral load samples played a vital role in the positive progress recorded in Nigeria.

4.3 Improvement in Viral Load Suppression Rate

One of the indicators that shows a favourable response to the ART medication for those placed on antiretroviral drugs is the viral load suppression rate. The viral load suppression rate is described as a threshold of <1000 RNA copies/ml used to define suppressed viral load, while a patient on ART for about six months still with a threshold of >1000 RNA copies per ml is defined as non-suppressed viral load (Shiferaw et al., 2019). We have earlier mentioned that the United Nations AIDS, the Joint Program on HIV/AIDS, has established the third 95 of the 95-95-95 that those receiving ART should have HIV-RNA viral suppression (UNAIDS, 2014). Shiferaw et al. (2019), in their studies of viral load suppression rate in Ethiopia amongst children, discovered that there was a high rate of non-suppressed HIV viral load among children studied. They concluded that the odds of having a non-suppressed viral load were higher in NVP-based treatment users. Hence, comprehensive management and follow-up of children on ART and testing for resistance and viral load could help reduce the problem in advance. The data obtained for Nigeria in 2022 indicated a suppression rate of 96%, surpassing the UNAID target of 95 by 1%. However, when the target was 90-90-90, a study in Vietnam by Rangarajan et al. (2016) showed that Viral load suppression in the four provinces studied was 93% overall and ranged from 88% to 100%. This high suppression rate exceeds the UNAIDS 90-90-90 target.

5 Conclusion and Recommendation

5.1 NiSRN is a Collaborative Effort Between Stakeholders Nationwide

i. It is a fact that sample transportation involves several stakeholders, ranging from the facility personnel, where the samples are collected from the patients, the State Ministry of Health, Federal Ministry of Health, Implementing Partners, Funding Agencies, third-party logistics companies, and others. To achieve the above result, some engagements are done daily between the facility focal persons and the specimen pick-up personnel. Monthly critical performance indicators review meetings between the management of third-party logistics companies, the agency managing the specimen referral network, and the quarterly stakeholders meeting to review and strategize for improvement. Stakeholders' engagement has fostered a cordial relationship between all stakeholders. Segarra-Ona, Peiro-Signes, and Verma (2020) captured that the new competitive environment urges companies to move from what is called the "company-centric" value creation to the "co-creation of value." This idea necessitated the stakeholders' collaboration in co-creating NiSRN and operationalization. In essence, any group or individual that has the potential to influence or be impacted by the accomplishment of the organization's goals is considered a stakeholder.

ii. NiSRN has played a crucial role in surpassing UNAIDS' third 95 target. UNAIDS unveiled a new set of ambitious goals in December 2020: By 2025, 95% of all individuals living with HIV will know their status, 95% of those diagnosed with the virus will receive continuous antiretroviral therapy and 95% of those on therapy will have viral suppression (Frescura et al., 2022) as a strategy to end AIDS by 2030 (United Nations, n.d). Since then, all countries that receive support from funding agencies have strived to meet these targets, Nigeria not being an exception. This continued the country's commitment to the 2014 Australia declaration by UNAIDS for the 90-90-90 strategies by 2020. Since 2021, Nigeria has been consistent in its drive to meet the UNAIDS targets of reducing the burden of HIV through various mechanisms. The efforts in setting up a national integrated specimen referral network have paid off handsomely. In 2021, a 90% suppression rate was achieved. In 2022, the suppression rate was 94%, while in 2023, it reached 96%, meeting the 95% target set by the UNAIDS. Achieving the 95-95-95 targets would have benefits associated with personal advantages for HIV-positive individuals, such as improved quality of life and lower rates of illness and death. Everyone has an equal right to a healthy life, including those who are living with HIV. As such, everyone should have access to ART. Ensuring access to HIV medication for PLHIV is a concrete action in reducing inequities within the global AIDS response to fulfill further the rights to health for all, as described by Eisinger, Dieffenbach, & Fauci (2019) and Eisinger & Fauci (2018) in Cane (2022), in their paper.

iii. NiSRN should be continually supported by PEPFAR & GF. Currently, Nigeria receives substantial support from the donor communities for her HIV programs. Olakunde and Ndukwe (2015) agreed that HIV financing in Nigeria is heavily donor-dependent. Most HIV funding in Nigeria comes from the US President's Emergency Plan for AIDS Relief (PEPFAR), with the USAID, Centre of Disease Control and

Prevention, and Department of Defense as the vehicles of implementation through several implementation partners. January 24, 2018, the United States Embassy in Nigeria reported that since 2003, the US government, through PEPFAR, has invested more than $85 billion in the global HIV/AIDS response, with Nigeria accounting for more than $6 billion (Nigeria US Embassy, 2018). The Global Fund has made a similar investment in the HIV program in Nigeria, as support for NiSRN also comes from the Global Fund. This study suggests that the funding agencies should continue this support as Nigeria is still in the woods economically.

iv. The Nigerian Government should prioritize the development of sustainable strategies and innovations that will keep the NiSRN service in place even after the support from the development partners is no more. It is a fact that one day, the support from PEPFAR and the Global fund will cease, as can be seen from the recent dwindling commitment of funds. Health is wealth, and understandably, how a country finances its healthcare system is a crucial determinant of the health of its citizenry (Olakunde, 2012). Examination of the various healthcare funding mechanisms revealed tax revenue, out-of-pocket payments, donor funding, and health insurance as the available sources (Obansa & Orimisan, 2013; Olakunde, 2012). This study encourages the Nigerian Government to intentionally provide funding for sample referral services by direct budget provision, donation by organizations as social responsibility services, or in-built minimal percentages into the laboratory reagent revolving fund system dedicated to specimen referral services. This last point agrees with the argument of Akintoyese, Olusegun, Albert, Joseph, and Rasak (2020) that alternative funding for healthcare through the community is necessary for achieving health for all.

v. Other countries struggling to meet the UNAIDS third 95 can learn from Nigeria's experience and implement similar initiatives. Some countries have made significant progress in achieving the UNAIDS 95-95-95. This progress needs to be maintained and improved upon if ending HIV in 2030 is to be achieved. According to Boakaye and Adjorlolo (2023), Ghana is struggling to meet this target when they mentioned that while Ghana has made significant strides in its HIV/AIDS response, achieving the 95-95-95 targets is a challenging yet realistic goal. Gulf Cooperation Council Countries (GCCC), according to Awaidy, Ghazy, and Mahomed (2023), have made great strides toward fulfilling the 95-95-95 targets, but the interim 2025 overall UNAIDS targets still need to be met.

Limitation

- This study could not disaggregate patients on treatment tested more than once a year.
- The data used for the studies are mainly from the 17 PCR labs supported by PEPFAR or the Global Fund. Data from the private sector healthcare providing HIV viral load testing was not part of this study.
- This study did not account for samples that may have been transported outside the NiSRN mechanism.

Acknowledgments. We want to thank the Federal Ministry of Health (FMOH) Medical Laboratory Services Division for overseeing the NiSRN operation in the country. We equally thank and appreciate USAID and the Global Fund for their support in developing and operating the NISRN in Nigeria. We also acknowledge with gratitude the 17 PCR laboratories in Nigeria that provided bimonthly logistics management information that served as the primary source of data analyzed during this study. Similarly, we appreciate that CHAI provides technical support for managing the National Laboratory Information Management System (LIMS) that warehouses the data from all the PCR laboratories in Nigeria supported through the PEPFAR and the Global Fund Mechanisms. We duly appreciate the staff of the GHSC-PSM Laboratory Logistics Advisors all over the country and the Central team of the Laboratory and Logistics Department that coordinates the NiSRN affairs, especially Rosemary Ekpeh and her team.

Interests and Financial Support. The opinions and findings in this research are the author's own, and they may not necessarily reflect those of the USAID or GHSC-PSM. This work has no financial inducement or support from anywhere and is with no conflict of interest.

References

ASLM. http://www.aslm.org/resource-centre/hiv-viral-load-testing/aids-2016-aslm-satellite-session-scaling%E2%80%90up-access-to-hiv-viral-load-testing/. AIDS 2016 ASLM Satellite Session: Scaling-up Access to HIV Viral Load Testing – 20 July 2016. Accessed 25 Jan 2024

Aguezzoul, A.: Third-party logistics selection problem: a literature review on criteria and methods. Omega **49**(1), 69–78 (2014)

Akintoyese, O.I., Olusegun, O.J., Albert, A.O., Joseph, O.E., Rasak, B.: Advancing alternative health care financing through effective community partnership: a necessity for universal health coverage in Nigeria. Cogent Soc. Sci. **6**(1), 1776946 (2020)

Awaidy, S.A., Ghazy, R.M., Mahomed, O.: Progress of the Gulf Cooperation Council (GCC) countries towards achieving the 95–95-95 UNAIDS targets: a review. J. Epidemiol. Glob. Health **13**(3), 397–406 (2023)

Awofala, A.A., Ogundele, O.E.: HIV epidemiology in Nigeria. Saudi J. Biol. Sci. **25**(4), 697–703 (2018)

Balogun, A.S.: HIV/AIDS epidemic in the history of Nigeria, 1986–2007. J. Hist. Soc. Nigeria **19**(2010), 166–176 (2014)

Boakye, D.S., Adjorlolo, S.: Achieving the UNAIDS 95-95-95 treatment target by 2025 in Ghana: a myth or a reality? Glob. Health Action **16**(1), 2271708 (2023)

Boyd, A.T., et al.: Expanding access to HIV services during the COVID-19 pandemic—Nigeria, 2020. AIDS Res. Ther. **18**(1), 1–8 (2021)

Cane, T.: Working with HIV today. J. Pract. Teach. Learn. **19**(1), 1–2 (2022)

Dalhatu, I., et al.: Outcomes of Nigeria's HIV/AIDS treatment program for patients initiated on antiretroviral treatment between 2004–2012. PloS One, **11**(11), e0165528 (2017)

Eisinger, R.W., Fauci, A.S.: Ending the HIV/AIDS pandemic. Emerg. Infect. Dis. **24**(3), 413 (2018)

Eisinger, R.W., Dieffenbach C.W., Fauci, A.S.: HIV viral load and transmissibility of HIV infection: undetectable equals untransmittable. JAMA **321**(5), 451–452 (2019). https://doi.org/10.1001/jama.2018.21167

Entonu, P.E., Agwale, S.M.: A review of the epidemiology, prevention, and treatment of Human Immunodeficiency Virus in Nigeria. Braz. J. Infect. Dis. **11**(6), 579–590 (2007). https://doi.org/10.1590/S1413-86702007000600011

Evangelista, P.: Environmental sustainability practices in the transport and logistics service industry: an exploratory case study investigation. Res. Transp. Bus. Manag. **12**, 63–72 (2014)

Farahani, R.Z., Rezapour, S., Drezner, T., Fallah, S.: Competitive supply chain network design: an overview of classifications, models, solution techniques and applications. Omega **45**, 92–118 (2014)

Faruna, T., Akintunde, E., Odelola, B.: Leveraging private sector transportation/logistics services to improve Nigeria's National Integrated Specimen Referral Network. Bus. Manag. Dyn. **8**(7), 8–16 (2019)

Fauci, A.S.: An HIV vaccine is essential for ending the HIV/AIDS pandemic. JAMA **318**(16), 1535–1536 (2017)

Fauci, A.S., Marston, H.D.: Ending the HIV–AIDS pandemic—follow the Science. N. Engl. J. Med. **373**(23), 2197–2199 (2015)

FMOH. Integrated National Guidelines for HIV Prevention Treatment and Care. In: National AIDS/STIs Control Programme, editor. Abuja: FMOH, Abuja (2014)

Frescura, L., et al.: Achieving the 95 95 95 targets for all: a pathway to ending AIDS. PLoS ONE **17**(8), e0272405 (2022). https://doi.org/10.1371/journal.pone.0272405

HEFDC (2020). https://hefdcgroup.com/. National Integrated Specimen Referral Network Evaluation: hefdcgroup.com. Accessed 18 Jan 2024

Joint United Nations Programme on HIV/AIDS (UNAIDS): Country fact sheet: HIV and AIDS estimates. Geneva: UNAIDS (2020)

Joloba, M., et al.: Strengthening the tuberculosis specimen referral network in Uganda: the role of public-private partnerships. J. Infectious Dis. **213**(suppl_2), S41–S46 (2016)

Kebede, Y., et al.: Improved specimen-referral system and increased access to quality laboratory services in Ethiopia: the role of the public-private partnership. J. Infectious Dis. **213**(suppl_2), S59–S64 (2016)

Kiyaga, C., et al.: Uganda's new national laboratory sample transport system: a successful model for improving access to diagnostic services for early infant HIV diagnosis and other programs. PLoS One, **8**(11), e78609 (2013)

Leuschner, R., Carter, C.R., Goldsby, T.J., Rogers, Z.S.: Third-party logistics: a meta-analytic review and investigation of its impact on performance. J. Supply Chain Manag. **50**(1), 21–43 (2014)

Louis, F.J., et al.: Specimen referral network to rapidly scale up CD4 testing: the hub and spoke model for Haiti. J. AIDS & Clin. Res. **6**(8), 1000488 (2015)

Lydon, P., Raubenheimer, T., Arnot-Krüger, M., Zaffran, M.: Outsourcing vaccine logistics to the private sector: the evidence and lessons learned from the Western Cape Province in South Africa. Vaccine **33**(29), 3429–3434 (2015)

Maloni, M.J., Carter, C.R.: Opportunities for research in third-party logistics. Transp. J. **45**(2), 23–38 (2006)

NACA. https://naca.gov.ng/nigeria-prevalence-rate/ Nigeria prevalence rates. Accessed 07 Sept 2023

National Agency for the Control of AIDS (NACA). https://naca.gov.ng/anti-retroviral-therapy, Antiretroviral Therapy. Accessed 15 Oct 2023

Obansa, S.A.J., Orimisan, A.: Health care financing in Nigeria: prospects and challenges. Mediterr. J. Soc. Sci. **4**(1), 221–236 (2013)

Ofem, B.I.: A review of the criteria for defining urban areas in Nigeria. J. Hum. Ecol. **37**(3), 167–171 (2012)

Okoroiwu, H.U., et al.: Thirty-five years (1986–2021) of HIV/AIDS in Nigeria: bibliometric and scoping analysis. AIDS Res. Ther. **19**(1), 1–15 (2022)

Olakunde, B.O.: Public health care financing in Nigeria: which way forward. Ann. Nigerian Med. **6**(1), 4 (2012)

Olakunde, B.O., Ndukwe, C.D.: Improved domestic funding enhances the sustainability of the HIV/AIDS response in Nigeria. Ann. Glob. Health **81**(5), 684–688 (2015)

Onovo, A.A., et al.: Estimation of HIV prevalence and burden in Nigeria: a Bayesian predictive modeling study. E Clin. Med. **62**, 102098 (2023). https://doi.org/10.1016/j.eclinm.2023.102098. PMID: 37538543; PMCID: PMC10393599

Rangarajan, S., et al.: Factors associated with HIV viral load suppression on antiretroviral therapy in Vietnam. J. Virus Eradication **2**(2), 94–101 (2016)

Sangadi, G.E., Muhereza, A., Aloyo, J., Karamagi, E., Rahimzai, M.: Addressing the 3rd 90 gaps through integrated health delivery camps in 4 health facilities in Nwoya District Uganda (2017). https://www.popline.org/node/666978. Accessed 01 Nov 2023

Shiferaw, M.B., et al.: Viral suppression rate among children tested for HIV viral load at the Amhara Public Health Institute, Bahir Dar Ethiopia. BMC Infectious Dis. **19**(419), 1–6 (2019)

Simchi-Levi, D., Kaminsky, P.: Managing the Supply Chain: The Definitive Guide for the Business Professional. Irwin McGraw-Hill, Boston (2004)

The Nigeria US Embassy. https://ng.usembassy.gov/pepfar/. Accessed 09 Jan 2024

UNAIDS (n.d.). What is World AIDS Day? https://www.unaids.org/en/World_AIDS_Day. Accessed 7 Sept 2023

UNAIDS (2014) UNAIDS. 95-95-95 An Ambitious Treatment Target to help end the AIDS epidemic. Geneva, Switzerland 2020. https://www.unaids.org/sites/default/files/media_asset/201506_JC2743_Understanding_FastTrack_en.pdf

UNAIDS (2020) UNAIDS. 95-95-95 An Ambitious Treatment Target to help end the AIDS epidemic. Geneva, Switzerland 2020. https://www.unaids.org/sites/default/files/media_asset/201506_JC2743_Understanding_FastTrack_en.pdf

United Nations: Transforming our world: the 2030 Agenda for Sustainable Development. Accessed 9 Jan 2024

Voyles, J., et al.: Moving beyond too little, too late: managing emerging infectious diseases in wild populations requires international policy and partnerships. EcoHealth **12**(3), 404–407 (2015)

World Health Organization. Scaling up antiretroviral therapy in resource-limited settings (2003 REVISION), pp. 9–10. WHO, Geneva (2004)

World Health Organization (2016). https://apps.who.int/iris/bitstream/handle/10665/208825/97892?sequence=1 Consolidated guidelines on the use of antiretroviral drugs for treating and preventing HIV infection: recommendations for a public health approach. Accessed 25 Aug 2023

World Health Organization. Consolidated guidelines on the use of antiretroviral drugs for treating and preventing HIV infection: recommendations for a public health approach. World Health Organization (2016). https://apps.who.int/iris/bitstream/handle/10665/208825/97892?sequence=1

Zwetyenga, J.S.L.G., et al.: Laboratory core capacities to be improved in two Central Asian countries through addressing national sample referral mechanisms. PANORAMA **23**(1), 4–7 (2018)

Challenges the Members of Bidding and Negotiating Committees Face During the Public Procurement Processes

Georgios Koligiannis(✉), Maria Drakaki, and Panagiotis Tzionas

International Hellenic University, Thermi, Greece
gkoligiannis@ihu.edu.gr

Abstract. Prior research has explored procurement performance in public entities. However, there seems to be a gap in the challenges members of the procurement committees face during the bidding process. During the bidding processes, procurement committees have to cope with several challenges to evaluate the offers submitted by the economic operators. In order to explore the challenges these committees face, a survey questionnaire was designed and sent to personnel who have been members of negotiation and procurement committees in the public sector. The survey questionnaire gathered data from experts in the field in Greece to provide solutions to public entities that could help the members of procurement committees become more flexible and effective in their processes. Greece has recently modified the procurement rules that public organisations have to abide by. The study found that the negotiation and procurement committee members feel less stress when they have more field experience and knowledge of the procurement laws. The study also revealed that the members of the committees face more challenges when the bidding documents are not precise enough for the potential economic operators, creating risks in the performance of the process.

Keywords: Bidding · challenges · public procurement · suppliers

1 Introduction

Public procurement aims to provide items and services to the public according to the national state's procurement laws and directives promulgated. The public procurement framework in Greece changed in 2016, and several changes have been applied compared to the previous procurement law. This outcome led to several changes in all the stages of the public procurement processes. However, several challenges still exist, and the members of the bidding and negotiating committees face them every day as they are the organ that evaluates the bids and proposes to the contracting authorities if a contract should be assigned to an economic operator or the process should be cancelled or cancelled and repeated with the same terms or with modified terms. The aforementioned highlights the importance of this stage of the procurement process as the members of the bidding and negotiating committees have to evaluate in depth all the bidding documents submitted by the economic operators according to the terms and conditions of

I. Kostavelis et al. (Eds.): ICSC 2024, CCIS 2110, pp. 309–323, 2025.
https://doi.org/10.1007/978-3-031-69344-1_23

the contracting authority's notice. This paper will focus on the specific stage of the procurement process. It will add to the contemporary literature by presenting the challenges faced by the members of the bidding and negotiating committees in public procurement processes and the consequences of these challenges in the outcome. The authors also aim to propose measures to overcome the existing challenges and measures that could help the members of the bidding and negotiation committees collaborate more effectively with other departments involved in the public procurement processes. In order to tackle the aforementioned issues, the authors will try to explore essential concepts such as personnel training, time constraints, limited expertise, and the existing procurement framework.

The research paper is structured as follows. Section 2 presents recent literature on public procurement processes. Section 3 explains the conceptual model conceived by the authors to answer the research questions. Section 4 describes the methodology applied and how the primary data were collected. Section 5 demonstrates the research results. In Sect. 6, the authors discuss the findings. Section 7 presents the limitations of the research project, and the authors conclude in Sect. 8.

2 Literature Review

The European Commission states that more than 250.000 public buyers spend 14% of GDP on infrastructure projects, services, and products [3]. Consequently, public procurement affects a nation's economy as growth and investment are boosted, unemployment decreases, and public funding is used. Directives 2014/24/EU and 2014/25/EU were promulgated by the European Commission to create a productive environment for the bidding processes [2]. Public procurement managers use competitive bidding as the usual process [5]. According to the Greek procurement law, two awarding criteria exist in public procurement processes: the most economically advantageous tender and the lowest price. Prior scientific research has highlighted that severe problems in an organisation's operations could result from disruptions in the supply of services and products due to incorrect decisions about supplier selection [7]. Recent research has also investigated public procurement initiatives during the era of COVID-19 in Greece [6]. The authors above found that for effective public procurement in future force majeure events, the best way is to sign framework agreements with more than one economic operator, implement central procurement, and utilise the newly established Public Buyers Community in the European Union. Prior research conducted by Aparicio-Arias and Moreno [1] investigated the factors that negatively affect public procurement of relief items during disasters. As mentioned above, in their study focused on Chile and New Zealand, the authors found that pressure on procurement teams, corruption, competition, price variation, supplier and market restrictions, lack of proper technology, and the centralism of public procurement structure negatively affect public procurement. The risk of corruption in public procurement has also been highlighted by several authors [4, 8, 9, 11]. For instance, assigning a high weight to a criterion that solely one potential economic operator could meet to favour him is a typical corruption case. Corruption in public procurement could be mitigated by enhancing official training, according to Gnoffo [4]. However, to the authors' knowledge, no prior scientific research has tried to investigate the challenges that the members of the bidding and negotiating committees face in public procurement processes.

3 Conceptual Framework

To tackle the research aims and present the relationships among the main concepts that structure the project under research, the authors designed a conceptual model as presented in Fig. 1. More precisely, to the authors' knowledge, the members of the bidding and negotiation committees face several challenges in the public procurement processes, including but not limited to lack of expertise, time constraints, and unclear evaluation criteria. Several other challenges exist, and the current project aims to investigate them in depth. These challenges affect decision-making and the efficiency of the process, which aims to procure the items/ services of the best quality and in a cost-effective way. An excellent way to overcome some challenges is to improve the collaboration between these committees and the departments involved in the public procurement processes, such as the end users and the legal and finance departments.

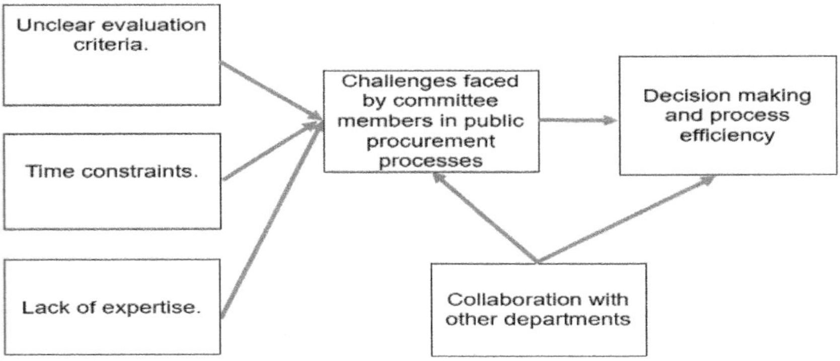

Fig. 1. Conceptual framework (Conceived by the authors)

4 Data/Methodology

The study has an exploratory nature as the authors aim to investigate the challenges the evaluation committees face during the process and propose strategies that could help them improve their actions. The authors in the methodology used a case study as the investigation refers to the public procurement processes conducted under the Greek procurement framework. In order to gather primary data and add to the existing scientific literature, the author designed a survey questionnaire containing the questions presented in Table 1. The questionnaire contained multiple-choice, Likert scale, and open-ended questions to capture respondents' experience on the project under research. It should also be mentioned that the survey questionnaire was designed to allow the respondents to answer only 5 to 10 min to attract more respondents. The survey questionnaire was designed with Google Forms, a free online software that helped the authors gather data from people across Greece. The questionnaire was e-mailed to procurement managers in the Greek public sector and people with prior experience as members of evaluation and negotiation committees in public procurement processes. In order to increase the sample, the questionnaire was also shared on Linkedin for ten days between 15 March and 29 March. Overall, 25 answers were collected. The authors explained to the respondents that all the data collected would be solely used for scientific purposes. Anonymity was provided to them to help the respondents express their point of view freely without bias, which complies with the research ethics. It should also be mentioned that no incentives were provided to the participants of the survey questionnaire, which complied with the standard research ethics. The authors used descriptive statistics to present the research findings and help the readers easily understand them. The authors also used the qualitative

Table 1. Questions formulated for the survey questionnaire (Created by the authors)

Question No	Description	Type of question
No1	How many years of experience do you have in public procurement processes?	Multiple choice
No2	To what extent do you think the current public procurement regulations are clear and easy to understand?	Likert-scale
No3	How often do you encounter difficulties in interpreting the bidding documents provided by economic operators (suppliers)?	Likert-scale
No4	Which of the following challenges are most common during the evaluation of the bids?	Multiple choice
No5	How satisfied are you with the level of training provided to committee members on public procurement processes?	Likert-scale
No6	How frequently do you experience delays in the public procurement processes due to factors outside of the committees' control?	Likert-scale
No7	What are the main consequences of these delays in the public procurement process?	Multiple choice
No8	Describe the biggest challenge you face when serving on a bidding and negotiation committee in public procurement processes	Open-ended
No9	Do you have any suggestions for improvements to the public procurement process that would make it easier and more efficient for committee members to fulfil their duties?	Open-ended
No10	How can bidding and negotiation committes collaborate more effectively with other departments involved in public procurement (e.g., finance, legal, and technical specialists)?	Open-ended

data collected from questions 9 to 11 of the survey questionnaire to highlight the main themes and propose the best strategies to the contracting authorities and policymakers participating in public procurement processes (Fig. 2).

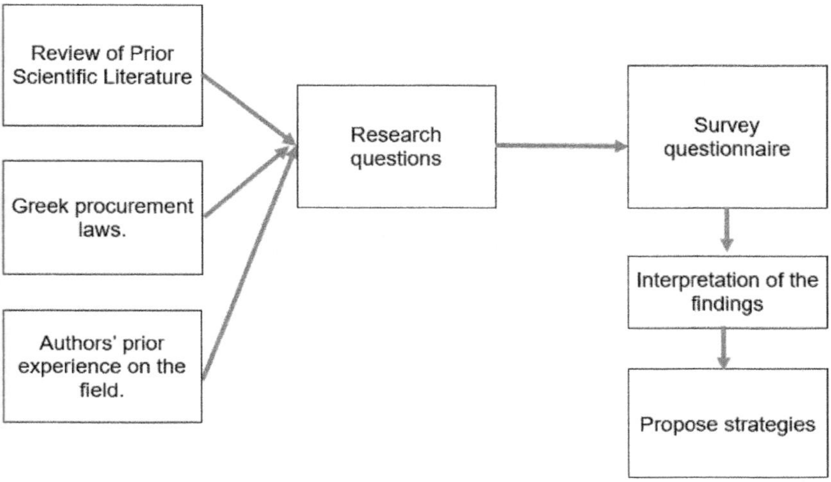

Fig. 2. Research strategy (Created by the authors)

5 Results/Findings

As illustrated in Fig. 3, 20% of the survey respondents have more than 15 years of experience in public procurement processes, 24% of them have 10 to 15 years of experience, 16% of them have between 5 to 10 years of experience, and the rest have less than 5 years experience in the field. The high proportion of experienced professionals who participated in the study highlights the validity of the research findings that policymakers could use.

As seen in Fig. 4, 68% of the survey respondents believe that public procurement regulations are clear and easy to understand. The remaining 32% strongly believe that they are not entirely clear.

The survey questionnaire results are pretty interesting in the Likert scale question, "How often do you encounter difficulties interpreting the bidding documents provided by the economic operators?". As seen in Fig. 5, 8% of the respondents answered always in every bidding process, 28% of the participants often, the majority of the survey respondents answered "often", and only 12% answered "rarely". It should also be mentioned that none of the respondents answered "never" in this question.

The survey respondents were also asked to select the most common challenge during the evaluation of the bids. As presented in the following pie chart, 34% of the respondents selected the "lack of clear evaluation criteria", 26% of them the "difficulty obtaining necessary information from the suppliers", and the rest 40% believed that the insufficient time for a thorough evaluation is a significant challenge (Fig. 6).

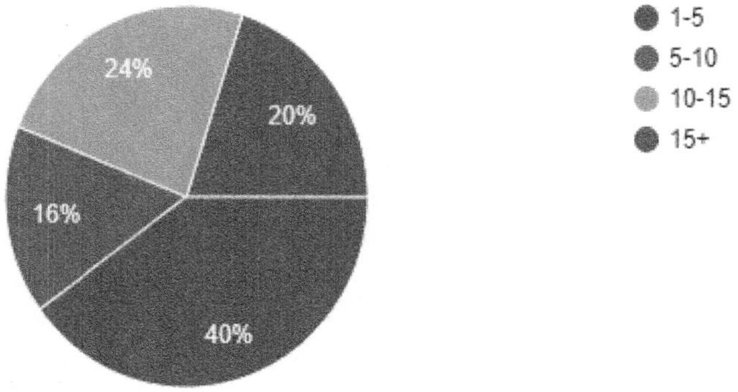

Fig. 3. Years of working experience (Created by the authors)

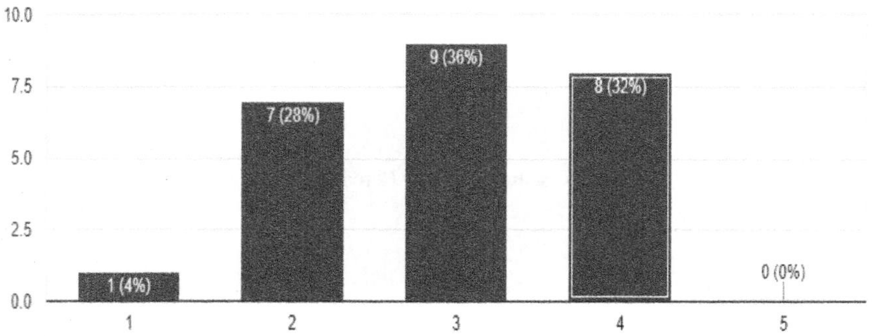

Fig. 4. To what extent do you think the current public procurement regulations are clear and easy to understand? (Created by the authors)

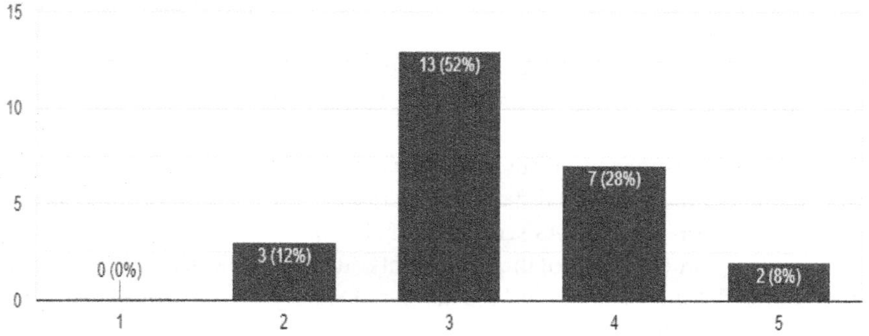

Fig. 5. How often do you encounter difficulties in interpreting the bidding documents provided by economic operators (suppliers)? (Created by the authors)

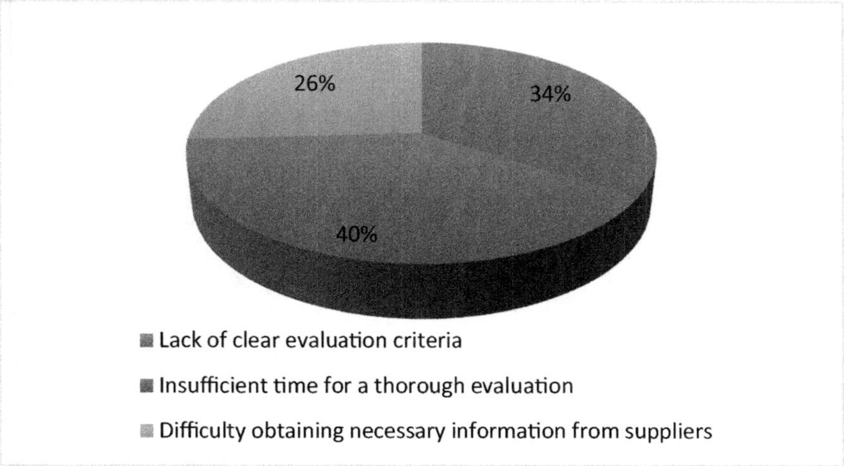

Fig. 6. Which challenges are most common during the evaluation of the bids? (Created by the authors)

The survey respondents were also asked to vote on how satisfied they were with the level of training provided to committee members on public procurement processes. As illustrated in Fig. 7, 16% of the respondents answered "very dissatisfied", 48% answered "dissatisfied", 28% answered "neutral", and the rest 8% answered "satisfied".

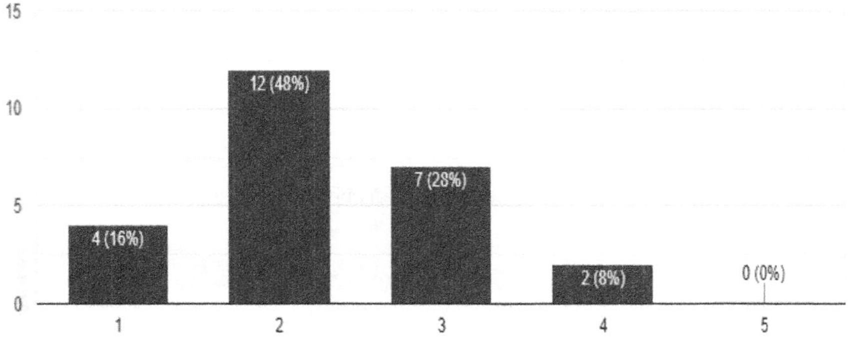

Fig. 7. How satisfied are you with the level of training provided to committee members on public procurement processes? (Created by the authors)

As illustrated in the following figure, the survey respondents were also asked to answer the following question: "How frequently do they experience delays in the public procurement processes due to factors outside of the committee's control?". As depicted in Fig. 8, 12% of the survey respondents answered "always", 44% answered "often", 28% answered "sometimes", and the rest 16% answered "rarely".

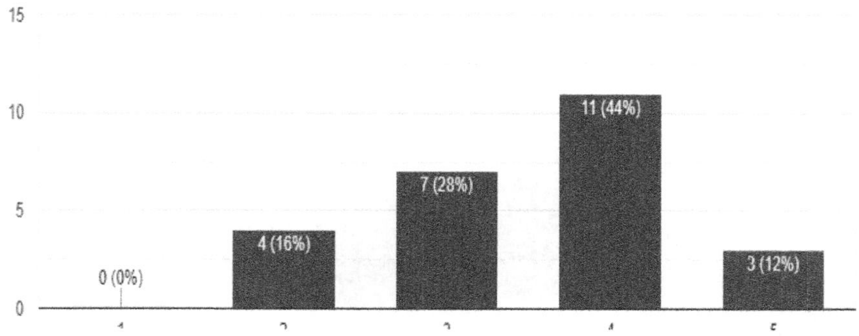

Fig. 8. How frequently do you experience delays in the public procurement processes due to factors outside of the committee's control? (Created by the authors)

As presented in the following pie chart, 60% of the survey respondents highlighted that the main consequence of delays in the public procurement processes due to factors outside of the committees' control led to project completion delays. 32% of the respondents chose "difficulty attracting qualified bidders" as the proper answer, and the remaining 8% responded "increased project costs" (Fig. 9).

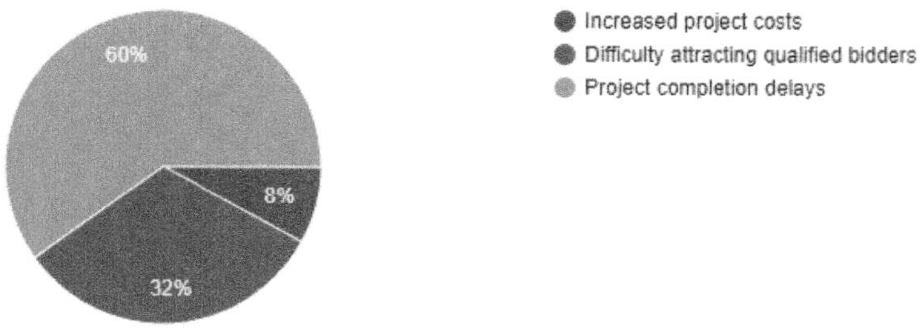

Fig. 9. What are the main consequences of delays in public procurement processes? (Created by the authors)

The primary quotes of the participants related to the question, "Describe the biggest challenge you face when serving on a bidding and negotiation committee in public procurement processes." are presented in Table 2.

Regarding the suggestions for improvements to the public procurement process that would make it easier and more efficient for committee members to fulfil their duties?, the participants voiced the views presented in Table 3.

Regarding how bidding and negotiation committees could collaborate more effectively with other departments involved in public procurement, the survey questionnaire respondents voiced the views presented in Table 4.

Table 2. Quotes retrieved from the participants in the question "Describe the biggest challenge you face when serving on a bidding and negotiation committee in public procurement processes." (Created by the authors)

Quotes	Theme identified
"Clarify the rules."	Define the terms and conditions
"Complete freedom of speaking one's mind"	Freedom of speaking
"The clear interpretation of the legislation regarding the extence of the clarifications that we could ask from the economic operators, especially when we face contradictory verdicts from the supreme legal authorities on this issue."	Interpretation of the legislation
"The process is often complex and requires careful planning and cooperation with other committee members. At the same time, compliance with the time constraints and procedures set by the legal framework governing fiscal contracts must be ensured. The evaluation and comparison of bids requires attention to detail and objectivity, as well as the ability to negotiate with other potential contractors without compromising the transparency of the process."	Constraints by the legal framework and the time
"Insufficient training and experience of committee members."	Insufficient training
"The biggest challenge is time constrains."	Time constraints
"People that are not willing to take initiatives. Also people are not willing to promote the procurement so in the end one or two companies are offering solutions so the price is high and the offerings are few."	No initiatives
"Time management"	Time constraints
"The successful completion of the process"	Completing the process successfully
"Unclear terms provided by the contracting authority and insufficient time for comprehensive evaluation of the bids."	Unclear terms and insufficient time
"Little flexibility in the requirements that actually lead to little if not only one choice. This cause plasmatic raise of the biding price."	Limited flexibility
"Limited time for the examination of the offers and complexity of the declarations"	Insufficient time

(*continued*)

Table 2. (*continued*)

Quotes	Theme identified
"Unclear Specifications & Requirements"	Unclear specifications
"In my point of view, the biggest challenge is optimal cooperation of committee members and the definition of mutually acceptable goals that will lead to a successful negotiation."	Optimal cooperation of the committee members
"Consensus between all members"	Optimal cooperation of the committee members
"The law"	Law restrictions

Table 3. Quotes were retrieved from the participants in the question, "What can be done to solve the challenges identified by the members of the bidding committees? (Created by the authors)

Quotes	Themes identified
"Extended training"	Better training
"Simplified toolbox (both digitally and regulatory)"	Simplified regulatory framework
"The reevaluation of the restrictions of the committee service (time), since I believe the ideal amount of time shall be 2 years. In terms of experience and efficiency, since in a period of 2 years usually there is not a repetition on the bidding subjects."	Reevaluation of the committees period
"Have a unique Database of providers"	Database of qualified suppliers
"Improvement in digital processes."	Improved digital processes
"Training programs for tender committee members can enhance their understanding of the procedures, laws and regulations governing public procurement, thus enhancing their ability to carry out their duties professionally."	Better training
"Two months express training of committee members before the commencement of their tasks."	Better training
"It should be processed exclusively by specialised personnel"	Specialised personnel
"Counter understaffing"	Counter understaffing

(*continued*)

Table 3. (*continued*)

Quotes	Themes identified
"Use of multicriteria decision making"	Using multicriteria decision-making
"Multi-faceted training of organisation's personnel to create a pool of efficient personnel who will ultimately form effective committees capable of addressing any challenge."	Better training in order to create a pool of efficient personnel
"Simplify the bidding documents to make it more attractive and easier for small and medium enterprises. Severe penalties for the unreliable providers in order to create an inner motivation for credibility"	Simplify the bidding documents
"more available time and training for committee members"	More time for the evaluation
"Establish a Feedback System"	Establishing a feedback system
"The clear definition of the specific terms of each procurement that are acceptable and the framework within each committee can operate, to fulfill their duty."	Defining the terms and conditions
"More Seminars & to become priority."	Better training

Table 4. How can bidding and negotiation committees collaborate more effectively with other departments involved in public procurement? (e.g., finance, legal, technical specialists?) (Created by the authors)

Quotes	Themes identified
"Open line of communication, development of an online tool of FAQ for the members with possibly a forum for showing and discussing case studies and solutions to possible scenarios"	Creating an online tool for FAQ
"A Parallel, to the bidding, transaction operational system could make the collaboration of those factors more efficient. That would not be public and could be used to automatise the communication procedures (eg, upload questions to the legal sector, technical spesificarions and receive the relevant answers)."	Creating an online tool for better cooperation

(*continued*)

Table 4. *(continued)*

Quotes	Themes identified
"Training and educating committee members on issues such as legal requirements and technical details can enhance their ability to work effectively with other departments."	Better training
"Allocating experienced points of contact between all relevant parties."	Experienced points of contact
"Should have meetings long before the process in order to organise how they will and can evaluate the process. The person that wrote the procurement paper should present the idea and the scope to all of them."	Meetings long before preparing the bidding process
"By having dedicated duties and by avoiding being double-hatted"	Dedicated duties
"Through better information sharing."	Better information sharing
"The committees should be surrounded by members from critical organisation departments who will function as advisory personnel, providing their expertise to the public procurement process."	Experienced advisory personnel
"Negotiation procedures should not be a matter of a specific division or person, but of a capable group of stakeholders that combine the experience of every engaged actor such as legal, financial or technical. Only a group that combines experts of all the aspects to be taken into account could be effective."	Experienced members
"Representatives of the other departments should participate as members in the committees"	Better representation of the departments in the committees
"Better Workforce Education"	Better training
"By using meetings in which the committee will raise its concerns and express questions that arise during the negotiation project."	Meetings during the projects

6 Results/Findings

The research findings highlight that the participants' point of view on the clarity of public procurement regulations is divided. This means some people believe the procurement framework is not easy or clear to understand. Further investigation should be conducted to trace which articles of the procurement directives need clarification from the proper authorities as they affect the members of the bidding committee's decisions. The above-mentioned findings of the study are also supported by the primary data collected and presented briefly in Fig. 5. More precisely, the survey questionnaire respondents highlighted that 36% of them always or often encounter difficulties interpreting bidding documents submitted by the economic operators in the public procurement processes. This could mean that the contracting authorities may not have defined in detail all the documents that need to be submitted by the economic operators without causing any potential problems to them. Suppose the members of the bidding committees misinterpret the submitted bids. In that case, the economic operators could be disqualified, discouraging several other qualified enterprises from participating in future bidding processes. The study added to the literature by underlying the importance of improving the clarity of the bidding documents. For instance, the contracting authorities could facilitate the process by using plain language and providing templates to the economic operators with the proper clarifications.

The study also found that the most prevalent challenges were the lack of clear evaluation criteria, difficulties obtaining necessary information from the economic operators, and insufficient time for thorough evaluation. These findings could help policymakers and procurement managers in contracting authorities formulate measurable, objective, and transparent criteria. The findings could also help the contracting authorities provide clarification documents to the potential economic operators when asked and extend the submission dates accordingly. The state could also evaluate if the period that the bidding committees have to evaluate the bids is enough to execute the given task.

Another critical finding is that the survey questionnaire respondents highlighted that they are not trained enough to cope with their duties. This means the contracting authorities must invest in their training to get the best results for the public good.

The study also added to the contemporary literature by highlighting that delays in public procurement processes are expected due to factors outside the bidding committees' control. According to the study, such delays lead to project completion delays, difficulties in attracting qualified suppliers, and increased project costs. This means that further investigation should be conducted to tackle these challenges.

The study also highlighted that the members of the bidding committees face the following challenges: unclear specifications, terms and conditions, limited interpretation of the procurement legislation, insufficient training, time constraints, law restrictions, and optimal cooperation of the committee members. Unclear specifications always raise questions not only to the potential economic operators but also to the committee members who act transparently and fairly. Limited interpretation of the procurement legislation is a major issue as the members of the committees have several questions about specific articles in the law, which affects the evaluation of the submitted documents. For instance, several questions have arisen from committee members on the limits of clarifying the documents that have been submitted in a bidding process. Should an economic operator be disqualified, or should clarifications be asked from the committee members? Insufficient training has always been a significant challenge in every sector, let alone the public procurement process. However, it should be considered that training should be provided by experienced personnel and people with a legal background in procurement regulations. It should also be considered that much time is needed to train all the people who participate in public procurement processes efficiently. The study also highlighted that time constraints are another challenge as the committees try to evaluate the submitted offers within a specific time framework defined in the procurement laws. This means that in periods of high workload, these members have to cope with the pressure of providing their evaluation to the contracting authority. Optimal cooperation of the committee members has always been a challenge, as every person acts according to the procurement directives, and how these directives are interpreted and according to prior experience is also a challenge. The aforementioned statement means that all the committee members may have a common goal; however, they do not share the same experience, background, or flexibility, leading to a challenging working environment.

Concerning the measures that need to be applied in order to overcome the challenges mentioned, the study identified the following: better training, simplified regulatory framework, countering understaffing, defining the terms and conditions accordingly, establishing a feedback system, more time for the evaluation and using multicriteria decision making. A simplified regulatory framework and transparent terms and specifications would help the committee members have fewer queries on the process and the documents submitted by the economic operators. Multicriteria decision-making would help the committee members promote value-for-money solutions to the contracting authority; however, grading several factors is also challenging. For instance, Wang and Chang [10], highlighted the challenges of using multicriteria decision-making in tendering processes, such as selecting experienced committee members, unfamiliarity with purchasing operations, and low adaptability to administrative culture. Time restrictions always put more pressure on committee members; however, there should always be a limit on the time to complete the evaluation of the bidding documents.

The study also added to the literature by exploring how the department could collaborate more effectively to make the procurement processes more efficient. It was found that the processes would lead to better results if an online tool for frequently asked questions was introduced, where experienced people would help the committees in every step of the process. It has also been highlighted that organising meetings long before starting the process and during the negotiations could lead to better results. The experts also highlighted that better representation of the departments in the committees would help the committees have a more holistic approach and become more effective. Better information sharing is another significant finding, as it would help the contracting authorities design the process to protect the suppliers and the contracting authority best.

7 Limitations

The main limitation of the research project is that only 25 respondents participated and helped the authors collect primary data. However, it should be mentioned that the survey questionnaire respondents have many years of experience in public procurement processes. Moreover, the authors partially tackled the mentioned limitation by targeting the chosen population, who had much experience in complex procurement processes, such as procuring relief items during disaster response. Future research could include a larger sample size to confirm the present findings.

8 Conclusions

The authors aimed to explore the challenges that the members of the bidding and negotiating committees face in public procurement processes and how they could be mitigated. In order to tackle the research aim, the authors focused their investigation on Greece's case study and designed a survey questionnaire to gather the primary data. The experts who participated in the study highlighted that major challenges are unclear specifications, terms and conditions, limited interpretation of the procurement legislation, insufficient training, time constraints, law restrictions, and the lack of optimal cooperation among the committee members. The experts also suggested that better training, simplified regulatory framework, countering understaffing, defining the terms and conditions accordingly, establishing a feedback system, more time for the evaluation and using multicriteria decision-making would solve the challenges that they face during the bidding and negotiating processes.

Acknowledgements. The study was not funded.

Disclosure of Interests. The authors have no competing interests.

References

1. Aparicio-Arias, R., Moreno, J.: Factors influencing public procurement during disasters: the cases of Chile and New Zealand. J. Public Procure. **21**(2), 206–219 (2021). https://doi.org/10.1108/jopp-01-2021-0002
2. European Commission: Directive 2014/24/EU of the European Parliament and of the council of 26 February 2014 on public procurement and repealing Directive 2004/18/EC text with EEA relevance. Official Journal of the European Union, vol. L94, no. 65 (2014)
3. European Commission: Public procurement, Internal Market, Industry, Entrepreneurship and SMEs (2023). Available at: https://single-market-economy.ec.europa.eu/single-market/public-procurement_en. Accessed 18 Mar 2023
4. Gnoffo, S.: A dynamic performance management approach to frame corruption in public procurement: a case study. J. Public Procure. **21**(1), 75–96 (2021). https://doi.org/10.1108/jopp-08-2020-0063
5. Johnson, P.F.: Purchasing and Supply Management. McGraw Hill, New York (2024)
6. Koligiannis, G., Drakaki, M., Tzionas, P.: Public Procurement Initiatives during the COVID-19 pandemic and lessons learned: the case study of Greece. J. Public Procure. **24**(1), 70–90 (2023). https://doi.org/10.1108/jopp-08-2023-0058
7. Piramuthu, S.: Knowledge-based framework for automated dynamic supply chain configuration. Eur. J. Oper. Res. **165**(1), 219–230 (2005). https://doi.org/10.1016/j.ejor.2003.12.023
8. Rustiarini, N.W., et al.: Why people commit public procurement fraud? the fraud diamond view. J. Public Procure (2019). https://doi.org/10.1108/jopp-02-2019-0012. ahead-of-print
9. Sabet, D.M.: Bidding despite corruption: evidence from Honduras. J. Public Procure. **21**(4), 399–417 (2021). https://doi.org/10.1108/jopp-07-2020-0058
10. Wang, W.C., Chang, F.C.: A study on developing the optimal procuring model for earthquake restoration in Taiwan. Chin. Inst. Civ. Hydraul. Eng. J. **27**(4), 28–43 (2001)
11. Williams-Elegbe, S.: Systemic corruption and public procurement in developing countries: Are there any solutions? J. Public Procure. **18**(2), 131–147 (2018). https://doi.org/10.1108/jopp-06-2018-009

Revolutionizing Secondary Vocational Education: Advancements in Supply Chain Management Curriculum Design and Learning Goals

Mylonas Dimitrios[1(✉)], Folinas Dimitris[1], and Fragkaki Zafeiro[2]

[1] International Hellenic University, Panagioti Kanelopoulou 2, 601 00 Katerini, Greece
dimmylonas@gmail.com, folinasd@ihu.gr

[2] Disciplinary Board of the Regional Directorate of Education of Central Macedonia, Certified With Professional Competence of Integrity Counselor, Aristotle University of Thessaloniki, Thessaloniki, Greece

Abstract. The teaching of the Thematic Fields related to the Supply Chain, based on the New Curriculum (CS) in the Vocational High School (Sector of Management and Economy - specialization "Warehouse and Supply Systems" should have as a fundamental methodological principle the effort to increase the active participation of students. The learning outcomes and the skills that, based on the new supply chain management systems, students will be asked to develop will be the starting point for the teaching practice and how it is designed and implemented. The appropriate use of educational activities (indicatively: case studies, small-scale investigations, simulations, role-playing, real data analysis, and decision-making) by teachers can not only enhance students' efforts to acquire knowledge on the effective organization, coordination, and management of the flow of products and information in the supply chain and to develop skills but also help them to learn autonomously, to cooperate, to communicate.

In the context of the new Supply Chain Curriculum, the role of the teacher will change. They will not only be asked to implement, but to plan, experiment, organize, and put information to the test. He/she will also be called upon to create a supportive learning environment, encouraging the active involvement of pupils in individual and group activities and encouraging each pupil to chart his/her learning path. This environment should facilitate a learner-centered approach to knowledge, students' self-activity, their participation in groups, and the linking of knowledge with everyday knowledge and experience. It should also promote respect, self-esteem, cooperative learning, combining the freedom of speech with the ethics of dialogue, and thus transforming the relationships between pupils and between pupils and teacher into a field of mutual respect, trust, and care, in which each pupil can develop cognitively, emotionally, and morally.

The teaching of integrity and corruption issues through the New Curricula in the Supply Chain will enable students, tomorrow's citizens of Greece and the world, to cooperate with Civil Society, face the risks of corruption, and enhance public trust in the processes and public economic and social policies.

Keywords: Learner-centred approach · New Curricula · Vocational education and training · Supply chain · Learning activities

I. Kostavelis et al. (Eds.): ICSC 2024, CCIS 2110, pp. 324–332, 2025.
https://doi.org/10.1007/978-3-031-69344-1_24

1 Introduction

With the development of the new Curricula in Secondary Education, the foundations are laid for quality education, which activates students without discrimination. The aim is to create a modern school that is open to society, to new cultural conditions and scientific developments, and to the essential link between theory and practice.

The new curricula of the Management and Economics Section of the Vocational High Schools, which includes the specialization 'Warehouse and Supply Systems Clerk', must be student-centred, functional, and open to the emergence of timeless values, activating students so that they can experience their adolescent life in an authentic way and become creative people and conscious citizens of tomorrow.

Modern curricula compared to traditional curricula are based on learning outcomes. What differs in learning outcomes-based curricula from traditional curricula is the following elements:

- learning combines knowledge and skills with personal and socio-cultural competences,
- knowledge is defined within a broader context and is interdisciplinary, and
- learning takes place in a variety of contexts and through different methods.

In addition, learning outcomes-based curricula increase students' autonomy by enabling them to shape their own pathways and choices. In addition, they contribute to improving students' integration into the labor market. Evidence shows that pupils have a better appreciation of expectations, are more committed to their goals and are more actively involved in the learning and assessment process. These curricula are considered more useful, as they link theoretical and practical learning more closely.

In these new curricula, information, and communication technologies (ICT) are increasingly being used to create digital learning environments and simulate real working conditions. Learning outcomes-based curricula can promote teaching and learning practices that meet the needs of all students. In the hands of teachers, they are important tools for the development of autonomous and active citizens with well-developed critical thinking.

In the modern context, priorities in education and learning are constantly changing, as schools are called upon to respond to the ever-changing and growing needs of the social context and the subjects of learning and to adapt to the challenges of rapid scientific and technological developments and achievements. The new curricula aim to modernize and reorientate the reality of school education so that it is in line with scientific, pedagogical, and technological developments and the constantly emerging requirements of the society of the future.

2 The New Curriculum (PS) at the Vocational Lyceum (Sector of Management and Economy - Specialization "Warehouse and Supply Systems")

Teaching strategies consist of teaching techniques/methods that can be used either independently or as part of an overall strategy, as mentioned earlier. All teaching methods have advantages and disadvantages, depending on the objectives of the course, the time available, the available teaching aids, the skills, and the cognitive level of the students. Their effectiveness is determined by the way they are applied in teaching practice [1, 2].

The basic methods/techniques used in teaching the Economics courses in the Supply Chain are indicatively [3]:

- Lecture.
- The discussion or dialogue.
- The debate or discussion.
- The brainstorming technique.
- The group collaborative teaching.
- The case study method.
- The method of playful teaching.
- The project method.
- The 5W1H method (a questioning approach and a problem-solving method that answers all the basic elements within a problem which are what, who, when, where, why, and how).

The play-based teaching method, mainly in the form of role-playing (strategy games) or simulations, makes a significant contribution to experiential learning and the approach to economic phenomena. It is an effective teaching method for courses in the supply chain. However, there must be educational time available to implement it [1, 4, 5].

In the context of the new Programme of Studies in the courses of the Supply Chain (Logistics), emphasis is placed on the cultivation of "economic literacy", which constitutes the fundamental knowledge base of the future, economically informed, active citizen. Achieving these objectives requires a range of skills, the development of which the teaching of the subject of logistics also aims to develop.

It also focuses on the reflection of the teacher and the redesign of the educational project, the identification and correction of problems and arrhythmias in the learning process, as well as the continuous exploration of how skills, cognitive, psycho-emotional, or other objectives of the New Curricula can be achieved [1]. The proposed curriculum design for the Management and Economics Sector (grades 2 and 3) (Tables 1 and 2).

The Programmes of Studies (PoS) in the specialty "Warehouse and Supply Systems" are expected to reflect the emerging priorities, values, choices, and directions of modern Greek society, to reflect the characteristics that society and "economic education" wants the cultured citizen of the future and the creative person to possess and to favor the development of individuals capable of meeting the challenges of modern times. Consequently, the Programmes of Studies must be in harmony with the spirit, conditions and needs of the times and modern society and the achievements of economic analysis, technology, and science, as well as the needs and requirements of modern pedagogy.

The main horizontal orientations of the Programmes of Studies are to support students to [4]:

- acquire the skills of reflective people who learn how to learn, how to investigate and how to become creative and effective,
- cultivate skills with which to use their knowledge and produce new knowledge,
- make decisions based on scientific evidence,
- take initiative and function autonomously in the classroom and in their lives,

Table 1. Class B - Department of Management and Economics (T: Theory L: Labs)

n	Courses	Hours
1	Introduction to Marketing	2T + 2L
2	Introduction to Tourism	2T
3	Introduction to Logistics	3T
4	Spreadsheets	2T
5	Introduction to Business Administration and Management	2E
6	Economic Mathematics and Statistics	2T
7	Circular Economy - Sustainability and Sustainable Development	2T
8	Entrepreneurship and Innovation	2T
9	English	2T
10	Introduction to Marketing	2T
	Total	23

Table 2. Class C - Warehouse and Supply Systems Worker (T: Theory L: Labs)

n	Courses	Hours
1	Principles of Economic Science	2T + 2L
2	Principles of Organization and Management	2T
3	Organisation and Management of Warehouses	3T
4	Transport Organisation and Management	2T
5	Logistics Applications	2E
6	Accounting Applications	2T
	Total	23

- acquire self-esteem, self-confidence, empathy, so that they can relate and communicate with others,
- recognize values and become aware of principles to acquire a sense of responsibility and prepare themselves as active citizens, and
- participate in events and practices that reflect the need to mobilize everyone to tackle the major challenges facing modern societies (waste of natural resources, pollution, refugees, epidemics, pandemics, crises, etc.).

The Programmes of Studies provides the opportunity for all students to learn to support and/or plan their personal development. The necessary time and opportunities are therefore provided to enable all students to acquire basic knowledge, skills, abilities, and attitudes related to the subject of logistics.

The Programmes of Studies links the subjects to the wider lives of the pupils, the local and wider community, incorporating elements of contemporary everyday life to foster acceptance and understanding through collegiality. A significant part of the PoS is required to be devoted to the cultivation of 'modern skills', those considered necessary for the smooth and prosperous development of 21st century citizenship. Modern skills are divided into vertical or hard skills, which are linked to knowledge and achievements that can be measured, and horizontal or soft skills, also known as subjective, interpersonal skills that are acquired through life experience and are much more difficult to quantify, as they are related to the way we connect and interact with other people [4].

Considering the priorities, in supply chain management the emphasis shifts from the subject matter, teachers, lecturers and the teaching process to the students and the expected outcomes. For the development of the PoS, it is necessary to consider the basic parameters such as: the purpose, objectives, and duration of the curricula, as defined for each broader and more specific subject area. The curricula to be developed by the Management and Economics Department of the PESA, specialization "Supply Chain", and therefore the subjects (courses) defined in it, should meet the following requirements to the greatest possible extent: Scientific validity, Completeness - Coherence - Relevance, Didactic appropriateness, Flexibility, Simple and understandable language, Respect for democratic values, globally focused knowledge content [4].

The Programmes of Studies are required to contribute dynamically to changing the school climate, to inspire teachers with appropriate instructions, ways and means, so that the classroom becomes a laboratory for research, communication, action and expression, to help students to realize communicative competence, cooperativeness, self-awareness, responsibility, tolerance, discipline, a sense of justice, democratic sensitivity, fair play, solidarity, problem solving, exploratory learning, digital literacy and a host of other important skills necessary for the future citizen of a democratic society of our time [4].

The basic didactic orientation of the PoS is the use of digital technologies as tools for research and learning in their full range. This is also recommended by a recent EU Directive (Digital Education Action Plan 2021–2027) which sets the goal for every classroom (by the year 2027) to be digital (this concerns infrastructure, content, and practices).

At the same time, Programmes of Studies are open and flexible, to allow students to seamlessly acquire the necessary creative and cognitive autonomy and to build a conscious and responsible attitude to the acquisition of knowledge, the learning process, and their economic realization, while at the same time providing the teacher with the possibility to discreetly guide the learning process.

The Curricula (Curricula) of the Department of Management and Economics, specialization in Supply Chain is based on the six (6) pillars of learning for the 21st century (UNESCO learning pillars) (Table 3).

Table 3. Content of 21st century learning pillars [6, 7]

n	Courses	Concerns all procedures and practices that:
1	I'm learning to do	Lead people to experience, know and transform knowledge to make sustainability a way of life
2	I am learning to be	Lead to a fusion of knowledge and action to build a sustainable future
3	Learning to live together sustainably	Lead people to self-realization, self-regulation and foster a sense of being rather than having
4	I am learning to transform myself and society	Lead to a peaceful and non-discriminatory society and to coexistence
5	I am learning to give	Transform unsustainable values and attitudes and undertake to change society towards sustainability
6	I'm learning to do	Promote solidarity and caring attitudes to meet human needs as students gain autonomy and meaning for their learning and participation in society

3 Skills of Logistics/Supply Chain Graduates - Linking the MAs to the Acquisition of These Skills

Working in the logistics sector requires the graduate of the specialty "Warehouse and Supply Systems Clerk" to have a set of basic skills, such as:

- Basic knowledge of economics and production.
- Knowledge of basic logistics and logistics management skills.
- Knowledge of economic and business administration and knowledge of business processes and logistics.
- Skills in the development of business processes, including knowledge of the latest developments in the field of retailing.
- Communication skills.
- Ability to record supply chain processes (flows, times).
- Knowledge of commercial procedures and customer service and monitoring of commercial agreements.
- Problem-solving skills.
- Teamwork skills to create synergies with customers and suppliers.
- Negotiation skills.
- Negotiation skills.
- Skills in document management and handling of paperwork and compliance with procurement rules.

However, these skills are not enough to succeed in today's logistics processes. The development of additional skills such as strategic and creative thinking, leadership skills, understanding of the global market, risk forecasting and management, communication skills and team spirit are equally important.

The subjects that should be taught in the specialization of Warehouse and Supply Systems Officers in secondary vocational education to fully meet the needs of the profession of Logistics System Officer are:

- Procurement.
- Ordering process.
- Distribution channels.
- Stock control.
- Demand forecasting.
- Transportation.
- Warehousing.
- Selection and warehouse location.
- Materials management.
- Support in components and services.
- Packaging.
- Defects and scrap.
- Management of returned products.
- Customer services.
- Accounting principles - Costing.
- Information Systems.
- Green Supply Chains.
- Humanitarian Supply Chain.
- Maritime Logistics.
- Sustainable Development and Circular Economy.
- Total Quality Management.

Storage and transport are the most important items based on market needs.

The five most important challenges in modern markets for the logistics-supply chain sector are: lack of transparency along the supply chain, the necessity of planning a long-time horizon, the co-volatility of demand, the existence of multiple channels for purchasing and distribution of products. To all this must be added important geopolitical, economic, and social factors, such as natural disasters, wars, fluctuations in currency exchange rates, cultural differences, etc., which require great flexibility and significant investment in modern technological solutions and skilled human resources by international supply chains.

Given the increasing use of systems and technological solutions throughout the supply chain, it is important for logistics managers to be familiar with new technologies. Understanding how the company, for example, uses business information systems for warehouse and inventory management and integrated enterprise resource planning (ERP) systems, leads to more efficient use and full exploitation of their potential. But also, the knowledge of new technologies, such as 3D printing, drones, the Internet of Things, robotics and automation, cloud computing, etc., will have a significant impact on the adoption of a new way of operating supply chains soon [8, 9]. Finally, knowledge of the subjects of communication and negotiation can be considered important. For every logistics executive, good communication with customers, partners as well as with his/her own team members is considered (and not without reason) as one of the most critical success factors. Negotiation skills are also essential for achieving better results.

4 Conclusions

The economists-teachers who teach the courses of Supply Studies need to take time to trace the possibilities, thoughts, experiences, and particular needs of students, so that, on the one hand, they can couple economic theory with their experience, and, on the other hand, they can redirect their personal view of economic reality towards the validity of scientific discourse. To achieve this, the eco-monologist-teacher should use teaching methods that will consistently attract the students' interest, activate their participation, intuition, and imagination, and motivate them to investigate economic phenomena and problems individually and in groups [1, 2, 4].

The applied Curricula in the field of Management and Economics are distinguished in terms of the emphasis on knowledge memorization. The adoption of curricula and corresponding educational material for the cultivation of competences that combine knowledge, skills, critical thinking, and values will significantly improve the learning outcomes of secondary vocational education. There is an urgent need for a comprehensive redesign of the curricula of the Management and Economics Sector, based on contemporary needs, across the whole spectrum of education and training. Basic parameters of the international and European framework must be considered, to the extent that they affect the indigenous development and economy, while the specific characteristics and prospects of the country's productive development (at national, regional, and local level), as well as the existing funding possibilities in each case, are a key factor in the entire planning process. Finally, account must also be taken of modern scientific and pedagogical developments, which must be followed in any change in the sensitive area of secondary education.

With these data, it seems that the new curricula that will be developed for the Sector of Management and Economics and for all its specializations should lead to the expansion of the professional outlets of the graduates of the Sector in the Greek economy and production, without excluding corresponding outlets on a European and international scale. From a pedagogical point of view, the new curricula must be designed after careful study of the aims and objectives of each educational level and of the initial professional integration. They must also be in line with technological developments and limited to the necessary curriculum [10].

Overall, the curricula must contribute to the multidimensional development of young people's personalities so that they can participate critically and creatively in social life, have confidence in themselves, be able to integrate adequately and with dignity into the profession, assert their rights, be able to keep abreast of technological developments and, in general, be integrated into society as full democratic citizens.

References

1. Mylonas, D., Vouzaxakis, G., Xanthi, H., Sycas, Th., Symacesis, S.: Teacher's guide Principles of High School Economics. Institute of Educational Policy (2021)

2. Mylonas, D., Vouzaxakis, G., Xanthi, H., Sikas, Th., Syracassis, S.: Curriculum Principles of Economic Science, 3rd grade. Institute of Educational Policy (2022)
3. Magoula, T.: Introduction to the Teaching of Economics. Gutenberg Publications, Athens (2009)
4. Mylonas, D., Folinas, D.: New Curricula in the field of Management and Economics of Vocational High Schools. Institute of Educational Policy. Institute of Educational Policy (2022)
5. Mylonas, D.: New curricula in technical vocational education: a case study in the new curricula of the sector of management and economics of vocational high schools. In: 1st Panhellenic Conference Curricula - School Manuals: From the Past to the Present and the Future, EKEDISY Museum of School Life and Education, Pedagogical Society of Greece, PIERCE - American College of Greece, Athens, Athens, Proceedings of the Conference, 4–6 March 2016, vol. B, pp. 594–604 (2016). ISBN: 978-618-81132-4-4
6. Makrakis, V., Kostoula-Makraki, N.: A teaching-learning model that applies problem-based learning with the help of ICT. In: Anastasiadis, A.E. (ed.) 9th Panhellenic Conference on ICT in Education, Crete, 6–7 October 2014, pp. 921–933 (2014)
7. Makrakis, V.: Unlocking the potential and relevance of ICT in the development of sustainable - just curricula and society. Cult. Knowl. **5**(2), 103–122 (2016)
8. Vouzaxakis, G.: Deconstruction and restructuring of the curriculum of economics courses in secondary education towards sustainable development with the support of ICT (Unpublished doctoral thesis). University of Crete, Rethymnon (2018)
9. Bousiosiou, D., Tjrovouzis P. The technological skills of secondary school teachers of economics for the integration of information and communication technologies in teaching Practice. In: ICT in Education, Proceedings of the 3rd ETPE Conference, 26–29 Sept 2002, vol. B, pp. 584–593 (2002)
10. Synmakesis, S.: Financial education in primary and secondary education. Xenophon. J. Econ. Second. Educ. (4) (2019)

The Advent of AI in Modern Supply Chain

Konstantinos A. Tsintotas[1(✉)], Stavros N. Moutsis[1], Ioannis Kansizoglou[1], Fotios K. Konstantinidis[2], and Antonios Gasteratos[1]

[1] Department of Production and Management Engineering, Democritus University of Thrace, 12 Vas. Sophias, 671 32 Xanthi, Greece
{ktsintot,smoutsis,ikansizo,agaster}@pme.duth.gr
[2] Institute of Communication and Computer Systems, 9 Iroon. Polytechnique Str., Gr-157 73 Zografou, Athens, Greece
fotios.konstantinidis@iccs.gr

Abstract. In the era of Industry 5.0, marked by cutting-edge technologies that enhance manufacturing processes, the supply chain constitutes a pivotal component that connects manufacturers with consumers. This work focuses on the emergence of artificial intelligence (AI) in various applications, including demand forecasting, inventory optimization, logistics, predictive maintenance, and risk management. These bring numerous benefits to modern businesses, such as enhancing operational efficiency, decision-making, and customer satisfaction. To this end, we highlight the strategic balance required between upcoming challenges, current opportunities, and prospects based on this technological advancement.

1 Introduction

In the Industry 5.0 era, where next-generation technologies are used to optimize manufacturing operations [57], the supply chain can be portrayed as a dimension that closes the gap between factories and consumers [31]. It can be considered the strategic coordination of various organizational business functions with external partners for efficiently planning, producing, transporting, and delivering products or services to customers [13,39]. In particular, it involves a network of interconnected entities, including suppliers, manufacturers, distributors, retailers, and logistics providers (see Fig. 1), that collaborate to optimize the flow of materials, information, and finances across the entire supply chain [6,24]. Hence, its main objectives include the enhancement of operational effectiveness, cost reduction, and lead times, while, through the timely delivery of goods and services [47,67], customer satisfaction is ensured [20,60].

Yet, recent supply chain models encompass technology integration, data analytics, and collaboration among various stakeholders. As modern systems aim at real-time and end-to-end visibility, flexibility, and responsiveness to market demands [16,56], advanced technologies, such as artificial intelligence

I. Kostavelis et al. (Eds.): ICSC 2024, CCIS 2110, pp. 333–343, 2025.
https://doi.org/10.1007/978-3-031-69344-1_25

Fig. 1. Supply chain management, including consumers, retailers, distributors, etc., and artificial intelligence are two factors that aim to improve the efficiency and effectiveness of modern business frameworks.

(AI) [36,42], internet of things (IoT) [18,33,58], machine vision [30,32,41], and blockchain [61], are adopted aiming to improve the efficiency and effectiveness of today's business performance.

Among the technologies mentioned above, AI refers to machine and deep learning techniques that learn from experience and training, *e.g.*, reward-penalty methods, and supervised learning to apply cognitive functions [44]. These approaches utilize algorithms, data, and computational power to process information, adapt to changing circumstances, and improve a system [54]. Other AI-based methodologies beyond machine and deep learning methods encompass heuristic pipelines [40]. These pipelines are structured frameworks aimed at enhancing specific functions, such as path-finding [55,59], a crucial tool extensively employed in optimizing supply chain operations [35,64]. Therefore, combining modern tools with recent supply chain models represents a workflow shift that reshapes companies' processes regarding their provided products and services [36,51]. To this end, as AI emerges as a transformative force[5], offering unprecedented possibilities for efficiency increase [17,48] and optimized decision-making [11], this paper delves into its profound impact on contemporary supply chains, exploring how advanced algorithms redefine traditional practices. By examining its applications, challenges, and opportunities, we provide a thorough understanding of AI's advent and its importance for businesses and stakeholders.

The rest of the paper is organized as follows. Section 2 discusses the application sector where AI is adopted in the supply chain. Next, the current challenges and opportunities are given. Section 4 describes its benefits and impact, while subsequently, we examine the future perspectives and conclude our work.

2 AI Applications in Supply Chain

This section presents the practical implementations of AI within the modern supply chain, as shown in Fig. 2. More specifically, we explore applications in which the proposed technology revolutionizes traditional processes, *i.e.*, from demand forecasting and inventory optimization to logistics and predictive maintenance to risk management.

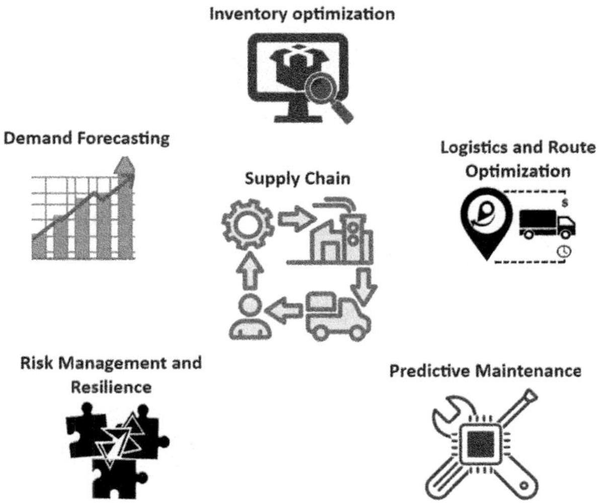

Fig. 2. Artificial intelligence applications in modern supply chains cover the processes of demand forecasting, inventory optimization, logistics and route optimization, predictive maintenance, risk management, and resilience.

Demand forecasting enables organizations to optimize inventory levels, reduce stockouts, and minimize excess products. As machine [1,2], and deep [23] learning [38] leverage historical data, market trends, and external factors to generate more accurate predictions, AI-based frameworks can adapt in dynamic consumer behaviors, seasonal variations, and unexpected disruptions, At the same time, its proactive decision-making capabilities for demand planning allow for a more responsive supply chain that aligns seamlessly with evolving customer demands and market dynamics.

Inventory optimization techniques minimize carrying costs, avoid stockouts, and ensure optimal stock levels [3] while permitting unprecedented efficiency and cost-effectiveness [45]. Combined with machine vision, they can detect the capacity and availability of warehouses to update the work orders [9,28]. This way, organizations streamline their operations and enhance customer satisfaction by ensuring that products are readily available when and where needed.

Logistics and route optimization exploits AI to harness real-time data, traffic patterns, and historical information to create efficient and adaptive route plans [22]. This method improves delivery speed and overall resource utilization while reducing fuel consumption and environmental impact. At the same time, predictive analytics against potential disruptions allow agile adjustments in route planning when unforeseen challenges come through [65].

Predictive maintenance constitutes the process that optimizes the life-cycle management of critical infrastructure. Hence, cutting-edge AI-based solutions allow the transition from traditional reactive maintenance to a proactive and cost-effective approach [8,34]. This way, equipment failures are predicted by analyzing historical performance data, sensor readings, and operational patterns. As a result, AI-driven predictive maintenance reduces downtime, extends machinery's lifespan, and minimizes unexpected disruptions. Accordingly, AI-powered monitoring provides real-time insights, permitting organizations to schedule the corresponding activities strategically, allocate resources efficiently, and ultimately enhance the reliability and longevity of supply chain parts [50].

Risk management and resilience examines diverse datasets encompassing geopolitical events and external factors to identify potential risks and vulnerabilities in the supply chain [21]. Therefore, organizations leverage modern tools to assess and mitigate risks proactively, ensuring adaptability in the face of unexpected disturbances [10]. Through real-time monitoring, informed decisions are enabled swiftly amid uncertainties; ergo, it becomes evident that the synergy of AI and strategic planning is instrumental against the complexities of the business environment.

3 Challenges and Opportunities

The following section explains how AI affects the current model and presents the upcoming challenges and opportunities that demand consideration. It is worth noting that success in the transformative journey of supply chains lies in the strategic balance between challenges and AI's immense opportunities.

3.1 Opportunities

Organizations leverage AI to optimize processes, reduce costs, and enhance customer satisfaction through predictive analytics, real-time insights, and adaptive decision-making [7]. The prospect of improved demand forecasting, streamlined logistics, and agile response mechanisms places businesses ahead in an ever-evolving market. At the same time, the potential for data-driven insights enables them to make strategic decisions, fostering a competitive edge in the dynamic business landscape.

3.2 Challenges

Nevertheless, these opportunities are accompanied by challenges that organizations must adeptly address to harness AI [19]. To begin with, integrating such technology seamlessly into existing infrastructure requires detailed planning for mitigating potential disruptions. In addition, privacy and data security concerns are significant as they raise ethical considerations surrounding AI since organizations handle vast amounts of sensitive information [52]. Finally, the need for skilled professionals in AI-based pipelines poses a major human resource challenge [53].

4 Benefits and Impacts

While the benefits are evident, it is crucial to acknowledge that AI's impacts extend beyond operational realms. This section discusses how it redefines supply chain processes, unlocking new possibilities and fundamentally altering businesses' operations. More specifically, we show the transformative influence that touches organizational culture, market positioning, and interaction between businesses and their supply chain ecosystem.

Operational efficiency is achieved through applications in demand forecasting, inventory optimization, and logistics. Organizations can streamline operations by automating repetitive tasks, optimizing processes, and providing real-time insights, reducing lead times and operational costs [14].

Enhanced decision-making constitutes one of the impacts that lies in AI's ability. Through advanced analytics and machine learning algorithms, organizations access data-driven insights that enable more informed and strategic decisions [11]. As a result, this improves day-to-day operations and supports long-term planning and risk management.

Improved Customer Satisfaction originates from AI capability to accurately forecast customer demands, ensure product availability, and reduce stockouts and overstock situations. Therefore, optimized logistics and efficient supply chain processes permit timely deliveries that increase customer loyalty [49].

Adaptability and resilience is performed as organizations can respond swiftly to market changes and unforeseen disruptions by identifying real-time patterns and trends. Such adaptability enriches the general stability of the supply chain, guaranteeing continuity in the face of challenges [12].

Cost savings and resource optimization is based on AI's ability to optimize processes, reduce inefficiencies, and enhance resource allocation. Organizations gain a more sustainable and cost-effective supply chain ecosystem by minimizing excess inventory and optimizing transportation routes [15].

5 Future Perspectives and Implications

This section explores the emerging trends and broader implications that AI introduces to the landscape of the modern supply chain, as it becomes evident that the integration of AI is not merely a technological evolution but a catalyst toward this goal.

Continued technological advancements as AI applications evolve accordingly. In particular, technological advancement suggests a perpetual journey of refinement and expansion, from more sophisticated machine learning algorithms [25] to integrating emerging technologies like quantum computing [63].

Interconnected ecosystems concerns the shape of a more interconnected and collaborative ecosystem beyond individual organizations. As AI facilitates seamless communication and data sharing among various stakeholders, we anticipate a future where the entire supply chain operates as a unified, intelligent network [66].

Sustainability and ethical considerations are likely to leverage AI to optimize resource usage [62], reduce environmental impact [43], and enhance the moral dimensions of their supply chain practices. Striking a balance between technological advancements and responsible, ethical AI usage will be vital [37].

Human-AI collaboration is another perspective of the continuous evolving landscape [4,46]. Since AI streamlines routine tasks and decision-making processes, human intuition, creativity, and critical thinking remain invaluable. The future of the supply chain sees a harmonious integration where AI models augment human capabilities rather than replace them [27].

Resilience in the face of disruptions originates from the advanced predictive analytics [26], scenario planning, and adaptive decision-making, which will fortify supply chains, enabling organizations to steer uncertainties quickly.

Strategic shifts and competitive Dynamics that adeptly leverage AI to gain actionable insights, optimize processes [29], and enhance customer experiences will emerge as industry leaders, reshaping market landscapes.

6 Conclusion

In conclusion, integrating AI into the modern supply chain heralds a paradigm shift with profound implications. As we have explored the evolution of supply chain management and the fundamental principles of AI, it is evident that the synergy between these domains can revolutionize operational efficiency, decision-making processes, and overall resilience. Despite the challenges posed by data security and integration complexities, the opportunities presented by AI applications in demand forecasting, inventory management, and logistics optimization are compelling. Therefore, organizations must strategically embrace and invest in AI technologies to remain competitive in an ever-evolving global market. Last, the future of the modern supply chain is intricately linked to the continued exploration and implementation of AI, promising increased efficiency and a new era of adaptability and responsiveness.

Acknowledgment. This work is supported by the project TAEDR-0535864 "Network of Excellence for the Development, Dissemination, and Application of Digital Transformation Technologies in the Greek Manufacturing Industry," carried out within the framework of the National Recovery and Resilience Plan Greece 2.0, funded by the European Union-NextGenerationEU.

References

1. Aamer, A., Eka Yani, L.P., Alan Priyatna, I.M.: (2020) Data analytics in the supply chain management: Review of machine learning applications in demand forecasting. Operat. Supply Chain Manag. Int. J. **14**(1): 1–13. https://doi.org/10.31387/oscm0440281
2. Abolghasemi, M., Beh, E., Tarr, G., Gerlach, R.: Demand forecasting in supply chain: the impact of demand volatility in the presence of promotion. Comput. Ind. Eng. **142**, 106380 (2020). https://doi.org/10.1016/j.cie.2020.106380
3. Albayrak Ünal, Ö., Erkayman, B., Usanmaz, B.: Applications of artificial intelligence in inventory management: A systematic review of the literature. Archives of Computational Methods in Engineering **30**(4), 2605–2625 (2023)
4. An, S., Che, G., Guo, J., Xu, Y., Wang, G., Tsintotas, K.A., Zhang, F., Ye, J., Fu, C., Zhu, H., et al.: An open-source robotic chinese chess player. Int. Conf. Intelli. Rob. Syst. **26**, 6238–6245 (2023)
5. An, S., Zhou, F., Yang, M., Zhu, H., Fu, C., Tsintotas, K.A.: Real-time monocular human depth estimation and segmentation on embedded systems. In: in proc. IEEE/RSJ International Conference Intelligent Robots and Systems. pp. 55–62 (2021)
6. Anderson, D.L., Britt, F.F., Favre, D.J.: The 7 principles of supply chain management. Supply Chain Manag. Rev. **11**(3), 41–46 (2007)
7. Awan, U., Kanwal, N., Alawi, S., Huiskonen, J., Dahanayake, A.: Artificial intelligence for supply chain success in the era of data analytics. The fourth industrial revolution: Implementation of artificial intelligence for growing business success pp. 3–21 (2021)
8. Balakera, N., Konstantinidis, F.K., Tsimiklis, G., Latsa, E., Amditis, A.: Iiot network system from data collection to cyber-physical system transmission under the industry 5.0 era. In: in proc. Int. Congress on Information and Communication Technology. pp. 929–941. Springer (2023)
9. Balaska, V., Folinas, D., Konstantinidis, F.K., Gasteratos, A.: Smart counting of unboxed stocks in the warehouse 4.0 ecosystem. In: Proc. IEEE Int. Conf. on Imaging Systems and Techniques (IST). pp. 1–6. IEEE (2022)

10. Baryannis, G., Validi, S., Dani, S., Antoniou, G.: Supply chain risk management and artificial intelligence: state of the art and future research directions. Int. J. of Prod. Res. **57**(7), 2179–2202 (2019)
11. Belhadi, A., Kamble, S., Fosso Wamba, S., Queiroz, M.M.: Building supply-chain resilience: an artificial intelligence-based technique and decision-making framework. Int. J. Prod. Res. **60**(14), 4487–4507 (2022)
12. Belhadi, A., Mani, V., Kamble, S.S., Khan, S.A.R., Verma, S.: Artificial intelligence-driven innovation for enhancing supply chain resilience and performance under the effect of supply chain dynamism: an empirical investigation Annals of Operations Research pp. 1–26 (2021)
13. Chatzoglou, P., Chatzoudes, D., Ioakeimidou, D., Tokoutsi, A.: Generation z: Factors affecting the use of social networking sites (snss). In: in proceedings International Workshop on Semantic and Social Media Adaptation and Personalization. pp. 1–6 (2020)
14. Dash, R., McMurtrey, M., Rebman, C., Kar, U.K.: Application of artificial intelligence in automation of supply chain management. J. Strat. Innov. Sustain. **14**(3), 43–53 (2019)
15. Dittakavi, R.S.S.: Ai-optimized cost-aware design strategies for resource-efficient applications. J. Sci. Technol. **4**(1), 1–10 (2023)
16. Dolgui, A., Ivanov, D.: 5g in digital supply chain and operations management: fostering flexibility, end-to-end connectivity and real-time visibility through internet-of-everything. Int. J. Prod. Res. **60**(2), 442–451 (2022). https://doi.org/10.1080/00207543.2021.2002969
17. Du, X., Shi, G., Zhao, Y.: The path of artificial intelligence technology to reduce cost and increase efficiency of e-commerce supply chain. In: in proc. Int. Conf. on Software and e-Business. pp. 28–32 (2022)
18. Fornes-Leal, A., Lacalle, I., Palau, C., Szmeja, P., Ganzha, M., Konstantinidis, F., Garro, E.: Tactile iot architecture for the iot–edge–cloud continuum: The assist-iot approach. Shaping the Future of IoT with Edge Intelligence p. 37
19. Fosso Wamba, S., Queiroz, M.M., Guthrie, C., Braganza, A.: Industry experiences of artificial intelligence (ai): Benefits and challenges in operations and supply chain management (2022)
20. Gunasekaran, A., Patel, C., Tirtiroglu, E.: Performance measures and metrics in a supply chain environment. Int. J. Operat. Prod. Manag. **21**(1/2), 71–87 (2001)
21. Ho, W., Zheng, T., Yildiz, H., Talluri, S.: Supply chain risk management: a literature review. Int. J. Prod. Res. **53**(16), 5031–5069 (2015)
22. Hu, W.C., Wu, H.T., Cho, H.H., Tseng, F.H.: Optimal route planning system for logistics vehicles based on artificial intelligence. J. Int. Technol. **21**(3), 757–764 (2020)
23. Husna, A., Amin, S.H., Shah, B.: Demand forecasting in supply chain management using different deep learning methods. In: Demand forecasting and order planning in supply chains and humanitarian logistics, pp. 140–170 (2021)
24. Ioakeimidou, D., Chatzoudes, D., Symeonidis, S., Chatzoglou, P.: Hra Adoption Via Organizational Analytics Maturity: Examining the Role of Institutional Theory, Resource-Based View and Diffusion of Innovation. Int. J, Manpower (2023)
25. Kansizoglou, I., Bampis, L., Gasteratos, A.: Deep feature space: a geometrical perspective. IEEE Trans. Patt. Anal. Mach. Intell. **44**(10), 6823–6838 (2021)
26. Kansizoglou, I., Bampis, L., Gasteratos, A.: Do neural network weights account for classes centers? IEEE Trans. Neural Networks and Learning Systems (2022)

27. Kansizoglou, I., Misirlis, E., Tsintotas, K., Gasteratos, A.: Continuous emotion recognition for long-term behavior modeling through recurrent neural networks. Technologies **10**(3), 59 (2022)
28. Konstantinidis, F.K., Balaska, V., Symeonidis, S., Mouroutsos, S.G., Gasteratos, A.: Arowa: An autonomous robot framework for warehouse 4.0 health and safety inspection operations. In: in proc. Med. Conf. on Control and Automation. pp. 494–499. IEEE (2022)
29. Konstantinidis, F.K., Kansizoglou, I., Santavas, N., Mouroutsos, S.G., Gasteratos, A.: Marma: a mobile augmented reality maintenance assistant for fast-track repair procedures in the context of industry 4.0. Machines **8**(4), 88 (2020)
30. Konstantinidis, F.K., Kansizoglou, I., Tsintotas, K.A., Mouroutsos, S.G., Gasteratos, A.: The role of machine vision in industry 4.0: a textile manufacturing perspective. Culture **4**, 5 (2021)
31. Konstantinidis, F.K., Myrillas, N., Mouroutsos, S.G., Koulouriotis, D., Gasteratos, A.: Assessment of industry 4.0 for modern manufacturing ecosystem: a systematic survey of surveys. Machines **10**(9), 746 (2022)
32. Konstantinidis, F.K., Myrillas, N., Tsintotas, K.A., Mouroutsos, S.G., Gasteratos, A.: A technology maturity assessment framework for industry 5.0 machine vision systems based on systematic literature review in automotive manufacturing. Int. J. Prod. Res. **17**, 1–37 (2023)
33. Krotov, V.: The internet of things and new business opportunities. Bus. Horiz. **60**(6), 831–841 (2017)
34. Lee, W.J., Wu, H., Yun, H., Kim, H., Jun, M.B., Sutherland, J.W.: Predictive maintenance of machine tool systems using artificial intelligence techniques applied to machine condition data. Proced. Cirp. **80**, 506–511 (2019)
35. Liu, Y., Chen, M., Huang, H.: Multi-agent pathfinding based on improved cooperative a* in kiva system. In: Proceeding Internaltional Conference Control, Automation and Robotics. pp. 633–638 (2019). 10.1109/ICCAR.2019.8813319
36. Loureiro, S.M.C., Guerreiro, J., Tussyadiah, I.: Artificial intelligence in business: state of the art and future research agenda. J. Busin. Res. **129**, 911–926 (2021). https://doi.org/10.1016/j.jbusres.2020.11.001
37. Lu, Q., Zhu, L., Xu, X., Whittle, J.: Responsible-ai-by-design: a pattern collection for designing responsible AI systems. IEEE Software (2023)
38. Mediavilla, M.A., Dietrich, F., Palm, D.: Review and analysis of artificial intelligence methods for demand forecasting in supply chain management. Proced. CIRP **107**, 1126–1131 (2022). https://doi.org/10.1016/j.procir.2022.05.119
39. Mentzer, J.T., DeWitt, W., Keebler, J.S., Min, S., Nix, N.W., Smith, C.D., Zacharia, Z.G.: Defining supply chain management. J. Busin. Log. **22**(2), 1–25 (2001)
40. Moutsis, S.N., Tsintotas, K.A., Gasteratos, A.: PIPTO: precise inertial-based pipeline for threshold-based fall detection using three-axis accelerometers. Sensors **23**(18) (2023). https://doi.org/10.3390/s23187951
41. Moutsis, S.N., Tsintotas, K.A., Kansizoglou, I., An, S., Aloimonos, Y., Gasteratos, A.: Fall detection paradigm for embedded devices based on yolov8. In: in proc. IEEE Int. Conf. Imaging Systems and Techniques. pp. 1–6 (2023). https://doi.org/10.1109/IST59124.2023.10355696
42. Moutsis, S.N., Tsintotas, K.A., Kansizoglou, I., Gasteratos, A.: Evaluating the performance of mobile-convolutional neural networks for spatial and temporal human action recognition analysis. Robotics **12**(6), 167 (2023)

43. Oikonomou, K.M., Kansizoglou, I., Gasteratos, A.: A hybrid reinforcement learning approach with a spiking actor network for efficient robotic arm target reaching IEEE Rob. Autom. Lett. (2023)
44. Papapetros, I.T., Oikonomou, K.M., Kansizoglou, I., Tsintotas, K.A., Gasteratos, A.: Semantic-based visual vocabulary for loop closure detection. In: Proceedngs IEEE International Conference Imaging Systems and Techniques. pp. 1–5 (2023)
45. Praveen, U., Farnaz, G., Hatim, G.: Inventory management and cost reduction of supply chain processes using ai based time-series forecasting and ann modeling. Proced. Manuf. **38**, 256–263 (2019)
46. Psarommatis, F., Azamfirei, V., Konstantinidis, F.K.: A rula-based assessment framework based on machine vision and zero-defect manufacturing 4.0 initiative. Automation, Robotics & Communications for Industry 4.0/5.0 p. 197 (2023)
47. Qiao, H., Lin, X., Zhou, X., Jiang, M.: Research on joint decision-making of timely delivery, product quality and marketing in supply chain based on differential game. Sustainability **14**(17), 10774 (2022)
48. Rai, R., Tiwari, M.K., Ivanov, D., Dolgui, A.: Machine learning in manufacturing and industry 4.0 applications (2021)
49. Rane, N.: Enhancing customer loyalty through artificial intelligence (ai), internet of things (iot), and big data technologies: Improving customer satisfaction, engagement, relationship, and experience. Internet of Things (IoT), and Big Data Technologies: Improving Customer Satisfaction, Engagement, Relationship, and Experience (2023)
50. Serradilla, O., Zugasti, E., Rodriguez, J., Zurutuza, U.: Deep learning models for predictive maintenance: a survey, comparison, challenges and prospects. Appl. Intell. **52**(10), 10934–10964 (2022)
51. Shah, H.M., Gardas, B.B., Narwane, V.S., Mehta, H.S.: The contemporary state of big data analytics and artificial intelligence towards intelligent supply chain risk management: a comprehensive review. Kybernetes **52**(5), 1643–1697 (2023)
52. Sobb, T., Turnbull, B., Moustafa, N.: (2020) Supply chain 40: a survey of cyber security challenges solutions and future directions. Electronics **9**(11): 1864
53. Sofia, M., Fraboni, F., De Angelis, M., Puzzo, G., Giusino, D., Pietrantoni, L., et al.: The impact of artificial intelligence on workers' skills: Upskilling and reskilling in organisations. Inform. Sci. Int. J. Emerg. Trans. **26**, 39–68 (2023)
54. Tsintotas, K.A., An, S., Papapetros, I.T., Konstantinidis, F.K., Sirakoulis, G.C., Gasteratos, A.: Dimensionality reduction through visual data resampling for low-storage loop-closure detection. In: Proceedings IEEE International Conference Imaging Systems and Techniques. pp. 1–6 (2022)
55. Tsintotas, K.A., Bampis, L., Gasteratos, A.: Online Appearance-Based Place Recognition and Mapping: Their Role in Autonomous Navigation, vol. 133. Springer Nature (2022)
56. Tsintotas, K.A., Kansizoglou, I., Konstantinidis, F.K., Mouroutsos, S.G., Syrakoulis, G.C., Psarommatis, F., Aloimonos, Y., Gasteratos, A.: Active vision: a promising technology for achieving zero-defect manufacturing. Proc. Comput. Sci. **232**, 2821–2830 (2024)
57. Tsintotas, K.A., Kansizoglou, I., Pastra, K., Aloimonos, Y., Gasteratos, A., Sirakoulis, G.C., Sandini, G.: Editorial: Enhanced human modeling in robotics for socially-aware place navigation (2024)
58. Tsintotas, K.A., Moutsis, S.N., Konstantinidis, Fotios K. Gasteratos, A.: Toward smart supply chain: Adopting internet of things and digital twins. In: AIP Conf. Proc. AIP Publishing (2024)

59. Tziola, A.A., Loizou, S.G.: Autonomous task planning for heterogeneous multi-agent systems. In: in proc. IEEE Int. Conf. Robotics and Automation. pp. 3490–3496 (2023)
60. Vavatsikos, A., Saridou, A., Mavridis, A., Ioakeimidou, D., Chatzoglou, P.: A robust multicriteria customers satisfaction analysis framework for airline services providers evaluation. Available at SSRN 4772855
61. Viriyasitavat, W., Hoonsopon, D.: Blockchain characteristics and consensus in modern business processes. J. Ind. Inform. Integr. **13**, 32–39 (2019). https://doi.org/10.1016/j.jii.2018.07.004
62. Wang, W., Zhang, J., Cao, Y., Shen, Y., Tao, D.: Towards data-efficient detection transformers. In: European Conference Computer Vision. pp. 88–105 (2022)
63. Weinberg, S.J., Sanches, F., Ide, T., Kamiya, K., Correll, R.: Supply chain logistics with quantum and classical annealing algorithms. Sci. Rep. **13**(1), 4770 (2023)
64. Weise, J., Mostaghim, S.: A scalable many-objective pathfinding benchmark suite. IEEE Trans. Evolut. Computat. **26**(1), 188–194 (2022). https://doi.org/10.1109/TEVC.2021.3089050
65. Woschank, M., Rauch, E., Zsifkovits, H.: A review of further directions for artificial intelligence, machine learning, and deep learning in smart logistics. Sustainability **12**(9), 3760 (2020)
66. Xie, Y., Yin, Y., Xue, W., Shi, H., Chong, D.: Intelligent supply chain performance measurement in industry 40. Syst. Res. Behav. Sci. **37**(4), 711–718 (2020)
67. Zhou, H., Shou, Y., Zhai, X., Li, L., Wood, C., Wu, X.: Supply chain practice and information quality: a supply chain strategy study. Int. J. Prod. Econom. **147**, 624–633 (2014). https://doi.org/10.1016/j.ijpe.2013.08.025

Author Index

I. Kostavelis et al. (Eds.): ICSC 2024, CCIS 2110, pp. 345–347, 2025.
https://doi.org/10.1007/978-3-031-69344-1